ACHIEVING YOUR GOALS

Malcolm Kahn
University of Miami

Sue Kahn
Miami-Dade College

andYOU.com
1762 Norcross Road
Erie, PA 16510-3838
USA

For product information and customer support, contact andYOU.com
at 1-866-690-ANDU or visit us at andYOU.com.

Connect with us on Facebook and Twitter:

 http://www.facebook.com/andyoucom

 http://www.twitter.com/andyoucom

Printed in the U.S.A.

ISBN 13: 978-1-938260-15-5
ISBN 10: 1-938260-15-5

1 2 3 4 5 6 7 8 9 10-WEB-18 17 16 15 14

Brief
TABLE of CONTENTS

TABLE of CONTENTS

PART TWO:
THE LEARNING EXPERIENCE AND YOU

CHAPTER 3

MANAGING YOUR TIME: A "POSITIVE" APPROACH

CHAPTER 6

SUCCEEDING ON EXAMS

CHAPTER 7

RESEARCHING AND WRITING AN
ACADEMIC PAPER: AN INTRODUCTION

ABOUT the AUTHORS

This book had its beginnings with our individual experiences counseling first-year university students with adjustment problems and teaching at-risk new community college students. Over the dinner table, we had many conversations about what was and was not working for our students and about how we could help them succeed. Our discussions led us to insights into the practical steps new students can take to adapt both personally and academically to the demands of college. A few years ago, our conversations turned to the idea of sharing our accumulated knowledge and understanding with a broader population of first-year students. We realized that the combination of our experiences in counseling and teaching along with our academic backgrounds produced the perfect fit to write a textbook aimed at helping first-year students succeed.

MORE ABOUT EACH OF US

Malcolm Kahn, Ph.D., ABPP is an expert in the personal adjustment factors that can help new students succeed. He gained this expertise predominantly through counseling hundreds of new students at the University of Miami as well as teaching first-year experience and psychology classes. In his role as Director of the University of Miami Counseling Center, Malcolm arranged many outreach programs targeting first-year students. Malcolm earned a B.A. in psychology from Johns Hopkins University and a Ph.D. in clinical psychology from Southern Illinois University, Carbondale. A clinical psychologist, board certified by the American Board of Professional Psychology, Malcolm is a Life Fellow of the Society for Personality Assessment and Fellow of the Academy of Clinical Psychology. He has served on the Governing Board of the Association for University and College Counseling Center Directors.

Sue Kahn, Ph.D. is an experienced professor, researcher, and author of issues central to the success of new college students. In her position at Miami-Dade College, Sue has specialized in teaching reading skills, English, and study skills to an at-risk diverse student population. She has presented numerous papers at professional organizations, including the International Reading Association, the Florida Reading Association, and the Florida Developmental Education Association. Sue earned a B.A. and M.A. in English from Southern Illinois University, Carbondale, and a Ph.D. in reading and learning disabilities from the University of Miami. In addition to publishing research articles, Sue co-authored a textbook for underprepared college students, *College Reading Skills and Strategies*, published by St. Martin's Press.

PREFACE

TO THE INSTRUCTORS

Regardless of their background, new students transitioning to college confront an array of often bewildering challenges. Many of today's students have been away from school for several years, juggle a full-time or part-time job, have major family responsibilities, and have difficulty adjusting to the campus or classroom. *College Success and YOU: Achieving Your Goals* is designed to help you help your students overcome these kinds of obstacles and achieve success.

We have synthesized our knowledge of how challenges evolve for new college students into a didactically meaningful structure for the text. The Introduction provides an icebreaker so new students can meet one another. It also sets the tone for the rest of the book by familiarizing students with the concepts of goal setting, the themes of positive psychology, and the importance of taking personal responsibility. The chapters are categorized into sequential units (The Discovery Experience and You, The Learning Experience and You, The Personal Experience and You, The Social Experience and You, and The Planning Experience and You) which represent the natural unfolding of challenges faced by new college students, from their initial feelings of uncertainty to the anticipation of their sophomore, junior, senior (and beyond) years. Since students develop best through a positive framework, we have infused this text with positive psychology, explaining how students can apply their personal strengths and potential to achieving their college goals.

Our textbook offers a variety of pedagogical aids to enhance student learning and your instructional efforts. Since students learn best through a structured approach, each chapter presents a consistent chapter format. The units and chapters are designed to be interchangeable, allowing for your ability to organize the course to represent your preferred sequence and to accommodate the specific needs of any class. The chapter activities target college success with pragmatic content and feature creative, engaging, active learning components. The varied and engaging exercises can be used both in your classroom and as homework assignments. These activities and exercises tap all the levels of Bloom's taxonomy as well as key learning styles. The layout of each chapter (including the cartoons, photos, charts, graphs) enhances and extends the contents of the chapter.

We are confident that along with your guidance, students who conscientiously read, understand, and apply the concepts contained within these chapters will succeed in achieving their college goals.

TO THE STUDENTS

Welcome to college! We hope you are enjoying your new campus and all that it offers. However, we realize just how challenging it can be for you to settle in. When we started college ourselves, we felt a little lost and had a lot of doubts. But we stuck with it until we figured out what we had to do to succeed. Throughout our careers, we figured it out a lot more through teaching and counseling hundreds of new students. In this book, we share with you many useful strategies and techniques to help you succeed in college. We are certain that if you conscientiously read this text and complete the exercises, you will figure it out, too.

As we prepared to write this textbook, we asked new students to list the issues that challenged them the most during their first month of college. Their leading concerns included getting enough sleep, managing money, getting along with roommates, and taking time to study. We cover those important topics in great depth in this book. If any of these issues are plaguing you right now, you can learn strategies to handle them by locating their page number in the Index and reading ahead. That's true for other topics as well. In fact, we believe that this book can serve as a reference throughout your college years and beyond for such practical topics as preparing for a job interview, managing time, speaking in front of a group, resolving conflicts, and implementing a budget.

Despite the challenges, most of us who attended college in the past envy your current status as a new student and the exciting journey that you will take. We wrote this book to help you succeed in your journey. We are cheering for you. If you read, understand, and apply the concepts in the chapters, we are confident you will achieve your college goals.

Features

Here are descriptions of the text's special features which we designed to help you learn and adjust.

Table of Contents

The chapters are sequenced in the following units intended to correlate with your evolution as a first-year student: The Discovery Experience and You, the Learning Experience and You, the Personal Experience and You, the Social Experience and You, and the Planning Experience and You.

Positive Approach

We infused our text with a positive psychology theme to call your attention to your personal strengths. Rather than focusing on a person's weaknesses, the positive psychology approach emphasizes self-esteem, optimism, success, and happiness.

Goals

Each chapter starts off with a few major goals that you can achieve through the chapter's content and your work in the classroom.

Self-Assessments

We created a wide variety of Self-Assessment activities to engage you in understanding your current status on topics covered in each chapter. For example, in Chapter 12, you will learn about diversity by finding out how similar or different you are when compared to your best friend.

End of Chapter Activities

Here are the activities you will find at the end of each chapter and their purpose:

Critical Thinking—We present five thought-provoking questions which ask you to apply an active evaluation of information using careful, thoughtful, and reasoned judgments. Faculty members and prospective employers highly value critical thinking ability.

Online Learning—Taking an online class requires some different attitudes and behaviors from traditional classes. In Online Learning, we provide information to help distance learners understand how to cope with the unique challenges they face.

Thinking Critically About . . . Succeeding on Exams

Critical thinking involves an active evaluation of information using careful, thoughtful, and reasoned judgments.

1. This chapter opens with a section titled "Is This Going to Be on the Test?" As exams approach, students often ask professors that question. Provide a convincing argument that such a question is irrelevant.

2. Compare and contrast a student's preparation for success on an exam with a contestant's preparation for success on *American Idol*.

3. Explain why constructing a practice test is a good learning activity.

4. Discuss the limitations of tests. How are tests insufficient to evaluate a student's development and knowledge?

5. Recommend actions that your college can take to minimize cheating on tests. What are the implications of cheating on tests in college for a student's subsequent actions in the "real" world?

Chapter Challenge—Each Chapter Challenge presents a case study of a first-year student facing a specific dilemma. For example, in Chapter 4, Amy is unsure how to manage the impossibly heavy reading load in her history and biology classes. After reading the background and description of the student's challenge, you will be asked a series of questions pertaining to possible solutions.

?? Can You Recall It?

Directions: To review your understanding of the chapter, choose the correct term from the list below and fill it in on the blank. You will not use every term.

syllabus	plagiarism	audited
elective	motivation	master's degree
defamation	PhD	associate professor
prerequisite	tenure	dean's list

1. Copying someone else's work and passing it off as your own is called _____.

2. Professor Martin's earning a/an _____ indicates that she received a graduate research degree that enables her to be called "Dr. Martin."

3. _____ occurs when false statements hurt a person's reputation.

4. High enough grades might qualify you for the _____.

5. Vince has increased his enthusiasm and energy for his studies after encouragement from his academic advisor. Vince's reaction is an example of increased _____.

6. _____ is the name for lifetime status awarded to a faculty member because of that faculty member's scholarly achievements.

7. A/An _____ class involves sitting in on the class but not receiving credit or a grade.

8. The guide for a course that provides the schedule for lecture topics, assignments, and exams as well as special information about the professor's expectations is called a/an _____.

Key Chapter Strategies—This section presents a brief list summarizing the major tips for success covered in a chapter.

Can You Recall It?—These eight-item fill-in-the-blank quizzes allow you to test yourself to make sure you understand the major concepts presented in a chapter.

Web Activity—For this section, you will be asked to research the Internet to find resources about topics covered in a chapter.

Reflection Time—Reflection Time poses questions for introspection to you about your unique attitudes and behaviors, and you are asked to write your responses as if you are writing in a journal.

CollegeSuccess.andYOU.com

At *CollegeSuccess.andYOU.com* you can find tools and resources that will expand your learning beyond the pages of this textbook. At this premium website you can:

- Make the interactive **Online Version** of the textbook your own with highlighting, note-taking, and bookmarking capabilities.

- Interact with your classmates and students across the country taking the *College Success & YOU* course on the **Discussion Board.**

- Receive instant feedback on the **Can You Recall It?** questions and selected **Exercises** in the text.

- Explore additional resources through relevant **Website Links.**

- Enhance your understanding of concepts by viewing **Animated Graphics.**

- **Download** exercises and other activities from the textbook so you can complete assignments and prepare for tests.

- Look up key terms from the textbook in the **Glossary.**

Instructor's Manual and Test Bank

The Instructor's Manual and Test Bank provides activities, journal questions, discussion topics, case studies, links to relevant videos and a number of multiple-choice, true-false, matching, short answer, and essay questions for every chapter in the book.

ACKNOWLEDGMENTS

Larson Texts

This book would not exist without the efforts of the staff at Larson Texts, our publisher. We are very grateful for their hard work on this textbook. A very special thank you goes to Ron Larson for giving us the opportunity to write this textbook, which is the second in a series of supportive textbooks for college students. He has had an amazingly productive career as a professor, prolific author, and publisher. Ron is a true visionary and an example of how hard work combined with ability creates success.

Dan Bruce, our editor at Larson Texts, has worked closely with us and the rest of the Larson team to coordinate all phases of the publication process. He has been an excellent communicator who carefully managed the steps toward publication. We thank Dan for moving this process forward while always showing sensitivity to us.

Jeannine Lawless, our developmental editor, performed the "nuts and bolts" operations to prepare the text for publication. Jeannine thoughtfully negotiated with us to achieve the best result possible. We are indebted to Jeannine for her outstanding work throughout the publication process.

Two other editors served important roles in this project, and we thank them as well. Barbara Resch, the copyeditor, monitored our writing and applied the *Chicago Manual of Style* to maintain consistency. We learned a great deal during the permissions process from Kathy Zander, the permissions editor, and we thank her.

It truly takes a team to publish a textbook, and the Larson Team is a champion.

Our Personal Support Network

So many people provided us with encouragement throughout the time between when we began to write this textbook and its publication. We particularly express our deep appreciation to Irene, Brooke, Wilma, Frank, Iris, Arthur, Allison, Andi, Lloyd, Lauren, Greg, Ed, Carolyn, Harry, Len, Mitch, Art, Dave, and Cookie for their continuous support and interest. We additionally thank our other friends, family, and colleagues for their enduring encouragement and constructive ideas.

Reviewers

We greatly appreciate the helpful comments and suggestions provided by the following faculty members and administrators who critically evaluated all or part of our manuscript. This book has greatly benefitted from their contributions.

Scott Amundsen
University of North Carolina, Wilmington

Andres Armijo
University of New Mexico

Paula Bradberry
Arkansas State University

Sherry Miller Brown
University of Pittsburgh

Licia Calloway
The Citadel

Lorna Catford
Sonoma State University

Sheryl Duquette
Erie Community College

John Fisher
Northwest Missouri State University

Margaret Garroway
Howard Community College

Melissa Gomez
Austin Peay State University

Rhonda Hall
West Virginia University

Peggy Jolly
University of Alabama at Birmingham

Laurel Koehler
Georgia Military College

Alice Lanning
University of Oklahoma

Courtney Milleson
Amarillo College

Yvonne Mitkos
Southern Illinois University, Edwardsville

Debbie Naquin
Northern Virginia Community College

Susan Rock
Long Island University/C.W Post Campus

Jonathan Schwartz
University of Hawaii-West Oahu

Karen Smith
East Carolina University

Wayne Smith
Spokane Falls Community College

Cheryl Spector
California State University Northbridge

William E. Thompson
Texas A&M University-Commerce

Dae Vasek
Baylor University

Arthur Webb
Oklahoma State University

Barbara Wilson
Saint Leo University

Brenda Winn
Texas Tech University

Jennifer Wright
University of Central Florida

Daniel Zelinski
Richard Bland College

DEDICATION

We dedicate this book to our son Daniel, a model of college success, whose inspiration and support helped us achieve our goal.

We also dedicate this book to you—the faculty and students who use this book. This book is written for you.

Introduction

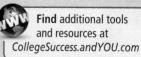

Find additional tools and resources at *CollegeSuccess.andYOU.com*

Self-Assessment: Who Are You?

Step 1: Fill in the empty blanks in the paragraph below. Sometimes there will be choices available and sometimes not. You will have a brief description of your unique identity when you have finished.

My full name is _____. I like to be called _____ by my friends and family. I am _____ years old, and I am from _____ (your hometown and state). I was previously a student at _____ (name of your school before this one). My favorite fun activity is _____. My three best personal characteristics are _____, _____, and _____. I think I learn best by _____ _____

(choose one: *listening*, *reading* and *observing*, or *using a hands-on, active approach*).

Step 2: Your professor will pair you with another student in the class. Each of you copy the other person's responses from Step 1 in the space below.

My classmate's full name is _____. My classmate likes to be called _____ by his or her friends and family. My classmate is _____ years old and is from _____ (his or her hometown and state). My classmate was previously a student at _____ (name of his or her school before this one). My classmate's favorite fun activity is _____. My classmate's three best personal characteristics are _____, _____,and _____. My classmate thinks he or she learns best by _____ (choose one: *listening*, *reading* and *observing*, or *using a hands-on, active approach*).

Step 3: You will introduce your classmate to the rest of the class by sharing his or her responses when your professor requests you to do so. Your classmate will similarly introduce you by sharing your responses. After the introductions, discuss the following items:

1. Who comes from the hometown farthest away?
2. Who comes from the same town as the college?
3. Who are the oldest and the youngest?
4. What are some of the unique fun activities?
5. How many students prefer to learn by
   listening? _____
   reading and observing? _____
   using a hands-on, active approach? _____

What are your
GOALS?

Goals are objectives, desired results, outcomes—something you work toward. Goals can be long-term or short-term depending on the amount of time they take to achieve. Research shows that it is important to set goals that are clear and challenging.[1] Having clear, challenging goals helps you set priorities, organize efforts, stay focused, and keep motivated.

This textbook is designed to assist you in achieving the key goals necessary to become a successful college student. Each chapter begins by listing goals for you. As you read the chapter, complete the exercises, and have class discussions, you will be working to achieve these chapter goals. If you learn the material presented in this textbook, you will have mastered at least forty goals essential to college success.

But what about your own goals? How do you set these goals? One way is to use the SMART goal system[2] explained in the following chart.

SPECIFIC	■ The goal is clear, precise, and well-defined.
MEASURABLE	■ The goal has explicit criteria, is manageable, and is quantifiable.
ATTAINABLE	■ The goal makes you reach, is something you can reasonably work toward, and is an achievable challenge.
REALISTIC	■ The goal is relevant and not too difficult or too easy.
TIMELY	■ The goal has a deadline, and time frame, or an end point.

As you can tell, SMART is a mnemonic device—a memory trick to help you recall information. The *S* stands for "**S**pecific," *M* stands for "**M**easurable," *A* stands for "**A**ttainable," *R* stands for "**R**ealistic," and *T* stands for **T**imely. **SMART** is an easy-to-remember method for you to use to create meaningful, reachable, long-term and short-term goals. You can set SMART goals that are relevant to academic success, personal achievement, career accomplishments, and lifelong desires. Setting goals following the SMART technique allows you to develop a plan of action so that you can be motivated to progress forward successfully. Setting goals creates motivation; motivation creates the drive to push forward; the drive to push forward creates hard work leading to achievement. The cycle of setting goals and working to achieve them can become a habit that leads you to a lifetime of success.

EXERCISE 1   What is Your SMART Goal?

Directions: For this activity, set an academic goal that you would like to achieve for an assignment you have due or for an approaching test (or any other upcoming academic responsibility). Fill in the SMART Goal Questionnaire that follows. Be prepared to discuss in class your goal and each step for its accomplishment. You may need to revise your goal and/or the steps to achieve it as you rethink your answers. Space at the end of the SMART Goal Questionnaire is provided for you to revise or restate your original goal.

Write your goal: _____

_____

1. **S**pecific: What are you going to do? What goal do you want to accomplish? Be very detailed. Instead of saying, "I need to improve in math," say, "I will increase my number of correct answers on the math problem set for Chapter 2." See the next step to make this statement measurable.

   _____

   _____

2. **M**easurable: How are you going to measure whether the goal is achieved? Give a specific indicator, such as a quantity, a grade, or a number. For example, "I will get all my answers correct for the math problem set for Chapter 2."

   _____

   _____

3. **A**ttainable: Is it possible? What are the skills, attitudes, performances, abilities, or resources necessary for you to accomplish this goal? Will this goal challenge but not overwhelm you?

   _____

   _____

4. **R**ealistic: Is the goal so difficult that it can seem that you are not making progress? Is the goal too easy? Does the goal relate to one of your academic responsibilities?

   _____

   _____

5. **T**imely: Do you have a specific deadline for accomplishing the goal? Be sure to give a specific date or time.

   _____

   _____

Revised or restated goal: _____

_____

Your goal won't magically happen just because you wrote it down. But now that you have a SMART goal, you understand exactly what you want and how to accomplish it. All that's left is to do it!

Use the resource links to find additional information at *CollegeSuccess.andYOU.com*

Acquiring Control

Hopefully, your transition to college is smooth and easy. However, attending college inevitably involves a set of major changes in your life. These changes can seem very stressful. You might feel so overwhelmed that your life seems out of control. You are likely to benefit most from college and achieve your goals if you can minimize stress by establishing a sense of control during your many new experiences.

The originator of modern stress theory is Hans Selye of McGill University.[3] Selye shows us that even very positive changes in our lives, such as going to college, can be extremely stressful. He coined the term **eustress** to identify the stress that comes from good events, such as starting college, getting married, obtaining a new job, or winning a big lottery jackpot.

The good news is that Selye suggests ways to manage eustress so that you can enjoy and succeed in your new role. The secret to this success is to gain as much control as possible over the demands that are made on you. So, as a eustressed college student, you can be successful in achieving your goals by taking control of your college experience. You can gain more by following these four suggestions:

1. View the varied demands of college as challenges and opportunities, not as pains or ordeals. Using positive terms in your mind, such as *challenges* and *opportunities* instead of more negative descriptions will enable you to maintain a constructive attitude for achieving your goals.

2. You identified your three best personal characteristics in Part I of the "Self-Assessment" activity at the beginning of this Introduction. These are your greatest personal strengths. Along with your other special attributes, these strengths will give you the inner resources to deal effectively with the challenges and opportunities that you will face as a college student.

3. Set SMART goals for yourself that will help you stay on track. Having clear and challenging goals keeps you working with more purpose and direction—which means less worry and stress.

4. Applying the information that you will learn from your class and this textbook is the final key ingredient. This textbook is written to provide you with the skills and knowledge that you need to help you become successful in your college career.

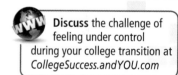

Discuss the challenge of feeling under control during your college transition at *CollegeSuccess.andYOU.com*

Combining a positive attitude, your inner strengths, and the strategies learned from class and this textbook will help you take control and succeed in achieving your college goals.

Understanding the College Scene: Right from the Start

1

In this chapter, you will move toward achieving your goals by

- learning about the administration, the faculty, and the support staff.

- discovering what you need to know about academic jargon, your rights and responsibilities as a student, and your campus website.

- recognizing the importance of your motivation.

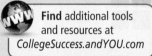

Find additional tools and resources at *CollegeSuccess.andYOU.com*

Self-Assessment:
Challenges and Opportunities

Step 1: Describe the three greatest challenges that you have faced since you arrived on campus.

1. _____
_____
_____

2. _____
_____
_____

3. _____
_____
_____

Step 2: Think about these challenges. Can you identify some solutions? Explain your solution to each of the challenges presented above. If you aren't sure how to handle some of the challenges, get suggestions from friends, family, an advisor, your professor, or college staff members.

1. _____
_____
_____

2. _____
_____
_____

3. _____
_____
_____

Step 3: Describe the three best experiences you have had since arriving on campus.

1. _____
_____
_____

2. _____
_____
_____

3. _____
_____

Top Ten Tips from Seniors

Challenges occur in any major new situation. Handling these challenges constructively will give you a positive start as you begin college. When confronted with college adjustment challenges, more-experienced students can be especially helpful sources of useful advice. Here are ten tips from experienced students to help as you transition to college life:

Discuss the Top Ten Tips from Seniors at *CollegeSuccess.andYOU.com*

1. Find a few friends, including one or two you can count on.
2. If you party, always stick with a friend and don't let him or her out of your sight. This arrangement can keep you out of trouble.
3. Give a high priority to keeping up with your school assignments; it's easy to get behind and tough to catch up.
4. Get involved in school activities and attend big events like football games; you'll be happier if you get involved.
5. Stay healthy by exercising, eating right, and getting enough sleep.
6. Set up a plan for keeping in touch with your family; take control and communicate regularly.
7. Figure out how to manage your time and money as soon as you can. Plan ahead.
8. Having a part-time job can be a good way to meet people and earn your own spending money.
9. Be patient if everything isn't perfect right away; it will work out if you give it time.
10. Smile!

As you begin your college journey, you will benefit by becoming familiar with key aspects of academic life. College environments feature a richness of thought and the pursuit and sharing of knowledge. In your role as a student, you will be asked to think analytically and critically. Just as Socrates, the ancient Greek philosopher and teacher, insisted that his students question everything about the world around them, your professors will challenge you to develop an intellectual curiosity that leads you to become an engaged citizen and a lifelong learner. Additionally, in the transition to college, you will find yourself in an environment that features little structure with many distractions, while simultaneously requiring considerable autonomy. Accepting personal responsibility for your academic and nonacademic behavior will help you adjust to campus life.

In your early days on campus, you have probably already encountered such strange titles as **provost**, **registrar**, and **bursar**. It will be helpful for you to understand the titles and roles of college personnel who teach, advise, and support students and how to interact effectively with them. A great resource for accessing information about your college is its website. To understand the information you access, you will need to grasp the unique educational jargon used on your campus. Additionally, a major factor that will help you succeed in achieving your goals is motivation. The most successful students maintain an inner drive and desire to be the best that they can be. This chapter provides the basic information you need relating to a college's framework and personnel; unique features such as college jargon, your rights and responsibilities, and your campus website; and the significance of motivation to your success.

Colleges are divided into many different categories. The box below helps you identify your school's category and the nature of its programs.

Categories of Colleges

Note: While this textbook refers to all undergraduate schools as colleges, *you probably attend one of the following major types.*

Universities — Universities provide undergraduate degrees. They also offer professional degrees (such as those in law and medicine) and graduate degrees through the doctoral degree. Faculty members at universities are often deeply committed to research, and students are encouraged to participate.

Colleges — Colleges emphasize undergraduate education culminating with a bachelor's degree. While colleges typically do not have graduate or professional programs, some may have master's degree programs. Colleges do not typically expect faculty to conduct extensive independent research.

Community Colleges — Community colleges are two-year schools, and students earn an associate's degree upon graduation. This degree can be a step along the way to a bachelor's degree via a transfer to a four-year college or university program, or it can be a terminal degree in career specialties such as fire science or medical technology.

Career or Technical Colleges — These schools emphasize training for particular career goals such as becoming a fashion designer or a chef. Some schools are highly specialized in one type of field, while others maintain programs in a variety of occupational specialties. Faculty members must either have expertise in a specialty area or support the general educational experience.

Online Colleges and Universities — The educational programs of these colleges are presented exclusively or chiefly online, and communication between students and faculty members usually occurs over the Internet. Otherwise, the types of programs offered by these schools and their faculties can be similar to any of those schools previously mentioned.

Other Distinctions:
Some colleges are **public**, meaning that they are run under the authority of a state or federal agency, while other colleges are **private**. Most private colleges are nonprofit institutions, although some are operated for profit. Usually, public colleges charge lower amounts for tuition than private colleges do. Also, some private schools are managed by a religious organization.

Schools can vary in identity or focus. For example, a few colleges only admit women or men. Also, some schools have historically emphasized admission and instruction of certain minority or religious groups. In terms of focus, there are some colleges that only offer liberal arts. Others offer specialized educational concentrations in fields such as the arts, military science, mining, engineering, or agriculture.

YOUR COLLEGE WANTS YOU TO SUCCEED?

The administration, faculty, and support staff of your college would like you to be successful by acquiring new knowledge, enjoying your experience, and graduating on time. A college thrives when its students thrive. People who work at a college usually take great pride in their students. Additionally, colleges are seen as successful when most students who enter eventually graduate. As a result, these officials have a vested interest in your success.

Colleges have created many support services and procedures to help you achieve your goals. Just as you probably went through a lot of hassles to get to this point, the college administration put forth its share of effort to attract you, arrange your enrollment, and orient you. Now that you have begun classes, your college will continue to assist you in achieving your goals. It can be very helpful to take advantage of some of the many opportunities that a college provides.

To facilitate your success, colleges are organized into a rather complex framework that you will need to understand. Generally, this framework includes the administration, the faculty, and the support staff.

The Administration

Along with overseeing a school's core academic mission, a college administration is also responsible for maintaining the backbone of the school, including its traditions, support services, and facilities.

At the peak of a college's bureaucracy is typically a board of trustees, chiefly consisting of prominent citizens from a variety of fields. The president of the college reports to the board of trustees but manages the school on an everyday basis. Some large schools may also have a chancellor with special administrative powers. Additionally, there are usually several top administrators, with titles such as provost or vice president, who manage particular divisions for the president.

The academic division of the college may have one of a wide variety of organizational structures. You will usually encounter academic departments run by a chairperson. The departments may be grouped by topic, with each cluster of related departments (such as engineering departments) managed by a dean. Academic advisors, who can be very helpful to you, will ordinarily fall under the leadership of a department chairperson or academic dean.

In addition to the academic division, administrators also manage such important functions as facilities maintenance, fundraising, information technology, student services, athletics, human resources, public safety, and business services. As you can imagine, your school would not run as smoothly for students without these important behind-the-scenes administrative officers.

Student Affairs

For students, one of the most significant nonacademic administrative units is **Student Affairs**. Usually run by a vice president or dean, this division is responsible for many key areas of student life. Student Affairs typically includes such important departments as Housing, Health and Counseling Services, Wellness Center, Dean of Students, Student Activities, and Multicultural Student Office.

Multiple Choices: The Student Affairs Department will organize many opportunities for your campus involvement.

"Good morning, and welcome to Abnormal Psychology."

The professionals who work in Student Affairs have selected a career dedicated to providing services to college students. They view their work as supporting you as you work toward your college goals. If you interact with Student Affairs staff members, you will probably find that they really care about your welfare and are willing to extend themselves to enhance your life at college.

The Faculty

People who become college faculty members usually enjoy the subjects they teach and are true experts in them. They could have had outstanding careers in the private sector in many fields, ranging from engineering to music. However, they chose to work at a college campus in large part because they enjoy sharing their knowledge with students. They very much want their students to succeed; in fact, a great thrill for many faculty members is watching former students receive their diplomas at graduation ceremonies. With these attitudes, most faculty members will be as helpful to students as possible, while simultaneously fostering independent learning.

EXERCISE 1   Who Teaches You?

Directions: You will find it helpful to have information available about each of the faculty members who serve as your professors. Fill in the name, office hours, office location, phone number, and email address for each of your professors in the chart below. You may want to store this information in your phone or computer.

Course	Professor	Office Hours	Office Location	Phone	Email

It may be useful for you to understand the different categories of faculty members. Most college faculty members have earned at least a master's degree, which usually requires about two years of education past the undergraduate degree, or a doctoral degree (usually a **PhD**, doctor of philosophy, or **EdD**, doctor of education), which requires at least four additional years of study. The PhD is a research degree, and the EdD is earned exclusively in the field of education.

Full-time faculty members are ranked according to their seniority and academic accomplishments. While these positions may or may not be correlated with enthusiasm and teaching ability, it might be helpful for you to be aware of academic ranks. Keeping in mind that not all college faculties include each of these positions, here are the major titles for college teachers and their typical criteria:

A. **Full Professors:** Full Professors are the most accomplished faculty members in their scholarly work.

B. **Associate Professors:** Experienced faculty members who are either on the road to becoming full professors or who have not produced enough scholarly work to reach the rank of full professor often have the title of associate professor.

C. **Assistant Professors:** As less-experienced or less-accomplished faculty members, assistant professors often have recently obtained graduate degrees.

D. **Lecturers, Instructors, and Adjuncts:** This group includes full-time faculty members who specialize exclusively in teaching and part-time faculty members who often have other full-time jobs related to their teaching specialties.

E. **Teaching Assistants:** Graduate students who acquire teaching experience and financial support for their teaching are usually referred to as *teaching assistants* (TAs). TAs are resources for students who are confused about a class topic or who need help preparing for an exam.

You may hear the term *tenured* applied to some associate professors and professors. **Tenured** faculty members essentially have lifetime contracts with the school based on their achievements.

Secrets for Success with Professors

Interacting with professors can be different from dealing with high school teachers. While each professor will be unique in his or her preferences, here are some general tips to help you get along with faculty members:

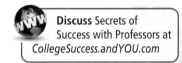
Discuss Secrets of Success with Professors at *CollegeSuccess.andYOU.com*

- Carefully study each course syllabus. A **syllabus** features the schedule of assignments and exams as well as that professor's particular rules. You should receive the syllabus when your course begins, either in print, online, or both. As soon as you receive the syllabus, you can write exam dates and assignment due dates into your planner. That will help you arrange your "to do" schedule. Also, you will get a feeling for the professor's specific expectations from the syllabus.

- Even if the syllabus does not mandate attendance, most professors assume students will come to every class and arrive on time. If you need to miss a class, follow any required guidelines to notify the professor.

- Avoid making excuses, except when they are really authentic. Most professors are experienced and skilled at spotting false excuses.

- Find out how to refer to each of your instructors and teaching assistants according to their preferences. Many PhD and EdD faculty members favor "Dr. _____," while other faculty members may ask to be addressed as "Professor," "Mr.," "Mrs.," "Ms.," or even by their first name.

- Participate in class, when appropriate, and act in a respectful manner.

- Be aware of your professor's policy about electronic devices. Some professors do not permit laptops or PDAs in the classroom because of the potential for student distractibility.

- When in the classroom, turn off and put away cell phones and other mobile communication devices.

- Complete assignments as scheduled on the syllabus. A good idea is to maintain a calendar on the computer or use an academic planner and fill in the important dates for all assignment due dates, exams, and quizzes.

■ You might be surprised that many professors enjoy getting to know their students. You can meet with your teachers during their office hours or make a separate appointment. It might be a good idea to meet with each of your teachers during the first month of class; at the minimum, they will probably learn your name. If you do well in class, a professor who knows you can provide a recommendation for you or even become your mentor. Remember, many faculty members teach in part because they enjoy being helpful and imparting their knowledge to the next generation.

■ Many college teachers are willing to answer questions by email. If you send emails to your professors, you can benefit by writing in a much more formal style than you use with your friends. Think of an email to a professor as being like a business letter and be sure to take into consideration the teacher's point of view.

Selecting Professors for a Class

You were probably assigned teachers for your initial college classes. However, you may have some choices when you register in the future. You may be able to select not only your classes but your professors. Consider which qualities, such as teaching style, personality, or type of assignments you are looking for. Friends, especially more experienced students, can provide valuable advice about professors. Additionally, you can learn about the qualities of college teachers from formal teacher evaluations, which may be posted on your college's website. Sometimes faculty members are so popular that a waiting list occurs for their classes.

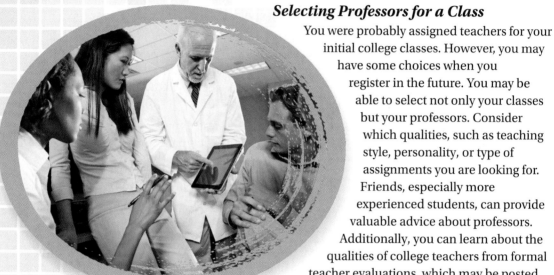

Getting to Know You: Meeting with your professors gives them the opportunity to get to know you.

The Support Staff

A college campus is similar to a small city focused on the welfare of its citizens. For a college, though, the citizens are its students. Thus, for any college to operate effectively, a large number of support staff employees indirectly or directly provide services to students. A college support staff usually includes a wide variety of employees including secretaries, receptionists, purchasing agents, technicians, record clerks, cooks, cashiers, and groundskeepers. Reflecting back on their college years, alumni often remember a support staff member, such as a special cafeteria worker or an administrative assistant, who was particularly kind and friendly to them. As with faculty members, such personnel usually choose to work at a college because they enjoy interacting with students or providing indirect support to their educational development. Members of the support staff can often provide you with the most help in managing the everyday details and complications you encounter. When you need their help during your journey through college, you will find that these employees will respond best when you treat them with respect and appreciation.

SUCCEED

The uniqueness of the college experience includes a great deal of information that may be unfamiliar to a new student. Understanding college jargon, your rights and responsibilities, and the usefulness of your campus website will empower you to gain familiarity with some of the most important features of the college experience.

College Jargon

In your first year of college, you will encounter unfamiliar terms that were not used in high school. Historically, students at each college develop their own set of unique phrases and colloquialisms that would not be understood outside that environment. For example, the term *hook* designates a grade of C on one campus. Another example occurs at UCLA, where every four years students revise a book called *u.c.l.a. slang*.[1] As you become involved in your studies, you will benefit by understanding some of the common academic terms that are used on your campus. The following passage about the academic concerns of Michelle, a typical freshman, should enable you to figure out the meaning of some key terms you are likely to encounter.

Michelle is currently taking fifteen credits. She isn't receiving a regular grade for one of her classes. The grade for this class is **pass/fail**, so she is confident she will be able to pass. However, she is very worried about her chemistry class because she did not study chemistry in high school. She thinks that she might get such a low grade in chemistry that she would be placed on **academic probation**. On the other hand, without chemistry, she figures that she can achieve such high grades that she might qualify for the **dean's list**. She must make a decision about dropping chemistry since the **drop date** is right around the corner. Michelle is undecided about her career path. Since she had not decided on a **major**, she was designated **undeclared**. Recently, she decided to concentrate on both biology and psychology. She has decided to declare herself to have an **interdisciplinary major** so that she can concentrate on both of her two favorite subjects. To select a substitute course for chemistry, she will analyze her **transcript** after her first year in college. She might decide to fulfill a **prerequisite** for one of her majors. She might also take a Spanish class, which would help her complete the necessary courses for a **minor** in foreign languages. Or she might choose an **elective** that is not required for either her major or minor. If she has time, Michelle may ask her chemistry professor if she can just sit in on his class and **audit** it. Michelle has one other big problem. One of her loans has not come through yet, and the **Bursar's Office** has sent her a note that it will put a **hold on registration** for next semester if her tuition and fees bill is not paid by the end of the month.

Learning the Lingo

Step 1: In the table below, list five academic terms that were unfamiliar to you before you began college. Across from each term, write your best understanding of its definition. An example word and definition are provided. <u>Use no more than two terms from the above passage about Michelle.</u>

Academic Term	Meaning
Audit	Registering for and sitting in on a class without getting a grade or receiving credit
1.	
2.	
3.	
4.	
5.	

Step 2: Be prepared to share and discuss in class your five terms.

Student Rights and Responsibilities

Your rights and responsibilities as a student are usually spelled out in detail in a student handbook, probably available on your school's website. On most campuses, the Office of the Dean of Students is responsible for publishing the student handbook and administering the resulting policies and regulations. It is a very good idea for all new students to browse through the student handbook and read topics of particular relevance. When you first glance at the content, it will appear to be a code of conduct, full of rules and possible penalties. However, the student handbook also informs you of some unique rights and responsibilities.

Student Rights

Colleges must abide by the **Family Educational Rights and Privacy Act (FERPA)**,[2] which protects your educational and financial records since you are considered a responsible adult (if you are eighteen or over). Unless you are claimed by a parent as a tax dependent on a federal tax return, no one outside of the college, including your family, can ordinarily see your academic records, including grades. If you are claimed as a tax dependent, your grades and other official academic reports may be available to your parents. In order to share your records with anyone else, you must sign an authorization for the college to release those records.

Generally, students 18 or older can be assured that records from campus health facilities are confidential. This means that parents are not entitled to be informed about your health condition without your consent, except in emergencies. Usually, the campus health and counseling services have "consent to treatment" forms explaining these policies, which you must sign at the time of your first appointment.

At most schools, student rights also include freedom from discrimination based on factors that may include age, race, national origin, sexual orientation, religion, and disability status. Colleges also usually have a formal written policy to protect students from harassment by others, including unwelcome sexual behavior.

Rules of Engagement: The "student rights and responsibilities" handbook is your guide to acceptable academic and social conduct.

Freedom of Speech

It is important to understand your freedom to speak openly on campus. **The First Amendment** of the U.S. Constitution affords individuals the right to free speech, without regard to political or philosophical preferences. Colleges are famous for cherishing the free exchange of ideas. Many campuses work to create intellectually safe environments in which members of the college community are free to express wide-ranging viewpoints inside and outside the classroom.

However, there are limits and exceptions to free speech on college campuses. Many colleges have campus speech codes that prohibit hateful or threatening speech. Also, be aware that if you lie about someone, you can be sued for defamation. **Defamation** is making a false factual statement in any format, including over the Internet, about someone that is harmful to that person's reputation. You cannot be sued for statements of opinion or for statements that can be proven to be true.

Hear Ye, Hear Ye: The right to express divergent points of view is an important part of campus life.

Student Responsibilities

With your rights comes a variety of responsibilities. There is a famous saying "Knowledge is power." Being aware of these responsibilities can help you make good choices on your path to college success. Some of the more interesting and relevant responsibilities are listed below:

- Many colleges and universities have honor codes to preserve academic integrity, punish offenders, and protect the value of earned degrees. College professors are typically very savvy about the prevention of cheating by their students. With the availability of the Internet, some students are tempted to **plagiarize** (copy other peoples' words and pass them off as their own) in college papers. To combat this problem, professors have ready access to methods for detecting plagiarism.

- "Going green" is often supported on college campuses. Other students and college staff members will guide you to sustain resources and maintain ecological sensitivity.

- On most campuses, students are responsible for always carrying their college ID cards with them. Often, these cards identify you as a student who is eligible for student services or events. The student ID cards may have money or meal plans attached to them. They may also be used for security purposes to identify who legitimately belongs on campus. You should be aware that because of national security issues, getting caught with a fake ID can be considered a federal felony with possibly serious penalties.

- You are expected to follow state laws related to alcohol use and, if eligible to drink, to use alcohol responsibly. Also, it is important to know that federal law permits colleges to notify parents if a student is caught violating alcohol policy.[3]

- Most campuses have instituted systems to notify students through email, text messages, cell phones, or sirens when a campus emergency occurs. It is your responsibility to become aware of your school's system and participate in it.

Using Your College Website

You probably already have recognized the importance of accessing information through your college's "cyberinfrastructure." The administrators of most colleges have spent enormous amounts of money and time to develop their systems. Here are three website resources that provide you with essential information:

- **Online Course Catalog or Bulletin** — The key features of a **course catalog** are a list and description of courses, requirements for a major in a program of study, the course numbering procedures, criteria for graduation, and an explanation of the grading system. It is also likely to provide information about leaves of absence, advanced standing, study abroad, and other special circumstances. Familiarizing yourself early in your college career with the wealth of information in this source will greatly benefit you.

- **Online Academic Calendar** — The academic calendar features dates for the beginning and end of semesters or terms, deadlines for dropping courses, the final exam schedule, and a list of holidays and breaks. Insert key dates from the academic calendar into your planner at the beginning of each semester/term.

- **Online Library** — The library website typically includes the catalog of holdings as well as an abundance of sources of information to help you complete your research assignments. Librarians will offer support to assist you if you have trouble finding what you need.

EXERCISE 3 Catalog Surfing

Step 1: Find your college's online catalog/bulletin and academic calendar. Then answer the following questions based on those online resources.

1. What is the course number and title for this class?

   _____

2. When do final exams for this semester/term begin, and when do they end?

   _____

3. How many points does an A count as in a grade point average?

   _____

4. What is the last day to drop a class this semester/term without an academic penalty?

   _____

5. How many credits does your college require for graduation?

   _____

6. When does preregistration begin for the next academic semester/term?

   _____

Step 2: Be prepared to discuss your answers in class.

GARFIELD © 2002 Paws, Inc. Reprinted with permission of UNIVERSAL UCLICK. All rights reserved.

The MOTIVATION to succeed

Psychologists have learned that performance is based on a combination of ability and motivation. Since you are attending this college, you probably have the ability to succeed. Given that assumption, motivation represents the key ingredient that can determine your level of success. To help you gauge your motivation, the following exercise will measure your current drive for success in college.

EXERCISE 4 **The Motivation Thermometer**

Step 1: For each statement, indicate the extent to which that statement is *currently true* for you by circling "Agree," "Somewhat Agree," "Somewhat Disagree," or "Disagree."

1. I have bought my textbooks and thoroughly examined each of them.

   Agree   Somewhat Agree   Somewhat Disagree   Disagree

2. I want to accomplish great things while I am a student here.

   Agree   Somewhat Agree   Somewhat Disagree   Disagree

3. I plan to attend all my classes regularly.

   Agree   Somewhat Agree   Somewhat Disagree   Disagree

4. I am striving for straight As.

   Agree   Somewhat Agree   Somewhat Disagree   Disagree

5. I have looked at the holdings of a library on this campus.

   Agree   Somewhat Agree   Somewhat Disagree   Disagree

6. I have communicated with one of my professors before or after class or outside the classroom.

   Agree   Somewhat Agree   Somewhat Disagree   Disagree

7. I am confident in my study skills.

   Agree   Somewhat Agree   Somewhat Disagree   Disagree

8. I have started to arrange for a part-time job or an extracurricular activity.

   Agree   Somewhat Agree   Somewhat Disagree   Disagree

9. I have had at least one conversation with another student here about one of my classes.

   Agree   Somewhat Agree   Somewhat Disagree   Disagree

10. I regularly use an academic planner.

    Agree   Somewhat Agree   Somewhat Disagree   Disagree

11. I am successful at managing my time.

    Agree   Somewhat Agree   Somewhat Disagree   Disagree

12. I like the challenge of a difficult class.

    Agree   Somewhat Agree   Somewhat Disagree   Disagree

13. I have begun to think about the classes to take for next semester/term.

    Agree   Somewhat Agree   Somewhat Disagree   Disagree

14. I don't spend hours wasting time on the computer or cell phone.

    Agree   Somewhat Agree   Somewhat Disagree   Disagree

15. I think about the next exam every time I attend class.

    Agree   Somewhat Agree   Somewhat Disagree   Disagree

16. I am up-to-date right now for all my assignments.

    Agree   Somewhat Agree   Somewhat Disagree   Disagree

17. I like to learn new things.

    Agree   Somewhat Agree   Somewhat Disagree   Disagree

18. When I sit down to study, I am focused and not easily distracted.

    Agree   Somewhat Agree   Somewhat Disagree   Disagree

19. I always pay attention in class and listen carefully to the professor.

    Agree   Somewhat Agree   Somewhat Disagree   Disagree

20. I have already found one or more quiet places on campus to study.

    Agree   Somewhat Agree   Somewhat Disagree   Disagree

Step 2: Calculate your *Degree of Motivation Score*. For each item, give yourself

> **5** points if you circled "Agree,"
>
> **4** points if you circled "Somewhat Agree,"
>
> **3** points if you circled "Somewhat Disagree," and
>
> **2** points if you circled "Disagree."

Add all your points to determine your *Degree of Motivation Score*.

Item	Number of Points	Item	Number of Points
1.	_____	11.	_____
2.	_____	12.	_____
3.	_____	13.	_____
4.	_____	14.	_____
5.	_____	15.	_____
6.	_____	16.	_____
7.	_____	17.	_____
8.	_____	18.	_____
9.	_____	19.	_____
10.	_____	20.	_____
		Total Points:	_____

Step 3: Circle the number for your Total Points on the *Motivation Thermometer* on the next page. Then, analyze your *Degree of Motivation* by matching your level of drive to the number in the scale.

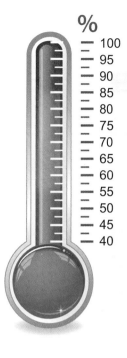

Score	Level of Drive
86 to 100	The red area suggests you have a hot level of drive for success in college.
70 to 85	The orange area suggests you have a moderately hot level of drive for success in college.
55 to 69	The green area suggests you have a moderately cool level of drive for success in college.
40 to 54	The blue area suggests you have a cool level of drive for success in college.

Step 4: Discuss in class what a student can do to overcome a low level of drive, including setting up SMART goals (see the Introduction).

Status Check

While it may seem early, it is probably a good time to reflect on how life is going for you in your role as a college student. The exercise below represents a status check. Think about your responses and their implications for you. Your answers can help give you some perspective on where you have been and where you are heading.

EXERCISE 5 **Status Check for Your Attitudes and Experiences**

Step 1: Fill in the blank in each sentence to express your true feelings and attitudes about your college experience thus far. Use as many words as you need.

1. The person on campus I would most like to meet is _____.

2. I feel most optimistic that I will _____ while I am a student here.

3. I should express my appreciation to_____ for helping me to get to this point.

4. The biggest change for me since I came to college has been _____. _____

5. The most fun I have had so far as a college student is _____. _____

6. The course that worries me the most is _____.

7. I expect to get my highest grade in _____.

8. A campus extracurricular activity that appeals to me is _____.

9. I miss _____.

10. Since I have been a student here, I have been most surprised by _____

Step 2: Be prepared to share your responses in class. It may be helpful to reflect periodically on your experiences and adjustment as your college years unfold.

Use the resource links to find additional information at *CollegeSuccess.andYOU.com*

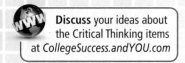
Discuss your ideas about the Critical Thinking items at *CollegeSuccess.andYOU.com*

Thinking Critically About . . . Understanding the College Scene: Right From the Start

Critical thinking involves an active evaluation of information using careful, thoughtful, and reasoned judgments.

1. **External motivation** means finding sources of motivation outside yourself (for example, "good grades"), while **internal motivation** means finding sources of motivation from within yourself (for example, "ambition"). Judge whether external or internal motivators are more useful for achieving a goal.

2. Explain how your college's administration has helped you adjust to your early experiences as a college student.

3. Based on your first impressions, how are college professors similar to and different from high school teachers?

4. Analyze what factors make a college class more or less motivating.

5. Compare and contrast the needs of a college community to the needs of a small city.

Online Learning

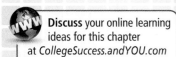
Discuss your online learning ideas for this chapter at *CollegeSuccess.andYOU.com*

Just as for traditional classes, online students are expected to meet all the academic demands of the class in a timely manner. Success in online classes requires not only adequate computer skills but also the self-discipline and personal responsibility to manage an unstructured learning environment. Online classes usually consume more dedicated time than you expect, so prioritizing your schedule to accommodate online learning may be a challenge.

Don't be surprised if you take at least one class online during your undergraduate years. In recent years, approximately 20% of college students in the United States were enrolled in an online class.[4] The trend toward more online education is expected to continue.

One major format for online classes allows the student to have course material available at any time, 24/7, and interact with the instructor and other students via designated chat sites or email. Another major format presents classes with video instruction in real time. The teacher is separated in space from the students but not in time. This format permits the possibility of some form of immediate interactions between the faculty member and students or among students. At some institutions, there are also hybrid classes in which students meet in class part of the week and online another part of the week. While some students may take online classes from a location that is many miles from campus, students in residence may elect or need to take an online class. For example, a student may take a required course in the 24/7 format because of a conflict with another scheduled class. A point to remember is that the online professor may be able to monitor the frequency and time involved in every login for each student.

CHAPTER CHALLENGE

ARE YOU AS SMART AS A COLLEGE FRESHMAN?

When some students begin college, they worry that they are at a disadvantage because of their educational backgrounds. They may believe, for example, that their high school preparation was not as good as that of their fellow students. Others may feel confident in one specialized area but insecure about their other classes. And some new students may have taken time off between high school and college, making them feel rusty in the role of a student. The transition to college can be enhanced by becoming familiar with the college scene and maintaining a positive outlook.

A CASE STUDY: FACING THE CHALLENGE OF . . .
ARE YOU AS SMART AS A COLLEGE FRESHMAN?

Jerry never really cared about getting good grades during high school. No one in his family had attended college, so he wasn't planning to go either. As Jerry grew up, he spent a lot of his free time in his room concentrating on his passion, reading superhero comics and graphic novels. He had many friends around the world with the same interest, and he loved sharing his opinions with them over the Internet. During high school, Jerry rarely did homework but still got decent grades in all his courses except math, which he found totally boring. Around this same time, Jerry started a blog about superheroes that received many hits. He occasionally even included his own original drawings as part of the blog. Aside from his online friends, Jerry hung out at a comic book store where he knew most of the customers. After graduating from high school, he took a full-time job managing the comic book store. Dreaming about becoming a comic book artist, he realized after one year of work that he would need to go to college to achieve his goal. He decided to work part-time while beginning his studies at the local community college. Jerry was very worried about succeeding in college since he had never been close to anyone who had gone to college, and he knew very little about life as a college student.

OVERCOMING THE CHALLENGE OF . . .
ARE YOU AS SMART AS A COLLEGE FRESHMAN?

Be prepared to discuss your answers to the following items: (1) What are some of the challenges of being a first-generation college student like Jerry? Provide some recommendations for Jerry to assist him in becoming familiar with key aspects of college life. (2) Jerry discovers he is as smart as a college freshman when he gets an A and the comment "Nicely done" on his first English essay. Assume that Jerry wants to talk with his professor about taking a class in creative writing. How should he proceed? (3) Identify the skills Jerry would have developed related to his passion for comic books and graphic novels. How can these skills contribute to his college success?

Key Chapter Strategies

- Carefully study the syllabus for each one of your classes.
- Participate in class or meet with your professors so they get to know you.
- Begin gathering recommendations from other students about really good classes or professors.
- Familiarize yourself with the student rights and responsibilities handbook.
- Use your campus website to access course information, the academic calendar, and the library.
- Insert key dates from the academic calendar into your planner.
- Keep your motivation going strong.
- Read these books to help you start off right: *Chicken Soup for the College Soul: Inspiring Stories for College Students* by Jack Canfield, Mark Victor Hansen, Kimberly Kirberger, Dan Clark, and James Malinchuks; and *Navigating Your Freshman Year* by Students Helping Students[6].

Can You Recall It?

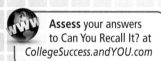

Assess your answers to Can You Recall It? at *CollegeSuccess.andYOU.com*

Directions: To review your understanding of the chapter, choose the correct term from the list below and fill it in on the blank. You will not use every term.

syllabus	plagiarism	audited
elective	motivation	master's degree
defamation	PhD	associate professor
prerequisite	tenure	dean's list

1. Copying someone else's work and passing it off as your own is called _____ .

2. Professor Martin's earning a/an _____ indicates that she received a graduate research degree that enables her to be called "Dr. Martin."

3. _____ occurs when false statements hurt a person's reputation.

4. High enough grades might qualify you for the _____.

5. Vince has increased his enthusiasm and energy for his studies after encouragement from his academic advisor. Vince's reaction is an example of increased _____.

6. _____ is the name for lifetime status awarded to a faculty member because of that faculty member's scholarly achievements.

7. A/An _____ class involves sitting in on the class but not receiving credit or a grade.

8. The guide for a course that provides the schedule for lecture topics, assignments, and exams as well as special information about the professor's expectations is called a/an _____.

Web Activity: Learning More About Your College

Directions: Your college probably has a rich and special history. Use the college website to answer the questions that follow. If necessary, you can also use search engines and online reference sources. Write below the exact website addresses where you found the answers.

1. When was your college founded and by whom? _____

   Website address: _____

2. Identify your school's motto. _____

   Website address: _____

3. Name a successful and/or famous person who graduated from your college. _____

   Website address: _____

4. How many students were enrolled in your school during the last academic year? _____

   Website address: _____

5. Who is the president of your college? _____

   Website address: _____

Reflection Time

Achieving Your Goals by Understanding the College Scene: Right from the Start

The ancient Chinese philosopher Lao Tse said, "A journey of a thousand miles must begin with a single step."[7] Based on the information in this chapter, list and discuss three steps that you can take to help you succeed "Right from the Start."

_____

_____

_____

_____

_____

_____

_____

_____

_____

_____

_____

2

Becoming Familiar with Campus Resources

In this chapter, you will move toward achieving your goals by

- identifying offices that provide academic support.

- gaining awareness of the wide range of available student activities and services.

- understanding the campus services provided to maintain your health and protect your safety.

Find additional tools and resources at *CollegeSuccess.andYOU.com*

Self-Assessment: How Was Your Visit?

Step 1: From the list below, select one campus resource that you have not yet used or visited. Note that the particular office providing a given resource may have a different name on your campus from those listed below.

A. Academic Support Service (a tutoring or learning lab)

B. Career Center

C. Counseling Center

D. Financial Aid Office

E. Wellness Center

Step 2: After your visit, answer the following questions:

1. Write the specific name of the center/office you visited.

_____

2. In which building is the center/office located?

_____

3. From your understanding, what are the services offered by the center/office you visited?

_____

_____

_____

4. In two or three sentences, describe your experience while visiting the center/office you selected.

_____

_____

_____

5. In the future, how might you use the services of the center/office you visited?

_____

_____

_____

Step 3: Be prepared to share your experiences with your classmates. Use this opportunity not only to learn more about the campus resource you visited but also to discover information about the other campus resources listed above.

Because the administrators of your college want you to succeed academically and thrive personally, the school offers a wealth of services designed to support your college experience. These services are provided by highly specialized offices managed by professionals who have had advanced training in their fields. An enormous bonus is that no additional cost is usually required to make use of campus resources, because you have already paid for these services through tuition and fees.

Campus resources for students include offices that support academic work, promote life outside the classroom, and emphasize health and safety. During your college years, you will probably have a reason to use the services of many, but not necessarily all, of these agencies. Also, not every college has all of these resources for its students. For example, colleges without student residence halls are less likely to have a health service than colleges with residence halls. Additionally, colleges use a variety of names to designate student support services, so you will need to learn the specific names on your campus. The most common names for student support services are used in this chapter.

Being willing to visit these campus resources through your own initiative, as well as taking the time to use them, can help you achieve your goals. Some campus administrators and professors believe that immature students are reluctant to use campus services because of worry or embarrassment over what their friends may think. In contrast, using these services demonstrates your willingness to assume personal responsibility and independence. Before you read the rest of this chapter, preview the following list of resources, activities, and services that are featured.

Campus Resources and Services

Academic Resources and Services
Registrar's Office
Academic Advising
Disabilities Office
Academic Support
    Reading-Learning Lab
    Tutoring Service
    Math Center
    Writing Center
    Foreign Language Lab
    Computer Lab
    English as a Second
        Language Lab
Bookstore
Library
Study Abroad
ROTC

Student Activities and Services
Activities
    Student organizations
    Volunteering
    Performing arts
    Competitive teams
Support Services
    Financial Aid Office
    Bursar's Office/
        Student Accounts Office
    Career Center
    Dean of Students Office
    Residential Life
    Multicultural Student Office
    International Student Office

Resources for Your Health and Safety
Physical Care
    Wellness Center
    Health Service
Mental Care
    Counseling Center
    Chaplains
    Sexual harassment policy

Safety
    Campus Police Department

ACADEMIC RESOURCES

Here are some useful resources that exist on many college campuses. These services are designed to provide you with support for your academic experiences.

Registrar's Office

The Registrar's Office is one of the many important college offices on campus. This office is responsible for course registration, which is usually managed online, in person, by fax, or by telephone. Because certain classes may be very popular or fulfill necessary requirements, registering as early as possible may have a significant benefit.

The Registrar's Office is also responsible for managing the academic calendar. Being aware of the academic calendar and meeting all applicable deadlines can preserve your academic record and even save you late fees or extra tuition costs. One of the Registrar Office's major challenges involves the scheduling of classes and classrooms. Most typically, weekday classes are scheduled either Monday, Wednesday, and Friday (MWF) or Tuesday and Thursday (TR).

Another critical function of the Registrar's Office consists of maintaining students' academic records. It accumulates and distributes grade reports. Transcripts summarizing all these grade reports are sent upon student request to prospective employers or educational programs by the Registrar's Office. This office also verifies that students on the verge of graduation have met all of the school's academic requirements.

Will's Suggestions for Getting a Great Schedule

William is a graduating senior from Michigan State University who has made devising a perfect schedule into an art form. Here are his top tips:

1. Get advised early and register as soon as possible to avoid getting shut out of the classes you want.
2. Read student evaluations of faculty and talk to other students about their experiences.
3. Find out if any students receive preference for early registration, such as athletes, residence hall assistants, or student government officers. Even if you don't qualify now, maybe you will later.
4. Use the "Goldilocks Principle." Take a balance of difficult and easy classes that makes your schedule "just right."
5. Arrange a schedule that gives you enough flexibility for work, extracurricular activities, class assignments, and personal time.
6. If you select several reading-intensive classes, choose some others that have lower reading loads.
7. Consider the location of your classes if they are back-to-back, so you have enough time to get from one to another.
8. Check out the size of the class in advance and choose a section according to your preferences.
9. In semesters full of your heaviest classes, take a more fun elective.
10. It's okay to take your sleep needs into account; if you hate waking up early, try to avoid 8:00 A.M. classes.

Academic Advising

Your **academic advisor** has the critical role of helping you select a favorable schedule while fulfilling your graduation requirements. An advisor may have been assigned to you before you arrived on campus and helped you sign up for classes. Working with a competent advisor can be very beneficial. Advisors usually know the reputation of particular professors and classes, so they can recommend classes to take or avoid. They also can guide you about preparing for educational or career opportunities after graduation. <u>Because academic advisors can guide you in your choice of classes and keep you on track for graduation, request an academic advisor as soon as possible if you don't have one.</u>

Advisors may be faculty members, full-time professional advisors, or peer counselors. **Peer counselors** are advanced undergraduate students trained to advise newer students. If you have not yet selected a major, you may have a more general advisor until you are assigned an advisor in your field of study after you select a major.

Students who are performing poorly in a class or feeling overwhelmed may decide to drop that class around midterm. You must ordinarily obtain your advisor's consent and signature before you can drop any class. An advisor can help you evaluate your plan thoroughly before completing the drop. The advisor could, for instance, arrange tutoring if you simply need help to succeed in the class.

To work most effectively with an advisor, students should initiate and show up for regular appointments with the advisor around the time class registration becomes available. At most schools, students are *not* contacted first by their advisor. When you initially meet with your advisor, help the advisor understand your background, your academic strengths and weaknesses, and your educational goals. Experienced students usually review the course catalog and their degree requirements before their advisement meeting. Then they bring a list of the classes they are considering and a set of questions for the advisor to the meeting.

Popular Questions for an Advisor

1. "What can I do to prepare for my appointments with you?"
2. "How do I declare or change a major?"
3. "Can a student have more than one major?"
4. "Do I meet the requirements for this class?"
5. "Are there any graduation requirements that you think I should be fulfilling now?"
6. "If I want to study abroad, when should I fit that in?"
7. "Can I get credit for a course that I might take at another college this summer?"
8. "What is the highest number of credits I can take in one semester?"
9. "When do I apply to graduate?"
10. "Are there any classes you think I should take that I haven't taken yet?"

Disabilities Office

According to the **Americans with Disabilities Act (ADA)**, most colleges must have a Disabilities Office to arrange accommodations for students who have physical, learning, or psychological disabilities.[1] To use these accommodations, students need to register with the office and provide documentation from doctors to verify their disabilities. The professional staff at the Disabilities Office will then decide the nature of the accommodation that is appropriate for each student's needs. For example, a student who is documented to have attention deficit disorder (ADD) may be provided with a note-taker or be administered exams without time constraints in a room with no distractions. Any request for special accommodations needs to be made as soon as possible.

Academic Support

The following academic support departments are designed to enhance all students' abilities to learn effectively in their classes and to perform well on tests. Here are examples of services that appear on many campuses, though the specific titles vary. Sometimes several of these services may be incorporated into one office.

Class Coaching: If you need help in a class, qualified tutors can provide academic support.

Reading-Learning Lab

The Reading-Learning Lab usually provides individual or group help with learning skills at a student's request. A lab may sponsor seminars on such topics as time management, organization skills, reading comprehension, note-taking, and study skills. Programs may also be offered about strategies for taking college exams or standardized tests for professional or graduate schools. While these offices are primarily designed to target students who feel academically challenged, students with high grades sometimes take advantage of academic support services to boost their skills even further.

Tutoring Service

The Tutoring Service provides individual or small group tutoring for specific classes. Usually, advanced students who have already succeeded in those classes are hired to provide the tutoring. On many campuses, tutoring is free. Students must officially request tutoring through these offices, and it is ideal to make that request as early as possible. Tutoring is most likely to be available for introductory and intermediate classes but is less likely for advanced classes. Some colleges also offer free access to a national online college tutoring site.

Math Center

With mathematics classes often required but perceived as challenging for many students, colleges furnish ample support to help students succeed. A popular form of math support combines regular individual or group tutoring by advanced students with walk-in help for solving specific problems. Study sessions for specific exams may also be offered. Additionally, some math centers conduct workshops on topics such as introducing students to the use of specialized calculators.

Writing Center

These agencies offer help in enhancing writing skills. Students can arrange for individualized assistance in improving the organization of papers, the correction of grammar and punctuation, or editing. In the Writing Center, an expert will usually be available to review writing assignments for classes and provide suggestions for improvement.

Foreign Language Lab

Students enrolled in a foreign language course are given an opportunity to improve their conversational skills by using the interactive media provided in a language lab. These labs also usually include the availability of videos and computer programs in foreign languages.

Computer Lab

The Computer Lab features hardware and software beyond what students usually bring to college. For example, the Computer Lab will probably have scanners or statistical packages that you need for particular academic assignments. Knowledgeable computer assistants typically staff the Computer Lab to help you understand how to use the equipment and programs.

English as a Second Language (ESL) Lab

For students whose original language is not English, many colleges provide English as a Second Language (ESL) classes, labs, workshops, and tutoring to prepare for classes requiring English. If you need this help, check with your academic advisor or your college's general academic support program.

Bookstore

The campus bookstore stocks virtually all the books and educational materials faculty members assign to classes. Additionally, the bookstore sells school supplies, popular literature, and clothing with the school's logo. Many campus bookstores today are run by national chains, such as Follett or Barnes and Noble. These stores usually sell both new and used textbooks and may be the only bookseller that can accept financial aid vouchers. Buying textbooks online has become very popular because prices are frequently lower than those at the campus bookstore. However, students buying books online should be careful to purchase the exact edition that the professor requires because editions of texts often change every few years. Also, it's a good idea to make sure that you can receive a text ordered online by the time you will need it for a class.

Library

The campus library embodies the core academic mission of a college. The library's staff aims to make scholarly information available to students and faculty through its collection of books and journals as well as its ever-expanding digital resources. You should also be aware that some professors place library materials on reserve for exclusive use by students in their classes.

During your college years, you are very likely to be assigned a research paper that will lead you to use the resources at the library. You may not realize that campus librarians have selected their careers in part because they like to be helpful. Therefore, a reference librarian will be eager to provide help in your research, if you ask.

Investigating the Library

Step 1: Visit your campus library. If your campus has more than one library, select whichever one you prefer. Answer the following questions about the library you visit.

1. What is the name of the library?

   _____

2. What are the library's days and hours of operation?

   _____

3. Identify a special event (exhibition, lecture, or workshop) at this library.

   _____

4. Where is the best place to study at the library, and why do you think so?

   _____

5. Is it possible for you to print, copy, or scan documents in the library?
   _____ If yes, what are the fees?_____

6. Check out a book relevant to a class you are currently taking and complete these items:

   1. Title of book _____
   2. Author(s) _____
   3. Library call number _____
   4. Relevant class for this book _____
   5. Briefly explain how the information in this book can help you in your class.

      _____

      _____

7. What surprises you the most about this library?

   _____

   _____

   _____

Step 2: Visit and browse the library's website. You will need to use the website to answer the questions below.

1. What is the exact web address for this library?

   _____

2. What information, such as a student ID number, must you provide in order to gain full access to this website?

   _____

3. List two searchable databases or online catalogs that are available to you through the library's website.

   _____

Step 3: For the next class, you may be asked to share your answers with your classmates. Be sure to bring to class the book that you checked out from the library.

Study Abroad

Because they place an increasing value on globalization, many colleges maintain study abroad offices that arrange for a semester or a yearlong international educational experience. Some schools even help defray the costs for a student to study internationally. A number of colleges have developed partnerships with institutions around the world. For students, living and attending college in another country can build confidence, provide educational experience unavailable back home, develop friendships, encourage appreciation and knowledge of another culture, and advance communication skills in a foreign language. If you are interested in studying abroad but do not want to spend an entire semester away, your college may provide briefer classes led by faculty members from your school. Recent research by the University of Minnesota reports that studying abroad for only a month or less can produce some benefits comparable to those from a longer period of study.[2]

Tour de France: You can expand your experiences by studying abroad.

ROTC (Reserve Officer Training Corps)

ROTC programs, offered by many colleges, involve courses of study and training associated with a specific military branch, including the U.S. Army, Navy, Marine Corps, and Air Force. Successful completion of these programs results in commission as an officer following college. Students usually participate in these programs while maintaining a regular academic curriculum. Students enrolled in ROTC receive significant financial help with tuition and expenses. Retired General Colin Powell, who joined ROTC at New York's City College, said that he gained the important quality of self-discipline through his ROTC program (aside from starting him on the path to an illustrious career as a general and secretary of state).[3]

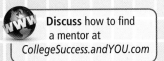

Discuss how to find a mentor at *CollegeSuccess.andYOU.com*

Finding a Mentor

A personal mentor can be a remarkable asset for a college student. A **mentor** is usually a person who has already succeeded with the opportunities and challenges you are facing, and who can advise you how to maximize your potential. You may be able to model yourself after your mentor. You can find a mentor among the staff and faculty as well as among students or professionals who have already succeeded in your field of study. Why would such individuals agree to mentor a college student? Along with experiencing the joy of helping another person succeed, the mentor also may have had a personal advisor when he or she was a student and may be proud to assume the role. In your search for a mentor, you might seek out a professor who has shown particular interest in your academic and professional development. Or you may be able to work closely with a graduate student or faculty member by volunteering to assist with a research project. You can also find potential mentors at meetings related to your field of study that are attended by alumni or professionals from the community. You might be pleasantly surprised when you ask someone to become your mentor.

Additional Academic Resources Available at Your College

Your college may have educational resources beyond those mentioned here. Your professor may suggest other resources, or you may discover them on your own. Use this space to identify and describe up to five other academic resources that are available to you.

First Academic Resource

Name: _____

Services to students: _____

_____

Second Academic Resource

Name: _____

Services to students: _____

_____

Third Academic Resource

Name: _____

Services to students: _____

_____

Fourth Academic Resource

Name: _____

Services to students: _____

_____

Fifth Academic Resource

Name: _____

Services to students: _____

_____

Student ACTIVITIES and SERVICES

Most colleges provide a variety of enriching activities and supportive services. Understanding a representative sample of student activities and services will enable you to identify those that you want or need to access.

Activities

A college student who actively engages in extracurricular pursuits is much more likely to achieve success than a less-active student. Usually, colleges provide plenty of opportunities for student engagement. Major categories of activities at colleges include student organizations, volunteering, performing arts, and competitive teams. Along with many other benefits, participation in such activities can develop leadership skills and social relationships.

As a new college student, you may initially be attracted to more activities than you can successfully manage. However, you will inevitably discover your passions and become involved specifically where your interests lie.

Student Organizations

Most colleges boast of a wide range of student organizations. As examples, students can become involved in organizations related to academic or career interests, cultural or religious identification, student media, sororities or fraternities, student government, politics, and hobbies. Typically, student organizations must have a sponsor from the faculty, staff, or alumni. Official student organizations may receive funding from a student programming council, supervised by a college administrator.

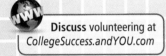

Discuss volunteering at *CollegeSuccess.andYOU.com*

At most colleges, the Student Activities Office manages the funding and provides support for student organizations. This office also arranges leadership training programs for students who aspire to become officers in their organizations. Leaders in student organizations often qualify to join honor societies.

Volunteering—Civic Engagement

Thousands of college students are promoting positive social change through their volunteer efforts on campus and in their communities. At the same time, volunteers benefit by mastering new skills, ranging from construction to tutoring to environmental advocacy, while developing self-esteem through feeling good about their accomplishments and genuine caring for others. Opportunities for civic engagement are usually coordinated by a single office on campus. Service learning classes also feature volunteer assignments. Additionally, many students use breaks from classes to travel to other parts of the country as part of formal programs to build houses for the needy, clean up the environment, plant trees, or provide other similar services.

With these significant volunteer contributions, communities hosting colleges are very fortunate. However, college towns also provide many important services and opportunities to students. On the next page is a list of some of the major community resources.

Constructive Project: You can help your community and enrich yourself by participating in volunteer projects.

Community Resources	
Banks	Political participation
Libraries	Specialized health care
Hair salons/barber shops	Part-time jobs
Shops	Movies and entertainment
Restaurants	Recreational opportunities
Transportation	Museums

Performing Arts

Talented students may become engaged in artistic activities such as campus theater, music, dance, journalism, creative writing, broadcasting, and filmmaking. These activities are typically open to anyone from any major, but you may need to demonstrate the necessary talent in order to participate. Although requiring a significant time commitment, participation in the arts can enable you to work closely together with similarly talented students, can prepare you for a career in that field, and may simply be fun!

Competitive Teams

While most colleges recruit significant numbers of student-athletes for intercollegiate sports teams, other students participate with those teams as managers, cheerleaders, training assistants, ticket clerks, marching band members, and broadcasters. Along with intercollegiate teams, many colleges support **club teams**, which are non-varsity teams that usually are managed by students and compete in equestrian, bowling, skiing, triathlon, and other competitive sports with teams from other colleges. Colleges also feature a wide array of intramural competitions in which teams of students at a college compete with each other. Additionally, schools may sponsor non-athletic teams in activities such as debate, chess, web design, Model United Nations, and engineering.

EXERCISE 2 **Implementing Involvement**

Step 1: List and briefly describe three meetings or campus events that you have attended since you arrived on campus.

1. Name of a meeting or event you attended.

_____

_____

Why did you decide to attend this meeting or event?

_____

_____

Explain how well this meeting or event did or did not meet your expectations and what you learned.

_____

_____

_____

2. Name of a meeting or event you attended.

_____

Why did you decide to attend this meeting or event?

_____

_____

Explain how well this meeting or event did or did not meet your expectations and what you learned.

_____

_____

3. Name of a meeting or event you attended.

_____

Why did you decide to attend this meeting or event?

_____

_____

Explain how well this meeting or event did or did not meet your expectations and what you learned.

_____

_____

_____

Step 2: Name two campus organizations or activities you might like to join. Then explain why each organization or activity appeals to you and how engaged in it you wish to become.

1. Name of a campus organization or activity you would like to join.

_____

Explain why this organization or activity appeals to you and how engaged in it you wish to become.

_____

_____

_____

2. Name of a campus organization or activity you would like to join.

_____

Explain why this organization or activity appeals to you and how engaged in it you wish to become.

_____

Step 3: Be prepared to discuss in class your experiences with campus meetings or events. Also, be prepared to discuss your interest in specific campus organizations and activities.

Support Services

Financial Aid

A recent study found that 69.9% of college freshmen report that they receive financial aid in the form of scholarships or grants.[4] The specialists at your school's Financial Aid Office help interpret and apply an extremely complex set of rules to administer this assistance. The Financial Aid Office is responsible for processing loans, grants or scholarships, and government-subsidized jobs given to students to help them pay for their education. Students must pay back loans but ordinarily do not have to pay back grants or scholarships. If you plan to renew or apply for financial support for the next academic year, it will be helpful for you to do as much research on your own as possible and then check with your Financial Aid Office around January of this academic year to find out exactly what will be available for you. Your family may also be required to meet deadlines in submitting tax forms and other detailed financial information. Because some scholarships may require that you maintain a certain grade point average, you will want to understand such criteria.

In case you are having financial problems this year, you may be able to find a job through the student employment section of financial aid. For U.S. citizens meeting certain financial requirements, federally funded work-study positions may be available. With these jobs, students can earn an hourly wage subsidized by the federal government. Unsubsidized part-time jobs are usually also available around campus for students who do not qualify for college work-study programs.

Bursar's Office

Just as the Registrar's Office keeps track of your academic record, the Bursar's Office, or Student Accounts Office, maintains your financial records. The Bursar's Office sends out bills to students or their families and is responsible for collecting the payments. Miscellaneous charges, such as an unpaid library or parking fine, may be added to the costs of tuition and fees. This office may also offer a debit card that can be used for meals and other campus purchases.

Career Center

The Career Center on your campus is a useful place to visit early in your college years. You will probably be surprised at the array of resources designed by this center primarily to help students find appropriate jobs after they graduate. The Career Center emphasizes the value in starting the process of career development as early as the first year on campus. The center and its website will help guide you in the development of a résumé that you will need to constantly update as your accomplishments grow. This office may also help you identify appropriate internships while you are a student. Eventually, the professionals at this office may arrange interviews for you either in their office or at job fairs they organize.

Dean of Students Office

On many campuses, the Dean of Students Office represents the nucleus for student support services. As a result, you can probably consult a staff member in this office for a connection to the best resource on campus for fulfilling a certain need or solving a particular problem. The scope of the Dean of Students Office varies tremendously from campus to campus. However, this office is almost always responsible for the administration of the college's manual of student rights and responsibilities. Student academic and personal integrity is a key value upheld by the dean and his or her staff. When a student violates campus community standards, the Dean of Students Office will hold hearings involving possible disciplinary sanctions against that student. Even though the dean of students may be viewed as the disciplinary dean, the person in that role is usually respected as the guardian of fair treatment and protection for all students.

Residential Life

Residential Life is an administrative unit that strives to enhance the college experience for students living in campus housing. Among the members of a residence hall staff, residence hall assistants (RAs), who are advanced undergraduates, have the most direct and regular contact with residents. Usually, an RA is responsible for programming, maintaining rules, resolving conflicts, providing peer counseling, and building a community for students living together in one area of a dorm. Because they have recently been freshmen themselves, RAs can be very helpful advisors about a wide variety of concerns related to college adjustment.

Multicultural Student Office

Because most campuses have very diversified student bodies, the Multicultural Student Office is designed to support students of varied minority backgrounds. On some campuses, these offices are called ALANA (which stands for African American, Latino(a), Asian American, and Native American). In addition to providing academic support for student success and progress toward graduation, multicultural or ALANA offices encourage a sense of community and pride among members of the groups represented. One of the most important roles for these agencies is the promotion of harmony and mutual respect through dialogue and programs involving students from many different backgrounds.

International Student Office

If you are a student from another country, the International Student Office provides an important lifeline for you on campus. Your initial contacts with this office probably came through information sent to you while you were still back home. Upon your arrival on campus, the staff of this office probably welcomed you during an orientation program in which you met other international students. In addition to providing ongoing programs designed for international students, one of this office's most critical functions is making sure that immigration requirements are being processed correctly. Because the rules for immigration are complicated, the International Student Office can help you understand how to comply with the requirements. This office also attempts to serve as a liaison with your country's official representatives in the United States.

EXERCISE 3 Map Quest

As you learn about the nature of the many helpful offices at your school, you will benefit by identifying their locations. Most schools have a Transportation and Parking Office to manage travel around campus. You probably were given a paper map provided by this department during orientation, and you also can access a map on your school's website. By now, these maps may have enabled you to devise an effective route for getting to your classes and back. It is possible during these trips that you are passing the buildings housing important campus functions without realizing it.

Step 1: Get a copy of your campus map. Either use one that you received when you arrived on campus or print one from your college's website. Follow the directions in the items below. You will need to mark on the map, so use a copy that you can write on. Bring your map to class with the following information marked on it:

1. To indicate *your starting point*, draw a circle around *one* of the following: your residence hall; the parking lot where you often park your car; the subway, bus, or train stop where you usually arrive on campus; or the campus entrance you typically use. Write "#1" next to the circle you draw.

2. Draw a circle around the building in which this class is located. Write "#2" next to the circle you draw.

3. Draw a circle around the location of the library that you used to answer the questions in Exercise 1. Write "#3" next to the circle you draw.

4. Draw a circle around a place where you might eat lunch. Write "#4" next to the circle you draw.

Step 2: On the map, draw a line connecting #1 to #2 to #3 to #4 to show a path you could travel to get from your starting point to your final destination, a place where you might eat lunch.

Step 3: In the space below, list three buildings you would pass by on your path. For each building, write the name of the building and its main purpose. Also, place a check mark next to these three buildings on your map.

1. Name of building: _____

Building's purpose: _____

2. Name of building: _____

Building's purpose: _____

3. Name of building: _____

Building's purpose: _____

Step 4: In class, be prepared to discuss your map, route, and the buildings passed. Your professor may pair you with another student to share/compare information.

Additional Student Activities and Services Available at Your College

Your college may have student activities and services beyond those mentioned here. Your professor may suggest other activities and services, or you may discover them on your own. Use this space to identify and describe up to five other student activities and services that are available to you.

First Student Activity or Service

Name: _____

Services to students: _____

_____

Second Student Activity or Service

Name: _____

Services to students: _____

_____

Third Student Activity or Service

Name: _____

Services to students: _____

_____

Fourth Student Activity or Service

Name: _____

Services to students: _____

_____

Fifth Student Activity or Service

Name: _____

Services to students: _____

_____

Resources for your HEALTH and SAFETY

While a college's mission emphasizes educating students and cultivating their personal development, the school's administration recognizes that health and safety are necessary for students to achieve these goals. These concerns are particularly relevant at colleges with many students living away from their families. To assist students on these campuses as well as at many commuter colleges, important physical care, mental care, and security services are provided.

Physical Care

Wellness Center

The campus Wellness Center is typically much more than a gym where you can work out to keep yourself physically fit. The **wellness philosophy** is a holistic viewpoint that promotes your total personal development.[5] This philosophy encompasses the dimensions of social, spiritual, intellectual, physical, and emotional development while encouraging you to give back to others. To foster your growth in these dimensions, the Wellness Center offers or cosponsors many educational programs on topics like nutrition, stress management, and meditation to complement the core fitness activities. Regularly taking part in the programs and fitness activities of the Wellness Center can enhance your experience as a college student and teach you good habits for the future. The best approach to getting started is to make an appointment with a Wellness Center professional to assist you in establishing the right wellness program for you.

All's Well: The Wellness Center offers you opportunities to stay fit and healthy.

Health Service

At most colleges with residence halls, the Health Service is provided to take care of students' health needs. You might want to think of the Health Service staff as primary care providers like your family doctor or general practitioner back home. In fact, you can benefit by finding one health service professional you prefer and continuing your care with that provider. The Health Service nurses, physicians, and other assorted health professionals attempt to prevent illness and resolve students' medical issues. If your needs are beyond their general practice capabilities, they are likely to refer you to a specialist in the larger community. Members of the Health Service staff usually check to make sure you have the proper immunizations before you arrive on campus. The Health Service also usually manages campus health insurance plans for students. You can check about the fees to use your campus Health Service.

Mental Care

Counseling Center

In all probability, your college years will be the only time in your life when you can access free or low-cost expert mental health services. College administrations support campus counseling services because they realize that the coinciding demands on students of a college education and the development of independence or management of a job or family can be stressful. Staffed by caring psychologists, psychiatrists, social workers, and mental health counselors, these offices usually offer short-term interventions, such as therapy and psychiatric medicine, to help you deal with adjustment concerns that may be interfering with your ability to be the best student that you can be. Because of the high demand for the services of these centers, students with long-term problems are sometimes referred off campus. The determination for what kind of help will work best is made at the first appointment. If you are interested, you can check out your Counseling Center's website to find out how to make that important first appointment.

Chaplains

Many colleges—both those affiliated with a specific religion and those that are nonde-nominational colleges—have campus chaplains available to assist students in fulfilling their spiritual needs. Often headquartered at religious houses on campus, chaplains lead services and foster religious awareness throughout the college community with activities and programming. Chaplains may provide consultation to individual students about spiritually related issues, such as handling a loved one's death, intermarriage, and a change of faith. Sometimes a particularly wise and caring chaplain becomes a popular campus advisor, even with students from other religions. Chaplains also may be responsible for coordinating special religious needs such as class absences for religious observances and special dietary restrictions. Along with their belief in a higher power, chaplains promote ideals for students including hope and optimism, purpose in life, love, and morality. Participating in the services and programs of a religious house offers students a good opportunity to meet people with similar beliefs. Students whose specific religious group lacks representation on campus may obtain a recommendation for an off-campus house of worship from a campus chaplain.

Sexual Harassment Policy

As an outcome of the Civil Rights Act of 1964, colleges in the United States have established sexual harassment policies to protect students and employees from unwanted sexual gestures and comments.[6] According to a recent study published by the American Association of University Women, one-third of first-year college students of both sexes report experiencing sexual harassment.[7] Most frequently, men report being teased about being gay while women report being the target of sexual jokes, comments, and touching. Offensive remarks made online may be included in the definition of sexual harassment. Sexual harassment can occur when victims of such behavior suffer from a hostile environment that is interfering with their academic performance and personal comfort. Another form of sexual harassment arises when a person uses a position of power, such as being a professor, to extract sexual favors from a student. A specific office on campus is designated to investigate complaints of sexual harassment. You can find out about the location of this office from your school's website or from the Dean of Students Office.

Safety

Campus Police Department

Colleges take the responsibility for protecting students and students' property very seriously. Departments with names such as Campus Security, Public Safety, or College Police are charged with the significant task of preventing crime on campus and offering protection to students. To accomplish these goals, campus police officials ask students to keep their dorm doors locked, avoid walking alone at night, hide valuables in car trunks, and engrave or label important possessions. Officers patrol the campus and respond to trouble upon request. Many campus security offices also offer escorts for students who must walk alone at night. While the most frequent crimes on campus are theft and alcohol violations, bodily crimes also occur. Especially concerned with sexual assault, campus police departments usually sponsor special programs to prevent these attacks.

The Guardians: The Campus Police Department works to keep your campus safe.

> To protect yourself when you are out on campus, Captain Bob Chaffee of the Colorado State University Police Department recommends adopting the vigilance of cats. He notes "cats are never tense. Their ears are open all the time. They are always paying attention. They're not panicky or stressed. They just always pay attention. It's just being certain of what's around you."[8]

Additional Resources for Your Health and Safety Available at Your College

Your college may have health and safety resources beyond those mentioned here. Your professor may suggest other resources, or you may discover them on your own. Use this space to identify and describe up to three other health and safety resources that are available to you.

First Health and Safety Resource

Name: _____

Services to students: _____

_____

Second Health and Safety Resource

Name: _____

Services to students: _____

_____

Third Health and Safety Resource

Name: _____

Services to students: _____

_____

Step 1: Assume that friends contact you for advice about where to get assistance on campus for ten different concerns. Your friends do not have the advantage of taking this class. Recommend which resource, activity, or service is best for your friends to contact for each of the ten concerns. Choose from the list below of all the resources, activities, and services included in this chapter. Write your recommendation in the space provided.

Academic Resources and Services
Registrar's Office
Academic Advising
Disabilities Office
Academic Support
    Reading-Learning Lab
    Tutoring Service
    Math Center
    Writing Center
    Foreign Language Lab
    Computer Lab
    English as a Second
        Language Lab
Bookstore
Library
Study Abroad
ROTC

Student Activities and Services
Activities
    Student organizations
    Volunteering
    Performing arts
    Competitive teams
Support Services
    Financial Aid Office
    Bursar's Office/
        Student Accounts Office
    Career Center
    Dean of Students Office
    Residential Life
    Multicultural Student Office
    International Student Office

Resources for Your Health and Safety
Physical Care
    Wellness Center
    Health Service
Mental Care
    Counseling Center
    Chaplains
    Sexual harassment policy

Safety
    Campus Police Department

1. "I am not sure if my tuition and fees are paid in full."

   Recommendation: _____

2. "My philosophy class has caused me to have religious concerns."

   Recommendation: _____

3. "I need help preparing for an interview for a summer internship."

   Recommendation: _____

4. "I feel sad all the time."

   Recommendation: _____

5. "All I do is eat, study, and go to class. I need to get physically fit."

   Recommendation: _____

6. "I am tired of getting obscene phone calls that I know are coming from another student."

   Recommendation: _____

7. "You remember I was diagnosed with attention deficit disorder? I'm so distractible I can't seem to concentrate on exams even though I'm keeping up with my meds. Maybe I need more time to take exams."

   Recommendation: _____

8. "I don't know which foreign language class I need to take to graduate."

   Recommendation: _____

9. "I'm having trouble keeping up with all my reading assignments. I think I need to learn how to read faster and better."

   Recommendation: _____

10. "I want to transfer to another school and I need a transcript, but I don't know where to go to get one."

   Recommendation: _____

Step 2: Be prepared to discuss in class the resource, activity, or service you recommend for each of your friends' concerns.

From resources to
RESOURCEFUL

This chapter is intended to supply you with the information about campus resources you will need to take advantage of your educational opportunities and achieve your goals. Incorporating your willingness to use these resources with your unique personal qualities can help lead you to success.

Use the resource links to find additional information at *CollegeSuccess.andYOU.com*

Thinking Critically About . . .
Campus Resources

Critical thinking involves an active evaluation of information using careful, thoughtful, and reasoned judgments.

1. If you become a billionaire and decide to donate money to one of the campus resources at your college, which one would you choose and why? Explain how you would recommend the money be used to improve your choice.

2. Colleges provide campus resources as a part of your tuition and fees. Some students argue that they would prefer lower tuition and fees even though there would be a reduction in the number and kind of resources available. Take a position on this issue (for or against reducing costs leading to a reduction in campus resources) and make a convincing argument.

3. Invent a new campus resource. Formulate a purpose for the resource and justify its necessity.

4. Look into a crystal ball and predict which five campus resources you are most likely to use during your college years. For those five resources, rank-order them from the resource you think you will use most frequently to the one you are likely to use the least. Explain why you rank-order them in this way.

5. Colleges often use campus resources as recruitment tools for prospective students. Judge which five resources on your campus to include in a tour. Explain how each of these resources creates a positive impression for prospective students.

Discuss your ideas about the Critical Thinking items at *CollegeSuccess.andYOU.com*

Online Learning

Discuss your online learning ideas for this chapter at *CollegeSuccess.andYOU.com*

While students taking online classes from a distance cannot avail themselves of some campus resources, others are readily available through the Internet. For example, distance-learning students writing assigned research papers can access many references through a library's website. Effective communications with the Registrar's, Bursar's, Academic Advising, and Financial Aid Offices also may be conducted online. In contrast, resources such as health care and student activities are probably unavailable for distance learners. To provide counseling to these students, the Counseling Center at George Mason University experimented with distance counseling using video transmissions, and some other centers have introduced this alternative. Students engaged in distance learning must replace recreational resources, including the campus Wellness Center and student activities, with comparable services in their home communities. Check your college's website to discover the services available to you.

CHAPTER CHALLENGE

FEELING LOST AS A NEW STUDENT ON CAMPUS

The transition to becoming a new student on a college campus can seem very lonely at first until the right opportunities for social bonding come into focus. Patience is often required; resisting impatience and maintaining an optimistic attitude are great virtues for eventually getting connected. After all, many new students have been forced to give up the securities of their social networks as well as their family support systems when they arrive at college. In their quest to develop new friendships, some students just happen to meet compatible people right away in settings like orientation, class, or their dorm floors. When other less-fortunate students see those lucky few happily hanging out together, they often are envious, yearning to belong to their own comfortable social group again. The good news on most campuses is the abundance of opportunities for students to meet like-minded people.

A CASE STUDY: THE CHALLENGE OF . . .
FEELING LOST AS A NEW STUDENT ON CAMPUS

Coming from a small, rural town, Margot felt overwhelmed when she moved into a dorm at a large state university of approximately 40,000 students about two hours from her hometown. Margot is a lively, outgoing girl who had starred in several high school theater productions. She expected to develop new friendships easily and had reason to believe through summer emails that her roommate would become a close friend. However, during orientation, Margot discovered that her roommate was a computer science major who was nice enough, but they didn't really share many of the same interests. Several of the girls on Margot's floor came from the largest city in the state and seemed to already know each other. They rebuffed Margot's efforts to hang out with them. When she phoned home after the first week of classes, she couldn't help but cry to her parents about her feelings of isolation and rejection. She emailed her best friend, who had started college in another state; she was sympathetic and advised Margot to hang in there.

OVERCOMING THE CHALLENGE OF . . .
FEELING LOST AS A NEW STUDENT ON CAMPUS

Be prepared to discuss your answers to the following items: (1) Identify three campus resources that can help Margot connect with other students. Explain specifically how each resource can be helpful. (2) Formulate actions that freshmen can take to reduce feelings of loneliness. (3) Predict what a fulfilling social life might be like for Margot during her sophomore year.

Key Chapter Strategies

- Take the time and initiative to use campus resources as needed.
- Become involved in student organizations and activities.
- Make sure you have regular consultations with your academic advisor. If an advisor has not been assigned, ask for one immediately.
- Find a mentor and meet periodically with that person.
- Librarians like to help; consult one when you have any reference questions.
- Begin to investigate your college's study abroad program.
- Consult this book for more information: *Getting the Best Out of College* by Peter Feaver, Sue Wasiolek, and Anne Crossman.[9]

? ? Can You Recall It?

Assess your answers to Can You Recall It? at *CollegeSuccess.andYOU.com*

Directions: To review your understanding of the chapter, choose the correct term from the list below and fill it in on the blank. You will not use every term.

Dean of Students	**federal work study**	**Bursar**
ADA	**multicultural**	**ROTC**
wellness	**sexual harassment**	**mentoring**
Registrar	**ESL**	**public safety**

1. The Civil Rights Act of 1964 resulted in _____ policies.

2. The _____ Office is in charge of student discipline.

3. A national program sponsored by the U.S. government that helps pay students' wages for work on campus is_____.

4. _____ is an academic program that trains future military officers.

5. The office responsible for providing you with a copy of your transcript is the Office of the _____.

6. ALANA is an office on many campuses that offers services to _____ students.

7. A/An _____ laboratory helps students who are non-native speakers of English improve their skills in English.

8. The _____ philosophy promotes the positive development of such major aspects of a person's life as fitness, spirituality, socialization, and intellect.

Web Activity: Site Inspection

Directions: In this chapter, you have learned some general facts about a wide variety of campus resources. It will prove helpful for you to follow up that general information with more specific information about those offices on your campus. To accomplish this goal, read the website of any three resources on your campus that have been described in this chapter. Name each resource whose website you have reviewed and then answer the questions below.

I. First Resource: _____

Website address: _____

    1. What is the major function of the resource? _____

    _____

    2. What are the office's hours? _____

    _____

    3. In which building is this office located? _____

    _____

    4. Name the director of the office or the person in charge. _____

    _____

II. Second Resource: _____

Website address: _____

    1. What is the major function of the resource? _____

    _____

    2. What are the office's hours? _____

    _____

    3. In which building is this office located? _____

    _____

    4. Name the director of the office or the person in charge. _____

    _____

III. Third Resource: _____

Website address: _____

    1. What is the major function of the resource? _____

    _____

    2. What are the office's hours? _____

    _____

    3. In which building is this office located? _____

    _____

    4. Name the director of the office or the person in charge. _____

    _____

Reflection Time

Achieving Your Goals by Becoming
Familiar with Campus Resources

Create an advertising slogan for one of your campus resources. Try to write an effective slogan by making it accurate, concise, distinctive, and memorable. Explain how your slogan captures the main benefits of the campus resource and why this slogan would motivate students to want to visit and use that resource.

_____

_____

_____

_____

_____

_____

_____

_____

_____

_____

_____

_____

_____

_____

_____

_____

_____

_____

_____

_____

_____

_____

_____

_____

_____

_____

Managing Your Time: A "Positive" Approach

3

In this chapter, you will move toward achieving your goals by

- facing the challenges of managing a college schedule.

- empowering yourself to gain control over your schedule through the **POSITIVE** approach to time management.

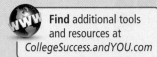

Find additional tools and resources at *CollegeSuccess.andYOU.com*

Self-Assessment:
What Is Your Typical Daily Schedule?

Step 1: For this "Self-Assessment" activity, choose a typical day you will be attending classes. Beginning with that particular morning, fill in the boxes labeled "Activities" on the schedule with your activities (including eating and sleeping) for the next twenty-four hours. Complete all the boxes for the full twenty-four hours. See **Step 2** for a chart giving examples of possible activities for the boxes. Of course, you may have different activities from those listed.

Your Schedule for _____ **(date)**

Time	Activities
7:00 A.M.– 8:00 A.M.	
8:00 A.M.– 9:00 A.M.	
9:00 A.M.– 10:00 A.M.	
10:00 A.M.– 11:00 A.M.	
11:00 A.M.– Noon	
Noon– 1:00 P.M.	
1:00 P.M.– 2:00 P.M.	
2:00 P.M.– 3:00 P.M.	
3:00 P.M.– 4:00 P.M.	
4:00 P.M.– 5:00 P.M.	
5:00 P.M.– 6:00 P.M.	
6:00 P.M.– 7:00 P.M.	
7:00 P.M.– 8:00 P.M.	
8:00 P.M.– 9:00 P.M.	
9:00 P.M.– 10:00 P.M.	
10:00 P.M.– 11:00 P.M.	
11:00 P.M.– Midnight	

Time	Activities
Midnight–1:00 A.M.	
1:00 A.M.–2:00 A.M.	
2:00 A.M.–3:00 A.M.	
3:00 A.M.–4:00 A.M.	
4:00 A.M.–5:00 A.M.	
5:00 A.M.–6:00 A.M.	
6:00 A.M.–7:00 A.M.	

Step 2: Review your schedule and fill in the amount of time that you spent on any of the following activities. Your total should equal twenty-four hours.

Activity	Amount of Time
Attending class	
Studying outside of class	
Traveling to and from school and work	
Working at a job	
Participating in extracurricular activities	
Engaging in exercise or recreation	
Communicating by cell phone, text message, email, Facebook, etc.	
Taking care of personal hygiene	
Sleeping	
Eating	
Spending time with friends	
Performing housekeeping, family, or personal responsibilities	
Doing something else, such as (please specify: _____ _____)	

Step 3: Answer the following questions about the sample daily schedule that you just completed.

1. Give specific examples of how you think you used your time effectively during these twenty-four hours.

   _____

   _____

   _____

   _____

   _____

2. Give specific examples of how you think you used your time ineffectively during these twenty-four hours.

   _____

   _____

   _____

   _____

   _____

3. What would you plan to change in the future to make your schedule more helpful to you?

   _____

   _____

   _____

   _____

   _____

4. How much time per day do you think you should spend on schoolwork to maximize the likelihood that you will achieve your college goals?

   _____

   _____

   _____

   _____

   _____

Managing a College Schedule: IT'S ABOUT TIME

Now that you have thought about your current schedule, you may feel that you need more control of your time to help you become successful and happy as a student. Before you begin to learn about how to accomplish this goal of time management, consider these two first-year students with dramatically different schedules. These two extreme examples will help you understand some important time management issues.

Two Extreme Examples

Student #1: Manny

Manny is an 18-year-old freshman whose hometown is about 150 miles away from his college. He is the first person in his family to attend college. Manny was a good student in high school, but his weakest subject was math. He and his parents are worried that he must take a more advanced math class in his first semester of college. Because he has never lived away from home before, his parents are also concerned about his adjustment to living on campus and all the new responsibilities that will be involved. With these issues in mind, Manny and his parents have decided that he should only take twelve credits during his first semester. His other classes, besides math, are English, Spanish, and history. Manny has decided not to look for a part-time job or participate in extracurricular activities until he proves that he can succeed in his classes.

Distractors: Managing your college schedule can be challenging.

Student #2: Liz

Liz just got married. She is a 28-year-old commuter student who had been working full-time as a dentist's receptionist before her marriage. She and her new husband calculated their budget and agreed that she could work part-time in her previous job, thirty hours a week, and go to school full-time, taking as many credits as possible in a semester so she could graduate quickly. Liz has signed up for eighteen credits in her first semester. Her goal is to become a nurse. She realizes that some of the classes will require additional hours because of labs. At the suggestion of her advisor, Liz joined the National Student Nurses Association, which meets for an hour weekly on her campus. She is worried about succeeding in the first year of nursing classes, maintaining her thirty hours of part-time work a week, spending a great deal of time commuting, and keeping up with her new household responsibilities.

Comment on Manny and Liz

There is a marked contrast in time commitments between Manny and Liz. Because Manny attends class twelve hours a week and also must attend a floor meeting for his dorm for one hour a week, he has a **fixed time commitment** on his weekly schedule of thirteen hours. Liz attends class eighteen hours a week and works part-time thirty hours a week with a club meeting for an hour every week, meaning that she has a fixed time commitment of forty-nine hours a week. Manny and Liz face very different problems in managing their college schedules.

EXERCISE 1 **Which Schedule Is More Challenging?**

Step 1: Answer the questions below.

1. Which of these two students' schedules do you think is more challenging in terms of adjusting to academic demands such as studying and completing assignments? Check one:

Manny's schedule: _____

Liz's schedule: _____

2. Explain in two or three sentences the reason(s) for your choice of Manny's schedule or Liz's schedule.

   _____

   _____

3. What problems in college adjustment do you think will affect the student who you believe has the more challenging schedule?

   _____

   _____

4. Which of these schedules does your current schedule most closely resemble and how?

   _____

   _____

Step 2: Review the following analysis of the time management issues faced by Manny and Liz.

There is no correct answer to Question 1 above. Many time management experts would argue that Manny has the more challenging schedule because he has too much free time. It is extremely difficult for most 18-year-old college freshmen to adjust effectively to so much free, unstructured time—that takes a lot of maturity. A student like Manny was accustomed to having a more structured life during high school: waking up early each morning at the same time for eight hours of school, possibly working or else participating in sports or extracurricular activities after school, and doing homework in the evenings, especially when urged by family members. The challenge to complete academic assignments in college is often great for a first-year student like Manny who has so much free, unstructured time. Manny's ability to manage his time could be helped by a part-time job or extracurricular activities. Increasing his time commitments will provide him with more structure, which is actually an aid to effective time management.

It certainly could also be argued, however, that Liz's situation is more difficult because her schedule is so overloaded, and she just got married. Along with being limited in the amount of time available for schoolwork, Liz may also suffer from fatigue and stress. To manage her schedule successfully, Liz probably should drop at least one class and, if feasible, reduce her workload.

As you can tell, first-year students such as Liz and Manny experience very different time management challenges. Both can profit from learning the **POSITIVE** approach to time management, a method that provides useful strategies for all students.

What is "POSITIVE" time management?

POSITIVE time management is a step-by-step method designed so that you can use your strengths to become a better student and yet still have time for non-academic activities. The technique emphasizes learning how to make decisions about which activities are most important to you and then how to arrange enough time to complete those activities while still fulfilling your other needs. Learning **POSITIVE** time management will be useful for you in achieving your goals in your everyday life, in college, and in your career.

You have already begun to recognize the importance of your daily schedule through the "Self-Assessment" activity at the beginning of this chapter. As you explore **POSITIVE** time management, you will learn the steps to managing your unique schedule so that you can achieve your educational goals while reducing wasted time and still having time for fun and social activities.

Each letter in the word **POSITIVE** represents a step in time management:

off the mark .com   by Mark Parisi

SLEEP, PLAY, EAT, SLEEP, SLEEP, PLAY, PLAY, SLEEP, SLEEP, SLEEP, EAT, SLEEP, PLAY, SLEEP, P,

TIME MANAGEMENT FOR CATS

P = Prioritizing tasks
O = Operating efficiently
S = Scheduling time
I = Itemizing a "To Do" list
T = Tackling procrastination
I = Ignoring distractions
V = Visualizing success
E = Enjoying your achievements

Now you'll learn more about each of these steps toward effective time management. Applying these steps can help you succeed in becoming an organized, productive student.

Prioritizing Tasks

While the amount of time available for all of us is a constant twenty-four hours per day, you have many daily choices in your schedule beyond the fixed commitments of classes or work. For example, you can talk on the cell phone, watch TV, spend time with friends, exercise, or browse the Internet. However, students intent on achieving their college goals usually decide to give priority to the completion of their academic assignments and to studying. These students place the completion of their class work as priority number one, while planning ahead enough to also allow for personal time.

Educators recommend at least two hours of study per week for each credit.[1] That means if you are taking twelve credits, you will need to set aside at least twenty-four hours in an average week for schoolwork. However, if you are taking eighteen credits, you will need a minimum of thirty-six hours dedicated to schoolwork.

You should note that the number of hours for study will vary from week to week according to the particular academic demands at any given time. Before exams or when papers are due, you will need to put more time into your classes. However, you might also experience some lighter weeks when you can reduce your academic work hours.

During any given week, non-academic activities might become important to you. For example, you might need to go to a medical appointment or an interview for a job. Spending your time on such matters is certainly important, and with planning, you can accommodate them in your schedule without sacrificing other priorities.

Operating Efficiently

Has this ever happened to you? You sit there trying to read your textbook—but as the minutes pass, you feel like you are just staring at the page as your mind wanders, with no progress in your schoolwork. Although you know that you still have plenty of time, you are beginning to think that you will never finish your work.

Cyril Northcote Parkinson, a British author, points out that work often expands to fill the time available to finish it. This observation is known as **Parkinson's Law**, which suggests that people have a tendency to take longer than necessary to complete a task when they know that more time is readily available.[2] Parkinson's Law means that students with open schedules often take longer to complete their assignments than necessary. Sitting in your room reading or studying a textbook and feeling like you are not making progress is unpleasant, and it's a waste of time that could be devoted to something more productive or enjoyable.

The application of the **POSITIVE** system of time management allows you to prioritize your studies while also giving you the time to perform some of your other favorite or necessary activities. A key to such success is understanding the concept of efficiency. The ideal mind-set for getting work done is known as *efficiency*. The field of industrial psychology has defined **efficiency** as getting the most output or productivity for the least input or work. That almost sounds too good to be true—getting more done *and* working less time! However, efficient students can learn to get the work done well so that they can go on to whatever else is important to them.

Avoiding Inefficiency: If you use your time efficiently, you spend fewer hours to get more work done.

Some students recognize that they have more trouble concentrating during the morning, during the afternoon, or during the evening. You may find that you can work consistently better during one of these time periods, sometimes referred to as your **biological prime time**. You will probably be more efficient if you arrange the work that requires your greatest concentration during your biological prime time.

✓ *Are You* **POSITIVE?**

1. Rate your current ability to **Operate efficiently**. Circle your choice.

   Very Weak   Somewhat Weak   Somewhat Strong   Very Strong

2. What two strategies can you implement to improve your ability to **Operate efficiently?**

   First strategy: _____

   _____

   Second strategy: _____

   _____

   Be prepared to share your strategies in class.

Scheduling Time

Now that you understand the importance of how to **P**rioritize tasks and **O**perate efficiently, you are ready to develop a schedule for your next week, the third step in the **POSITIVE** approach to time management. Creating a weekly schedule might seem unexciting, but it is extremely helpful. To get the most out of your schedule, you need to know a magic number.

The Magic Number Is . . . 168

If you can remember the **number 168**, you will be moving toward accomplishing the task of time management. Why is 168 a magic number? It represents the total number of hours in a week—twenty-four hours multiplied by seven days. Everyone has 168 hours in a week. To gain control of your schedule, you will need to work with one week, or 168 hours, at a time. Once you gain control of your schedule through manipulating the hours of the magic number, you will have moved toward becoming a more successful student.

EXERCISE 2 **What Is Your Schedule?**

Step 1: Use the blank schedule below to begin to prepare your own weekly schedule. Fill in the boxes representing only your fixed, regular school or employment commitments (for example, your classes, scheduled meetings, or job) for each day. You are not expected to fill in every box.

Time Management Weekly Schedule Planner
(fixed, regular time commitments)

	Sun	Mon	Tues	Wed	Thurs	Fri	Sat
7:00 A.M.–8:00 A.M.							
8:00 A.M.–9:00 A.M.							
9:00 A.M.–10:00 A.M.							
10:00 A.M.–11:00 A.M.							
11:00 A.M.–Noon							
Noon–1:00 P.M.							
1:00 P.M.–2:00 P.M.							
2:00 P.M.–3:00 P.M.							
3:00 P.M.–4:00 P.M.							
4:00 P.M.–5:00 P.M.							
5:00 P.M.–6:00 P.M.							
6:00 P.M.–7:00 P.M.							
7:00 P.M.–8:00 P.M.							
8:00 P.M.–9:00 P.M.							
9:00 P.M.–10:00 P.M.							
10:00 P.M.–11:00 P.M.							
11:00 P.M.–Midnight							

	Sun	Mon	Tues	Wed	Thurs	Fri	Sat
Midnight–1:00 A.M.							
1:00 A.M.–2:00 A.M.							
2:00 A.M.–3:00 A.M.							
3:00 A.M.–4:00 A.M.							
4:00 A.M.–5:00 A.M.							
5:00 A.M.–6:00 A.M.							
6:00 A.M.–7:00 A.M.							

When preparing a weekly schedule, some students like to use a daily or weekly planner. While you can buy such scheduling books at a bookstore or an office supply store, you might prefer to use more modern technology to help with your scheduling. Some of the communication devices that you use every day may include features that can assist you with time management. For example, very useful calendar programs can be accessed via your computer. A popular program is Microsoft Outlook, which allows you to schedule your activities in Windows through a user-friendly format. Google Calendar, accessible with a Gmail account, provides similar calendar functions. Many smartphones also have calendar datebook apps that you can use to schedule activities and arrange reminders.

1. Rate your current ability to **Schedule time**. Circle your choice.

Very Weak   Somewhat Weak   Somewhat Strong   Very Strong

2. What two strategies can you implement to improve your ability to **Schedule time**?

First strategy: _____

_____

Second strategy: _____

_____

Be prepared to share your strategies in class.

Scratch-Offs: Creating a "To Do" list and deleting items as you complete them facilitates the management of your tasks.

Itemizing a "To Do" List

"To Do" lists are checklists of academic activities or personal obligations that you need to complete. Regular fixed time commitments, such as the classes and jobs that you wrote into your weekly schedule in Exercise 2, are not usually included in a "To Do" list. The items in the "To Do" list need to be rank-ordered when you plan your schedule each week.

Many students maintain and update their "To Do" lists through such means as a computer, smartphone, or planner. You will probably find it very rewarding to be able to delete or cross off items from your "To Do" list as you complete them.

Some items in a "To Do" list require immediate attention, and others may not need to be completed for several weeks. Moreover, some items can be divided into several smaller steps. For example, if you are writing an academic paper, you can divide it into steps such as choosing your topic, completing a literature review, structuring an outline, and writing a first draft.

A sample "To Do" list of schoolwork priorities follows. You will notice that the items chiefly are designated for completion in the following week, but the anticipated date of completion for items taking longer is also included.

Sample "To Do" List of Academic Priorities

"To Do" List	Estimated Time Required	Expected Date of Completion
History text—read Ch. 4	2 hours	Tuesday evening
Math problem set	2 hours	Monday evening
History paper—research	3 hours	Thursday afternoon
English essay	2 hours	Tuesday evening
Spanish text—read Ch. 7	2 hours	Monday afternoon
Spanish text—read Ch. 8	2 hours	Saturday afternoon
History paper—outline	2 hours	Saturday afternoon
History exam—study	3 hours	Thursday evening
Math exam—study	5 hours	Wednesday evening
Completion of history paper	15 hours	Two weeks from Sunday

Preparing an Academic "To Do" List

Step 1: Prepare a "To Do" list for yourself for the next calendar week, starting with tomorrow as your first day. Follow the same format as the sample "To Do" list given at the bottom of page 58. You may have to add lines or spaces.

My "To Do" List of Academic Priorities

"To Do" List	Estimated Time Required	Expected Date of Completion

Step 2: Go back to the schedule of fixed commitments that you completed in Exercise 2 on page 56. Fill in the empty boxes in Exercise 2 with each academic "To Do" item you listed above. Write with a different color than you used before for filling in these priorities, if you can. Note that you may divide your preparation hours for a particular class into different days, if you prefer. Following is an example of what your "Time Management Weekly Schedule Planner" might look like. In this example, the regular fixed commitments are written in black and the academic "To Do" priorities are written in red.

Time Management Weekly Schedule
(black = fixed commitments; red = "To Do" priorities)

	Sun	Mon	Tues	Wed	Thurs	Fri	Sat
7:00 A.M.–8:00 A.M.							
8:00 A.M.–9:00 A.M.							
9:00 A.M.–10:00 A.M.		Job		Job		Job	
10:00 A.M.–11:00 A.M.		Job	Spanish class	Job	Spanish class	Job	
11:00 A.M.–Noon		English class	Spanish lab	English class	Spanish lab	English class	

	Sun	Mon	Tues	Wed	Thurs	Fri	Sat
Noon–1:00 P.M.							
1:00 P.M.–2:00 P.M.		Read spanish	Job	Job	History research	Job	History outline
2:00 P.M.–3:00 P.M.		Read spanish	Job	Job	History research	Job	History outline
3:00 P.M.–4:00 P.M.			Job	Job	History research	Job	Read spanish
4:00 P.M.–5:00 P.M.		History class	Math class	History class	Math class	History class	Read spanish
5:00 P.M.–6:00 P.M.							
6:00 P.M.–7:00 P.M.							
7:00 P.M.–8:00 P.M.	Meeting			Study math			
8:00 P.M.–9:00 P.M.		Math prob. set	Read history	Study math	Study history		
9:00 P.M.–10:00 P.M.		Math prob. set	Read history	Study math	Study history		
10:00 P.M.–11:00 P.M.			English essay	Study math	Study history		
11:00 P.M.–Midnight.			English essay	Study math			
Midnight–1:00 A.M.							
1:00 A.M.–2:00 A.M.							
2:00 A.M.–3:00 A.M.							
3:00 A.M.–4:00 A.M.							
4:00 A.M.–5:00 A.M.							
5:00 A.M.–6:00 A.M.							
6:00 A.M.–7:00 A.M.							

Step 3: Be prepared to discuss in class the time challenges that arise from combining your "To Do" list with your already established fixed time commitments, which include your classes, job, and meetings. How does having your schedule for the week written out in a schedule planner help you with time management?

Now you should have a clear idea of your academic schedule for the upcoming week. Of course, your personal needs such as sleeping, eating, maintaining health and hygiene, and getting to and from class will also be important parts of your weekly schedule. Hopefully, you will have free time on your schedule that will allow you to fulfill your academic and personal priorities for the week while having some time for leisure. Having some free time each week to unwind and do fun things that are very different from schoolwork will actually help you become a more efficient student.

Are You POSITIVE?

1. Rate your current ability to **Itemize a "To Do" list**. Circle your choice.

   Very Weak   Somewhat Weak   Somewhat Strong   Very Strong

2. What two strategies can you implement to improve your ability to **Itemize a "To Do" list**?

   First strategy: _____

   Second strategy: _____

Be prepared to share your strategies in class.

Tackling Procrastination

You have now read about the first four parts of the **POSITIVE** time management system. You have studied **P**rioritizing tasks, **O**perating efficiently, **S**cheduling time, and **I**temizing a "To Do" list. Now you will **T**ackle procrastination. **Procrastination** is delaying the completion of something that should be finished now.

Annie will serve as a clear example of a well-intentioned first-year student who lets herself become a victim of procrastination.

During the third week of her first college semester, Annie realizes that she is falling behind in her class assignments. She decides to spend the entire evening alone in the library catching up. She needs to write an essay for English composition class, complete a problem set for precalculus, and read a chapter for world history. To write the essay, she brings her laptop to the library. As she starts to write, however, she remembers that she wants to update her Facebook page. She does that before returning to her essay. When Annie begins struggling with a good first sentence, she decides to work on her math problem set. She manages to complete three of the eight items before going to get a snack. When she returns to her desk, she begins reading the world history chapter but finds the politics of ancient Greece very boring. She gets through half the chapter before going back to her essay. She writes two paragraphs but feels very dissatisfied with her work; she knows she won't get a good grade on her essay and wishes she had more time to devote to writing. Because she decides she may feel more inspired to write later, she goes back to math and finishes two more problems before feeling frustrated about having spent so much time in the library and getting so few tasks done. She returns to her dorm room feeling defeated for accomplishing so little.

In this example, Annie is procrastinating. She keeps putting off the work for her assignments until—three weeks into the semester—she feels herself falling behind. Then she procrastinates more as she wastes her study time by falling into a cycle of putting off the completion of her assignments until frustration sets in.

Cycles of procrastination (like Annie's) are prevalent in many college students. For students with uncommitted, unstructured time, it is very tempting to put off today what presumably can be done tomorrow. Some students get into a semester-long pattern of procrastination with disastrous results.[3] The graphic below shows some of the leading reasons for procrastination in college students.

Reasons for Procrastination

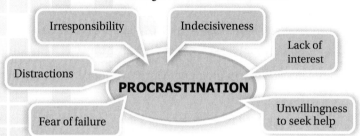

Fortunately, the principles of **POSITIVE** time management provide excellent solutions to the procrastination temptation. Prioritizing academic tasks, scheduling their completion, and sticking to that "To Do" list will allow you to have free hours to do whatever you want, with no concern about schoolwork hanging over your head. If a student like Annie applies the **POSITIVE** time management technique, she will learn to complete her assignments in a well-organized manner and, as a result, be less frustrated and feel better about herself.

Tackling procrastination really is equivalent to taking care of yourself and your needs.[4] Here are some statements that you can make to yourself inside your head that provide strategies to help you overcome the temptation to procrastinate.

Self-Talk to Tackle Procrastination

- "It doesn't have to be perfect."
- "I can work for a while even if I'm tired."
- "The sooner that I finish, the sooner I'll be able to have some fun."
- "If I really concentrate, I can get this finished."
- "Maybe I can break this big assignment into small parts and do the first part right now."
- "If I get my work done, I will make myself happier and more optimistic."
- "I'll give myself a little reward (such as downloading a song or watching some TV) after I finish studying."
- "I will make changes in my attitude right now, not starting tomorrow."
- "I will enjoy crossing tasks off my 'To Do' list."
- "I'll just stop worrying about failing and get this job done."
- "I need some extra help; I'll ask my professor."
- "I will be responsible to myself and get this assignment done."

Ignoring Distractions

A key to successful time management is the ability to ignore distractions. The **POSITIVE** approach has already helped you learn how to prioritize tasks and plan a schedule, but distractions can get in the way. College life is full of ready-made distractions.

Let's begin with an example of a freshman, Ray, who is taking twelve credits and intends to devote two hours to studying that night after spending the afternoon playing video games. As he begins studying, two friends stop by and ask if he wants to go off campus with them to get a pizza. Although hesitating, Ray simply can't resist, especially when he realizes that he can use part of his available time the next day to catch up. In this example, Ray is allowing a distraction to interfere with his study, a situation that may repeat itself again and again until his opportunity to study is lost. With the pizza invitation, Ray could tell his friends that he will be able to join them after he completes two hours of studying. If that works, Ray will have a much less worried outlook and the pizza will taste even better.

It is worth remembering that you have the capacity for a lot of control over your study environment, including the ability to turn off, hide, or work away from your entertainment and communication devices. In a 2013 article in *eCampus News*, Larry Rosen, a psychology professor at California State University, reports research findings that show how easily students are distracted in their studying environment by iPods, tablets, laptops, smartphones, and Facebook. He suggests that students will improve focus and concentration by periodically taking complete technology breaks for at least 15 minutes while completing assignments.[5]

You may also have to accommodate distractions from your living environment. For example, if your roommate is making too much noise, you can study in a less-distracting place such as a quiet corner of the library. Additionally, some of you may have distractions from family members, such as children. Perhaps you are a single parent struggling to find a quiet opportunity to study. You may find that your best study time takes place after the children go to sleep when you can minimize distractions.

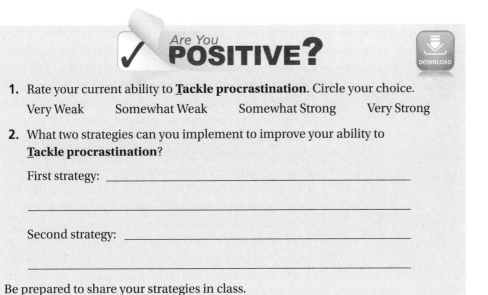

Staying Focused: You have the power to overcome distractions.

To Multitask or Not to Multitask?

With the availability of modern technology, performing several activities at once, or **multitasking**, is very common among college students. The typical scene of students walking to and from classes while talking on the cell phone is probably the most visible form of multitasking. There are probably some students who can adeptly switch back and forth between tasks and believe that they are performing each task well, or at least, well enough. When it comes to completing schoolwork efficiently, however, avoiding multitasking is the best strategy.[6]

One first-year student complained to his advisor that he just could not concentrate on his studies. When asked to describe how and where he studies, he explained that he studies in front of his computer every evening while waiting for communications from his girlfriend. He noted that he couldn't remember what he reads and makes little progress in his schoolwork as he "talks" to his girlfriend. In this case, the student is attempting to multitask with little success. To concentrate on his studies without distraction, he could study in another location with his communication devices turned off.

Using the principles of **POSITIVE** time management, you will have assigned certain times specifically for studying. You will probably be happier and more successful if you study during the times you have allotted and save your other activities for the designated free time on your schedule.

1 + 1 = 0: When it comes to schoolwork, multitasking leads to no one task being done well.

Are You POSITIVE?

1. Rate your current ability to **Ignore distractions**. Circle your choice.

   Very Weak   Somewhat Weak   Somewhat Strong   Very Strong

2. What two strategies can you implement to improve your ability to **Ignore distractions**?

   First strategy: _____

   _____

   Second strategy: _____

   _____

   Be prepared to share your strategies in class.

Discuss "To Multitask or Not to Multitask" at *CollegeSuccess.andYOU.com*

Visualizing Success

The next step in the **POSITIVE** approach to time management is visualization. **Visualization** is a technique that uses the imagination to help people achieve their goals. By visualizing an event or a situation as we would like for it to be, we can help ourselves achieve it. When you are struggling to study or complete an assignment, you might pause for a moment to visualize the outcome you are seeking, such as the completed chapters you are assigned to read or the finished paper.

Thoughts are forms of energy. If you can create a positive visualization by imagining overcoming the struggle to manage your time, you can help yourself achieve that goal. The energy becomes a more positive force to guide you to success.

To visualize yourself as an efficient and successful student, you will need to follow some basic steps:

1. Create a clear picture or idea of what you want to achieve.

2. Focus positively on the goal and how you will reach it.

3. Affirm to yourself what you will accomplish.

By following these simple steps, you can "see" what you want to accomplish. Just as with anything else, such a positive visualization of school success is likely to help lead to a positive result.

EXERCISE 4 **Visualizing Success**

Step 1: Think about a recent struggle you have had with managing your time. For example, it may involve trying to finish a reading assignment or working to complete a problem set.

1. What is the subject area, and what struggle have you experienced?

   _____

   _____

Step 2: Describe the image in your mind for each of the three basic steps for visualization:

1. What is a clear picture or idea of what you want to achieve?

   _____

   _____

2. Focus positively on the goal and how you will reach it. What outcome are you seeking? _____

   _____

3. Affirm to yourself what you will accomplish. State "firmly" what you will do to achieve the outcome you are seeking. "I will _____

   _____

   _____

Practicing these visualization steps regularly can lead you to better time management. You might decide to create a **SMART** goal as a part of your visualization. **SMART** goal setting is explained in the "Introduction" to this textbook on page xxi.

Are You POSITIVE?

1. Rate your current ability to **Visualize success**. Circle your choice.

   Very Weak   Somewhat Weak   Somewhat Strong   Very Strong

2. What two strategies can you implement to improve your ability to **Visualize success**?

   First strategy: _____

   _____

   Second strategy: _____

   _____

Be prepared to share your strategies in class.

Enjoying Your Achievements

Now you have arrived at the last step in the **POSITIVE** system for time management. Having followed all the guidelines and steps that brought you here, you are probably ready at last to enjoy your success as an organized student. Successful time management is one of the most important means to becoming a good student. By following the steps in **POSITIVE** time management, you will find yourself with designated times for all your work and school commitments, with additional hours designated as free. The free and open hours allow you to do whatever you want.

One way in which you might enjoy your achievement as an organized student is when friends notice and come to you for advice or suggestions on what they might do to manage their time as well as you do. You can glow in your success as you relate recommendations to them on what they can do to overcome their problems with time management.

EXERCISE 5   **Applying Time Management Principles**

Step 1: By this time, you have begun to feel mastery over your schedule. Imagine that your friends have noticed and are impressed. Three friends have come to you separately and in conversations with you have asked for advice about their time management problems. For each of these three scenarios, write your two best tips for your friends.

1. Gina complains that she has gotten into the habit of waiting until the last minute to study for her midterms and can't learn all the material in such a short time. What would you suggest to Gina?

   Tip 1: _____

   _____

   Tip 2: _____

   _____

2. Terrence started out with fifteen credits but dropped a class. Now he is taking twelve credits and has no other obligations or activities. He finds that he plays on the computer or spends time with his friends when he's not in classes, and he constantly puts off his studies because he feels like he has so much free time. As a result, he never seems to get his work done. What would you suggest to Terrence?

Tip 1: _____

_____

_____

Tip 2: _____

_____

_____

3. Kim is a very serious student who eventually wants to get into medical school. Besides her part-time job as a research assistant and her heavy involvement in extracurricular activities, she seems to spend almost all her time studying. In conversation with you, she says that she feels like she's not really concentrating very well when she studies, and she is afraid her lack of concentration will affect her grades. What would you suggest to Kim?

Tip 1: _____

_____

_____

Tip 2: _____

_____

_____

Step 2: Be prepared to share your tips with your classmates. In class, select which tips are most likely to help Gina, Terrence, and Kim.

✓ Are You **POSITIVE?**

1. Rate your current ability to **Enjoy your achievements**. Circle your choice.

   Very Weak   Somewhat Weak   Somewhat Strong   Very Strong

2. What two strategies can you implement to improve your ability to **Enjoy your achievements**?

   First strategy: _____

   _____

   Second strategy: _____

   _____

Be prepared to share your strategies in class.

Use the resource links to find additional information at *CollegeSuccess.andYOU.com*

Thinking Critically About . . . Time Management

Critical thinking involves an active evaluation of information using careful, thoughtful, and reasoned judgments.

1. Several years ago, Nike had a major advertising campaign featuring the slogan, "Just Do It." Evaluate the advantages and disadvantages of the use of that slogan by college students to overcome procrastination.

2. You are asked to speak to a group of high school students taking a tour of your college. One of them asks you how much studying you do each week, and if you have free time. Advise these students about the best way to manage their classes, possible jobs, and other responsibilities so that they can have free time available.

3. The use of electronic devices (including computers, smartphones, and tablets) has become a regular activity for college students. Compare and/or contrast the time-saving benefits today's electronic devices offer a student with the toll they may take as ways to waste time.

4. Experts report that using time management procedures contributes to a college student's stress reduction and sense of control. Analyze how the **POSITIVE** approach to time management can help college students reduce stress and gain a greater sense of control over their lives.

5. Compare and contrast the concepts of "spending time" and "spending money" for college students.

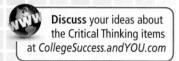
Discuss your ideas about the Critical Thinking items at *CollegeSuccess.andYOU.com*

Online Learning

"Distance learning requires students to be . . . better time managers . . ."
—**Doug Valentine**[7]

Online learners may need to apply time management skills to their schedules *even more* than students in face-to-face environments. The demands from family and jobs can overshadow the need to study for classes, so studying gets postponed, and then, postponed again. The on-campus learning environment does not surround you and become a part of your everyday awareness. Thus, studying may not be in the forefront of your consciousness.

The steps of **POSITIVE** time management offer you a workable method to manage your schedule. As a distance learner, you will find you have time for your family, for your job, *and* for your studying. The best part, though, is that if you follow **POSITIVE** time management suggestions, you will have hours in your schedule designated as free and open. These are *your* hours when you can find fulfillment in activities that are important to you.

Discuss your online learning ideas for this chapter at *CollegeSuccess.andYOU.com*

CHAPTER CHALLENGE

NO TIME-OUTS FOR STUDENT ATHLETES

In their early days of college, student athletes quickly learn that their time is filled. Their daily lives are dominated by athletic commitments, which can consume 30 to 40 hours a week beyond the time required for classes and studying. As with other freshmen, they also discover the increasing responsibilities of taking care of themselves while developing new relationships. However, student athletes are students first. They must maintain the minimum of a full-time course load with acceptable grades to stay eligible. With such difficult schedules, keeping a focus on learning and academic success can be very tough.

A CASE STUDY: FACING THE CHALLENGE OF . . . NO TIME-OUTS FOR STUDENT ATHLETES

An all-state lineman in high school, Robert was confident that he would succeed as a college football player. He hadn't really thought much about classes until they began. Almost immediately, he felt overwhelmed. He hadn't been expected to study much in high school, so he felt lost about completing his college assignments. On most weekdays during college football season, he was expected to attend class, meet with trainers, practice for four hours, attend a required study hall, meet with the line coach, and watch films of the upcoming opponent. During the second week of classes, he attended a session led by an athletic department advisor. Robert was shocked when the advisor suggested that he spend about twenty-four hours per week beyond classes for schoolwork. Robert knew he was capable of accomplishing what was expected of him; he just wasn't sure how he could keep everything straight, have enough study time, and not miss important deadlines.

OVERCOMING THE CHALLENGE OF . . . NO TIME-OUTS FOR STUDENT ATHLETES

Be prepared to discuss your answers to the following items: (1) Determine which specific steps of the **POSITIVE** time management system are more relevant for Robert. Why are these steps more relevant? (2) Compare and contrast the time management issues for an athlete like Robert with the time management issues for a student not involved in any activities besides classes. (3) Some argue that the time management structure necessary for college athletes to cope with their many daily obligations helps them adapt to college life better than other students. Explain why very busy athletes might have an advantage despite their hectic schedules.

Key Chapter Strategies

- Write out your schedule and update your "To Do" list at the beginning of each week.
- If your schedule includes too much free time, try to add a part-time job or a major extracurricular activity.
- If your schedule is overloaded, try to cut back on selected time commitments, if at all possible.
- Stay up-to-date on your regular assignments while keeping an eye on those that are longer term.
- Remember the magic number of 168 hours in a week. Those hours belong to you—to manage.
- Tailor your schedule to your style and needs.
- Read these helpful books on time management: *How to Get Control of Your Time and Life* by Alan Lakein[8] and *Best Practices: Time Management: Set Priorities to Get the Right Things Done* by John Hoover.[9]

Can You Recall It?

Assess your answers to Can You Recall It? at *CollegeSuccess.andYOU.com*

Directions: To review your understanding of the chapter, choose the correct term from the list below and fill it in on the blank. You will not use every term.

fixed time commitment	prioritizing	credit
procrastination	self-talk	visualizing
extracurricular activity	Parkinson's Law	"To Do" list
efficiency	multitasking	the magic number

1. The national recommendation is at least two hours of study per week for each _____ of class you take.

2. Deciding which academic activities to complete next is called _____.

3. _____ represents getting the most output for the least input.

4. Telling yourself, "I just don't feel like doing my studying now; I'll do it tomorrow," is a form of _____.

5. Janet is taking two hours to complete a job that she should have been able to complete in forty-five minutes. This expansion of work to fill the time available represents _____.

6. In the **POSITIVE** time management system, a job or a class will be categorized as a/an _____.

7. In the **POSITIVE** time management system, one of the steps involves _____ success, where you use your imagination to help you achieve your study goals.

8. If you study while you simultaneously sit at your computer exchanging instant messages, listening to music, eating a snack, and conversing with your roommate, you are _____.

Web Activity: Thinking Positively About Time Management

Directions: Using a search engine, find two quotations about time management. Use the key words "quotations about time management" or the key words "quotations about time" to enter into the search engine. Choose two motivational quotations. Provide the exact web addresses you used and write a brief interpretation of the quotations selected. An example follows.

Example Quotation: *"You can ask me for anything you like, except time." Napoleon Bonaparte*

Website address: www.inspirational-quotes.info/time.html

Interpretation: *The amount of time we have doesn't change. We have 168 hours in a week, so we can't get more than that. Therefore, Napoleon means we can ask for anything, but we can't ask for more time—we have only a specific, set amount.*

Quotation 1: _____

_____

_____

Website address: _____

_____

Interpretation: _____

_____

_____

_____

Quotation 2: _____

_____

_____

Website address: _____

_____

Interpretation: _____

_____

_____

Reflection Time

Achieving Your Goals by Using the POSITIVE Approach to Time Management

When you wait for a class to start, your friend to arrive, a bus to come, a meeting to begin, and so on, what do you do during those minutes? Think back through each weekday of last week. Beside each weekday listed below, write the circumstances for your waiting and approximately how many minutes were involved.

Monday	Tuesday	Wednesday	Thursday	Friday
1.	1.	1.	1.	1.
2.	2.	2.	2.	2.
3.	3.	3.	3.	3.
4.	4.	4.	4.	4.
5.	5.	5.	5.	5.
6.	6.	6.	6.	6.
7.	7.	7.	7.	7.
8.	8.	8.	8.	8.
9.	9.	9.	9.	9.
10.	10.	10.	10.	10.

How much total time do you estimate you spent waiting last week? _____
On the blanks below, discuss ways you can use this spare time constructively as a part of the **POSITIVE** approach to time management.

_____

_____

_____

_____

_____

_____

_____

_____

_____

_____

_____

_____

Getting the Most Out of Your Textbooks: Reading, Studying, and Remembering

4

In this chapter, you will move toward achieving your goals by

- strengthening and enriching your reading skills.

- learning how to study more efficiently.

- expanding your ability to remember information.

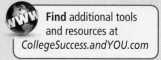

Find additional tools and resources at *CollegeSuccess.andYOU.com*

Self-Assessment:
Penny Wise

Step 1: On the left side below, draw from memory the "heads" side of a penny. On the right side below, draw from memory the "tails" side of a penny. Be sure that you don't look at a penny before you do the drawing. Rely only on what you can actually remember about a penny.

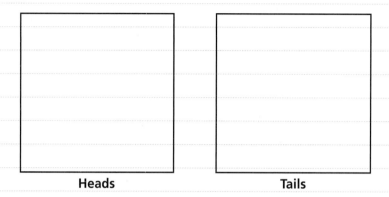

Heads   Tails

Step 2: Now you need to examine the penny carefully. You may use any penny that is commonly circulated. Read all of the information on the heads side and the tails side. Study both sides of the coin with the purpose of trying to remember their appearance so that later in this chapter you can draw each side again. This chapter deals with reading, studying, and remembering, and having a clear purpose or intent for reading, studying, and remembering is one of the major principles of learning. By purposefully reading, studying, and remembering the penny, you should be able to reproduce the heads side and the tails side with much more accuracy. Your purpose here is to be able to reproduce a more accurate drawing of the two sides of the penny later in this chapter.

The ability to read, study, and remember the information in your textbooks is inseparable from college success. Your professors will sometimes require you to read massive amounts of material that they will expect you to study and remember when test time arrives. Enriching and expanding your existing skills in reading, studying, and remembering combined with following the specific "how to" suggestions in this chapter will guide you to achieving the goals that you identified at the beginning of this book.

> "The more that you read, the more things you will know. The more that you learn, the more places you'll go."[1]
>
> Dr. Seuss, *I Can Read with My Eyes Shut*

The ultimate
READING SKILLS for college success

Most classes you take in college require you to read, sometimes enormous amounts of material. Much of your time will be taken by reading assignments given by your professors, who expect you to absorb a lot of information. Being able to read efficiently and with good comprehension will help you succeed.

Three key techniques are useful for college reading. These techniques are sequenced as first *pre-reading*, next *reading*, and then *reviewing*. Most of your reading assignments come from textbooks that accompany each class, and your professors will usually assign chapters or groups of chapters or articles to be read for the next class. Here is the process to follow when you have such a reading assignment.

PRE-READ	■ Follow the pre-reading steps. ■ Use your background information. ■ Look for unfamiliar vocabulary.
READ	■ Determine main ideas and major details. ■ Apply critical reading and thinking.
REVIEW	■ Paraphrase key ideas. ■ Visualize overall structure.

How to Pre-read Your Textbook Assignment

The purpose of **pre-reading**, which is sometimes called using **advance organizers**,[2] is to give you the opportunity to get a "bird's-eye" view of the entire assignment before you actually do the reading. Pre-reading is similar to looking both ways before you cross the street or turning on the lights before you enter an unfamiliar, dark room—it gives you a look at what's ahead. Pre-reading will probably take no more than about five minutes to complete once you understand how to proceed. Here are the steps to take when pre-reading a textbook assignment:

Step 1: Read the title and subtitle.

The title will provide the overall topic, and the subtitle will suggest the more specific focus. If there is no title or subtitle, check for introductory and concluding sections that serve the same function.

Step 2: Read the section called "Introduction" or the first paragraph.

This part will give you the plan for the passage and usually will contain the author's overall key ideas.

Coming Attractions: Pre-reading allows you to know what to expect before you actually read your textbook assignment.

Step 3: Read each dark, boldfaced heading (if there are any) and the first sentence of every paragraph.

The headings act as labels for that part of the passage, and the first sentence of each paragraph often expresses the main point.

Step 4: Identify any unfamiliar vocabulary.

Underline or highlight any unknown words you come across. Sometimes authors help readers by defining key words somewhere in a chapter or in a glossary at the end of a textbook. Be sure you know definitions for these words before you actually read the passage.

Step 5: Notice graphical or typographical aids.

For example, italics, an outline format, pictures, or graphs might be used. These aids are there for a reason: to provide you, the reader, with information.

Step 6: Read the last paragraph or the section called "Summary" or "Conclusion."

This part will give you a condensed version of the passage and might repeat the key points.

Step 7: Skim (read quickly) over any end-of-the-passage material.

Discussion/study questions, references, suggested readings, or websites might appear here. This material might be useful to you as you later study the passage. If there are discussion/study questions, skim them at this point to get an idea of what is important in the passage.

By pre-reading, you prepare yourself to do the actual reading in several ways. First, you get a look at the material before the real reading, which activates your **background information** (or your prior knowledge about the subject) as you prepare to do the actual reading. This process allows you to increase your understanding of the ideas being presented. Next, you get a preview of the key ideas that are going to be discussed so that you can anticipate information as you read. Also, you have the opportunity to locate any unfamiliar vocabulary, which you can then define before you do the actual reading of the assignment. When you are defining words, you can of course use a dictionary; however, other techniques might also be useful as you find words you don't know in your assignments.

Two Ways to Define Words without Using a Dictionary

Two strategies to discover the meaning of a word can help you as you read. Both strategies will save you time while you read, and both are useful when you don't have access to a dictionary.

Using Context Clues

Using **context clues** is the first way to figure out the meaning of a word. **Context** refers to the surrounding words in the sentence or paragraph, and the **clues** are the hints that are available to figure out a word's meaning. Here is an example of a word to define that doesn't have context clues available, and then the same word with context clues provided.

Word Wise: You can learn to define words without referring to a dictionary through the use of context clues and word parts.

Word without context clues: My brother Jason is *diffident.*

Word with context clues: Although Eric is loud and outgoing, my brother Jason is *diffident.*

The word *diffident* should have been easier to figure out with context clues. Did you define it as "quiet and shy?" In the example sentence with context clues, the opposite of *diffident* is provided: "loud and outgoing." Then, you think about what would be the opposite of "loud and outgoing," and you can guess "quiet and shy," which is correct.

Context clues are not always available in a sentence, but they occur frequently enough for you to be alert to their presence and use them to help you figure out words when a dictionary is not available. Here are four of the most common types of context clues with sample sentences given to illustrate their use.

Common Types of Context Clues

Type of Context Clue	Explanation	Example Sentence	Definition of Word
Definition Clue	The exact meaning of the word is provided.	The <u>feral</u> (wild) cats were caught.	<u>Feral</u> means "wild."
Contrast Clue	The opposite of the unknown word is given.	Although Eric is loud and outgoing, my brother Jason is <u>diffident.</u>	<u>Diffident</u> means "quiet and shy."
Example Clue	An example of the unknown word is given.	The <u>ostentatious</u> clothes she wore included a gold sequined dress and a big feathered hat.	<u>Ostentatious</u> means "excessively showy and glitzy; flashy."
Logic/ Inference Clue	Enough information is given in the sentence to make a good guess.	The message in the Chinese fortune cookie was <u>prescient</u> because I did win the lottery.	<u>Prescient</u> means "to have foreknowledge of events; able to predict accurately."

Here is a practice exercise on using context clues to show you how helpful these types of hints can be. The words are taken from the "Academic Word List," which contains 570 words that are the most common in college textbooks.[3]

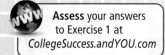

Assess your answers to Exercise 1 at *CollegeSuccess.andYOU.com*

EXERCISE 1 Context Clues Views

Step 1: For each item, choose the definition that is closest in meaning to the word. Write the letter of your answer in the space provided. <u>Don't</u> use a dictionary for this activity. In Step 1, the words have *no* context clues. In Step 2, you will have these exact words with the exact choices for answers, except you *will* have context clues available. After you finish both steps, check all of your answers (in class). You can determine the benefits of using context clues when you compare the results from Step 1 with the results from Step 2.

_____ **1.** empirical
  A. slanted in a certain way
  B. related to an empire
  C. collected by hand
  D. based on observation or experiment
  E. found in a book

_____ **2.** paradigm
  A. model; framework
  B. reply
  C. question
  D. search; examine
  E. hope

_____ **3.** albeit
  A. all over
  B. although
  C. so
  D. because
  E. since

_____ **4.** aggregate
  A. wonder
  B. sum total
  C. happiness
  D. aggravate
  E. greediness

_____ **5.** integral
  A. necessary
  B. numbers
  C. in between
  D. generous
  E. front

_____ **6.** subsidiary
  A. underground
  B. of major importance
  C. secondary level
  D. unfortunate
  E. low achieving

_____ **7.** analogous
  A. next
  B. behind
  C. vocal
  D. awkward
  E. similar

_____ **8.** regime
  A. king
  B. type of country
  C. island
  D. form of government
  E. military troop

_____ **9.** levy
  A. repair a leak in
  B. require a payment of
  C. fly
  D. fill a gap for
  E. flood

_____ **10.** inherently
  A. naturally
  B. quickly
  C. angrily
  D. attractively
  E. unpredictably

Step 2: Here are exactly the same words and choices from the preceding page. However, now you *do* have context clues to help you. For each item, choose the definition that is closest in meaning to the underlined word. Write the letter of your answer in the space provided. Remember, <u>don't</u> use a dictionary.

_____ **1.** A central concept in science is that all evidence must be <u>empirical</u>.
    A. slanted in a certain way
    B. related to an empire
    C. of secondary importance
    D. based on observation or experiment
    E. found in a book

_____ **2.** The cognitive <u>paradigm</u> in psychology emphasizes the way a person thinks.
    A. model; framework
    B. reply
    C. question
    D. search; examine
    E. hope

_____ **3.** He has a very good idea, <u>albeit</u> a very strange one.
    A. all over
    B. although
    C. so
    D. because
    E. since

_____ **4.** The <u>aggregate</u> of all her past experiences led her to turn down the blind date.
    A. wonder
    B. sum total
    C. happiness
    D. aggravate
    E. greediness

_____ **5.** An <u>integral</u> part of a car is a working battery.
    A. necessary
    B. numbers
    C. in between
    D. generous
    E. front

_____ **6.** The large clothing manufacturing plant announced plans to create a <u>subsidiary</u> company to produce only zippers.
    A. underground
    B. of major importance
    C. secondary level
    D. unfortunate
    E. low achieving

_____ **7.** A computer is <u>analogous</u> to the brain.
- A. next
- B. behind
- C. awkward
- D. vocal
- E. similar

_____ **8.** The old socialist <u>regime</u> was replaced by a democratic form of government.
- A. king
- B. type of country
- C. island
- D. form of government
- E. military troop

_____ **9.** The government can <u>levy</u> taxes for cigarettes or alcohol.
- A. repair a leak in
- B. require a payment of
- C. fly
- D. fill a gap for
- E. flood

_____ **10.** Cats are <u>inherently</u> curious.
- A. naturally
- B. quickly
- C. angrily
- D. attractively
- E. unpredictably

Step 3: Determine your scores by filling in the spaces below with the number correct for each step.

Number Correct

Step 1: _____ (out of ten)

Step 2: _____ (out of ten)

Step 4: After you go over the correct answers in class, discuss the value of using context clues to help figure out the definition of an unknown word.

The purpose of this activity is to illustrate that you can use context clues to help you figure out the definition of an unknown word. You can make looking for and using context clues a regular practice as you read assignments.

Using Word Parts

The second way to figure out a word's meaning when you don't have access to a dictionary is by using **word parts** (prefixes, roots, and suffixes). **Prefixes** contribute meaning at the beginning of a word, **suffixes** contribute meaning at the end of the word, and **roots** can appear at any position in the word to contribute meaning. The more meanings for word parts you know, the bigger your vocabulary. Consider the following long word consisting of prefixes, roots, and suffixes.

pneumonoultramicroscopicsilicovolcanoconiosis

What does this word mean? It means "a lung disease caused by breathing in fine silicate dust particles" and is derived from the meanings of the word parts that form it:

pneumono	=	lung
ultra	=	beyond, extremely
micro	=	small
scopic	=	see, look
silico	=	silicate (like sand)
volcano	=	eruption
coni	=	dust
osis	=	condition

Therefore, when the meanings of the word parts are combined together (a condition of a lung caused by inhaling extremely small, but able to be seen, eruptions of sand-like dust particles), you get the definition. Even if you have never seen this word before—but you know the meanings for the word parts—you can make a good guess at the correct definition.

There are many prefixes, roots, and suffixes, but the following list of fourteen words developed by James I. Brown is especially important.[4] The essential word parts for these words can be your guide to being able to analyze the meaning of over 14,000 words.

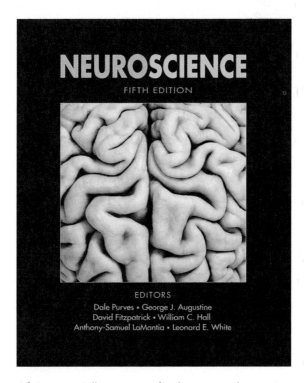

Of Course: College courses often have names that are combinations of word parts: astrophysics, microeconomics, biochemistry, thermodynamics, hydrogeology, and neuroscience.

Fourteen Words That Unlock the Meaning
to Over 14,000 Words

Words	Prefix	Meaning of Prefix (Common Example Words)	Root	Meaning of Root (Common Example Words)
Precept	pre-	"before" (<u>pre</u>mature, <u>pre</u>fix)	<u>cept</u>	"take, seize" (inter<u>cept</u>, con<u>cept</u>)
Detain	de-	"away, from" (<u>de</u>part, <u>de</u>rail)	<u>tain</u>	"have, hold" (con<u>tain</u>, re<u>tain</u>)
Intermittent	inter-	"between" (<u>inter</u>cept, <u>inter</u>act)	<u>mit(t)</u>	"send" (trans<u>mit</u>, ad<u>mit</u>)
Offer	of-	"to, toward" (<u>of</u>fend, <u>of</u>fense)	<u>fer</u>	"bear, carry" (trans<u>fer</u>, de<u>fer</u>)
Insist	in-	"into" (<u>in</u>doors, <u>in</u>put)	<u>sist</u>	"stand, endure" (per<u>sist</u>, con<u>sist</u>)
Monograph	mono-	"one, alone" (<u>mono</u>tone, <u>mono</u>logue)	<u>graph</u>	"write" (auto<u>graph</u>, para<u>graph</u>)
Epilogue	epi-	"upon" (<u>epi</u>center, <u>epi</u>graph)	<u>log(ue)</u>	"say," (mono<u>logue</u>, dia<u>logue</u>)
Aspect	as- ad-	"to, toward" (<u>as</u>pire, <u>ad</u>mit)	<u>(s)pect</u>	"see" (<u>spect</u>ator, circum<u>spect</u>)
Uncomplicate	un- com-	"not" "with, together" (<u>un</u>natural, <u>com</u>pany)	<u>pli(c)</u>	"fold, bend" (<u>pli</u>able, du<u>plic</u>ate)
Nonextend	non- ex-	"not" "out of" (<u>non</u>profit, <u>ex</u>it)	<u>tend</u>	"stretch" (con<u>tend</u>, in<u>tend</u>)
Reproduction	re- pro-	"back, again" "for, forward" (<u>re</u>read, <u>pro</u>ceed)	<u>duc(t)</u>	"lead" (con<u>duct</u>, de<u>duct</u>)
Indisposed	in- dis-	"not" "apart from" (<u>in</u>sane, <u>dis</u>appear)	<u>pos(e)</u>	"put, place" (pro<u>pose</u>, dis<u>pose</u>)
Oversufficient	over- suf- sub-	"above" "under" (<u>over</u>do, <u>suf</u>fix)	<u>fic, fac</u>	"make, do" (<u>fic</u>tion, <u>fac</u>tory)
Mistranscribe	mis- trans-	"wrong" "across, beyond" (<u>mis</u>spell, <u>trans</u>mit	<u>scrib(e)</u>	"write" (tran<u>scribe</u>, <u>scrib</u>ble)

Do you think this pre-reading step seemed to take a lot of time to complete? Along the way through this section, you slowed down to learn about using context clues and word parts. In fact, now that you understand pre-reading, this step will likely take you no more than about five minutes to complete. Doing pre-reading will create a curiosity about and interest in the upcoming information and empower you to do your best as you progress to the next step.

How to Read Your Textbook Assignment

After you have used your new skill of *pre-reading* the assignment, it is time to do more deliberate reading. More deliberate reading occurs when you apply all of your skills to the task of fully comprehending the material you have been assigned. The foundation skill of reading involves being able to figure out the main idea. The **main idea** refers to the overall controlling idea, whether it applies to a paragraph, an article, a chapter, or even a whole book.

To identify the main idea, ask yourself two questions. The first question is, "What is this passage about?" Try to provide one word or a few words that answer this question. The word or few words you use as an answer will identify the *topic*, or subject, of the assignment. The second question is, "What is this passage saying about _____?" On the blank, fill in the answer from Question 1—the one word or few words that identify the topic or subject of the passage. Now you are ready to answer Question 2. After you answer Question 2, you will have identified the main idea.

Also important to figure out are the major details. The **major details** represent the supporting facts or statements that prove or explain the main idea. To identify the major details, find the sections or statements that provide additional explanation for the overall main idea. Major details include the facts, examples, processes, reasons, and anecdotes that provide the support for the overall main point.

The diagram below illustrates the relationship between the overall main idea and the major supporting details.

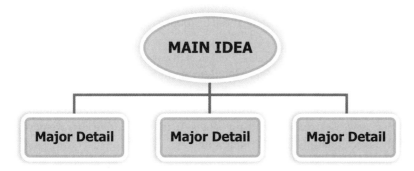

For example, the overall main idea of this chapter is to explain the techniques of reading, studying, and remembering information from textbooks. The first major detail of this chapter discusses reading, which involves the three key techniques of pre-reading, reading, and reviewing. Thus, a diagram of the chapter so far would look like this:

MAIN IDEA
Reading, Studying, and Remembering Textbook Information

Major Detail
✓ Pre-Reading – follow pre-read steps; activate background information; define unknown vocabulary.
✓ Reading – Identify main ideas and major details.

Major Detail
✓ Studying textbook information

Major Detail
✓ Remembering textbook information

You can apply this same procedure to just about any textbook that you are assigned to read. The main ideas and the major details will offer the information most professors want you to study and remember as you approach exam time. Along with the main ideas and major details of what you read, *critical reading* and *critical thinking* are important. **Critical reading** involves applying *critical thinking* when you are involved in the process of interpreting, evaluating, and criticizing what you read. While *critical reading* clarifies the full meaning and intentions of an author, **critical thinking** adds the reader's own evaluation and analysis of the material through careful, thoughtful, and reasoned judgments. For example, a critical reader might detect the expression of elation or disappointment about the outcome of the 2012 presidential election in a political science article; a critical thinker goes beyond detecting the author's biases to formulating his or her own reasoned judgments.

A study by ACT, a company that tests students, reports that critical reading is the key to college success.[5] College textbooks may have elaborate organization, the messages are more implied than stated, the relationships among ideas or characters are subtle, and the vocabulary is demanding and complicated. These textbooks require you to have critical reading ability.

Legal Reasoning: The preparation by lawyers and judges for courtroom deliberations exemplifies the importance of critical reading and critical thinking outside the classroom.

The process for critical reading has a great deal in common with the foundation skills of reading for the main ideas and major details explained above. In critical reading, the main ideas may be implied and not directly stated, but the procedure to identify the main ideas is still the same. The supporting details focus more on interpretations of the facts, examples, processes, reasons, and anecdotes. To make accurate interpretations, you need to apply critical reading and thinking skills.

Critical Thinking Applied to Reading

1. Understand the basics first. Be sure you comprehend the main ideas and the major supporting details.

2. Determine if **bias** (favoring one position or viewpoint) is present. Bias may be revealed by the author's use of positive or negative words.

3. Recognize the **tone** (the author's feelings toward the subject). Tone may be identified by deciding what feelings, or emotions, are communicated. Sorrow, hate, gratitude, joy—in fact, the whole range of human emotions—are possible tones.

4. Decide if the passage reveals more **facts** (provable statements) or more **opinions** (beliefs), or if it is mixed with both.

5. Draw accurate **inferences** (educated guesses) or **conclusions** (reasoned judgments). Do this by looking for as many clues or hints in the passage as you can find that you can add together to support a guess or judgment.

Critical reading also involves complex vocabulary. The focus is not so much on the literal meanings of the words, phrases, or statements in context. Instead, you will need to go beyond the page to understand the vocabulary. To analyze the meanings of the words, you again need to apply critical thinking.

Critical Thinking Applied to Vocabulary

1. Understand the literal meaning of the words first. Use context clues and word parts to help determine the definition, but check a dictionary if necessary.

2. Decide if the language is **figurative** (imaginative). Imaginative language makes comparisons in descriptive ways to create new effects or fresh insights. Figurative language involves creating impressions for the reader.

3. Identify the use of **denotation** (using the literal, dictionary definition of a word) or **connotation** (using judgments or feelings associated with the use of a word). Connotations are words that reveal a positive or negative bias.

4. Determine whether the words or phrases are everyday or **specialized usage**. Words and phrases have different meanings in different contexts. For example, the word *root* has different meanings in math (square root), biology (plant root), social science (historical root), and English (root word).

For Exercise 2, you will read a textbook passage about the history of abnormal psychology. The questions in the exercise combine reading for main ideas and major details with the more complex reading and vocabulary skills necessary for college success.

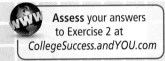

Assess your answers to Exercise 2 at CollegeSuccess.andYOU.com

EXERCISE 2 Caution: Critical Reading Skills at Work

Step 1: First, go over this passage using the pre-reading technique you have learned. Check for unknown vocabulary that you may need to define. Then read through the passage more deliberately, looking for the main ideas, the major details, and the complex ideas. The questions that follow the passage represent the type of analysis that college students are expected to be able to do.

In the history of abnormal psychology, milder behavior problems have been viewed very differently than more severe problems. For example, mood changes, poor self-esteem, uncontrolled anger, and general anxiety have only been recognized as legitimate signs of psychological disturbance during the last century. Previously, such symptoms were either ignored or considered voluntary and due to moral inferiority. In contrast, more severe mental problems had been blamed on possession by the Devil, and rituals were developed to exorcise the demons. Alternatively, men and women perceived as strange were labeled witches and burned.

During the Middle Ages in much of Europe, people suffering from insanity were at worst treated like animals and at best segregated from the general population and neglected. If they were "hospitalized," they joined the physically impaired and beggars in primitive institutions with deplorable living conditions. Some of these medieval "hospitals" had previously housed people who suffered from leprosy, a contagious disease that had largely disappeared. No treatment was available at these facilities; they simply housed the unwanted dregs of society.

By the 16th century in England, one advance in the understanding of mental illness occurred when a rudimentary psychiatric diagnostic system emerged. Two types of mentally incompetent people were recognized: idiots, who were intellectually limited, and lunatics, who were insane. The powerful monarchy agreed to take responsibility for such impaired individuals and house them in asylums.

In 1547, King Henry VIII ordered the opening in London of the Hospital of St. Mary's of Bethlehem, an asylum for idiots, lunatics, and other lost souls. St. Mary's of Bethlehem became one of the best-known asylums during the Middle Ages. While St. Mary's of Bethlehem did house people who suffered from severe mental impairment, it provided virtually no treatment or comfort. The word "asylum" indicates a place of sanctuary and protection. In fact, the inhabitants of St. Mary's of Bethlehem lived in very crowded conditions; had poor nutrition; and, if unruly, were kept in chains. Eventually, the idiots and lunatics of St. Mary's of Bethlehem became a tourist attraction that visitors paid a fee to observe. Interestingly, the word "bedlam" was soon coined from the local pronunciation of Bethlehem to describe the loud and chaotic environment that prevailed there. The founding of St. Mary's of Bethlehem spurred the development of many other asylums in Western Europe. However, more benign, dignified treatment did not emerge until the end of the 18th century.

Step 2: Choose the best answer for each item.

_____ **1.** What is the overall main idea of this passage?
   A. Religious thinking dominated during the Middle Ages.
   B. Mentally disturbed people provided the motivation for creating poorhouses during the Middle Ages.
   C. During the Middle Ages, people believed in magic, witches, and demons.
   D. The Middle Ages was a period of time when little effective treatment was available for psychological disorders.

_____ **2.** The word "bedlam" is derived from
   A. the word "asylum," which is what the poorhouses were called.
   B. the monks who used the word in their monasteries.
   C. the Hospital of St. Mary's of Bethlehem in London.
   D. the beds in which the patients were placed.

_____ **3.** The authors of this passage are
   A. biased against Christianity.
   B. neutral toward the treatment of mental illness in the Middle Ages.
   C. biased in favor of asylums.
   D. biased in favor of magic.

_____ **4.** The tone (that is, the authors' feeling toward the subject) is
   A. objective.
   B. sorrowful.
   C. frustrated.
   D. indignant.

_____ **5.** The reader can conclude that, for mental illness during the Middle Ages,
   A. hospitals offered the best treatment.
   B. treatment was not usually available.
   C. men received better treatment than women.
   D. asylums provided the best treatment.

_____ **6.** The reader can infer that if a person had a physical illness during the Middle Ages,
   A. the treatment was usually more successful than the one for mental illness.
   B. doctors offered quality care.
   C. the treatment was usually as unsuccessful as the one for mental illness.
   D. monks provided the best care.

_____ **7.** Identify this sentence as representing a statement of "fact" or "opinion": "The Hospital of St. Mary's of Bethlehem became one of the best-known asylums during the Middle Ages."
   A. fact
   B. opinion

_____ **8.** The authors of the passage are
   A. entertaining us with stories about witches, demons, and devils in the Middle Ages.
   B. informing us of the treatment of mental illness in the Middle Ages.
   C. persuading us that the Middle Ages represented a colorful, historical time.
   D. explaining the causes for mental illness in the Middle Ages.

_____ **9.** Which term best identifies how the last paragraph is organized?
   A. description
   B. cause-effect
   C. time
   D. comparison-contrast

_____ **10.** Which is the most appropriate title for this passage?
   A. "Mental Health Care during the Middle Ages"
   B. "History of Treatment for Psychological Diseases"
   C. "Spiritual Explanations of Psychological Disorders"
   D. "The Good Work of Asylums in the Middle Ages"

Step 3: After you go over the correct answers in class, discuss recommendations (including specific campus resources available) to help a student who has difficulty with this kind of analysis.

How to Review Your Textbook Assignment

After you have finished both the _pre-reading_ and the _reading_ of your assignment, it is important to _review_. **Reviewing** means going back over the assignment, from the beginning to the end, looking at each heading, subheading, and first sentence. Taking a few minutes to review will make a big difference in what you are able to remember later. Reviewing helps to lock the information into your brain before that information has a chance to escape.

Two techniques for reviewing will help you. The first technique for reviewing is to **paraphrase** (state in your own words) to yourself each point as you go. When paraphrasing, use your own words to say to yourself each main idea and major detail. The second technique is to try to **visualize** the overall structure of the assignment. Visualizing the structure helps you see how the ideas are all interrelated and makes it easier to recall later. Ask yourself, for example, if the author is comparing or contrasting, presenting reasons, providing processes, or defining concepts.

Complete the review of your assignment immediately after you have finished reading. Your inclination may be to breathe a sigh of relief, close the book, and go on to something else. However, it is best to resist this temptation, and complete the recommended review. The review will not have the same effect if you wait to do it later—even ten minutes later. To get the full benefit, review while the content of the assignment is still fresh in your mind. Review before other thoughts begin to interfere or compete with the information from the assignment. Reviewing may require some discipline to complete, but you will find that it can pay off.

Best STUDY PRACTICES for college success

Many students think of reading and studying as the same. They believe that time spent reading is time spent studying. However, reading is a process of discovery, of going through the material to identify the new concepts to be learned. Studying is the process of learning, of storing the new information in memory. Reading and studying certainly do overlap, but each has activities that are unique.

One of the best practices for studying is to be sure that you are organized before you begin the actual process of storing the new information to remember. Getting organized won't take too much time or effort, but the return for doing it will be considerable. You'll end up saving time. Be a "study smart" student by following the suggestions for organizing below.

Study Skill: Your studying will be most effective sitting at a well-lit desk in a quiet location.

"Study Smart" Suggestions for Organizing

Use a planner or a notebook. Keep track of schoolwork—assignments, due dates, exams, etc.

Find good study places. The location can be anywhere (except your bed), but make sure it has a writing surface, is well-lit, and is comfortable without distractions.

Keep all returned papers and tests. Use a pocket folder or some method to keep all returned papers and tests organized by class.

Plan time for a study session. Allow more time for a study session than you think you will need.

Vary the types of assignments. Read English, then do a math problem set, then read your history assignment.

Do the hardest work first. Get the most difficult assignment out of the way first, while you are still fresh.

Discuss the Study Smart Suggestions for Organizing at *CollegeSuccess.andYOU.com*

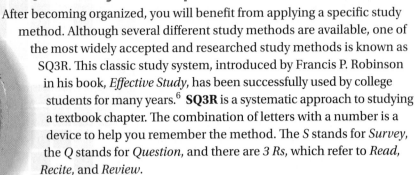

The SQ3R Study Technique

After becoming organized, you will benefit from applying a specific study method. Although several different study methods are available, one of the most widely accepted and researched study methods is known as SQ3R. This classic study system, introduced by Francis P. Robinson in his book, *Effective Study*, has been successfully used by college students for many years.[6] **SQ3R** is a systematic approach to studying a textbook chapter. The combination of letters with a number is a device to help you remember the method. The *S* stands for *Survey*, the *Q* stands for *Question*, and there are *3 Rs*, which refer to *Read*, *Recite*, and *Review*.

SQ3R works because repetition is an effective way for people to learn. When you were learning the alphabet, you sang the alphabet song over and over; when you learned the multiplication tables, you repeated them again and again. Study systems such as SQ3R provide the opportunity for repetition to ensure that learning occurs. Two research studies, one in *Contemporary Educational Psychology*[7] and one in *Psychological Science*,[8] support the use of the read-recite-review component of SQ3R for college students. The researchers of the second study conclude that this study method promotes "deep learning"[9] and recommend that college students "implement the method for remembering information."[10]

The Second *R*: One step in SQ3R is to *Recite* information to yourself to solidify what you are trying to learn.

Also, SQ3R works because it offers several advantages. First, it gives you a preview or survey of what's ahead as you read (very similar to pre-reading, which you already know about). Next, you feel that you are searching for specific information, which usually involves the main idea, rather than wandering around on a printed page. Finally, when you find the information you are searching for, you feel rewarded—you have accomplished something. And when you can remember this information at test time, you will feel even more rewarded.

Read through the next section a few times. It explains the details of the SQ3R study method, and the more familiar you become with it, the easier it will be to use.

SQ3R Overview

Step 1: S = Survey: Become familiar with the overall content of what you are getting ready to read.

1. Read the title and subtitle.
2. Read the "Introduction" or the first paragraph.
3. Read each dark, boldfaced heading and the first sentence of every paragraph.
4. Identify any unfamiliar vocabulary.
5. Notice graphical and typographical aids.
6. Read the last paragraph or the section called "Summary" or "Conclusion."
7. Skim (read quickly) any end-of-the-passage material.

(See "How to Pre-read Your Textbook Assignment" on page 76 for a more detailed explanation of how to survey.)

Step 2: Q = Question: Form questions as you read, which gives you a direct purpose for reading.

1. Convert each chapter heading or subheading into question form and then read that section to answer the question. Use "Who, What, When, Where, Why, or How" to begin the question.
2. Formulating the questions will make important points stand out.

Step 3: The first *R* is Read: Read each chapter section or subsection to answer the question you formulated from Step 2.

1. Actively search for the answers to the questions as you read.
2. Underline answers as you find them since these are the main ideas for each chapter section or subsection.

Step 4: The second *R* is Recite: After you read each section or subsection, stop to see if you can recall or recite to yourself the answer to the question.

1. Try to answer the question you formulated during Step 2 without looking at the text.
2. If you can't answer without looking back, then go back to check. Be sure you understand the answer.

Continue through the entire chapter, following Steps 2, 3, and 4 for each new chapter heading.

Step 5: The third *R* is Review: When you have finished the whole chapter, go back to the first question. See if you can remember the answer. Continue through the chapter using this format.

1. If you come to a section or subsection and you can't remember the answer, stop. Be sure you have the question clearly in mind and then reread to answer the question.
2. Test yourself this way through the entire chapter.

Here is an exercise to give you practice using SQ3R. You can use this technique for any textbook study assignment that you have for your classes, including this class.

EXERCISE 3 **Use SQ3R to Study a Textbook Assignment**

Step 1: Use SQ3R and the following worksheet (which you can find at this book's website for duplication for future use) for your next study assignment. You may use a chapter from any textbook, including this textbook, for the exercise.

Textbook Information

Textbook title: _____

Chapter number:_____ and chapter title: _____

Use SQ3R

S = Survey   Read the title of the chapter, the "Introduction," and each boldfaced heading; note unfamiliar vocabulary; observe pictures or graphs; read the last paragraph or "Summary" section; skim (read quickly) any end-of-the-passage material (review questions, etc.)

1. What is the chapter about?_____

2. According to each boldfaced heading, what major topics are covered in the chapter?

     1. _____

     2. _____

     3. _____

     4. _____

     5. _____

     6. _____

Q = Question   Turn each boldfaced heading into question form. Use "Who, What, When, Where, Why, or How" to begin the questions. Keep the same order of major topics listed above.

     1. _____

     2. _____

     3. _____

     4. _____

     5. _____

     6. _____

R = Read   Read each section of the chapter. As you finish each section, write (in your own words) the answer to your questions stated above. Keep the same order as the questions above.

1. _____
_____

2. _____
_____

3. _____
_____

4. _____
_____

5. _____
_____

6. _____
_____

R = Recite   As you finish reading a section of the chapter, look away from the book and the notes you wrote above. Recite to yourself the question and the answer. If you cannot recall, reread the section again.

R = Review   Now go back to the very first heading. See if you remember your question and your answer. Continue to the next heading and do the same. If you come to a section for which you cannot recall the question or answer, reread that section again and refer to your questions and answers above.

Step 2: Be prepared to discuss your use of the SQ3R technique in class.

Use a different worksheet for every chapter you must study. Then use the collected worksheets for reviews before exams.

Now that you are familiar with SQ3R, you can alter it to work more effectively for you. You can adapt, modify, or rearrange the steps in SQ3R to suit your own study preferences. Your goal is to have a systematic way to approach studying.

REMEMBERING

> Student #1: "I can't remember anything!"
> Student #2: "How long have you had this problem?"
> Student #1: "What problem?"

At the beginning of this chapter, you were asked to draw from memory the heads side and the tails side of any commonly circulated penny. Then you were asked to examine the penny and to read, study, and remember it. Your purpose was to be able to draw the heads side and the tails side again. Now see how much about the penny you can remember.

EXERCISE 4 **"Self-Assessment" Follow-Up: Penny Wise**

Step 1: On the left side below, draw from memory the heads side of a penny. On the right side below, draw from memory the tails side of a penny. Try to remember as much about the penny as you can. Your previous reading and studying of the penny will probably help you remember more key features of the penny than when you first drew it.

Heads	**Tails**

Step 2: Compare your accuracy for both the first time you drew the penny in the "Self-Assessment" activity (on page 74) and for this time you drew the penny. Check the box below for each item you correctly drew. Use the first of the box pairs for the first attempt and the second of the box pairs for the last time you drew the penny.

Heads

☐ ☐ Lincoln profile facing right

☐ ☐ "In God We Trust" across the top

☐ ☐ "Liberty" on left

☐ ☐ Year on lower right

Tails

☐ ☐ Lincoln Memorial Building or a *shield** centered

☐ ☐ "United States of America" across the top

☐ ☐ "E Pluribus Unum" above building or on the *shield**

☐ ☐ "One Cent" across the bottom

Note that beginning in 2010 a newly minted penny features a shield rather than the Lincoln Memorial on the tails side.

Step 3: Count your checks for the first and then the second attempts. You probably earned more points for the second attempt. Base your score on the second attempt. Use this scale to determine your Memory Index.

Memory Index
8 = Excellent
7 = Very Good
6 = Good
5 = Fair
4 and under = Study the penny and try again.

Intent to Remember

One important part of remembering is establishing an "**intent to remember**." Drawing the penny illustrates this idea. You probably didn't remember the details of the penny at first because you had no intention to remember them. You are more likely to remember better when you plan to do so. The same principle applies to your schoolwork. You must select the material from the textbooks and from the lectures that you intend to remember. In pre-reading, you learned to get a "bird's-eye" view in advance of the thorough reading, which helps you discover the main ideas and the major details that you should intend to remember. You also learned in SQ3R about formulating questions to guide your studying. Questioning involves changing each boldfaced heading into a question form and then reading to find the answer to the question. The answers to these questions represent the information that you would intend to remember.

Your first step to remembering, then, is to establish the intent to remember. Here are the main steps to take for enhancing memory.

Discuss the Positive Memory Steps for College Students at *CollegeSuccess.andYOU.com*

Positive Memory Steps for College Students

Step 1: **Intend to remember.** Engaging your brain by telling it you want to remember will help you stay focused.

Step 2: **Get enough rest.** If you aren't getting enough sleep, you may become tired while you are reading or studying. If you're burning the midnight oil, be sure to read and study when you are most alert. Take breaks to stay focused.

Step 3: **Concentrate.** Put all worries and distractions out of your mind. Tell yourself you can go back to these worries when you have free time.

Step 4: **Use a system to find specific information later.** For example, use sticky notes, markers, note cards, and pens and pencils. Have all materials assembled for your use.

Step 5: **Review right before sleep.** Go over any information you want to remember immediately before sleeping, which allows the brain to process this information and commit it to memory while you sleep.

Two Methods for Remembering

You can also apply some useful methods to help improve your memory. The first method to help you remember is to use a *mnemonic device*. **Mnemonic devices** are memory tricks, or aids, that you can devise to help you remember information. **POSITIVE** is a mnemonic device you have already learned in Chapter 3 to help you with the steps of time management. Mnemonics include rhymes, anagrams, words, silly sentences, nonsense words, and mental pictures that can aid in the recall of information. Another example of an already existing mnemonic device is "**P**lease **E**xcuse **M**y **D**ear **A**unt **S**ally," which reminds algebra students of the correct order of operations: **P**arentheses, **E**xponents, **M**ultiplication, **D**ivision, **A**ddition, **S**ubtraction. You can make up your own silly sentences or other mnemonic devices to help you remember many types of information.

A second method to help you remember is teaching someone else what you are trying to remember yourself. Consider this quote from Dr. William Glasser, a learning theorist:

We learn . . .
10% of what we read,
20% of what we hear,
30% of what we see,
50% of what we see and hear,
70% of what is discussed with others,
80% of what we experience personally,
95% of what we teach to someone else.[11]

To improve your ability to remember anything, then, teach the ideas or information you are trying to learn to someone else. Get your friends, parents, or roommates to listen to you as you "teach" them the concepts you want to remember. If you can explain the ideas clearly and thoroughly enough that they understand, you will have the ideas anchored in your own brain.

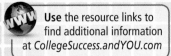

Lake Effect: A mnemonic device that students use to help them remember the names of the five Great Lakes is HOMES: Huron, Ontario, Michigan, Erie, and Superior.

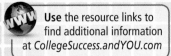
Use the resource links to find additional information at *CollegeSuccess.andYOU.com*

Thinking Critically About . . .
Getting the Most Out of Your Textbooks:
Reading, Studying, and Remembering

Critical thinking involves an active evaluation of information using careful, thoughtful, and reasoned judgments.

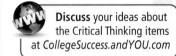

Discuss your ideas about the Critical Thinking items at *CollegeSuccess.andYOU.com*

1. Timothy is the go-to guy on his dorm floor for answering questions about the latest popular video game. As soon as a game is available, he gets it and begins to absorb the complex manual along with any relevant articles or comments he can find online. He manages to master the complicated games very quickly. At the same time, Timothy is failing his American history class. Speculate about how Timothy can master information for the video games but not for his class. Identify the skills that Timothy can transfer from reading about video games to reading about American history.

2. Create a mnemonic device to help you remember information from one of your classes. Evaluate the usefulness of mnemonic devices as a tool for aiding memory.

3. On the first day of your Introduction to Philosophy class, the professor alerts students that they will need to learn "the specialized language of philosophy" to pass the class. Develop a plan that will allow you to master the vocabulary of philosophy.

4. Freshmen who had achieved high grades in high school sometimes find themselves having difficulty understanding their college textbooks. Most of these students were not previously aware of having weaknesses in reading. Explain what students can do to improve their ability to understand college textbooks.

5. Assume that dictionaries were never created. Discuss how the absence of dictionaries would interfere with the educational development of students. Hypothesize what students might do to learn the meanings of words if dictionaries didn't exist.

Online Learning

Discuss your online learning ideas for this chapter at *CollegeSuccess.andYOU.com*

Online learners must rely heavily on their reading skills to achieve academic success. Aside from reading and studying textbooks, online students participate in class sessions by reading and responding to information on their computers. To succeed, online students may need to replace their habit of quickly scanning information on the computer screen with the focused, purposeful reading required for academic material.

Students enrolled in online classes may lack the opportunity to clarify lecture or reading content and the ability to access on-campus academic resources and support. As a result, they may be dependent solely on written material to help them understand course concepts. An option may be to form a study group with one or two other students in the online class.

Finding a quiet place to study can be a special challenge for online students learning at home or at some distance from campus. Noise and other distractions can interfere with the efforts of even the most dedicated student. When you are studying from home, you may need to work harder to find a quiet study place where you can concentrate. Public libraries, an outdoor park if the weather is good, or a quiet coffee shop may be suitable choices.

One of the best techniques for solidifying what you are trying to learn is to teach someone else. Many online students live with another person who would be a willing student. If that is not the case, you can ask a favor of a friend or fellow employee. A surprisingly effective alternative is simply to explain the material aloud as if another person might be listening.

Key Chapter Strategies

- Follow the pre-read, read, and review steps for your textbook reading assignments.
- Use context clues and word parts to analyze unknown words.
- Sharpen your critical thinking abilities for both reading and vocabulary.
- Be "study smart" by organizing your study materials and using a study method such as SQ3R.
- Establish an "intent to remember" information and then use mnemonic devices and teaching others as ways to anchor that information in your brain.
- Read these books for vocabulary development and for more information on memory: *Merriam-Webster's Vocabulary Builder* by Mary W. Cornog[12] and *Your Memory: How It Works and How to Improve It* by Kenneth L. Higbee.[13]

CHAPTER CHALLENGE

LEARNING TO LEARN

With the possible exception of Advanced Placement and other special classes, high school courses usually require students to learn far less material than college courses do. Consequently, many new college students taking full loads of demanding classes have not developed the study skills necessary for success. They are often unaware that educators have spent years developing very effective techniques to help students study and recall information from college classes and textbooks. Without knowledge of these techniques, college students can be at a serious disadvantage. Students can familiarize themselves with techniques such as SQ3R and the use of mnemonic devices through college success classes and programs at their school's academic support center.

A CASE STUDY: FACING THE CHALLENGE OF . . . LEARNING TO LEARN

High school was a breeze for Amy. Even though she earned high grades, she rarely felt challenged. She usually waited until the night before to read the chapters to be covered on the tests. She would not define this activity as studying, but it worked in high school. For Amy's first semester of college, she is signed up for English writing, college success, precalculus, European history, and biology. The assignments for the first three courses are highly structured, and she sets aside enough time to complete them when they are due. However, the history and biology classes require an enormous amount of reading, with many facts and concepts to remember. She is not sure how to learn all of the material required for these two classes.

OVERCOMING THE CHALLENGE OF . . . LEARNING TO LEARN

Be prepared to discuss your answers to the following items: (1) Contrast the reading demands for success in college with the reading demands for success in high school. Why is Amy challenged by her college reading requirements? (2) Imagine you are having a conversation with Amy about the SQ3R study technique. Explain to her the advantages of using this technique to study difficult subjects such as history and biology. (3) Out of frustration, Amy argues that some students in her class simply have better memories for names, dates, and events than she has. Convince Amy that she can better remember information by using special memory techniques.

Directions: To review your understanding of the chapter, choose the correct term from the list below and fill it on the blank. You will not use every term.

mnemonic device	pre-read	critical thinking
intent to remember	teach someone else	bias
word parts	figurative language	context clues
main ideas	SQ3R	survey

1. When authors favor one position or viewpoint in their writing, they are revealing _____ .

2. Sean is taking a test and isn't allowed to use a dictionary. If he finds a word he doesn't know, he might try using _____ and also using _____ to figure out the definition of the unknown word.

3. Readers look for _____ , which are the overall controlling ideas, whether they apply to a paragraph, an article, a chapter, or even the whole book.

4. A first step in trying to remember is to establish a/an _____. Engaging your brain to accomplish this step helps you stay focused.

5. A widely accepted and researched study method is known as _____ , which provides a systematic way to approach studying.

6. How do you complete this quote on learning and remembering from Dr. William Glasser, a learning theorist?
   We learn . . .
   10% of what we read,
   20% of what we hear,
   30% of what we see,
   50% of what we see and hear,
   70% of what is discussed with others,
   80% of what we experience personally,
   95% of what we _____ .

7. When you detect vocabulary that creates new effects or fresh insights in a descriptive, imaginative way, it is called _____ , which requires that you interpret and analyze the language.

8. Betsy needs to remember the sequence of colors in the visible spectrum or a simple rainbow. She uses Roy G. Biv, an example of a/an _____ , which stands for the colors, in order: **R**ed, **O**range, **Y**ellow, **G**reen, **B**lue, **I**ndigo, **V**iolet.

Directions: Editorial and political cartoonists capture current events by drawing funny cartoons with political and social commentary. Interpreting and analyzing these cartoons require the application of critical reading and thinking. Using a search engine, find a political or editorial cartoon about current events. Use the key words "editorial cartoons" or "political cartoons" to enter into the search engine. Choose a cartoon and print it out. Paste, glue, or tape the cartoon below and then write a paragraph about the cartoon explaining the humor. When writing the paragraph, you should be answering the question, "What can I infer from this cartoon?" or more simply, "Why is this cartoon funny?"

Paste, glue, or tape the editorial or political cartoon here. You might need to fold it.

Write your paragraph of interpretation and analysis here.

_____

_____

_____

_____

_____

_____

_____

_____

_____

_____

Reflection Time

Achieving Your Goals by Getting the Most Out of Your Textbooks: Reading, Studying, and Remembering

This chapter is about reading, studying, and remembering information from your college textbooks. The skills that you use to gather information from your textbooks are similar to the skills that you apply to general reading—so what do you read for interest when you have enough time? Do you read blogs, sports or fashion magazines, graphic novels, mysteries, or something else? Choose two categories of materials (such as those just listed) that you read for interest when you have time and give several reasons why they appeal to you. Each paragraph will be answering the question, "Why am I interested in reading . . . blogs? or sports or fashion magazines? or graphic novels? or mysteries? or . . .?"

_____

_____

_____

_____

_____

_____

_____

_____

_____

_____

_____

_____

_____

_____

_____

_____

_____

_____

_____

_____

_____

_____

_____

Learning Styles in the Classroom: Listening, Taking Notes, and Participating

In this chapter, you will move toward achieving your goals by

- developing positive classroom listening skills.

- enhancing note-taking from lectures and textbooks.

- establishing effective classroom participation techniques.

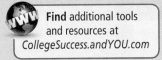

Find additional tools and resources at *CollegeSuccess.andYOU.com*

Self-Assessment:
And the Survey Says . . .

Each person has a preferred way of processing information, called a *learning style*. **Learning styles** are different approaches to learning. Do you learn best by seeing (**visual learner**), by listening (**auditory learner**), or by moving, doing, or touching (**kinesthetic/tactile learner**)? This "Self-Assessment" Learning Styles Survey will help you discover which type of learning style you prefer.

Step 1: For each item, select the alternative that best describes you. If no choice suits you exactly, select the one that is closest to your preference. Write the letter of your choice in the blank at the left.

_____ 1. When I need computer help, I
    A. look for pictures, tables, or diagrams.
    B. ask someone (my friend, the Help Desk technician, etc.).
    C. try a solution and see if it works.

_____ 2. To explain concepts in my classes, I like professors to use
    A. films and videos.
    B. lecturing and answering questions.
    C. hands-on activities.

_____ 3. When I am trying to relax, I prefer
    A. focusing on peaceful pictures.
    B. concentrating on restful music.
    C. performing a relaxation technique.

_____ 4. To get my new cell phone working, I am likely to
    A. carefully read through the instruction manual.
    B. talk to someone else about what to do.
    C. jump right in and begin to try to use it.

_____ 5. In chemistry class, I can best learn and remember an experimental procedure by
    A. observing the professor perform the experiment.
    B. listening to the professor describe how it is performed.
    C. doing the experiment by myself.

_____ 6. It is easiest for me to remember new people I have met by recalling
    A. their appearance, especially their faces.
    B. conversations we had.
    C. what we did together.

_____ 7. To memorize a lengthy scene from a Shakespearean play, I would repeatedly
    A. read the passage.
    B. listen to a recording of the passage.
    C. act out the scene.

8. To learn how to serve a tennis ball, I would want to
   A. watch the tennis instructor do it.
   B. have the tennis instructor tell me how to do it.
   C. just start hitting the ball until I get it right.

9. If someone gives me travel directions, I remember them by
   A. visualizing in my mind how to get there.
   B. repeating the directions to myself over again.
   C. creating a map to get there.

10. To solve a complicated algebra word problem, I would
   A. read and then reread the written problem.
   B. analyze it out loud to myself.
   C. use handy objects (paper clips, pencils, etc.) to
      represent the components of the problem.

11. When I read textbooks, I
   A. picture in my mind what I am reading.
   B. like to read out loud to myself.
   C. move my lips while I silently read.

12. If I am trying to spell a word correctly, I
   A. visualize how it looks in my mind.
   B. phonetically sound out the word.
   C. pretend to write out the letters sequentially with
      my fingers.

13. I enjoy learning most when I am
   A. reading books.
   B. listen to audio recordings.
   C. working with my hands.

14. To learn a complex new video game, I would most likely
   A. study the manual.
   B. talk to a friend who already knows the game.
   C. start playing and figure it out as I go.

15. To explain an electrical circuit to someone else, I would prefer
   A. using a diagram to show how it works.
   B. verbalizing how it works.
   C. demonstrating how it works.

Step 2: Count the total number of *A*s, *B*s, and *C*s you marked and enter the numbers on the lines in the diagram below.

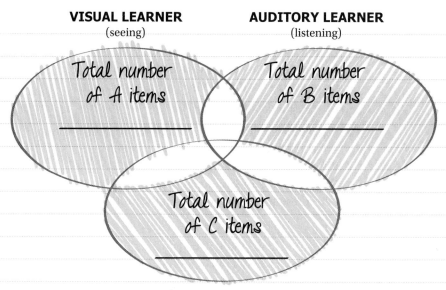

VISUAL LEARNER
(seeing)

AUDITORY LEARNER
(listening)

Total number
of A items
_____

Total number
of B items
_____

Total number
of C items
_____

KINESTHETIC/TACTILE LEARNER
(moving, doing, touching)

Step 3: Your highest score among the three choices on the "Self-Assessment" survey signals a preference for *visual learning, auditory learning,* or *kinesthetic/ tactile learning.* The A items indicate a *visual learner*, the B items indicate an *auditory learner*, and the C items indicate a *kinesthetic/tactile learner.* The diagram above shows overlapping circles because the learning styles are not discrete or separate; they overlap and flow into each other. As a student you will use all three styles of learning, but your highest score indicates a preference that you bring to your role as a college student. Now that you know how you learn best, consider the following chart with each learning style listed along with reading and learning strategies to use as part of each learning style.

VISUAL LEARNER (seeing)	AUDITORY LEARNER (listening)	KINESTHETIC/ TACTILE LEARNER (moving, doing, touching)
✓ Watch educational films or DVDs; use software when available.	✓ Talk out loud as part of studying.	✓ Create and take practice tests.
✓ Visualize images, concepts, information.	✓ Discuss/study with others.	✓ Use colored markers as you read/study.
✓ Pay attention to lectures by watching as well as by taking notes.	✓ Repeat information you are trying to learn.	✓ Move around while studying.
✓ Review by using study cards.	✓ Record lectures to listen to again.	✓ Write notes while listening to lectures.
		✓ Take action to keep focused, such as wearing a rubber band on your wrist to snap to get yourself back on task.

While learning theorists define and identify learning styles in many different ways, one of the most widely accepted views is that students prefer a visual learning style (seeing), an auditory learning style (listening), and/or a kinesthetic/tactile learning style (moving, doing, or touching).[1] Much of the material you are expected to learn as a college student comes from reading textbooks, which represents learning via the visual learning style. Thus, reading may appeal to you and come more naturally to you if you prefer the visual learning style; nevertheless, all college students must read textbooks and learn textbook information (see Chapter 4 for specific information on getting the most from your textbooks). Reading textbook assignments usually occurs outside the classroom. The rest of what you are expected to learn mainly occurs inside the classroom.

"As we start this semester, Professor Smith,
I just want you to know that I'm a visual
learner and trust that you will teach accordingly."

Now that you have identified your preferred learning style(s), you can understand why college classrooms might present challenges to some students. The traditional college classroom is structured around the lecture method of presentation. If you are an auditory learner, you are in great shape; but if you are a visual or kinesthetic/tactile learner, you will need to adapt to a professor's lecture method of presentation. Even though learning through listening may not be your most natural style, adapting to listening may be easier than you think. For example, even though you may have discovered that your preferred learning style is visual or kinesthetic/tactile, you can probably quote lyrics from songs. Since you most likely learned those lyrics through the listening learning style, you have proven that you are a learner who can adapt to another style.

This chapter will help you bolster the skills you need by applying what you know about your preferred learning style(s) to listening better in the classroom, to improving your note-taking from lectures and textbooks, and to participating more actively in the classroom.

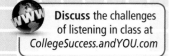
"LISTEN UP"
in the classroom

The classroom is one of the most important places to apply listening skills for a college student. The International Listening Association reports in a study that college students typically spend approximately 50% of their time in listening-related activities.[2] Although students rely on listening skills more than any other communication skill in the classroom, listening is rarely taught. Think back to your prior school days; do you recall learning about listening? Since the answer is probably "no," this section of the chapter provides a review of listening competencies and strategies with suggestions for those of you who are not strong auditory learners.

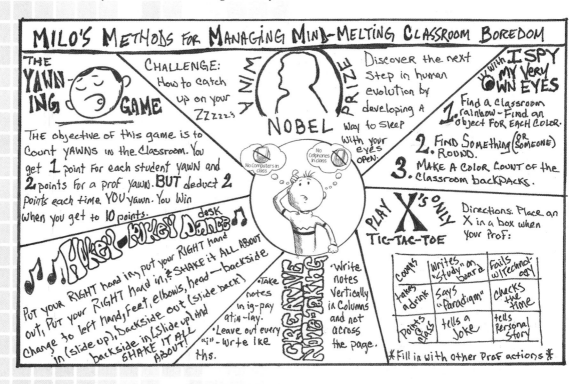

An analysis of how your professors teach will help you get a good idea about how you can improve your listening regardless of your preferred learning style. The following exercise asks you to observe a professor's teaching style. You will then use that information to see how you can adapt and improve your ability to listen to the professor's style of classroom teaching.

EXERCISE 1 **Turn the Table: Evaluate Your Professor**

Step 1: Choose one of your professors (other than the professor for this class) to analyze for his or her teaching style. As you pay attention in class, try to be aware of the way that professor teaches. After class, answer the following questions. You will learn how to apply this information to listening in Step 2.

1. What classroom or presentation aids (for example, the board, technology—presentation software, videos) did the professor use?

   _____

   _____

2. What kinds of voice patterns (soft, loud) or rates of speech (fast, slow) did the professor display? Did these vocal characteristics indicate changes of topic or emphasis for a particular point? How does the professor indicate important points?

   _____

   _____

3. Are there questions and answers, with exchanges taking place between the professor and the students in the classroom? Do students express their own opinions?

   _____

   _____

4. Are there any mannerisms or characteristics about the professor that you find distracting? If so, what are they?

   _____

   _____

5. Explain to what extent the professor stayed on the subject or wandered around while providing instruction.

   _____

   _____

6. How do you rate the classroom's physical environment (hot, noisy, crowded, bright, etc.)? List any distractions that bothered you.

   _____

   _____

Step 2: Consider the following comments and suggestions for each of the above questions. Listening recommendations are offered in each item.

Question 1: Sometimes professors use instructional aids to help them explain a complicated concept or emphasize a point. Good use of classroom aids can help keep the subject lively. Observe carefully what professors write on boards or display in the classroom—it is usually information they want to emphasize. Listen closely as a professor explains or emphasizes points using these types of aids.

Question 2: If a professor speaks too softly for you to hear, consider moving closer to the front of the room. Also, look for a professor's pattern of speech to signal a possible shift of topic or an emphasis on an important main idea. Listen for main ideas and major details in a speech or lecture just as you do when reading to detect them in textbooks. Check back in Chapter 4 for more information about identifying main ideas and major details.

Question 3: Listen carefully to what a speaker is saying in class, even if it is another student. Avoid letting emotion-laden words or biases influence your listening. Fully understand the speaker's point of view before accepting or rejecting it. The classroom is a place for a nonemotional interchange of ideas, so listen with an open mind.

Question 4: The responsibility for interest in what is being said lies with the listener. Finding fault with the professor does not excuse you from good listening. The message being conveyed is more important than *how* that message is conveyed.

Question 5: A professor who wanders around or digresses from the subject requires you to be an even more active listener than usual. Try not to daydream if the teacher goes off on a tangent. Keep yourself focused by anticipating what the next significant point will be. Make a game of predicting and give yourself a pat on the back if you are correct. Your listening will remain active if you are trying to discover the next major point.

Question 6: You might need to triumph over your environment. Students arriving late, papers being shuffled, and noises coming from hallways or other classrooms are all potential distractions, but avoid giving up your attention to these inconveniences. Listen with a purpose—identify what you expect to learn in class and then listen for these ideas as your professor speaks. Listening purposefully can help you forget about the environmental distractions.

Step 3: Discuss in class any methods you have successfully used to listen carefully in the classroom.

Listening competency in the classroom gives you the tools to accommodate your professor's teaching style, your learning style preference(s), and your learning environment. The listening competencies discussed in the comments and suggestions for each of the above items are summarized in the box below.

Summary of Listening Competencies for the College Classroom

1. Observe carefully what a professor writes on the board or otherwise displays in the classroom, since these actions usually signal important information. Listen closely as these concepts are explained.

2. As professors speak, listen for main ideas and major details. If you can't hear well enough, move closer to the front of the room.

3. Listen with an open mind. Examine opinions or points of view with full understanding before accepting or rejecting them.

4. Avoid allowing a speaker's mannerisms or characteristics to distract you from good listening. Focus on the content of the message rather than the delivery.

5. If a professor wanders off the topic, stay focused by listening for the next important point. Anticipating what comes next will help keep *your* mind from wandering.

6. Listen purposefully to overcome the distractions of your environment. Identify what you expect to learn and then listen for these ideas.

The Final Four Listening Strategies

Listening Behavior

Understanding and applying some listening strategies will also help you as you work to achieve your academic goals. The first strategy is to understand your own *listening behavior*. **Listening behavior** refers to a self-understanding of your attitudes and values toward listening. For example, if you have been told that you are a poor listener ("You never listen to me!" or "You're not listening!"), you may have developed a negative attitude toward listening. If you have been told often enough that you are a poor listener, you may behave accordingly. Your attitude toward listening may even be a factor in which learning style(s) you prefer. However, by recognizing the basis for your listening behavior, you can begin to develop a positive attitude toward listening in the classroom. Remember that hearing and listening are quite different. *Hearing* refers to processing the physical sounds made; *listening* refers to understanding what is said. It will be to your advantage as a college student not only to want to hear the information presented but also to listen to the information.

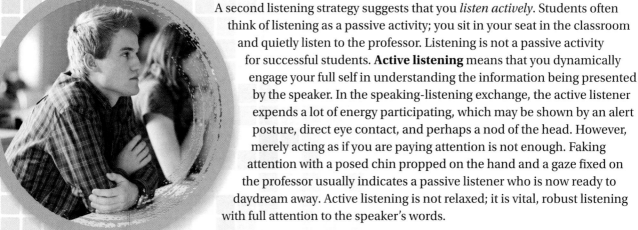

Active Listening

A second listening strategy suggests that you *listen actively*. Students often think of listening as a passive activity; you sit in your seat in the classroom and quietly listen to the professor. Listening is not a passive activity for successful students. **Active listening** means that you dynamically engage your full self in understanding the information being presented by the speaker. In the speaking-listening exchange, the active listener expends a lot of energy participating, which may be shown by an alert posture, direct eye contact, and perhaps a nod of the head. However, merely acting as if you are paying attention is not enough. Faking attention with a posed chin propped on the hand and a gaze fixed on the professor usually indicates a passive listener who is now ready to daydream away. Active listening is not relaxed; it is vital, robust listening with full attention to the speaker's words.

All Ears: Active listening can help you stay alert in the classroom.

Critical Listening

The next listening strategy is *critical listening*, which directly relates to critical thinking and reading.[3] See Chapter 4 to refresh your memory regarding critical thinking and critical reading skills. **Critical listening** means listening not only to understand or comprehend but also to evaluate information using careful, thoughtful, and reasoned judgments. This skill applies primarily to persuasive messages. As listeners, we are flooded with persuasive messages and arguments designed to influence our attitudes and behaviors.

In the classroom, you hear many opinions on a variety of topics from professors, students, and guest speakers. Professors, students, and guest speakers probably are not maliciously trying to influence your thinking, but an educated person is usually a careful listener. The critical listener must decide to accept or reject a message or argument according to valid criteria.

First, to judge the acceptability of a persuasive message you hear, consider a speaker's credibility. Ask yourself if the person has credentials in the area under discussion and if you would consider the speaker an expert in that area. Professors usually are experts in the areas they teach, but students or guests may not be as informed. Be wary of speakers who do not have the necessary educational background or expertise in the specific area of discussion.

Next, evaluate the validity of the speaker's argument. Listen for supporting data (statistics such as percentages, probabilities, averages); facts (provable statements); cases (supporting case studies); or other acceptable forms of support. The supporting evidence should be relevant to the argument and sufficient to support the message.

Then, analyze the message for the soundness of the argument. A speaker may use a **fallacy**, which is an error in reasoning, leading to a flawed argument. Fallacies such as **hasty generalizations** (drawing a conclusion with insufficient evidence), **bandwagon appeal** ("join the crowd" since everyone else believes or accepts this idea), and the **either/or fallacy** (assuming there are only two sides to an issue or only two possible choices available) are only a sampling of the many types of fallacies that a speaker might use to try to persuade a listener to accept a certain viewpoint or belief.

Three Types of Fallacies for Critical Listening

Type of Fallacy	Definition	Example
Hasty Generalization	Drawing a conclusion with insufficient evidence	Three students you talked to said they find PowerPoint format lectures boring so you conclude that all students find PowerPoint format lectures boring.
Bandwagon Appeal	"Joining the crowd" since everyone else believes or accepts this idea	A guest speaker says, "Everyone agrees that using bottled water is wasteful." Since the speaker says that everyone agrees, you are also expected to agree.
Either/Or Fallacy	Assuming there are only two sides to an issue or only two possible choices available	During class a student says, "TV violence must be allowed or totally banned," when actually ratings for various levels of violent actions can advise viewers.

Applying critical listening skills to persuasive messages will give you a reliable basis for evaluating the message. A professor who lectures with strong convictions can present a model for your engagement in critical listening analysis. You can carry this skill with you throughout life as you listen to and evaluate the claims of politicians, advertisements you hear on television, or a friend's point of view.

Note-Taking

The final listening strategy involves *note-taking*. Although software programs and technology gadgets (such as smart pens) are available to support the note-taking process, none of them can actually take notes—you must always write the notes yourself. You will have a lot of trouble recalling what you hear in class without taking notes. Taking notes also keeps you actively involved in listening to the professor. If you are not a strong auditory learner, taking notes can help you focus on the professor's message. Successful note-taking involves writing the key ideas expressed in the lecture; taking down what the professor writes on the board or otherwise displays in the classroom; writing questions you or your professors pose; and using a specific note-taking procedure, such as the Cornell Note-taking System, which is explained on page 115. Various suggestions for how to improve your note-taking follow in the next section.

Discuss the challenges of note-taking in the classroom at *CollegeSuccess.andYOU.com*

Listening to Podcast Lectures

Podcasts are audio or video presentations that you can access whenever you choose. Specifically, a podcast is a means of distributing audio and video files (known as *feeds*) via the Internet. A podcast allows you to hear or view the presentations when you want. If a professor uses podcasts, you can listen to or view a lecture through your computer or on a portable media player or other similar device.

Students who enjoy podcasts say that the convenience of listening at any time, even multitasking while walking on campus to classes, is a valuable feature. They also find it helpful to be able to fast-forward or rewind and listen to repeats of parts of lectures that are confusing. In fact, researchers at the State University of New York at Fredonia report that students who take notes from a podcast lecture have an advantage for test preparation over students who take notes during a live lecture. The researchers attribute this advantage to the possibility for students to listen again to the podcast.[4]

Other students say that it becomes too tempting to skip a class if the lecture is accessible on a podcast, and they end up missing the useful discussions that can continue after a lecture ends. They also miss the student-to-student interactions that often can help clarify confusing course concepts.

You can apply the same listening competencies and techniques that you are learning in this chapter to podcasts. You might need to be even more diligent in your listening to podcasts since so many more distractions can interfere. Also, recognize that not everything taught at colleges translates to podcasting. Some classes, such as lab courses and theater classes, won't work well as podcasts.

Simple solutions to NOTE-TAKING

Just as reading may be appealing and more natural for students who favor a visual learning style, and listening in class may be more natural to students who favor an auditory style, note-taking may be more natural to students who prefer a kinesthetic/tactile learning style. As college students, you usually take notes in two different contexts. The first circumstance in which you will need to take notes occurs during lectures. You have learned about listening to lectures, so now you will learn about a specific method to use to take notes from lectures. Second, when you read textbook assignments, you need to follow a procedure to record the information for later study and review. You have already learned about techniques that help you discover the important ideas as you read textbooks (see Chapter 4). Now you will learn ways to record that information for later review. Before you learn about procedures for note-taking either from lectures or from textbooks, here are some general note-taking basics for your consideration. If you use a laptop in the classroom, apply the same note-taking principles that you are learning in this chapter.

Basic Training for Taking Notes

- Use a large notebook (8½ by 11 inches). Small notebooks are easy to carry, but that is not your major objective. An 8½-by-11-inch page gives you enough room to indent plus take notes. Write on one side only—you want to be able to organize your papers at any time.

- Leave spaces blank as you move from one major idea to another. The spaces separate the ideas, and you might need extra room to fill in additional information later.

- Attend classes regularly. When you have to miss a class, arrange to get that day's notes.

- Write the date and the class at the top of each page. Keep all notes for one course separated from those for another course. Separate notebooks help with this suggestion.

- Don't try to write down everything. Take down the main ideas and major details. The minor points, such as examples, are supplementary and are not always necessary to write.

- Make your notes legible. You can use abbreviations and symbols, but be sure you can read and understand your own notes.

Now that you have reviewed the basics of note-taking, you are ready to increase your understanding of how to take notes from classroom lectures.

Secrets for Taking Notes from Lectures: A Proven Method

Although several note-taking methods exist—for example, you can use basic outlining or mapping procedures—one of the most widely used and respected systems of taking notes from lectures is the **Cornell Note-taking System**. This system was developed by experts at the Learning Strategies Center of Cornell University.[5] The Cornell System offers you an organized and concise way to take notes.

An Overview of What You Do

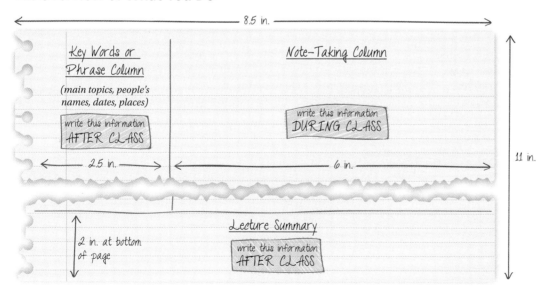

Before the Lecture

To use the Cornell Note-taking System, divide one sheet of regular 8½-by-11-inch paper into two columns by drawing one line from top to bottom. The line should be only about 2½ inches from the left side of the page. The lecture notes go in the right-side column, the wider column. Use the left-side column, the narrower column, for writing in key words or phrases (such as the main topics, people's names, dates or places, and so forth) after you finish taking the lecture notes. You should also designate the last four lines at the bottom of the notes for a brief summary of the day's key information.

During the Lecture

Leave the 2½-inch-wide left column blank for now. Write your notes, recording the main ideas and major details (see Chapter 4 for a discussion of main ideas and major details) in the wider column on the right side of the page. Skip lines to show the end of topics. Using abbreviations can save you time. Be sure to write legibly so that you can read your notes when you need to review them.

After the Lecture

Review your notes and make sure they are readable. Now fill in the left-side column with key words and phrases (the main topics, people's names, dates or places, and so forth). Then, fill in the last four lines with a summary of the lecture's key points. Do an immediate review of the lecture by covering over the right side column of notes, using your key words and phrases to recite to yourself the information in the notes. If you don't remember, reread your complete notes for that key word or phrase. At exam time, review by covering up your notes on the right-side column and going over all the key words and phrases to see if you can recall the corresponding information in the notes.

What Does the Cornell Note-taking System Look Like for a Real Class?

	Geography 335
	April 5, 2014
biome def.	biome – group of ecosystems with similar climate, plant, animal communities
6 types of biomes	6 basic types of terrestrial biomes (also are aquatic biomes)
	1 – tundra → cold, windy, dry
	2 – coniferous forest → cold, snow, somewhat dry
	3 – deciduous forest → cold winter, warm summer
	4 – grassland → cold winter, hot summer
	5 – desert → hot, dry
	6 – rain forest → warm, wet
biome names	biome often named for most dominant/common plant
coniferous	coniferous – cone-bearing trees
deciduous	deciduous – trees with leaves that shed

A biome is a major ecosystem consisting of similar climate conditions with similar plant and animal communities. There are six basic types of terrestrial biomes (tundra, coniferous forests, deciduous forests, grasslands, deserts, and rain forests). Biomes are often named for the dominant plant (coniferous, deciduous).

EXERCISE 2 Cornell Note-taking in Action

DOWNLOAD

Step 1: Use the following blank template to take notes in a class of your choice. Try this system to see how it works. To get more blank templates to use for your classes, go to the textbook website and print as many copies as you need.

Key Words or Phrase Column *(main topics, people's names, dates, places)*	Note-Taking Column

Lecture Summary

Step 2: Bring your notes to class and be prepared to discuss your experience using the Cornell Note-taking System.

Once a week, it is a good idea to review all the notes you have taken from the beginning of the semester. Cover over the notes on the right side of the page and use only the key words and phrases. Then, try to recite to yourself the information from the notes and reread as necessary. If you complete this review every week, you will continuously build your store of information, and you will be able to see the interrelationships of the ideas you are learning. You will be prepared for exam time by being up-to-date with all the concepts of the class that have been presented from the first week of the semester.

Using Laptops for Note-Taking in the Classroom
College educators and students are debating the usefulness of laptops in the classroom. Advantages and disadvantages exist for both the professor and the student. According to professors, laptops create distractions but increase the number of instructional techniques available. While students say laptops ease note-taking, they agree that laptops create distractions both for themselves (web surfing during class time) and for other students (who are stuck viewing this web surfing).

A study by Carrie B. Fried of Winona State University examined in-class laptop use in a large lecture course. Results suggest that students who use laptops spend considerable time multitasking, that laptop use creates distractions for both users and fellow students, and that laptop use negatively relates to overall course performance.[6]

Many colleges and individual professors are establishing laptop usage policies, so if you want to use a laptop, you need to review any policies that are in place for your school or your professor. If you do use a laptop in the classroom, apply the same note-taking principles that you are learning in this chapter. Although software applications can help support the note-taking process, they can't take notes for you. You can use the Cornell Note-taking System by creating a template. Follow the same procedures and advice for taking notes from a lecture in the classroom. Also, remember to be a mature, courteous laptop user in the classroom—both to your professor and to your classmates.

Four Main Methods for Taking Notes from Textbooks

The other type of note-taking you do for your college classes relates to reading textbook assignments. Although this type of activity generally occurs away from the classroom, note-taking from textbooks is a key skill for classroom success. While taking notes from textbooks is essential for all students, note-taking can provide extra support to auditory learners and kinesthetic/tactile learners in processing the visually presented material. You have learned about reading to determine the main ideas and major details of textbooks. When taking notes from textbooks, your ability to figure out the main ideas and major details is important since they form the content that you put into your notes. You might consider a quick review of main ideas and major details (see Chapter 4) if you think a refresher will help you decide which information to include in your textbook notes.

The four methods available for taking notes from textbooks are *underlining/highlighting, outlining, summarizing,* and *mapping.* No one method is better than the other; it is a matter of which ones you prefer to use. And as you will discover, each method requires you to locate the same information in your reading: the main ideas and the major details. The methods vary only in the way you format the information you discover.

Although a detailed explanation for each of these four methods follows below, here is a brief overview. When using **underlining/highlighting**, you mark the main ideas and major details in the book. However, if a book is rented or borrowed, you probably will not want to write directly in it. If that is the case, you will likely choose one of the next options. When **outlining**, you set the main ideas and major details in an outline format. When **summarizing**, you write the main ideas and major details in a paragraph form. And when **mapping**, you draw diagrams to represent the main ideas and major details. You may choose to vary the techniques you use depending on the assignment you are reading.

Method One: Underlining/Highlighting Information in Textbooks

When you underline or highlight words or sentences in textbooks for study purposes, you may wonder, "What am I supposed to mark?" The answer is that you underline or highlight the main ideas and major details. Not only is underlining/highlighting an effective way to keep track of important ideas, it is also a time-saver for you. Suppose that you are assigned a chapter in your biology text that takes you several hours to read. A month later, you need to review the chapter for an exam. If you underlined or highlighted the key ideas, you can review the chapter pretty quickly; if you didn't, you will have to reread the whole chapter again.

The following paragraph not only gives important tips on underlining and highlighting, it is also highlighted to illustrate for you how a student would go about marking the information.

Lighten Up: Using highlighters to mark main ideas and major details reminds you of important information.

Three tips will guide you as you underline or highlight the main ideas and major details in textbooks. Following these suggestions will help you become an efficient note-taker so that when exam time arrives, the information underlined or highlighted can serve as a record of what is important to learn and remember. This technique will save you time because you will need to reread only the marked information for study purposes. First, read totally through the paragraph or section before you mark the key ideas. It is only after you read completely through the passage that you can go back to mark the main ideas and major details. If you don't read first, you cannot know which sentences form these key ideas. Second, underline or highlight the right amount, which is about 20%–30% of the material. If you mark too much, you are probably not focusing on the important information, and if you mark too little, you are probably missing key ideas. Your purpose is to distinguish the important from the unimportant information. Third, underline or highlight accurately so that when you study the information, the marked parts make sense to you. If you randomly mark words and phrases as you read, then your review of the material becomes difficult or impossible because your underlining or highlighting won't make sense to you. You will end up being forced to reread a great deal of material.

Notice that when you read this paragraph, the main idea (the first sentence) and major details (the sentences beginning "First," "Second," and "Third") are marked; about 20%-30% of the paragraph is marked; and you can understand the meaning from reading the highlighted parts alone. These are the goals when using underlining or highlighting to mark textbooks.

Method Two: Outlining Information in Textbooks

Outlining represents another choice for taking notes from a textbook. When outlining, you list the main ideas and major details, showing their relationships to one another. The structure of your outline is important because it helps you instantly understand the relationships of the ideas. The standard form for outlining uses roman numerals, letters, numbers, and indentation. You don't have to follow an outline format precisely as long as your outline shows an organization of ideas that works for you. You can use words, phrases, or complete sentences, whichever is best for you. If you need to provide a formally organized outline for a research paper or an essay, then you will want to be sure that you carefully structure the outline. For now, as you use outlines for your personal studying, you can structure them informally to suit yourself. An outline usually follows a format similar to the one below:

I. First Main Idea

    A. Major Supporting Detail One

    B. Major Supporting Detail Two

        1. Minor Supporting Detail (if needed)

        2. Minor Supporting Detail (if needed)

II. Second Main Idea

Remember the paragraph that had tips for underlining or highlighting? When it is outlined, it looks something like this.

I. Three tips guide you for underlining or highlighting main ideas and major details.

    A. Read the passage completely through first before marking key ideas.

        1. Then go back to mark main ideas and major details.

        2. You can't know what to mark without first reading.

    B. Underline or highlight about 20%-30% of what you read.

    C. Underline or highlight accurately so that it makes sense when you review it.

Notice that when you read the outline, the main idea is identified by a roman numeral, the major details have capital letters, and the minor details are indicated by regular numbers. Each level of the outline gets indented to indicate a relationship so that when you look at it, you can instantly tell that the main idea is farthest left, major details are next, and minor details are the most indented. This procedure can be effectively used to format an outline for studying a textbook.

Method Three: Summarizing Information in Textbooks

A summary provides a condensed version of a longer passage. It is a shortened statement that preserves the key information (that is, the main ideas and major details) of the original passage. Often, a summary is written in a paragraph form that ties together these key ideas. Summaries do not include the reader's opinions or any information that is not in the original passage. Summaries do follow the organization of the passage by keeping the ideas in the same order as they appear in the original material. You might choose to summarize individual sections of chapters or even whole chapters.

For the paragraph on tips for underlining or highlighting information, a summary looks something like this.

> Three tips guide you for underlining or highlighting main ideas and major details. First, read completely through the material before you mark the key ideas. Second, underline or highlight about 20%–30% of what you read. Third, underline or highlight accurately so that the material marked makes sense when you are ready to study.

Sum It Up: Just as a search engine's results page gives a brief synopsis of each site's contents, a summary represents a condensed expression of longer ideas.

With this method, the main idea and major details are written in paragraph form and no minor details appear. Also, you will see that no extra information appears in the summary—it has only a brief version of the original. Additionally, the ideas are kept in exactly the same order as the original paragraph.

Method Four: Mapping Information in Textbooks

Mapping is a visual method of organizing information; students with a preferred visual learning style might appreciate this technique for note-taking over any of the others. Mapping involves drawing diagrams to show how main ideas and major details in a section of a chapter or a whole chapter are connected. In representing these key ideas, mapping maintains their relative importance and relationship to one another. Maps can take many different shapes or forms, and you are free to choose how to draw them to represent the ideas in the textbook. Here is a map of the paragraph on tips for underlining and highlighting information.

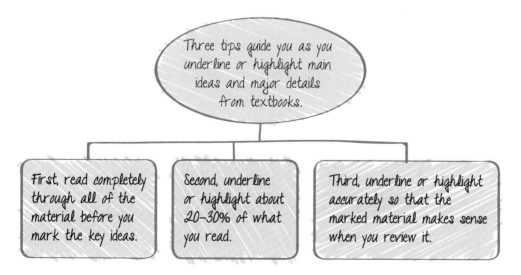

Three tips guide you as you underline or highlight main ideas and major details from textbooks.

First, read completely through all of the material before you mark the key ideas.

Second, underline or highlight about 20–30% of what you read.

Third, underline or highlight accurately so that the marked material makes sense when you review it.

You can choose boxes, circles, ovals, or just about any shape you prefer for mapping information. As you become skilled at mapping information, you can try various techniques to display the textbook information. You organize the map to include the main ideas and the major details with connections showing the relationships. And you do want to remember that your goal is to have the key ideas in a map form that will help you understand and study the information.

EXERCISE 3 Noting Results

Step 1: Choose *one* of the four methods for taking notes from textbooks: (1) underlining/highlighting, (2) outlining, (3) summarizing, or (4) mapping. Using any of your current textbooks, including this text, prepare notes for any one chapter. Bring the notes to class. If you choose underlining/highlighting, you will need to bring the textbook with the information marked on the pages in the book.

Step 2: Write the answers to the following questions. You will need to wait for class to answer some of the questions.

1. Which method of note-taking did you select? _____

    _____

2. Why did you choose the method you selected? _____

    _____

3. Which method of note-taking was most selected by members of your class?

    How many students in the class chose underlining/highlighting? _____

    summarizing? _____

    mapping? _____

4. What is a primary reason the other students chose the method they selected?

    For underlining/highlighting _____

    _____

    For outlining _____

    _____

    For summarizing _____

    _____

    For mapping _____

    _____

Step 3: Discuss in class if one note-taking method is better for some students than another method. For example, explain how one note-taking method matches a preferred learning style better than another note-taking method.

PARTICIPATION

getting started yesterday

Class participation is an interactive, exploratory process. Implementing focused and active listening will help you become a classroom participant. Some students look forward to participation in class, while others dread it. Regardless of your preferred learning style, a bit of stage fright is fairly common, so don't feel alone if you are nervous about speaking in class. Because a kinesthetic/tactile learner prefers "doing," participating in class may be more comfortable for someone with this learning style. Whether you favor a visual, auditory, or kinesthetic/tactile learning style, the following ideas can help you maximize your abilities to become an active classroom participant.

Why Participate

When you read your professor's syllabus (see Chapter 1), you may find that a certain amount of credit will be awarded for class participation. Not only will you learn more and enjoy class more if you participate, but also you will earn credit. The syllabus may even state that you are required to participate. For example, you may have to give a mandatory in-class oral presentation.

Are You Ready? To make class participation easier, you might prepare your question or comment ahead of time.

Class participation will also enable you to share your unique views. Participating encourages diverse viewpoints to be expressed and received. Sometimes discussions take unexpected turns as ideas change and unfold. A broadening of perspectives occurs as these classroom exchanges take place. The opportunity to understand a diversity of views is often what a college classroom discussion is all about.

Also, the best place to request clarification and expansion of class material or test preparation is in the classroom. You can raise questions or concerns for the professor to address. Since questions often generate a classroom discussion regarding concepts that are confusing, it is helpful to most students. Don't ever be afraid to ask what you consider a "dumb" question if you are confused, since other students probably are equally confused and have in mind the exact same question as you.

How to Participate If You Are Uncomfortable

The best first step for planning to take part in class is preparation. Get ready by reviewing your notes based on your listening (see the earlier section in this chapter, " 'Listen Up' in the Classroom") and then by organizing your contribution. You can start speaking in class by making a small contribution, such as agreeing or disagreeing with the discussion. Or you can request clarification or expansion of a point, such as asking for an example or additional information. You can then work up to more participation by asking a broader question of your own. You might prepare a question ahead of time for the topic of the day after reading in advance about that topic. After you are feeling comfortable, you can participate even more by answering a question that has been raised, by providing your own example for a discussion, or by explaining the reasons for your agreement or disagreement with someone else's point of view. The idea is to start small and then consciously try to work toward more contributions.

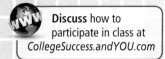

Discuss how to participate in class at *CollegeSuccess.andYOU.com*

Sometimes topics are controversial in the classroom, and the purpose of the class discussion aims to explore differing viewpoints while arriving at reasoned mutual understanding. Such an argument is not about who "wins" but instead emphasizes the development of ideas, the advancement of understanding, and the opportunity to think critically (see Chapter 4). During these kinds of discussions, it is important to be mannerly—to be courteous, to listen respectfully, to disagree politely, to keep the discussion open and friendly. A differing viewpoint doesn't signal being incorrect; a diversity of views is a hallmark of a great classroom discussion.

The Required Classroom Oral Presentation

To prepare yourself for a required oral presentation, follow the guidelines on the next page, which will serve you well in your presentation efforts. Everyone has to work hard to get ready to speak in a classroom, so don't think that you are the only person spending time preparing for the presentation. Thorough preparation will give you a sense of control that can help make you less nervous.

Delivering Your Address: Following an action plan for giving an oral presentation helps build your confidence.

Action Plan for Giving Classroom Presentations

1. **Being Prepared**
   - Have everything for your presentation ready—including any audiovisual aids.
   - Develop clear objectives or goals for the presentation.
   - Outline three to five main points.
   - Know the room. If it's not your classroom, visit it ahead of time to increase your comfort level.
   - Start with a bang. Have an introduction that gets attention. For example, use appropriate humor, quotes, stories, startling statistics, or audience participation.
   - Practice, practice, practice. Give the presentation several times, using the audiovisual aids. Ask a friend or family member to listen and give you feedback.
   - Visualize giving a successful presentation and receiving praise from your professor and other students.

2. **Delivering the Presentation**
   - Dress comfortably and appropriately.
   - Stay aware of your posture, voice tone, gestures, and body language.
   - Speak slowly and clearly enough for everyone to grasp your ideas and to hear you.
   - Face your audience and establish eye contact with as many people as possible.
   - Talk to your audience and not to a visual aid.
   - Realize that you probably know more about your specific topic than anyone else in the audience, including your professor. This thought can be comforting and confidence building.

3. **Answering Questions**
   - Invite questions, giving time for your audience to formulate them.
   - Anticipate specific questions and prepare a response.
   - Repeat a question you are asked, to be sure you understand it and to be sure the audience heard it.
   - Keep your answers brief and to the point.
   - Be honest; if you don't know an answer, say so.
   - Accept a last question and then go on to briefly summarize your main points.
   - Thank the other students and your professor for their attention.

Following this action plan will help bring out your capacity to speak effectively in front of others, a skill that may prove useful in your eventual career.

How to Relax for Classroom Presentations

The best advice for giving a successful classroom presentation is to be prepared and to relax. If relaxation seems like an impossible goal, you can take some positive steps toward reducing your anxiety. **Public speaking anxiety** refers to the fears, sometimes almost overwhelming, that some students might experience when they must "perform" or speak in public. The fear of not doing well can hold you back from accomplishing things that you are otherwise capable of achieving.

So how exactly do you go about relaxing for a required class presentation? First, be sure you have eaten, because hunger can contribute to anxiety. But avoid eating sugary foods or drinking caffeinated beverages (including soft drinks) since these will speed up your bodily reactions. You will probably already have enough energy going on without supplying any additional boosts.

Another helpful activity is to change the way you might be *thinking* about speaking in public. You might be *thinking* about how awful things could turn out and *thinking* about what others *think*. It isn't useful to think that your self-worth is wrapped up in one classroom presentation. Extremes—that you will either perform superbly with a perfectly exquisite presentation or that you will not utter one acceptable statement in the whole presentation—are not realistic. Instead of thinking that you must succeed with every single syllable, a better strategy is to focus on your topic and block out what others *might* be thinking. We can never know what others are really thinking, so worrying about it is too distracting. Why distract and worry yourself with that?

Since you are probably going to know more about your specific topic than anyone else in the classroom, including your professor, your listeners aren't likely to realize if you have made a mistake. Listeners will notice a mistake only if you call their attention to it. So if you make a mistake, just keep going and most likely no one will pay much attention to your error. Don't apologize by mentioning your mistake or your nervousness, since you are probably calling the listeners' attention to something they haven't noticed.

A moderate level of nervous anticipation can energize you to make a good effort. The other students will want you to succeed; they know that they will soon be in your same position, so they want you also to be successful. Harness your nervousness and turn it into positive energy and enthusiasm. Public speaking is an acquired skill; experience builds confidence, so the more oral presentations you do, the easier it will become. After you have finished your presentation, you can sit back, breathe a sigh of relief, and enjoy your moment of accomplishment—you did it!

Use the resource links to find additional information at *CollegeSuccess.andYOU.com*

Thinking Critically About . . .
Learning Styles in the Classroom:
Listening, Taking Notes, and Participating

Critical thinking involves an active evaluation of information using careful, thoughtful, and reasoned judgments.

1. Discuss your viewpoint on the advantages and disadvantages of using a laptop computer to take notes in the classroom.

2. Imagine that you are a professor meeting a class of students. What behaviors will indicate a motivated, interested student? Analyze how these behaviors create a positive academic image.

3. Produce a list of reasons students might give for not wanting to participate in class. For each reason, provide advice for what students might do to overcome their reluctance to participate.

4. Analyze how each of the learning styles (visual, auditory, and kinesthetic/tactile) relates to learning in college. Include a discussion of the implications of mismatches between a student's learning style and a professor's teaching style. Explore the match of a preferred learning style to a particular subject area of study (for example, science or literature).

5. How can the skills of listening, note-taking, and participating in the classroom during college be valuable after a student graduates?

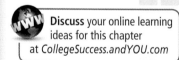

Discuss your ideas about the Critical Thinking items at *CollegeSuccess.andYOU.com*

Online Learning

In a typical college classroom, participation requires listening and speaking. For online learners, participation usually requires reading and writing, although sometimes online students listen to recorded lectures. In many classes, online learners may participate not only through threaded discussion of content with one another, but through interactions with the professor, with small groups or teams, or with a partner. If participation is required, you might be graded by criteria that include whether or not you made enough discussion comments that are accurate, original, relevant, and well written.

Even if online discussions are not required, they may be valuable. They allow you to participate at any time to seek clarification, discuss class topics, or initiate new ideas. You may feel more comfortable in online participation than classroom participation since it is easier to compose, edit, and refine your ideas before you express them online. You generally have a greater degree of anonymity online than in face-to-face settings, so participation may be less worrisome than speaking in the classroom. Nevertheless, before you hit the Send button or post a comment, it's a good idea to review your words to make sure they say just what you intend to communicate.

To help online students gain experience in speaking, some professors assign giving a brief presentation to a friend or neighbor. Students who are assigned such speaking requirements may be expected to write about their experiences.

Discuss your online learning ideas for this chapter at *CollegeSuccess.andYOU.com*

CHAPTER CHALLENGE

YOU DON'T HAVE THE RIGHT TO REMAIN SILENT

Many students arrive at college without any experience in speaking to groups of their peers. Therefore, it is understandable that some students become very nervous over the prospect of delivering a presentation to fellow students in a classroom setting. Yet some college professors require every student to give oral presentations in front of a class. For example, a history professor may assign term papers and then schedule students to describe the information from their papers to the other students in the class. At some colleges, students must take a public speaking class that requires them to give several speeches. Students with anxiety about speaking in front of groups can find these demands very stressful. Becoming comfortable with public speaking can be advantageous since many career fields require the ability to speak in front of professional groups, clients, or customers.

A CASE STUDY: FACING THE CHALLENGE OF . . .
YOU DON'T HAVE THE RIGHT TO REMAIN SILENT

David wanted to become an architect once he saw the soaring grace of the skyscrapers in New York City during a family vacation when he was eight years old. It looked like his career dreams would come true when he was accepted into the best architecture program in his state. Upon starting college, he was very optimistic that he would succeed in achieving his goals. As he sailed along during the early weeks of his first semester, he received a rude jolt to his confidence. His architecture design professor informed the class that all the students would have to give a 20-minute oral presentation in front of the class explaining their final designs for the semester. The presentation would count for a significant part of the final grade. David was scared. He had avoided any requirements for giving speeches during high school, so he had never given a class presentation before. David knew that he would be extremely nervous giving a speech, and he wasn't sure what to do.

OVERCOMING THE CHALLENGE OF . . .
YOU DON'T HAVE THE RIGHT TO REMAIN SILENT

Be prepared to discuss your answers to the following items: (1) David has the written speech for his final architecture design ready. Explain the steps David can take to prepare to deliver his class presentation. What are suggestions for David to follow while he delivers his speech? (2) What recommended actions can David take to try to overcome his anxiety about classroom presentations? (3) Speculate why David's design professor would require students to give a classroom presentation.

Key Chapter Strategies

■ Recognize and effectively use your preferred learning style(s) in your studies.

■ Listen actively and critically in class.

■ Take notes from lectures by following a specific method, such as the Cornell Note-taking System.

■ Take notes from textbooks by choosing to use (1) underlining/highlighting, (2) outlining, (3) summarizing, and/or (4) mapping.

■ Become an active classroom participant.

■ Implement an action plan for giving oral presentations.

■ For additional information, read *Blink: The Power of Thinking Without Thinking* by Malcolm Gladwell[7] and *Listening: The Forgotten Skill* (second ed.) by Madelyn Burley-Allen.[8]

Can You Recall It?

Directions: To review your understanding of the chapter, choose the correct term from the list below and fill it in on the blank. You will not use every term.

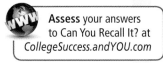
Assess your answers to Can You Recall It? at *CollegeSuccess.andYOU.com*

kinesthetic/tactile learner	classroom participation
outline	Cornell
anxieties	critical listener
auditory learner	Bandwagon
main ideas and major details	podcast
visual learner	listening

1. Josh attended a lecture filled with opinions and persuasive messages. Josh must be a/an _____ to judge and evaluate the worthiness of these views.

2. If you are a/an _____ , you prefer to learn by moving, doing, or touching.

3. Francisco's lecture notes are literally all over the page. He writes up and down the margins and fills the front and back of the paper with every detail and example. To help him, you suggest he might use the _____ Note-taking System.

4. When you take notes from a textbook, no matter what method you use, you include the _____ of what you read.

5. One way to take notes from a textbook is to write the notes in a/an _____ form.

6. College students spend approximately 50% of their time in _____ -related activities, so it's a surprise that this topic isn't often taught.

7. Many college students dread _____ since they feel awkward or uncomfortable about it.

8. A fallacy for critical listening involving "joining the crowd" is called the _____ Appeal.

Learning Styles in the Classroom: Listening, Taking Notes, and Participating **129**

Web Activity: YouTube and You

Directions: Go to YouTube (www.youtube.com) and enter the key words "learning styles" in the search box. Choose and watch a presentation on learning styles from among those available. Then fill in the information below.

1. Title of the presentation: _____

2. Exact web address of the presentation: _____

_____

3. What specifically was the presentation about? Give a short explanation of the content. _____

_____

_____

_____

_____

4. Evaluate the presentation. You can use the following criteria plus any others you wish to apply: Is it interesting and imaginative? Are there good visuals? Is it well structured? Is the presenter effective? Is the speech clear? Do background noises interfere? Are the transitions between segments smooth?

_____

_____

_____

_____

_____

_____

5. Briefly (in two or three sentences) discuss whether or not you enjoy learning information through a web presentation and why. _____

_____

_____

_____

_____

_____

_____

Reflection Time

Achieving Your Goals through Learning Styles in the Classroom: Listening, Taking Notes, and Participating

Choose any upcoming class session during which you plan to excel in listening, taking notes, and participating. Throughout the class, listen, take notes, and ask at least one question or make at least one comment. After the class, write three paragraphs answering each of the following questions. Paragraph 1: Explain how successful you were in listening. How did your preferred learning style(s) influence your listening? What can you do next time to improve your listening in the classroom? Paragraph 2: Explain how successful you were in taking notes. How did your preferred learning style(s) influence your note-taking? What can you do next time to improve your note-taking? Paragraph 3: Explain how successful you were in participating in class. How did your preferred learning style(s) influence your classroom participation? What can you do next time to improve your class participation?

_____

_____

_____

_____

_____

_____

_____

_____

_____

_____

_____

_____

_____

_____

_____

_____

_____

6

Succeeding on Exams

In this chapter, you will move toward achieving your goals by

- exploring how to manage test stress.

- understanding how to prepare for different types of tests and improving your test-taking strategies.

Find additional tools and resources at *CollegeSuccess.andYOU.com*

Self-Assessment: This Is Not a Test

Step 1: Circle the number for the item that most closely applies to you.

1. I preview the entire exam paper before beginning.
   - 1 = None of the time
   - 2 = Some of the time
   - 3 = Much of the time
   - 4 = Almost always

2. I carefully review and proofread the exam once I have finished.
   - 1 = None of the time
   - 2 = Some of the time
   - 3 = Much of the time
   - 4 = Almost always

3. I distribute my study time before the exam instead of cramming.
   - 1 = None of the time
   - 2 = Some of the time
   - 3 = Much of the time
   - 4 = Almost always

4. I read every question all the way through, including all the choices on a multiple-choice exam, before I answer.
   - 1 = None of the time
   - 2 = Some of the time
   - 3 = Much of the time
   - 4 = Almost always

5. I pay close attention to directions before I begin answering questions.
   - 1 = None of the time
   - 2 = Some of the time
   - 3 = Much of the time
   - 4 = Almost always

6. I budget my time on a test and use the point value of questions as a guide to how much time to spend on an item.
   - 1 = None of the time
   - 2 = Some of the time
   - 3 = Much of the time
   - 4 = Almost always

7. While studying, I predict questions that I think will be asked on a test and try to answer them.
   - 1 = None of the time
   - 2 = Some of the time
   - 3 = Much of the time
   - 4 = Almost always

8. I look for key words when answering true-false questions or essay questions.

    1 = None of the time
    2 = Some of the time
    3 = Much of the time
    4 = Almost always

9. I avoid changing answers unless I feel strongly that my first answer is wrong.

    1 = None of the time
    2 = Some of the time
    3 = Much of the time
    4 = Almost always

10. I answer easier questions first and persist until I answer all the questions.

    1 = None of the time
    2 = Some of the time
    3 = Much of the time
    4 = Almost always

11. My essay exam answers are grammatically correct, neat, and organized.

    1 = None of the time
    2 = Some of the time
    3 = Much of the time
    4 = Almost always

12. I take care of myself leading up to the exam, for instance, by eating well and getting enough sleep.

    1 = None of the time
    2 = Some of the time
    3 = Much of the time
    4 = Almost always

Step 2: Calculate your score by adding together the numbers you circled.

    My total score is _____.

Step 3: Analyze your score by matching your number to the scale.

Test-Taking Self-Analysis

12–35	Your test-taking skills need to improve for you to be the best college student that you can be. You may be able to obtain better grades by becoming more test-wise from the techniques suggested in this chapter.
36–41	You use test-taking skills to your advantage but not as much as you might. As you learn more about test-taking techniques in this chapter, you can boost your grades to higher levels.
42–48	You are aware of test-taking skills and use them to your advantage. Decide which skill areas from this chapter you can strengthen to become even more successful at taking tests.

Is this going to be ON THE TEST?

Exams can be scary and stressful. They may represent some of your biggest challenges in college. But they also can benefit you. You may never enjoy taking exams, but they provide you with opportunities to succeed and learn.

Professors use exams in part as a teaching tool. They realize that many students may not study as hard or learn as much without exams. Of course, they also use exam grades as a yardstick for comparing the amount of knowledge gained by students in their classes.

The key to success on exams involves gaining a sense of control and mastery over the testing process. You can acquire this mastery by learning the ideal test-taking attitudes and by developing strategies for conquering the various types of tests that professors use. If you combine effective studying with the suggestions from this chapter, you are likely to become confident and successful on the exams you must take.

Questions and Suggestions for Managing Test Stress

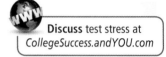
Discuss test stress at *CollegeSuccess.andYOU.com*

Many students report feeling very stressed before, during, and even after college exams. A little tension can heighten your awareness and sharpen your reflexes, allowing you to perform better—you might even be able to remember something that you otherwise couldn't recall. Although a certain amount of anxiety is normal and improves performance, sometimes you might feel so much worry that it overwhelms you and interferes with your ability to perform successfully on tests. The information in this section is organized as a series of questions and suggestions about managing test stress.

Before a Test

The following questions represent potential sources of stress; the suggestions following each question offer research-based and time-tested solutions to the testing worries you face. If you answer *no* to any of these questions, carefully consider the strategies offered in the suggestions. Determine which strategies suggested might apply to you.

Question: Are you prepared for the test?

Suggestion: Unfortunately, nothing can replace adequate preparation for the exam. Study in an organized manner by following a specific method, such as using SQ3R (see Chapter 4). Study efficiently by using techniques to remember, such as mnemonic devices (see Chapter 4). Learn effectively by listening carefully in class and by taking notes following a specific technique, such as the Cornell Note-taking System (see Chapter 5). Being up-to-date with the information you need to know for an exam will ease some of the nervousness you might feel as exam day approaches.

Additionally, begin your study well before the exam date. If you wait until the last minute to cram, you will increase your feelings of stress. **Cramming** is intensive, last-minute preparation for an exam in a short period of time. Cramming is very stressful since you will realize how much there is to learn and how little time is left to accomplish it. Cramming is also not an effective way to prepare for exams, both because you will be too stressed and because you will remember less. Consider making a vow to yourself that you will manage your time (see Chapter 3) so that you are prepared and can earn the grade you want.

Question: **Do you treat yourself well before the test?**

Suggestion: Your body is yours to keep healthy.

- First, be sure you get enough rest—go to bed early and try to get at least eight hours of sleep the night before your exam. If you feel overly tired, you won't be able to function at your best performance level.

- Second, practice healthful eating. Be sure to avoid sugary foods or caffeinated beverages. While some students believe these are helpful to their performance, consuming sugary foods and caffeinated beverages is usually counterproductive. They can speed up your body reactions and make you feel more stressed. They also can cause you to crash and feel tired after a while. Right before the test, have a healthful snack, such as a granola bar or some fruit, since hunger can make you feel tired and anxious.

- Third, keep up a schedule of exercise. Physical activity is shown to be a stress reducer. Even a brisk walk around campus before the exam will help reduce feelings of anxiety. Low-key physical activity before your exam might also help increase your alertness and sharpen your mind.

- Next, dress in a way that lifts your spirits and is comfortable. Be prepared to layer your clothing; for example, bring a jacket if you anticipate the room will be too cool.

- Finally, avoid taking medications that are not prescribed for you, especially so-called performance-enhancing drugs. Despite potential dangerous side effects, some students try these drugs, such as those developed for attention deficit disorder or as beta-blockers for heart problems. These drugs are not proven to be brain-boosters in healthy people and have many associated risks, including addiction.

In the end, if you treat your body kindly, it will amply return the favor so that you will feel energized, motivated, and able to perform your best.

Question: **Do you make specific arrangements to arrive on time for the test?**

Suggestion: Arriving late for a test creates unnecessary last minute stress. Set your alarm (or maybe two alarms) well ahead of time and get up early. Anticipate problems, such as slow traffic or unavailable parking, so that you give yourself plenty of time to get to the test. Arrive early so that you can select a seat with minimum distractions and organize your materials (consider having your pencils, paper, eraser, calculator, and other supplies ready the night before). Consciously relax your mind as you make these arrangements. Immediately before the test, avoid conversations with other students who seem like worried test-takers and who may stress you, even deliberately moving away from them for exam sessions. If you begin feeling anxious, pause and relax. Here are some ways to relax in a stressful situation:

- Take a deep breath, hold it, and then slowly release your breath along with the tension.

- Start at the top of your head, relaxing your face, jaw, shoulders, and hands, working all the way down your body to your feet.

- Stay calm for a moment, and then return to your task.

Wake-Up Call: Waking up early enough to give yourself plenty of time to get to your test helps reduce your stress level.

Question: **Do you rehearse for success before the test?**

Suggestion: Rehearsal is one of the most powerful means of reducing test stress because it can give you a sense of control over the testing situation. Make test preparation similar to a dress rehearsal for a play or a scrimmage for an athletic event by preparing and taking a practice test before the exam. If the professor gives you old exams or tells you what questions will be asked, use them for the practice test. Otherwise, anticipate the questions you might be asked and make up a test for yourself, or exchange practice questions with a friend from the class, or try to find questions on your subject on the Internet. Time yourself on the practice test to become accustomed to the time limitations you will have imposed. Additionally, to reduce stress even more for especially important exams, if possible, take the practice test in the classroom or location where the actual test will occur.

In addition to taking practice tests, visualize taking the actual test. Mentally imagine going through the test experience: See yourself confidently walking into the room, sitting at a desk, receiving the test, correctly answering the questions, and earning the grade you want. Repeat this visualization several times before the exam as a part of the rehearsal for the actual test session. Rehearsing for the test and visualizing success will help reduce your stressful feelings.

Preparing for Prime Time: Taking practice tests gets you ready for an exam just as a scrimmage gets football players ready for a big game.

Question: **Do you keep a positive attitude before the test?**

Suggestion: Keep a positive attitude as you prepare for the test and expect success. Consider setting a SMART goal (see the Introduction) to help you stay positive. If outside problems are interfering, tell yourself that no matter how pressing these issues may be, they can wait two hours while you take your test. Maintaining a positive attitude can help you succeed. Tell yourself:

- "I am ready for this test."
- "I have studied hard."
- "I will succeed."
- "I will do my best."
- "I am confident."
- "I know I can do this."

During a Test

The questions that follow are for you to consider as you analyze your thoughts and feelings for what you will do as you take a test. A *yes* answer suggests that you might benefit from applying the strategies offered in the suggestions that follow.

Question: **Are you feeling stress because you think you might go blank during the exam?**

Suggestion: Even though you have thoroughly studied and prepared, and you know the material, you may find that you freeze up on a question. If that happens, leave the question, go on to other questions or parts of the test, and plan to return later. As you work on other parts of the test, you will likely find yourself remembering the information necessary to answer the part where you felt blocked, and you can return to that question or section then. If you simply can't come up with the information you need, continue on to the other parts of the test, realizing that you can still perform well on the rest of the exam.

Another strategy to use if you fear that you might forget everything you know during the test is to perform what is called a *memory dump*.[1] A **memory dump** means that the first thing you do when you get the test is write down in the margins of the page every detail you want to remember for the test. You include all the definitions, rules, formulas, dates, mnemonic devices (see Chapter 4), or facts so that you don't have to worry about them as the test progresses. This list of information will provide memory cues to you as you answer test questions and will help you avoid going blank during the test. Use it when you know you will still have enough time to finish the test.

Question: **Are you worried about not getting a good enough grade?**

Suggestion: Just about every student will worry about getting back the grade from a test. Since you can't know the grade you will get, it's best not to try to predict. You have probably experienced trying to predict and finding that although you think you did very well on a test, when the grades are returned, you don't get the great grade you had expected. Or maybe it's the other way around. You think you have done poorly on a test, yet when the test paper comes back, you find that your grade is much higher than you expected. So why waste your time worrying about the grade you can't predict? The suggested approach is to do the very best you can during the test and let that effort represent your intention to earn the grade you want.

Question: **Do you feel stress when everyone else seems to finish, but you haven't?**

Suggestion: Everyone works at a different pace. Don't worry about your friend's style of work or about those of others in the class. Plan to use the entire exam period rather than trying to rush. Rushing through the test creates unnecessary anxiety that can cause you to unintentionally skip questions. But you also need to work at a steady pace through the test so that you have time to finish. Remember to bring a watch, clock, or timer other than your cell phone so that you can pace yourself as the test proceeds. Keep your eye on the clock while taking the test. Allow yourself enough time to finish the entire test. Avoid getting stuck on a question—just skip it, note it, and return if and when you can. While you want to complete the test, it's really not only about finishing— but about finishing as successfully as you can.

Question: **Do you let yourself get upset over a question that you think is extremely difficult or unfair?**

Suggestion: If you can't figure out an answer, remember that it's okay to get one question wrong. For most tests, you don't have to get every question correct to do well. Find the questions that you think are the easy ones, the questions with answers you know, and answer these first. Responding to the easy questions first will build your confidence and give you the momentum to get through the rest of the test. Use everything you know to your advantage, including good test-taking techniques.

Question: **Does stress overwhelm you so that you feel like you can't answer a single question?**

Suggestion: A certain amount of adrenaline (or that "psyched" feeling) is helpful, but if nervousness is overwhelming to you, then you need to distract yourself in some way to focus your attention away from these feelings of anxiety. For example, you might allow yourself a moment to daydream. Even though you may have been scolded for daydreaming in class when you were younger, now would be the time to forget that and allow yourself a moment to let your mind wander past the feeling of being overwhelmed by the material. Imagine yourself in a place of comfort and allow your body to relax. Feel the physical tension leaving and when you do, return to the task at hand. Find that one question you think you can answer correctly and answer that one question. Once you have succeeded with one question, you can continue on with the confidence that at least you answered one item correctly. As you continue with the test, if the overwhelming anxiety returns, pause and again relax your body, and tell yourself that you can and will succeed with the test. Focus on something in the room to help clear your mind, such as the texture of your desk or the colors of the floor and walls, and then return again to the test. Keep in mind that no one test will obliterate your success as a student. If feelings of overwhelming stress consistently interfere with your test-taking, consider seeking help from a counselor on campus.

After the Test

These questions are for you to consider regarding your feelings and actions after the test. When you answer *no* to questions, consider the ideas offered in the suggestions for strategies to help you overcome future test stress.

Question: **Do you reward yourself after the test?**

Suggestion: If you feel that you made a good effort on your exam, give yourself a reward. You met the challenge of the test, so you owe yourself something. Give yourself a treat, such as going to a movie or playing a fun video game. It doesn't need to be something lavish but something that you feel adequately reinforces your effort to do the best you could on the test.

Question: **Do you relax after the test?**

Suggestion: Kick back and relax by letting go of thoughts about the test after it is over. Avoid dwelling on mistakes you think you might have made. The test is finished, and there is nothing you can do about it now, so allow yourself to relax. Do something you enjoy. If you really did the very best you could do, there will be nothing to worry about. Avoid allowing yourself to stew and worry about the outcome of the test after it is over.

Take It Easy: Having some fun after a test rewards your good efforts and eases pressure you may have experienced.

Question: **Do you keep a good sense of humor after the test?**

Suggestion: Laughter is known to be a good stress reducer since the deep breathing that accompanies laughter reduces tension. You won't get angry or depressed if you are using your sense of humor to lighten your mood. After the test, engage in an activity that makes you laugh, such as watching your favorite comedy show or reading a book of funny cartoons. These activities will not only take your mind off the test but also will encourage you to have a good laugh, which will naturally reduce your anxiety and boost your spirits.

Question: **Do you stay calm even if you think you blew the test?**

Suggestion: You can't know for sure how you did on the test until your professor returns it to you. Sometimes you can end up getting a much better grade than you think you will; however, other times you might think you performed very poorly for good reasons. If you do get a low grade, it is time to ask yourself some questions. Did you prepare adequately? Did you carefully read and understand the test directions? Did you use the information you knew to the best advantage? Did you control your stress? Did you effectively manage your time? Think honestly about your answers to these questions and take action before the next test to help avoid a repeat of your poor test performance. Rather than dwell on your test or get frustrated and give up on success, take the lessons you have learned to heart so that you can succeed next time. Talking with your professor about recommendations for future tests or discussing with more successful students from the class about their test preparations might help you get ready for the next test. Also, this chapter is designed to help you succeed with tests, so use all the suggestions to your own advantage.

Question: **Are you present in class when the test is returned and reviewed?**

Suggestion: Students sometimes choose the day a test is returned to be absent; they wrongfully assume that nothing important will be happening on that day, and they believe they can find out their grade another time. Actually, test return day is one of the most important days of the semester for you. You can learn a lot from your current test results to help you on your next test. Everyone learns from mistakes, so you need to examine your test results with an eye on what you can do better next time. Why do you think you missed a question—misreading it, not preparing for it, or running out of time? Where did the questions originate—from the textbook, from class lectures, from outside readings? Be sure to understand what the professor wanted as an answer and observe the kinds of questions the professor likes to use. Save the test (if you can) for future study. Learning from your own test results is one of the best ways to make your next test a more positive and a less stress producing experience.

Overcoming test stress is difficult, and stress can never really be eliminated completely. Your goal is to keep it at a healthy level. Remember, you can only do your best. Use your stress energy to focus on the test and put the energy to work for you.

Learning from Tests: Being in class when tests are returned gives you insight into effective preparation for the next test.

EXERCISE 1 A Helping Hand

Step 1: Your friends have noticed that you remain calm and composed for exams, and they are impressed. Three friends have come to you for advice about their test stress. For each of these three scenarios, write your two best tips to help your friends.

1. Kenneth complains that he gets exceptionally nervous in the hours before exams begin. He tells you that his next exam is for a 10:00 A.M. class. He asks what he should do after he wakes up to help himself stay calm. What do you recommend to help Kenneth?

   Tip 1 _____

   _____

   _____

   Tip 2 _____

   _____

   _____

2. Jan is a very serious student who tells you that she is okay as she prepares for an exam. Her problem, she says, is during an exam when she feels panicky and freezes up. What do you recommend for Jan?

   Tip 1 _____

   _____

   _____

   Tip 2 _____

   _____

   _____

3. Nadia has trouble with overwhelming stress after her exam is over. She tells you she worries so much about the test afterward that she can't focus on anything else. What do you suggest to help her recover?

   Tip 1 _____

   _____

   _____

   Tip 2 _____

   _____

   _____

Step 2: Be prepared to discuss your tips in class. From the class discussion, decide which tips are best for Kenneth, Jan, and Nadia.

TEST-SMART TIPS 8 for taking
different types of tests

Study and preparation are absolutely necessary for test success. Nothing replaces effectively preparing for tests through study methods such as SQ3R and memory techniques. However, many students are surprised to learn that there is more to doing well on exams than learning the material. Test-taking skills can provide you with the edge you need to significantly increase your test performance. Knowing some of the techniques for answering questions can help you improve your test performance as well as assist you in developing a more positive attitude toward taking tests. Following are eight different types of tests you may be required to take, along with tips to help you become a test-smart student. Practice questions are provided to illustrate each type of test-taking skill along with correct answers and explanations to illustrate *why* an answer is correct.

PEANUTS © 1978 Peanuts Worldwide LLC. Dist. By UNIVERSAL UCLICK. Reprinted with permission. All rights reserved.

Test-Smart Tips for True-False Questions

1. Pay close attention to *key qualifying words*. **Key qualifying words** are terms that are all inclusive (include everyone or everything) or all exclusive (exclude everyone or everything) or provide a safe, middle position. Here are some examples of key qualifying words you may come across in true-false questions:

   ■ *all, most, some, few, none, no*
   ■ *always, usually, often, sometimes, rarely, never*
   ■ *great, much, little*
   ■ *more, equal, less*

   Terms that are extremes (such as *all, none, always, never*) tend to be false, while terms that express a midpoint (such as *some, few, sometimes*) tend to be true. One of these words will often determine whether a statement is marked true or false.

2. If *any* part of a statement is false, it makes the whole statement false. In other words, *every* part of a true statement must be true.

3. Be careful with negative and double negative statements. Questions that use negative words can be confusing. Consider circling negative words (*no, none, never, not, cannot*) and words with negative word parts (*in-, dis-, un-, il-, ir-*) so that you can spot when double negatives occur. For example, "It is (not) (unreasonable)" means "It is reasonable."

4. If you can't determine an answer, make your best guess; you have a 50% chance of being right. For those items, it is usually better to guess True than False, since it is more difficult for professors to write false statements than true statements. As a result, many tests will have more true items than false.

Demonstration True-False Questions (Try these questions.)

Directions: Answer T for True or F for False.

_____ 1. Constellations are never of any use to astronomers.

_____ 2. It is not unreasonable to believe that on most days the weather will be warmer in Miami than in Boston.

_____ 3. Annual plants live only one month while perennial plants live several years.

_____ 4. A ballet was adapted from Cervantes's famous book *Don Quixote*.

_____ 5. People sometimes try to cope with time stress by carefully planning their shopping trips.

Answers with Explanations for the True-False Questions

Question 1: The answer is False because of the key qualifying word *never*. Constellations are sometimes going to be useful to astronomers.

Question 2: The answer is True. Two negatives appear together (the word *not* and the word part *un-*) and cancel each other so that "not unreasonable" means "reasonable." It *is* reasonable to believe that on most days the weather will be warmer in Miami than in Boston.

Question 3: The answer is False. Although the second part of the statement ("perennial plants live several years") is true, the first part of the statement ("annual plants live only one month") is false. Since part of the statement is false, the entire statement is false.

Question 4: The answer is True. If this is information about which you have no idea, then the best practice is to answer true.

Question 5: The answer is True because of the key qualifying word *sometimes*. People do *sometimes* cope with time stress in this way.

Test-Smart Tips for Multiple-Choice Questions

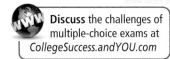

Discuss the challenges of multiple-choice exams at *CollegeSuccess.andYOU.com*

1. Read all the answer choices before you decide on one. Avoid the temptation to select the first choice that sounds good. On most multiple-choice tests, your job is to choose the best answer, and the last choice may be better than the one you were first considering.

2. Use a process of elimination to get rid of incorrect choices and narrow your guess range. If you can eliminate two choices as wrong, your chances of guessing accurately increase.

3. Look for two answer choices that are opposite from each other. One of these two is likely to be the correct answer.

4. Convert each item choice into a true-false option. Read the beginning of the multiple-choice statement (the stem) with each alternative to form a true-false sentence. Decide which alternative is true, and that will identify the correct answer.

5. Be careful with the choices "all of the above" and "none of the above." Don't select one of these unless more than one choice is correct or all choices are incorrect. If you know two or three options seem to be correct, then "all of the above" is a possibility. If you know two or three options seem to be incorrect, then "none of the above" is a possibility.

6. If you don't know the answer and can't eliminate any of the choices as incorrect, make a guess by selecting the longest, most complete choice. Professors tend to write the correct answer as carefully and completely as possible, and in doing so, the choice becomes longer and more detailed.

7. As a last resort, if you have absolutely no idea of the correct answer and the choices seem equally long and detailed, choose B or C. In the *Journal of Educational Measurement*, researchers report that test-makers have a tendency to place correct answers in middle positions.[2]

Demonstration Multiple-Choice Questions (Try these questions.)

Directions: Write the best answer on the line.

_____ 1. A rain forest is characterized by

    A. low amounts of precipitation.
    B. limited vegetation.
    C. no animal life.
    D. none of the above

_____ 2. In the *Canterbury Tales*, Chaucer

    A. focused on death.
    B. wrote about France.
    C. set up an interesting framework of stories about pilgrims gathered at an inn.
    D. wrote for children.

_____ 3. Which city is a state capital?

    A. Albany, New York
    B. Sacramento, California
    C. Atlanta, Georgia
    D. all of the above

_____ 4. The national government

    A. needs large amounts of money to enforce rules and to provide services and benefits.
    B. depends on states to provide all monies for budgets.
    C. needs no money to enforce rules and to provide services and benefits.
    D. taxes only members of Congress to secure money.

_____ 5. In Italian, one meaning of the word *genero* is

    A. fitting room.
    B. son-in-law.
    C. soccer stadium.
    D. daughter.

Question 1: The answer is D. A rain forest certainly has a lot of precipitation, an abundance of vegetation, and varied animal life. If you convert each choice item into a true-false statement, you will discover that each item is *false*. For example,

"A rain forest is characterized by low amounts of precipitation" is *false*.
"A rain forest is characterized by limited vegetation" is *false*.
"A rain forest is characterized by no animal life" is *false*.
Then you can choose answer D ("none of the above") as correct.

Question 2: The answer is C. If you don't know the answer, and none of the choices can be eliminated, make a guess by choosing the longest, most complete and detailed answer.

Question 3: The answer is D. Each city is the state capital. If you can identify at least two of these cities as capitals, then you can guess that D ("all of the above") is correct.

Question 4: The answer is A. When you find two items that are opposite each other (A is opposite to C), then one of them is likely correct. The one that makes the most sense for the national government is A.

Question 5: The answer is B. If you don't know the answer and all the choices are much the same in detail and length, choose B or C because test-makers often place correct answers in middle positions.

Test-Smart Tips for Short Answer/Identification/ Fill-in-the-Blank Questions

A professor's purpose for short answer, identification, and fill-in-the-blank questions is to confirm whether you have learned important facts relevant to the course. Short answer, identification, and fill-in-the-blank questions require you to write brief answers to specific course-related topics.

For Short Answer/Identification Questions

1. Plan your answer by jotting down brief notes to yourself before you begin to write. Organize your response so you can get in all the main ideas and major details (see Chapter 4) in a concise form.

2. Use point value as a clue to how detailed your answer must be. A question valued at ten points will require a much more detailed answer than a question that has a three-point value. Also, you can use the amount of space provided for an answer, especially if the space is different for different items, as a signal to judge how much information to write.

3. Read the question very carefully to be sure that you answer it fully. Short answer or identification questions may consist of multiple parts, and you want to be thorough in your response.

4. When you don't know an answer, skip it and keep going. After you finish the test, come back to this item. Other parts of the test may provide clues to help you formulate an answer.

5. If you don't know an answer, and no clues to a possible answer are provided on the test itself, make an educated guess. Making a common sense guess (not a random, off-the-wall guess or joke) might get you partial points, which is better than leaving an answer blank, resulting in zero points.

For Fill-in-the-Blank Questions

1. Fill-in-the-blank questions require you to supply an exact word or phrase to complete a sentence. The "Can You Recall It?" questions at the end of each chapter in this textbook are examples of this type of question. To answer these items, first read the entire sentence to yourself saying "blank" for the blank space. Then, using the context of the entire sentence to help you, reread the sentence and place the best word or phrase in the blank space. Whether or not choices for your response are provided, you will benefit from using the content of the whole sentence to decide on words or phrases for answers.

Demonstration Questions and Example Answers for Short Answer/Identification Questions (You aren't expected to answer these questions.)

Directions: Answer the following American history questions.

1. Briefly identify Dr. Martin Luther King, Jr. (2 points)
2. Describe the major contributions of Dr. Martin Luther King, Jr. (6 points)

Sample Answer for Question 1: Dr. King was an African-American minister and civil rights leader who led nonviolent protests against segregation and gave the famous "I Have a Dream" speech. He was assassinated in 1968.

Sample Answer for Question 2: Dr. King arranged a protest of segregation on buses in Montgomery, Alabama, in 1955. The protest involved a boycott of buses. Dr. King led the use of civil disobedience against racial discrimination, and people went to jail as part of the protest. In 1963, Dr. King helped lead a march of more than 200,000 people to support civil rights laws, and this is when he gave his famous "I Have a Dream" speech. The Civil Rights Act passed in 1964, and he deserves much of the credit.

Explanations for the Short Answer/Identification Questions

Question 1: This question is worth two points, so the answer is shorter, yet it includes the major details necessary to answer the question.

Question 2: This question is worth six points, so the answer is longer and more comprehensive with greater detail.

Test-Smart Tips for Matching Questions

1. Read the directions very carefully for matching questions. Sometimes professors provide more items in Column 2 than there are matches to be made from Column 1. Providing uneven numbers increases the difficulty of your task. Note how many extra nonmatching items you have so that as you progress, you eliminate those items that you are sure have no match.

2. Think about what you are being asked to match to get an overview of the subjects and topics that the questions cover. In reading over the items, decide if you are being asked to match terms and definitions, people and achievements, or dates and events to discover if there is a pattern.

3. An effective strategy is to complete the easiest matches first, crossing them off as they are used. This system reduces the chance of matching incorrectly for more difficult items.

4. Avoid choosing the first answer you find that seems correct since items later in the list may be better matches. Read over all the items to be matched first so that you know all the possibilities. Professors want the best match, not a somewhat correct match.

Demonstration Matching Questions (Try these questions.)

Directions: Match the astronomy term in Column 1 to its meaning in Column 2. There are more items in Column 2 than you will use. No item will be used more than once.

Column 1	Column 2
_____ **1.** atom	**A.** an event during which the Moon passes through the shadow of Earth, temporarily darkening its surface
_____ **2.** comet	**B.** a building block of matter
_____ **3.** cosmology	**C.** a blazing light
_____ **4.** flare	**D.** a small body, composed mainly of ice and dust, in an orbit around the Sun
_____ **5.** lunar eclipse	**E.** a wave that travels outward from the site of an earthquake
	F. an explosive event occurring in or near an active region on the Sun
	G. the study of the structure of the entire universe
	H. a phase of the Moon in which it appears as a complete circular disk in the sky

Answers with Explanations for the Matching Questions

Column 1 has five astronomy terms, and Column 2 has eight potential meanings, so you know that you will not be using three of the meanings from Column 2. Begin to answer with any of the items you know for sure and mark off the meanings from Column 2 as you use them. As you work your way through the five terms, the list of matching meanings will be reduced and you can make better educated guesses, if needed.

Question 1: The answer is B.

Question 2: The answer is D.

Question 3: The answer is G.

Question 4: The answer is F. For Question 4 ("flare"), a possible match is C ("a blazing light"), but as you read down the list of meanings, you will find a better answer for an astronomy test is F ("an explosive event occurring in or near an active region on the Sun").

Question 5: The answer is A.

For this matching set, you did not use three meanings from Column 2: C, E, H.

Test-Smart Tips for Open Book and Open Note Questions

Preparation is a key to success for an open book and open note test. You may think that since you can use your book and your notes, preparation is unnecessary. Actually, the open book and open note test will most likely be harder as well as require more study time and preparation than a closed book test. Because it is assumed you will have all information available, the test will be designed to gauge your understanding of the material.

1. Organize your material so that you can easily find what you need during the exam. For your textbooks, mark important pages with some system, such as color coding, paper clips, or sticky notes. For your class notes, organize by topic or by chronological sequence and number the pages. You can design an index for yourself of the textbook topics with page numbers and your class notes with topics and page numbers. Make your textbook and class notes as user friendly as possible to save you time during the test.

2. Bring to the exam all the resources your professor allows. For example, you may be able to create formula sheets or summary sheets with dates and names to use during the exam.

3. Focus on learning the main ideas and major details and know where in your textbook and class notes they are located.

4. Use short quotations from your textbook to support or illustrate a point if you are encouraged to do so, but avoid overquoting. Use a quotation to draw on the authority of the author or because you can't say it better and the quote exactly supports your discussion.

5. Plan your time. Quickly review all the questions and note how much time each question should take. First, answer the easy questions that you know without needing to check your references. Next, answer the more complex and difficult questions—the ones for which you must check your textbook and your class notes.

User Friendly: Being fully prepared and organized for your open book and open note test increases the likelihood of success.

Demonstration Open Book and Open Note Question (You aren't expected to answer this question.)

Directions: In statistics class, we have studied chi-square, the statistic that compares observed frequencies to expected frequencies. Apply chi-square to the following problem: In a marketing study, researchers surveyed 500 randomly selected college students about their preference for Coke or Pepsi. The researchers found that 300 preferred Coke. Determine if that number is statistically significant when the researchers expected no significant difference. Consult the table from your textbook with the critical values of chi-square to answer this question.

Explanation for the Open Book and Open Note Question

Statistics is an example of a class likely to feature open book tests. On the question above, you would have to consult tables of data in your textbook to solve the problem. To accomplish this task efficiently, you would need to have labeled the pages of the textbook with relevant formulas and tables before the test. Then you would be able to combine your knowledge of how to solve the problem with the data in the tables to calculate the correct answer. Organizing your textbook and notes ahead of time will save you time as you try to locate appropriate pages to use.

Test-Smart Tips for Oral Questions

Although oral tests are not as common as written ones, some types of classes such as foreign language and speech are more likely to use oral exams. An oral test can be formal or informal. The formal test will follow a set list of questions in a specific order. An informal test is more open and conversational although the professor will still expect correct responses to questions. For either type of oral test, you need to listen carefully to the question, and then answer specifically. You can find suggestions on how to relax during your oral exams in Chapter 5.

1. Be sure you know the time, date, and place of the test (if the test is not in your classroom). Verify the information with your professor. You may have had to sign up to be tested at a specific time. Find out about topics covered and if you are expected to use classroom boards or media.

2. Write practice questions for yourself and rehearse answers in front of a mirror, record your answers on audio or video, or practice with a classmate. Evaluate your body language, your voice, your composure, your eye contact, and your posture. See Chapter 5 for tips on classroom presentations, which are applicable here.

3. Speak directly to the question in complete sentences. Try not to give one word or two word answers, but avoid rambling. If you don't know an answer, state directly that you are unsure but briefly explain how you would find the answer or solve the problem. The professor may appreciate that you at least know how to go about locating an answer or what you might do to solve the problem, even if you don't know the exact answer.

4. Look and act professional: Turn off your electronic devices, dress appropriately, arrive early, and be polite.

5. Be sure to thank the professor when you are finished.

Q and A: Knowing your topic, rehearsing, and listening carefully to the questions before you answer are key steps for taking an oral exam.

**Demonstration Oral Exam Question
(You aren't expected to answer this question.)**

Directions: During this semester, we studied the architecture of sacred places. I will give you three places we have studied, and I want you to choose two and discuss both the sculptural and architectural features. The three sacred buildings are the Parthenon in Greece, the temple of Angkor Wat in Cambodia, and the Cathedral Notre-Dame in France.

Explanation for the Oral Exam Question

Be aware that the professor will probably vary the sacred places and rotate the choices from student to student. When answering, be sure you notice that you must choose two of the three locations to discuss. Also, notice that you are explaining both the sculptural and architectural features. Be as clear and specific as you can regarding the sculptural and architectural features of the two buildings you select. If you are allowed to use the classroom chalk board or white board, consider drawing representations of special architectural features; for example, you might draw columns and special sculptural features such as representations of Greek myths or gargoyles.

Test-Smart Tips for Take-Home Questions

A take-home test is more often used for classes in which there is an emphasis on problem solving, such as political science, management, or statistics. These tests are used to evaluate your understanding of concepts and your ability to interpret and apply information.

1. Know and follow all the rules. Are there word processing or typing requirements? What is the deadline for turning in the test? Can you consult any reference sources? Are you allowed to talk to classmates or others? A word of caution: Do not collaborate with classmates or anyone else for answers when you have been directed not to consult with anyone about the test. Recently, over one hundred Harvard students were threatened with suspensions or revocation of degrees for collaborating on take-home exams in an Introduction to Congress course.[3]

2. Decide if the problems posed by the test require solution by one method or another. In other words, you must decide what to read or look up. This decision becomes critical because it must be informed through a basic understanding of the concepts of the course.

3. Waiting until you have the test in your hand is not the time to study. It will be too late, so study and organize your materials ahead of time.

4. A take-home test often features essay questions. The hints in the next section for successfully writing essay answers apply to take-home essay questions.

5. After you finish the test, put it away for a while—even for just an hour or so. Then go back to review it. Read through your answers and decide if they are correct and complete. Did you consider all the alternatives? Have you made the correct choices? Recheck all your calculations and proofread all your answers before you submit your take-home test.

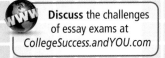
Discuss the challenges of essay exams at *CollegeSuccess.andYOU.com*

Test-Smart Tips for Essay Questions

The two factors that influence grades on essay tests are what you say and how you say it. You need both accurate information and an organized, logical, well-written essay. Careful reading of the essay question and writing a precise, organized answer are keys to success for the essay test.

1. Read the directions and questions carefully. The directions may tell you to answer all the questions or only three of the five questions. If you have a choice of questions to answer, choose all your questions at the beginning, basing your decision on how much you know about the topic and how much relevant information you will have to write. If any of the questions are confusing, consider asking your professor for clarification.

2. Plan your time. It's easy to get carried away with a topic you know well and end up spending the entire time on one essay answer. Decide how much time to spend on each question and stick to your plan. Save a few minutes at the end for proofreading. If you run out of time, jot down at least the key ideas you would have discussed. If your paper is blank, then the professor has no choice but to give you zero points, but if you have a few ideas written, you might earn partial credit.

3. Answer the easiest essay questions first. Doing this will help build your confidence, provide you with a foundation of points upon which to build, and leave you with extra time for the more difficult questions.

> Trace the major events leading to the signing of the Declaration of Independence.

Writing It Right: Carefully reading the questions gets you off to a good start for preparing your answers on an essay test.

4. Be sure to organize your answer. You can use the standard five paragraph structure:

- Paragraph One—Provide a brief overview of your essay.
- Paragraphs Two, Three, and Four—Focus on one main idea per paragraph that is central to your topic.
- Paragraph Five—Conclude with a brief summary of your main points.

Make the first and last paragraphs brief since you want to spend most of your time on the substance of your answer. Before you begin, make a quick outline to help you stay on track with the information for each paragraph. Avoid "padding" an answer with irrelevant, unnecessary information.

5. Try to be as neat as you can. Write legibly on one side of the paper. Not only will this be neater, but also it will allow you to go back to revise more easily. Your professor must grade many papers, so neatness counts toward your getting as many points as possible.

6. Remember to proofread your answers. Allow yourself a few minutes to read the questions again and then read your answer. Be sure you answered all parts of the question. Review, edit, and correct your writing. Look for misspellings, incomplete sentences, and mistakes in dates or facts.

7. When you don't know an answer, avoid leaving a page blank. Attempt an answer and maybe you can write something that is partly correct. Providing an attempted answer gives your professor the opportunity to give you some points for trying.

8. Notice the *key action words* used in essay questions. **Key action words** are the words that tell you how to organize and present your answers. Professors choose these words carefully and expect you to answer what you are asked. The following table lists commonly used key action words along with what they require. Sometimes essay questions have several parts, so look for these action words to indicate different parts for one question.

Key Action Words for Essay Questions

Analyze	Break down the topic into component parts and examine each part.
Clarify	Explain in abundant detail, using both major and minor details.
Compare	Show how items are similar or like one another. Emphasize likenesses, but differences may be mentioned.
Contrast	Show how items are different from one another.
Critique/Criticize	Judge what is good or right—or what is bad or wrong—about the topic.
Define	Provide an accurate meaning of the term with enough details and examples to demonstrate your understanding.
Describe	Create a detailed mental picture for the reader. Specifically tell how something looks or happens.
Discuss	Explain, review, analyze, and consider carefully the topic.
Enumerate/List	List and discuss the points in concise form one by one.
Evaluate	Provide the strengths and weaknesses, the pros and cons, or the advantages and limitations of a topic.
Explain	Give facts and details that both clarify and make understandable the idea or concept. This open-ended action word gives some flexibility in how to treat the question.
Illustrate	Use examples or instances that demonstrate or simplify the topic.
Interpret	Offer the meaning of something.
Justify	Provide reasons that support an action, event, policy, or belief.
Prove	Convince the reader by using evidence and argument to establish a concept or theory.
Relate	Use examples and analogies to show relationships— how things fit together.
Review	Cover the major points in an organized sequence, including your evaluation.
State/Specify	Assert and explain the main points in a brief, clear form.
Summarize	Cover the main ideas and major details including approximately 25% of the original information.
Trace	Provide the evaluation or progress of a trend, event, or process in chronological sequence.

Demonstration Essay Question
(You aren't expected to answer this question.)

Directions: Answer the following marketing question. Be sure to cite specific examples from the readings and the lectures to substantiate your answer.

Essay Question: Our marketing textbook refers to the concept of *social class.*[4] Define the concept of social class. Discuss the major social class groups in the United States and in this college community. Select two product classes (such as food, beverages, clothing, automobiles, furniture) and relate how each social class you identified for the United States might respond to marketing strategies for these products.

Explanation for Essay Question

1. This is a multipart essay question. Read the directions carefully and break down the question into its parts so that you address each issue in your answer. Look for and circle the key action words that direct you to answer in a certain way.

Parts to the Question	How to Answer
A. (Define) *social class.*	**A.** Provide an accurate meaning of social class with enough details and examples to show you understand.
B. (Discuss) the major social classes in the United States and your college community.	**B.** Explain, review, and analyze the major social classes of the United States and your college community.
C. Select two product classes and (relate) how each social class you identified for the United States might respond to marketing strategies for these products.	**C.** Choose your two product classes and for each, use examples and analogies to show relationships— how social classes you identified for the United States might respond to marketing strategies.

2. Plan your time so that you can address each part of the question. Use the standard five paragraph structure:

   Paragraph One: Preview what you intend to do in the essay: (1) provide the definition of *social class*, (2) discuss the major social classes of the United States and your college, and (3) relate how the social classes of the United States might respond to marketing strategies for two selected products.

   Paragraph Two: Define social class.

   Paragraph Three: Discuss the major social classes of the United States and your college.

   Paragraph Four: Relate how the social classes of the United States might respond to marketing strategies for the two selected products.

   Paragraph Five: Summarize your main points: Give a brief definition of *social class*; review the major social classes of the United States and your college; and relate how the social classes of the United States might respond to marketing strategies for the two selected products.

3. Try to write neatly, proofread your answers, and make corrections.

4. Congratulate yourself for producing an excellent essay answer.

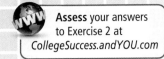 **Assess** your answers to Exercise 2 at *CollegeSuccess.andYOU.com*

EXERCISE 2 **Key In to Key Words**

Step 1: Read each situation. On the blank line, write the key word you would find if the professor wants you to write a response to an essay question. Choose from the following list of key words.

analyze	evaluate
contrast	illustrate
define	justify
describe	prove
enumerate/list	trace

_____ 1. Your science professor has explained in class how to proceed in collecting data for an experiment. The professor wants you to give the steps briefly, one after the other.

_____ 2. In art class, the professor wants you to examine two paintings and talk about the differences in style between them.

_____ 3. Your psychology professor spent many sessions telling the class about "personality." The professor wants to know if you understand the concept of personality.

_____ 4. The professor in your logic class wants you to establish that "all people are human."

_____ 5. Your Naval history professor wants you to talk about when and where the Navy had its beginning and then follow with its development and progress.

_____ 6. In government class, the professor wants you to give reasons why democracy is a better form of government than socialism.

_____ 7. In American literature class, you studied the book *Tom Sawyer*. The professor wants you to provide concrete examples of characters working together cooperatively.

_____ 8. Your class in the teaching of foreign languages has learned about the immersion system. The professor wants you to talk about both the advantages and disadvantages of teaching a language through the immersion system.

_____ 9. Your architecture professor took the class to visit a construction site for a new building. The professor wants to know if you remember the framing for the building foundation.

_____ 10. The professor of your economics class wants you to break down and examine the parts of the economic theory of free trade.

Step 2: Discuss your answers in class. Be prepared to justify your key word choice.

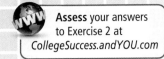 **Use** the resource links to find additional information at *CollegeSuccess.andYOU.com*

Celebrating Your Success on Exams

You are now ready to manage your test anxieties and triumph over the various types of tests your professor might use. Remember that the key to success on exams is gaining a sense of control over the testing process. You can gain this control by applying the ideal test-taking attitudes and by using the strategies for succeeding with different types of tests presented in this chapter.

Thinking Critically About . . .
Succeeding on Exams

Critical thinking involves an active evaluation of information using careful, thoughtful, and reasoned judgments.

1. This chapter opens with a section titled "Is This Going to Be on the Test?" As exams approach, students often ask professors that question. Provide a convincing argument that such a question is irrelevant.

2. Compare and contrast a student's preparation for success on an exam with a contestant's preparation for success on *American Idol*.

3. Explain why constructing a practice test is a good learning activity.

4. Discuss the limitations of tests. How are tests insufficient to evaluate a student's development and knowledge?

5. Recommend actions that your college can take to minimize cheating on tests. What are the implications of cheating on tests in college for a student's subsequent actions in the "real" world?

Discuss your ideas about the Critical Thinking items at *CollegeSuccess.andYOU.com*

Online Learning

Preparation for an online test is identical to preparation for a classroom test. For example, you need to apply principles of time management (see Chapter 3) and use effective study techniques (see Chapter 4) for both. Sometimes an online student is sent to a room or office to take a proctored test.

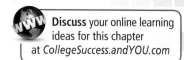

Discuss your online learning ideas for this chapter at *CollegeSuccess.andYOU.com*

Taking online tests differs, however, from taking classroom tests in a number of ways. Blackboard and other course management systems are often used to administer online tests and quizzes. If you are taking an exam online, you usually are prompted to follow a number of steps, such as closing all other windows and disabling pop-up blockers on your computer.

Occasionally online tests come with time limitations. If this is the situation, it is a good idea to be sure you set aside enough time for the test. Avoid waiting to take the test until the last possible moment before the test window closes. Also, you will want to let anyone you live with know that you are taking a test, and that you need some undisturbed time to finish it. Depending on how your professor has designed the exam, you will either be presented with one question at a time or you will receive the entire test all at once. Since you may not be allowed to revisit questions, it is a good idea to check your answers, make changes as necessary, and then submit your test responses after you have carefully reviewed each item. In case you get locked out of your online test, contact your professor, who can "clear your attempt" so you can begin the test again. Also, some systems require only a *single* mouse click, so a double-click will create a complication. Since you are on an honor system, it is important to maintain the integrity of your learning community by always taking your online tests in an ethical manner.

CHAPTER CHALLENGE

THE BIG TEST

Many students expect college exams to be much tougher than high school exams. Sometimes just the idea of a first pending midterm or final exam takes on an almost overwhelming stature. To prepare for such a challenge, motivated students typically combine their previous study techniques with tactics that they have heard are effective in college. Students quickly discover that they must find out what works best for them.

A CASE STUDY: FACING THE CHALLENGE OF . . .
THE BIG TEST

Tony, a first-semester student at his local college, was very pleased with his schedule. He was taking English composition, college algebra, photography, and American history. He was happy that American history was his only class with a large amount of reading since he found such classes especially difficult. The professor in Tony's American history class administered a brief, weekly multiple-choice quiz. In terms of the final grade, the quizzes would count for 20%; a midterm exam, 40%; and a final exam, 40%. As the midterm approached, Tony decided that he would do everything possible to get a high grade. He kept up-to-date with the reading, performed well on the weekly quizzes, and spent days reviewing the material before the big test. To complete his preparation, he pulled an all-nighter, reading over the text, reviewing his notes, and asking himself questions to make sure that he understood the material. The exam was scheduled for 9:00 A.M., so Tony arrived at school an hour early. Since he felt a bit groggy from sleep deprivation, he had three cups of coffee to make himself alert for the test. When Tony arrived at the classroom, he felt like he was in a fog. He could not think straight, and he felt very fidgety. Also, the test had essay questions for which he was completely unprepared. As a result, he performed much more poorly than he expected. He felt both disappointed and frustrated because he really thought that he was preparing in just the perfect way for the test.

OVERCOMING THE CHALLENGE OF . . .
THE BIG TEST

Be prepared to discuss your answers to the following items: (1) Evaluate what Tony did right in his test preparation and what he did wrong. (2) If Tony doesn't understand what caused his problems, recommend what he can do to find out. (3) Suggest test-smart actions that Tony can take to improve his performance on his next American history exam.

Key Chapter Strategies

- Take steps to control your stress before, during, and after an exam.
- Pay attention to key qualifying words, especially on true-false and multiple-choice questions.
- Read directions and test questions thoroughly before answering.
- Generally, answer easier questions first.
- Budget your time while taking an exam.
- Try not to leave anything blank.
- Write well-organized, accurate, logical, and grammatically correct answers on essay tests, paying close attention to the key action words in the questions.
- Proofread any test paper before submitting it.
- Maintain ethical behavior while taking any type of test.
- Read this book for more about testing: *No More Test Anxiety: Effective Steps for Taking Tests and Achieving Better Grades* by Ed Newman.[5]

  ## Can You Recall It?

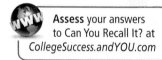

Directions: To review your understanding of the chapter, choose the correct term from the list below and fill it in on the blank. You will not use every term.

trace	proofreading
cramming	memory dump
multiple-choice	open book
short answer/identification	key qualifying words
matching	analyzing
true-false	key action words

Assess your answers to Can You Recall It? at *CollegeSuccess.andYOU.com*

1. *All*, *always*, *none*, and *never* are examples of _____ that might appear on a true-false test, usually resulting in a *false* answer.

2. Use point value as a clue to how detailed an answer to provide for a/an _____ test.

3. Marking your textbook and notes with sticky notes or paper clips so that you can quickly find information will be helpful to you on a/an _____ test.

4. You have a 50% chance of answering correctly if you have a/an _____ question.

5. _____ is a good idea for any test you take to be sure your answers are what you want them to be before submitting it.

6. If you write down in the margins of the paper everything you can remember after you receive your test, you are doing what is called a/an _____ .

7. _____ is never a good idea since it creates unnecessary stress and often results in poor grades.

8. Essay tests have _____ that tell you how to organize and present your answer.

Web Activity: Design a Test For Your Partner

Directions: Select a partner from this class who is enrolled in one of your other current classes. Your professor can help with finding a partner. You will design a brief exam for your partner related to the content of this other class. At the same time, your partner will design a similar exam for you. You will use a *specific* website (as opposed to a general information website) to obtain all the information for your test questions. Your partner can use a different website. You are going to write a ten-question test following the guidelines below. Provide the exact website address you used for this activity and write the questions and answers in the space provided.

Write the exact website address: _____

_____

Write your test topic: _____

_____

Step 1: Design questions according to the following guidelines: Create *two* (2) true-false questions; *two* (2) multiple-choice questions (with four choices each); *three* (3) matching items; *two* (2) fill-in-the-blank questions; and *one* (1) short answer/identification question, for a total of *ten* (10) items. If you need extra space, extend your writing into the margins or use separate paper.

True-False Questions:

1. _____

2. _____

Multiple-Choice Questions:

3. _____

   A._____

   B._____

   C._____

   D._____

4. _____

   A._____

   B._____

   C._____

   D._____

Matching Questions:

5. _____   A. _____

6. _____   B. _____

7. _____   C. _____

Fill-in-the-Blank Questions:

8. _____

9. _____

Short Answer/Identification Question:

10. _____

_____

_____

Step 2: Provide answers for your questions. For the short answer/identification question, write what you believe would be an acceptable answer for the question as you have designed it.

Answer Key:

1. _____
2. _____
3. _____
4. _____
5. _____
6. _____
7. _____
8. _____
9. _____
10. _____

_____

_____

_____

_____

Step 3: Bring your test to class where you will answer the questions your partner prepared, and your partner will answer the questions that you prepared.

Step 4: Be ready to discuss in class how writing practice questions can be an effective tool for preparing for an exam.

Achieving Your Goals by Succeeding on Exams

Think back to times when you have taken exams. Reflect on what you already do that helps you perform successfully on exams and what you can now begin to do, after reading this chapter, to improve your test-taking skills. Write a paragraph (or more) giving at least three positive steps you can take to enhance your college exam performance.

_____

_____

_____

_____

_____

_____

_____

_____

_____

_____

_____

_____

_____

_____

_____

_____

_____

_____

_____

_____

Researching and Writing an Academic Paper: An Introduction

In this chapter, you will move toward achieving your goals by

- determining the definition of an academic paper.

- applying the seven steps in the process of writing a college paper.

- finding out about plagiarism and how to write ethically.

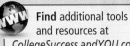

Find additional tools and resources at *CollegeSuccess.andYOU.com*

Self-Assessment:
Me, Myself, and I—Writing

Step 1: Fill in your answers for each item.

1. I can remember having to write papers for classes as far back as

   when I was in _____ grade.

2. The person who has helped me most with writing skills is/was

   _____ (name of person) who is/was my _____

   _____ (teacher, friend, relative, etc.).

3. The best advice that I have been given about writing is _____

   _____

   _____

   _____ .

4. I think I am a _____ (good/fair/bad) writer because

   _____

   _____ .

5. When I write, I am best at_____

   _____ .

6. If I am writing and I'm having difficulty, I usually _____

   _____ .

7. The writing I have done that has made me the most proud is

   _____

   _____ .

8. To become a successful writer of college papers, the three most
   important areas of improvement for me are these:

   (1) _____

   _____

   (2) _____

   _____

   (3) _____

   _____

9. If my friend is having trouble writing, I would recommend

_____

_____ .

10. The topic I most enjoy writing about is _____

_____ .

11. Communication through texting, tweeting, instant messaging, and emailing has influenced my writing by _____

_____

_____ .

12. Writing effectively after college can be important to me because

_____

_____

_____ .

Step 2: Review your answers from the "Self-Assessment" activity and check the box below that best describes your current status as a writer.

☐ **A Transitional Writer:** You are a reluctant writer who feels weak in almost all writing skill areas, including conventional grammar, spelling, and punctuation. With more work and practice in skill development, you hope to become a more willing, independent writer.

☐ **An Average Writer:** You are a willing writer who feels competent in most skill areas, but you still need help and support to produce a high-quality paper. With a little boost in skills, you will be ready to become an independent, experienced writer.

☐ **An Experienced Writer:** You are an independent writer who enjoys the writing process and has developed a sophisticated writing style. You are ready for the next writing assignment so that you can engage in an activity that you find satisfying and rewarding.

DEFINING
an academic paper

"What, exactly, is an academic paper?" "How is an academic paper different from what I have written in high school?" "Why do students have to write academic papers?" These may be some of the questions that are occurring to you as you think about the title of this chapter. First, the term *academic paper* covers many types of writing you may be required to do in your college classes, such as a research paper, an essay, a reaction paper, a literary analysis, or other types of written academic assignments. Most of these types of assignments ask that you read, think, analyze, argue, and write about ideas that are relevant for an academic community.

Second, the question "How is an academic paper different from what I have written in high school?" is answered by considering the audience for whom you are now writing. In college, your audience is composed of experts in the various disciplines that you will study. In contrast to many of your high school teachers, your professors are likely to hold advanced degrees in the areas they teach. Since you are writing for a sophisticated audience, you will benefit from learning to write in a sophisticated manner. The writing methods you used in high school will certainly be applicable in your college writing, but you will want to extend and refine your writing to meet the expectations of your professors.

Finally, "Why do students have to write academic papers?" has a frivolous answer, which you can probably guess: "Well, students write papers because the professors require them, of course." This might seem like the only answer for the question. However, the real reason students are asked to write academic papers is that producing these papers assists in the development of critical reading and thinking (see Chapter 4), analyzing, researching, arguing logically, and, of course, writing clearly. Every college has an English Department with faculty dedicated to the development of these necessary skills. These skills are all essential, both to becoming an educated person and to achieving your college goals. Additionally, they are skills that employers greatly value.

Write Here: Writing academic papers is an important part of your college career.

Six Simple but Powerful Prewriting Tips

1. Give yourself time. You need to take your time as you work on your paper so that you can review it later with a fresh perspective and a critical eye.

2. Try not to think of writing a big paper as an overwhelming task. Break it down into the seven manageable steps that you are about to learn.

3. Writing is not a talent for a chosen few; it is a learned skill that you can master. With some effort, you can become a superior writer.

4. Carefully read the directions specifying the requirements for a writing assignment before you begin. Be sure you fulfill these requirements as you proceed.

5. Consult your professor if you are unsure about any aspect of your paper, especially the selection of a topic. You want to be sure from the start that your topic is appropriate for your professor's expectations.

6. Become familiar with the language of the subject area about which you are writing. Each discipline has its own **jargon**, or specialized use of language. Avoid too much jargon in your writing, but become familiar enough that you use terms correctly.

The **PROCESS** FOR **WRITING** an academic paper

Step 1	Step 2	Step 3	Step 4
Choose a topic and narrow it	Develop a thesis statement	Complete a literature review and revise the thesis	Structure an outline

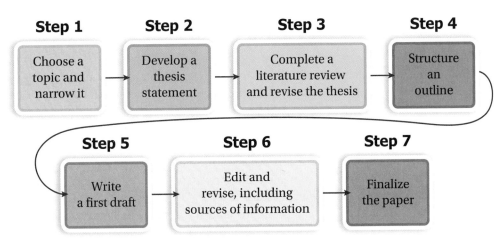

Step 5	Step 6	Step 7
Write a first draft	Edit and revise, including sources of information	Finalize the paper

The steps (or process) for writing an academic paper, shown above, are similar whether you are writing a research paper, an essay, a reaction paper, a literary analysis, or any other type of written academic assignment. The seven steps in the diagram are a guide to help you prepare an academic paper.

Step 1: Choose a Topic and Narrow It

In some cases, your professor may give you a topic. If this occurs, you will have no choice about what you write. More often, you will have the option of selecting your own topic within a given broad framework. For example, if you are taking a religion class, your professor may ask you to write a paper on comparative religions. Since "comparative religions" is a broad topic, you must narrow it to certain religions, and then specifically identify what aspects of these religions to explore in your paper. You would, then, begin with "comparative religions," and perhaps narrow to "Christianity and Buddhism," and narrow more specifically to "the concept of death/afterlife in Christianity and Buddhism." You could then begin to develop a thesis statement (explained in Step 2) and conduct a literature review (explained in Step 3) of that topic, being sure as you proceed that your paper will fulfill the requirements set by your professor. Narrowing a topic in this way can be viewed as an inverted triangle.

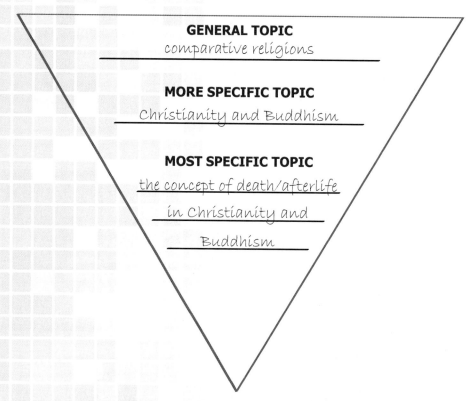

GENERAL TOPIC
comparative religions

MORE SPECIFIC TOPIC
Christianity and Buddhism

MOST SPECIFIC TOPIC
the concept of death/afterlife
in Christianity and
Buddhism

A common mistake, which you will want to avoid, occurs as you begin to decide on a topic. The mistake is to decide on a topic that is too general (or too broad) for your assignment. Choosing too broad of a topic makes it impossible to say everything necessary in the amount of space you have. Narrow your topic to one that is manageable for the number of pages appropriate for your paper. Keep moving from one category ("comparative religions") to a more narrow class within that category ("Christianity and Buddhism") to a more narrow class again ("the concept of death/afterlife in Christianity and Buddhism") until you arrive at a reasonable topic. "The concept of death/afterlife in Christianity and Buddhism" is a topic appropriate for a writing assignment requiring a five- to ten-page paper. The more pages you have, the broader your topic can be. However, it is possible to write a very long paper on a very specific topic. As a result, when in doubt, keep narrowing your topic until you have made it as specific as you think it needs to be to meet the requirements of your assignment.

EXERCISE 1 Narrower and Narrower

Step 1: You are going to begin with three general topics that you will narrow until they are appropriate for a five- to ten-page paper. Choose from the suggested general topics below or substitute any general topics of your own that are relevant to your classes. Narrow each until you think you have sufficiently focused on a topic that would be appropriate for a five- to ten-page paper. Consult reference materials, if necessary, in order to narrow the topic. Write your answers in the inverted triangles on pages 168–169. Follow this example.

Example: General Topic—constellations

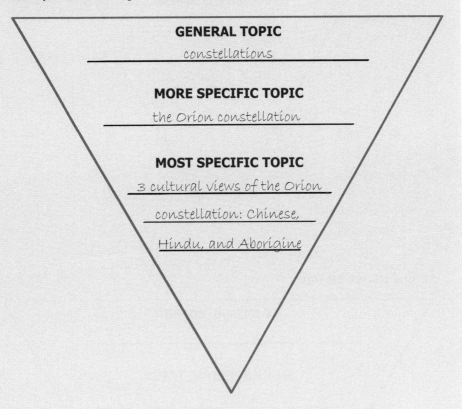

GENERAL TOPIC

constellations

MORE SPECIFIC TOPIC

the Orion constellation

MOST SPECIFIC TOPIC

3 cultural views of the Orion

constellation: Chinese,

Hindu, and Aborigine

Suggested General Topics (or substitute your own general topics)

1. the environment
2. music
3. historical documents
4. social justice
5. computers

6. unemployment
7. libraries
8. diets
9. space exploration
10. politics

First Narrowed Topic:

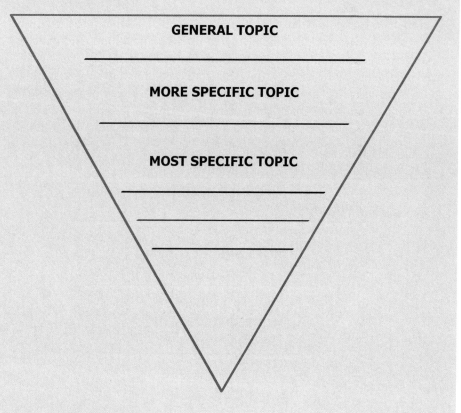

Second Narrowed Topic:

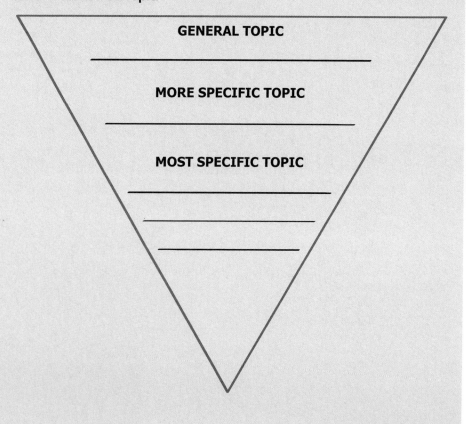

Third Narrowed Topic:

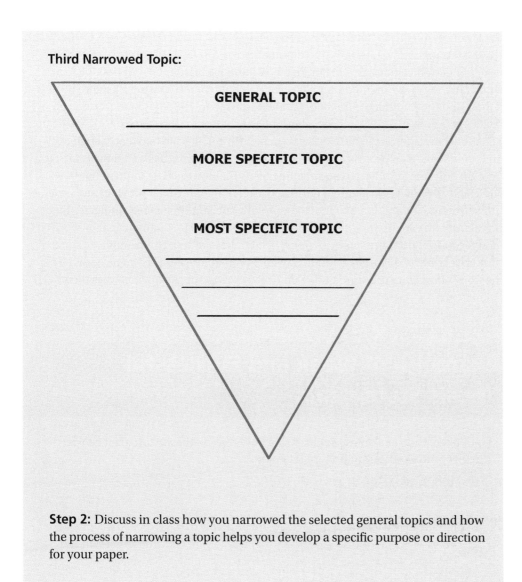

GENERAL TOPIC
_____

MORE SPECIFIC TOPIC
_____

MOST SPECIFIC TOPIC
_____

_____

_____

Step 2: Discuss in class how you narrowed the selected general topics and how the process of narrowing a topic helps you develop a specific purpose or direction for your paper.

Step 2: Develop a Thesis Statement

A **thesis statement** is the central thought or main point, sometimes stated in one sentence, for your paper's topic. Think of it as a map that guides both you, the writer, and the reader through your paper. A thesis statement performs the same function for a longer paper that a topic sentence, or main idea sentence (see Chapter 4), does for a paragraph. The thesis acts as a summary statement for the entire paper. Formulating a successful thesis statement will start you off to producing a successful paper; it will be the controlling force that guides you as you write the main body of your paper.

A good location to place your thesis statement is typically at the end of an introductory paragraph or section, especially in papers that are five-to-ten-pages long. Although this location isn't a requirement, it is still a good rule of thumb to place your thesis statement somewhere near the end of the first paragraph in shorter papers or in the last paragraph of the opening section in longer papers.

A successful thesis statement is (1) *unified*, (2) *specific*, and (3) *clear*. A **unified thesis statement** develops only one dominant idea. For example, this thesis statement is *not* unified since it has two major ideas: "Although Christianity and Buddhism are similar in their views on meditation and their relationships to historical figures (Christ and the Buddha), Christianity and Buddhism are different in their views on death and afterlife." The first idea is the similarity between Christianity and Buddhism, and the second idea is the different view on death and afterlife between Christianity and Buddhism. Your professor would want you to revise this thesis statement to develop only one key idea. To be **specific** means that the thesis statement has been sufficiently narrowed. Just as you narrowed a general topic in the previous step, you must structure the thesis statement to be equally specific. To be **clear** indicates that no vague words are used. When you are structuring a thesis statement, vague words or terms (*good*, *exciting*, and *many reasons*) need to be avoided. For example, to state "The novel *Northanger Abbey* by Jane Austen is very interesting" is vague because of the word *interesting*. Your professor would want you to specify in what ways the novel is "interesting."

Examples of Weak and Successful Thesis Statements

Here are some examples that illustrate how a weak thesis statement can be revised into a successful thesis statement.

Weak Thesis Statement	"Stress is a pervasive problem in our society."
Explanation of Weakness	The term *pervasive problem* needs to be made specific and clear. What pervasive problems exist?
Successful Thesis Statement	"Stress in our society affects job performance, relationships, and health."
Weak Thesis Statement	"Printing has a complex history and has brought about many reforms."
Explanation of Weakness	First, this thesis statement has two parts: (1) "printing has a complex history," and (2) "printing has brought about many reforms." A thesis needs to be unified, developing only one major idea. Second, each part is neither specific nor clear.
Successful Thesis Statement	"Printing modernized communication, bringing about reform in science, law, and commerce."

EXERCISE 2 Writing a Thesis Statement

Step 1: Choose one of the topics you narrowed from Exercise 1 and copy it into the inverted triangle below. In Step 2, you will write a thesis statement for this topic.

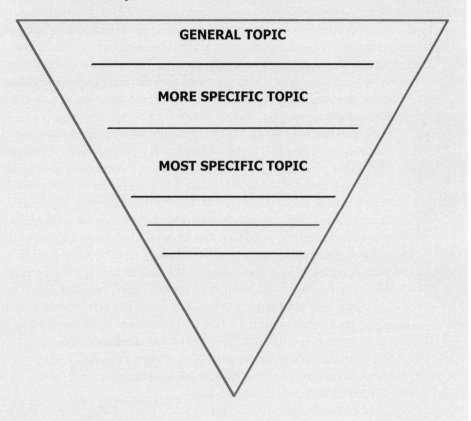

GENERAL TOPIC

_____

MORE SPECIFIC TOPIC

_____

MOST SPECIFIC TOPIC

_____

_____

_____

Step 2: Write a unified, specific, and clear thesis statement for the narrowed topic above. Consult the Internet or additional books and materials, if necessary, in order to construct a thesis statement.

Thesis statement: _____

_____

_____

_____

Step 3: In a class discussion, compare and contrast your thesis statement with the thesis statements your classmates have written. You may need to revise your thesis statement until it meets the criteria of being unified, specific, and clear.

Step 3: Complete a Literature Review and Revise the Thesis

To become familiar with the scope of your topic and to test the feasibility of your tentative thesis statement, it is now time to begin the research process. Your goal is to discover the collective body of knowledge that will offer support and credibility to your academic paper. You have many sources of information to consult as you review the literature necessary to prove, explain, or support your tentative thesis statement. At this time, the thesis statement is "tentative" because as you consult sources and read more about your topic, you might discover that a slight, or even a major, revision of your thesis idea is necessary.

As you consult sources of information, such as your campus and public libraries, the Internet, and government or business agencies, you need to set up a system for taking notes (see Chapter 5 for suggestions on note-taking) and a system for recording full bibliographic information. Sometimes students use note cards for this activity, and you might want to consider this system or develop a method of your own. Remember that any notes you take lacking bibliographic information will be useless since you won't be able to cite the source of the information in your academic paper. The full **bibliographic information** will include the author, title, place of publication, publisher, date of publication, page numbers, **URLs** (uniform resource locators, or web addresses, which are the string of letters, numbers, and symbols found in the address box on your computer screen), creation or modification dates on web pages, and your date of access. If you print information from the Internet to use as resources, it is wise to have your browser set to print the URL and date of access for every page.

Your professor will usually indicate which of several **citation styles** to use. These various styles use slightly different methods to list the author, title, publisher, and other necessary components of a bibliographic item. Some of the more commonly used styles include the following: (1) the APA (American Psychological Association) style, (2) the MLA (Modern Language Association) style, (3) the Chicago style, and (4) the Turabian style. Information about each of these citation styles can be accessed through the Internet or through your campus library.

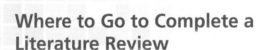

Library Visit: A library is an indispensable resource for completing a literature review.

Where to Go to Complete a Literature Review

Internet Sites

The Internet offers many possible sources, such as the links listed on the following page. The sources listed are not all that are available, but they are suggested as a guide for you to use. As you review websites, remember to take notes on information you obtain. Or if you print pages that are relevant for your paper, remember to include the URL and date of access for each page.

The *Chicago Manual of Style* 16 SIXTEENTH EDITION

The Essential Guide for Writers, Editors, and Publishers

In Style: A research paper requires the use of a consistent citation style.

1. **Search Engines—Single Databases**

   These search engines are designed to search for information on the Internet, providing web pages, pictures, and other types of files.

Ask.com	www.ask.com
Bing	www.bing.com
Google	www.google.com
Safari	www.safari.com
Yahoo	www.yahoo.com

2. **Search Engines—Multiple Databases**

   These engines search other search engines, such as those listed above, usually several at a time.

Dogpile	www.dogpile.com
Ixquick	www.ixquick.com
MetaCrawler	www.metacrawler.com

3. **Google Scholar**   http://scholar.google.com

   Google Scholar is a database of scholarly literature across many disciplines, including papers, theses, books, abstracts, and articles from academic publishers, professional organizations, universities, and other scholarly sources.

4. **Google Books**   http://books.google.com

   Google Books is a database of books scanned from various libraries and publishing companies. Sometimes the view is of a page (a limited preview), and sometimes there is access to the entire book.

5. **Proprietary Electronic Databases**

   These are fee-based databases for which you must have access provided by your college or university library. Since many schools provide their students with access to these sources, check to see which of these (or others) you have available.

   <u>Oxford English Dictionary</u>   www.oed.com
   The OED is a comprehensive dictionary of the English language.

   <u>LexisNexis</u>   www.lexisnexis.com
   LexisNexis is a database of newspapers, magazines, professional journals, legal documents, and business reports.

   <u>JSTOR</u>   www.jstor.org
   JSTOR is a database of selected academic journals and monographs ranging from American Studies to Zoology.

   <u>Web of Knowledge</u>   http://wokinfo.com/
   The Thomson Reuters (formerly ISI) Web of Knowledge is a database of selected academic journals in science, social science, and the arts and humanities.

   <u>ERIC</u>   www.eric.ed.gov
   ERIC (Education Resources Information Center) provides access to journals, books, conference papers, and other materials that are related to the field of education. Although there is free access to ERIC abstracts, to read an entire article you will need to use your library's electronic holdings.

6. **Your school's online library accesss**

   Each college or university has an online library with access to databases your library houses. Use an "index" menu to find which proprietary electronic databases from the list above (or others) you can use. If you have questions, consult a campus librarian who can assist you with your electronic search.

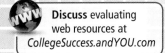
Discuss evaluating web resources at CollegeSuccess.andYOU.com

Caution: Evaluating Web Resources

Since anyone can post any information at any time on the Internet, caution is necessary when you are gathering information from websites. Before you decide to accept information found on *any* Internet site, you will want to ask and answer the following questions.

Author Questions

Who is the author? Is the person reputable in the scholarly community? Are the credentials of the author relevant for the subject? Has this person been mentioned by your professor or cited in textbooks or bibliographies you have seen?

Source Questions

Does this source directly relate to your thesis statement? Is the date for the source current enough for your need? Is this source too technical or too informal for your paper? Is the information sponsored by any particular group, organization, institution, corporation, or governmental body that might have reason for bias?

Two Tips for Internet Searching

1. Use *Wikipedia* (or other similar general websites) as a place to *begin* your research. *Wikipedia* can give you the background information you might need, such as important names, dates, and primary references, but it is *not* an authoritative source since anyone—even you—can modify entries. A recent research study reports that 82% of surveyed college students went to *Wikipedia* to research background information for a topic.[1] Use the information gained to move on to specific websites and to library resources.

2. If you're searching in a database, but you aren't sure what to enter into the search box, short phrases of two or three words ("home schooling") are better than many words ("how home schooling affects social development"). Sometimes combining words with "*and*" ("Internet and gambling") works better than using a phrase ("Internet gambling"), since using "*and*" finds articles with the words *Internet* and *gambling* appearing somewhere in the article but the phrase "Internet gambling" finds only articles with that exact phrase.

Where to Go Other Than the Internet

Your campus library is the best place to go for information after you complete your initial search on the Internet. Although the Internet provides access to an incredible array of sources, good, old-fashioned books and printed materials are valuable for gathering information for your paper. Moreover, librarians really *want* to help you; that is the job they have spent many years preparing to do. Librarians will guide you to which of the many sources your campus library offers that are appropriate for your topic, such as microfilm, microfiche, specialized reports, subject-area dictionaries, and encyclopedias, as well as books, magazines, newspapers, and journals. They will also explain to you how to find and use these various sources. Librarians will arrange to get books or other material for you through interlibrary loan if they are not available in your library. You will discover that a helpful librarian can be one of the best campus resources you can find.

Ready to Revise the Thesis Statement

The notes you have taken from various sources will guide you to revise the thesis statement as necessary and plan the organization for your paper. You might discover that you need to do either a minor or a major revision of the thesis statement. If you used note cards, try to group them together by subtopics. You can even write the subtopic designation in the upper corner of the card. Then, arrange the notes into a logical order or sequence. The thesis statement will probably dictate the order of organization, such as chronological, cause and effect, or comparison-contrast. In fact, you can use the information you learned about organizing an essay test answer (see Chapter 6) to help you decide how to organize your paper.

As you rework the thesis to represent the ideas you have acquired in your research, be sure to keep it unified (has one dominant idea), specific (is sufficiently narrow), and clear (uses no vague words). You will now have a successful thesis statement to act as a map that guides you and your reader through the various parts of your academic paper.

Step 4: Structure an Outline

Once you are satisfied that you have gathered sufficient information and have a successful thesis statement, you can create an outline. Using an outline will help you discover connections and relationships between various ideas that you couldn't recognize before. Also, you will become aware of information that isn't necessarily relevant to your thesis statement.

An informal outline, which lists the topics and subtopics of your paper with related notes, may be all you need before you begin the actual writing. In Chapter 5, you read about outlining. You learned to structure a three-level outline, consisting of Roman numerals for main ideas, capital letters for major details, and numbers for minor details. (For more information on figuring out main ideas, major details, and minor details, see Chapter 4.) The parts for such an outline appear like the one in this box.

I. First Main Idea
    A. Major Supporting Detail One
    B. Major Supporting Detail Two
        1. Minor Supporting Detail (if needed)
        2. Minor Supporting Detail (if needed)
II. Second Main Idea
    . . . and so forth.

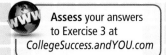

Assess your answers to Exercise 3 at *CollegeSuccess.andYOU.com*

EXERCISE 3 **Practice Outlining**

Step 1: Read the following passage taken from *Consumer Behavior and Marketing Strategy*,[2] a commonly used marketing textbook, and then follow the outline directions to fill in the missing blanks.

When people come into contact with a new culture or subculture, they may go through **four stages of acculturation** corresponding to four levels of cultural interpenetration [the amount and type of social interactions immigrants, movers, and marketers have with people in the host culture]. In the *honeymoon stage*, people are fascinated by the exotic foreign culture or subculture. Because cultural interpenetration is shallow and superficial, at this level little acculturation occurs. Tourists traveling to various regions of the United States may experience this stage.

If cultural interpenetration increases, people may enter a *rejection stage*, where they recognize that many of their old behaviors and meanings may be inadequate for acting in the new subculture. Some people may develop hostile attitudes toward the new subculture and reject its key values and meanings. Cultural conflicts tend to be maximal in this stage.

If cultural interpenetration continues and deepens, people may reach the *tolerance stage*. As they learn more cultural meanings and behaviors, they may begin to appreciate the new subculture, and cultural conflict will decrease.

Finally, in the *integration stage*, adjustment to subculture is adequate, although acculturation need not be complete or total. At this stage, people are able to function satisfactorily in the new culture or subculture, which is viewed as an alternative way of life and is valued for its good qualities.

Step 2: Fill in the missing blanks in the following three-level topic outline based on the passage on the previous page.

I. Four stages of acculturation
    A. Honeymoon stage with fascination for exotic foreign culture or subculture
        1. Shallow and superficial cultural interpretation
        2. Example of regional U.S. tourists

    B. _____
        1. Development of hostile attitudes toward new subculture with rejection of key values and meanings
        2. _____

    C. _____
        1. Development of cultural meanings and behaviors
        2. Decrease in cultural conflict

    D. _____
        1. _____
        2. Viewed as an alternative life and valued for its good qualities

Step 3: As you review your answers in class, discuss the value of preparing an outline for an academic paper.

Sometimes, however, your professor may require you to write a more formal outline to be submitted with your paper. If you are required to submit a formal outline, you may need a multilevel outline consisting of more than the three levels illustrated above. The *MLA Handbook for Writers of Research Papers* suggests the following six-level "descending parts of an outline".[3]

I.
    A.
        1.
            a.
              (1)
                (a)
                (b)
              (2)
            b.
        2.
    B.
II.

The final outline can be written as either a topic outline or a sentence outline. A **topic outline** uses only short phrases to express ideas, and a **sentence outline** uses complete sentences to show ideas more fully. If your professor does require an outline, be consistent in your development of it. Stay consistent with either a topic or a sentence outline.

Using an outline to help organize and structure your ideas will illustrate for you the strengths and weaknesses of your paper. You will be able to tell which material is not relevant for your thesis statement, and these portions should be cut from the paper. If parts of the outline appear to be weak in relationship to others, more research may be necessary to balance your presentation. As you can see, the outline gives you a "bird's-eye view" of your paper so that you can adjust and refine it before the actual writing begins.

Step 5: Write a First Draft

Using your outline as your guide and the notes you have taken when you completed the literature review, you will now write a first draft of your paper. Your paper should have the following suggested parts, which are explained below: (1) an introductory section with the thesis statement; (2) supporting and explanatory paragraphs; (3) a conclusion; and (4) citations, such as footnotes or endnotes and a bibliography.

An Introductory Section with the Thesis Statement

An **introductory section** includes either one paragraph (for a shorter paper) or a few paragraphs (for a longer paper) that catch the attention of the reader and contain the thesis statement. In the introductory section, you lead up to and then state the thesis. The opening paragraph or paragraphs might supply background information, a context for your ideas, essential definitions, or perhaps a story or a quotation that reflects your thesis idea. This introductory section provides the first impression for your reader, so you will want to take special care as you write. Actually, you might consider writing the introduction *after* you've written the rest of your paper, since some students discover they have a better overall grasp of their topic once the first draft is complete. Just be sure not to change any of the thesis statement ideas if you write the introductory section after the first draft; any changes made to the thesis statement affect the entire paper.

Supporting and Explanatory Paragraphs

The **supporting and explanatory paragraphs** expand on your thesis statement. These paragraphs form the body of your paper. Each paragraph will declare a point, usually stated as that paragraph's topic sentence (or main idea sentence—see Chapter 4). A **topic sentence** is similar to a thesis statement—except that it is the controlling sentence for an individual paragraph rather than an entire paper. Each paragraph in the body of the paper will develop a topic sentence, and each topic sentence indicates a relationship to the thesis idea. You will use quotations and evidence from the notes you have taken when completing the literature review as you write these paragraphs. Make your paragraphs strong with solid topic sentences connected to the thesis idea, with sufficient relevant quotes and evidence, and with a flow from paragraph to paragraph.

First Draft: The first draft is one of several drafts that you write for your paper.

A Conclusion

The **concluding section** summarizes the main points you have made in your paper. You draw together all the main points you presented and bring the paper to a close. Techniques for conclusions are similar to those for introductory sections. You can again consider background information related to your thesis, return to the key terms or definitions and how you have used them, or use a story or a quotation that summarizes or represents your thesis idea. Your goal in this final section is to connect back to your thesis statement with language that will demonstrate the importance of the thesis idea, provide a sense of completeness to your paper, and leave a positive final impression on your reader.

Footnotes or Endnotes and a Bibliography

Most professors will require you to use a **citation method** (how you identify sources of information such as books or the Internet) for the papers you write. Your professor will probably designate a specialized **citation style** for you to follow. If no one style (such as APA, MLA, Chicago, or Turabian) is required for your paper, you can choose whichever you prefer. You can learn more about these citation styles by searching the Internet, checking your campus library or consulting your professor.

The citation style you use displays and explains the documentation procedures for a footnote, an endnote, or a bibliography. **Footnotes** are placed at the bottom of each page and list the sources from which you have taken quotations or evidence that you have used on that page. Footnotes are called **endnotes** if they are accumulated as a consecutive list and placed at the end of your paper. The **bibliography**, sometimes called "Works Cited" or "References," appears at the very end of your paper. It alphabetically lists, by author, all the sources that you used to write the paper. Remember, if you keep careful records as you complete the literature review, preparing the bibliography will be relatively easy. Each source used in your paper appears in the bibliography in the correct citation style.

Bibliography

Allen, K. R. 1971. Relation between production and biomass. J. Fish. Res. Bd. Can. 28: 1573-1581.

Andrews, A. H., E. Cordes, and M. M. Mahoney. 2002. Age and growth and radiometric age validation of a deep-sea, habitat-forming gorgonian (*Primnoa resedaeformis*) from the Gulf of Alaska, p. 101 110. *In* L. Watling, and M. Risk (eds.), Biology of cold water corals. Hydrobiologia 471.

Bailey, E. P. 1993. Fox introductions on Alaskan islands: History, impacts on avifauna, and eradication. U.S. Fish Wildl. Serv. Res. Publ. 193. 54 p.

Bailey, K. M., R. D. Brodeur, N. Merati, and M. M. Yoklavich.1993. Predation on walleye pollock (*Theragra chalcogramma*) eggs and yolk-sac larvae by pelagic crustacean invertebrates in the western Gulf of Alaska. Fish. Oceanogr. 2: 30-39.

Barnes, R. D. 1980. Invertebrate zoology. Saunders College, Philadelphia. 1,089 p.

Bell, F. H. 1981. The Pacific halibut: the resource and its fishery. Anchorage: Alaska Northwest Publishing Company. 267 p.

Brodeur, R. D., and M. Terazaki. 1999. Springtime abundance of chaetognaths in the shelf region of the northern Gulf of Alaska, with observations on the vertical distribution and feeding of *Sagitta elegans*. Fish. Oceanogr. 8(2):93-103.

Caswell, H., S. Brault, A. J. Read, and T. D. Smith. 1998. Harbor porpoise and fisheries: An uncertainty analysis of incidental mortality. Ecol. Appl. 8: 1226-1238.

Christensen, V., and D. Pauly. 1992. Ecopath II - a software for balancing steady-state ecosystem models and calculating network characteristics. Ecol. Modell. 61: 169-185.

Clark, W. G., and S. R. Hare, 2003. Assessment of the Pacific halibut stock at the end of 2003. International Pacific Halibut Commission, P.O. Box 95009, Seattle, WA 98145-2009. Available at http://www.iphc.washington.edu/halcom/research/sa/papers/sa03.pdf. Accessed 11/9/2007.

Essington, T. E., J. F. Kitchell, and C. J. Walters, 2001. The von Bertalanffy growth function, bioenergetics, and the consumption rates of fish. Can. J. Fish. Aquat. Sci. 58: 2129-2138.

Feder, H. M., and S. C. Jewett, 1981. Feeding interactions in the eastern Bering Sea with emphasis on the benthos, p. 1,229-1,261. *In* D. W. Hood, and J. A. Calder (eds.), The eastern Bering Sea shelf: oceanography and resources, vol. 2. U.S. Dep. Commer., NOAA, Office of Marine Pollution Assessment, Univ. Washington Press, Seattle, WA.

Works Cited: The bibliography identifies all the reference sources you used in your paper.

Step 6: Edit and Revise, Including Sources of Information

Editing your own writing is one of the most important steps in the writing process. **Editing** involves having the courage to look critically at your own work, thinking about your reader's reactions, and making necessary changes. You may need to edit and rewrite three or four drafts of your paper to state ideas more clearly.

Try to leave your first draft alone for a while, so you can read it cold and as if it were unfamiliar to you. Put away the first draft for several hours or, if possible, a day or two, so the material you wrote seems somewhat new or fresh.

Although it might seem silly to you, read the paper out loud at some point in the editing step. Reading out loud allows you to consider every word you have written to note errors. Also, reading aloud allows you to listen for the flow of your ideas and the language you have used. You can edit changes as you notice your unintended mistakes, awkwardly worded phrases, or repetitions in word choices.

The following twenty-question editorial checklist will help you as you edit and revise your paper.

Twenty Questions for Editing Your Paper

Yes	No	
☐	☐	**1.** Did I narrow the topic enough for the required length of the paper?
☐	☐	**2.** Is my thesis statement unified, specific, and clear?
☐	☐	**3.** Did I fully develop each idea expressed in the thesis statement?
☐	☐	**4.** Does each paragraph in the body of the paper have a strong topic sentence?
☐	☐	**5.** Have I supported each topic sentence with sufficient and relevant quotes or evidence?
☐	☐	**6.** Does each paragraph have a clear relationship to the others?
☐	☐	**7.** Do I make a good first impression with an introductory section that includes the thesis statement?
☐	☐	**8.** Does my conclusion refer back to the thesis and leave a positive final impression?
☐	☐	**9.** Did I follow an organizational pattern in my paper? (See pages 152–153 to confirm your organizational pattern for the paper.)
☐	☐	**10.** Did I evaluate for credibility the Internet sources that I have included in my paper?

Yes	No	
☐	☐	**11.** Do I have a variety of sources of information for my paper?
☐	☐	**12.** Have I avoided misrepresentation in everything I wrote?
☐	☐	**13.** Did I follow my outline?
☐	☐	**14.** If I must submit my outline, is it correctly structured?
☐	☐	**15.** Have I used good grammar and correct spelling?
☐	☐	**16.** Are my word choices the best I can make?
☐	☐	**17.** Have I used correct formatting for each footnote or endnote?
☐	☐	**18.** Is every item in my bibliography in the correct format?
☐	☐	**19.** Is the citation style consistent throughout my paper?
☐	☐	**20.** Have I proofread and revised my paper to make it the best I can?

Step 7: Finalize the Paper

To prepare your final version of the paper, return to your assignment sheet. Recheck the due date, the format requirements, and any other specifications your professor has supplied. Review your paper for consistency with these requirements.

Your final version should be typed with a word processor using standard white 8½-by-11-inch paper (unless your professor specifies differently). Use appropriate top, bottom, and side margins and only one side of the paper. Use a standard font, double-spaced in 12-point size, unless your professor specifies otherwise. Take care not to play games with font size and margins to try to make your paper seem longer or shorter; your professor will probably notice. Be sure to keep a final version of the paper for yourself. If you have any questions about the techniques for word processing, you can check with both your professor for suggestions and with your campus Computer Lab. Computer Lab assistants can provide information you might need regarding use of word processing programs.

Proofread your final version more than once. If possible, have someone else also proofread your final version. Fresh eyes can sometimes find mistakes that you no longer notice. It is *not* a good idea to rely on computer spell-checkers for proofreading since spell-checkers read the following poem as correct.

SPELL CHECKER POEM

I have a spelling checker.
It came with my PC.
It plane lee marks four my revue
Miss steaks aye can knot sea.

Eye ran this poem threw it,
Your sure reel glad two no.
Its vary polished inn it's weigh.
My checker tolled me sew.

A checker is a bless sing,
It freeze yew lodes of thyme.
It helps me right awl stiles two reed,
And aides me when aye rime.

From Jerrold H. Zar, "Candidate for a Pullet Surprise," Journal of Irreproducible Results, January/February 1994, page 13, and Vol. 45, No. 5/6, 2000, page 20. See www.jir.com/pullet.html. Reprinted with permission.[4]

As you can see, this poem has many mistakes. So use this poem as a caution that computer spell-checkers are limited in usefulness.

After you have completed your last final review and you have handed in your paper on time, give yourself a reward for knowing that you have done your very best job possible.

A word about
PLAGIARISM

The word about plagiarism is *don't*. However, before you *don't* plagiarize, you need to understand what it is. The *MLA Handbook for Writers of Research Papers* (page 66) explains plagiarism as "a form of cheating that has been defined as 'the false assumption of authorship: the wrongful act of taking the product of another person's mind, and presenting it as one's own.' "[5]

From this definition, plagiarism can take these forms: (1) submitting another student's paper as your own, (2) presenting information from a source (such as a book, a journal, a magazine, a newspaper, a website, or a lecture) without proper bibliographic citation, (3) buying and turning in a paper from a service or a person, and (4) downloading and submitting as your own all or parts of a paper from a free academic paper website. With today's technology, there are hundreds of websites that offer research and paper services. The ability to cut and paste from websites has made plagiarism tempting and easy. Resist these temptations because professors have online technology that assists them in detecting plagiarism, such as www.Plagiarism.org and www.TurnItIn.com. If plagiarism in a paper is detected, your professor may give you a failing grade and refer you to your college's disciplinary board, which could recommend suspension or expulsion. Consult your student code of conduct to learn the consequences of plagiarism at your college.

Quote Directly, Summarize, Paraphrase

When you take material from any source, including the Internet, you must do one of the following: (1) **quote directly** word-for-word using indentation with single spacing and/or quotation marks around the entire passage, (2) **summarize** the information (see Chapter 5 for more information on writing a summary), or (3) **paraphrase**, which means restating the information in different words. Reference citations are necessary for each of these. Suppose, for example, that you are writing a paper on Picasso for your art class and you want to use the information in this passage from the book *The Arts: World Themes* by Geraldine Nagle.[6]

off the mark.com   by Mark Parisi

YOUR TERM PAPER ON "THE GROWING PROBLEM OF PLAGIARISM IN SOCIETY" IS EYE-OPENING...ESPECIALLY SINCE IT'S THE THIRD TIME I'VE SEEN IT...

> **Original Version:**
> What makes *Guernica* a masterpiece? Very simply, the originality of its theme and its style. Picasso turned an atrocity into a universal statement about the horrors of violence. To this end, he distorted observable reality by changing people, places, and things into abstract symbols—a creative process that is anything *but* simple. (p. 63)[7]

First, to *quote directly*, you would do the following.

> **Quoted Directly,**
> "What makes *Guernica* a masterpiece? Very simply, the originality of its theme and its style. Picasso turned an atrocity into a universal statement about the horrors of violence. To this end, he distorted observable reality by changing people, places, and things into abstract symbols—a creative process that is anything *but* simple" (Nagle 1997, 63).

Second, you can *summarize* the information as follows. When summarizing, you include the key ideas from the original.

> **Summarized Version:**
> Picasso's *Guernica* is a masterpiece because of its theme and style. Picasso distorted reality by changing everyday things into a representation of the horrors of violence, an extremely complex process (Nagle 1997).

Third, you can *paraphrase* by restating the information in different words. The original intent and ideas must be maintained in the restatement.

> **Paraphrased Version:**
> According to Nagle (1997), the ingenious *Guernica* reveals Picasso's mastery of the complexity of composition and expression by his converting everyday things into representations of horrible brutality.

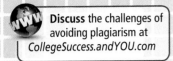

Discuss the challenges of avoiding plagiarism at *CollegeSuccess.andYOU.com*

Avoiding Plagiarism Problems

Sometimes, plagiarism results from procrastination. Maybe you put off your writing until you no longer have the time to produce your paper. The best solution for procrastination is to use good time management skills (see Chapter 3) as you plan a schedule to include writing your assigned paper.

Plagiarism also results from inexperience or lack of knowledge. Not knowing the rules about plagiarism is an unacceptable excuse for college students. The information in this chapter guides you on how to avoid plagiarism. You can familiarize yourself further by checking with your campus library or English Department. Tutorials on plagiarism are often available through these resources. Additionally, you can ask your professor. Your professor will be able either to answer your specific question or direct you to someone who can, such as a staff member at your campus Writing Center.

Academic writing must be honest. Severe penalties, ranging from course failure to even expulsion from your college, can result from academic fraud. The ability to write clearly, effectively, and ethically is a skill necessary not only for you to achieve your college goals but also for you to reach personal and professional success.

Use the resource links to find additional information at *CollegeSuccess.andYOU.com*

Thinking Critically About . . .
Researching and Writing an Academic Paper: An Introduction

Critical thinking involves an active evaluation of information using careful, thoughtful, and reasoned judgments.

1. Some people argue that students who plagiarize end up hurting themselves more than anyone else. Evaluate this opinion by providing a detailed explanation of your viewpoint.

2. You are selected to give advice to incoming students at your college about the importance of academic writing. How would you address the following two questions: What key elements are necessary to become an independent, competent writer? What are the benefits of becoming an independent, competent writer?

Discuss your ideas about the Critical Thinking items at *CollegeSuccess.andYOU.com*

3. Choose a controversial topic, such as whether alcohol should or should not be banned on college campuses. Select two websites, each with the opposite view—one in favor and one opposed to the controversial issue you choose. Compare and contrast the points of view and the soundness of the arguments made. Evaluate the quality of each of the two websites as a source for a research paper.

4. Students who write academic papers complain that preparing footnotes (or endnotes) and a bibliography ("Works Cited" or "References") is a hassle. Several different citation styles exist, and they can seem complex. Assess and explain the value of using a standardized system for documenting sources of information in an academic paper.

5. Many professors are strongly opposed to students using *Wikipedia* and *SparkNotes* as Internet resources for academic papers. Take a position on this issue (for or against using *Wikipedia* and *SparkNotes*) and make a convincing argument.

Online Learning

Discuss your online learning ideas for this chapter at *CollegeSuccess.andYOU.com*

If you are taking an online class, the procedure for writing an academic paper is the same as for a classroom student, but you may have more writing assignments to complete than students in traditional classes. Online learners must be very careful when submitting the final version of the paper to the professor. Upload times are sometimes long, so try to prepare the files in such a way as to make uploading smooth. Some professors forbid email attachments, so you may need to place your entire paper as plain text in the body of the email. Also, be sure you have clearly identified yourself as the person who submitted the paper, or else it might not get credited to you. Online learners usually have a great deal of interaction with professors, so asking questions is easy. You may be able to consult with campus librarians through email; however, if there is no campus librarian, consider seeking help from a community librarian. Practicing good time management skills in preparing your paper (see Chapter 3) will also be essential. Family demands and job necessities may interfere with distance learners' schedules, so give yourself enough time to complete the written assignment.

Key Chapter Strategies

- To keep the process manageable, follow the seven steps found in "The Process for Writing an Academic Paper."
- Narrow the topic and thesis statement appropriately for each writing assignment.
- Carefully construct the thesis statement since it acts as a guide for the entire paper.
- Be precise and consistent with bibliographic citations.
- Always acknowledge the contributions of others and the sources for your ideas.
- Use the twenty questions on page 180–181 to edit your paper.
- Proofread and revise your paper several times until it represents your best effort.
- Try to become an independent writer who finds writing enjoyable and rewarding.
- Visit the Purdue University Online Writing Lab website for many outstanding pointers about writing academic papers: *http//owl.english.purdue.edu/owl*.

CHAPTER CHALLENGE

A WRITER'S ROADBLOCKS

When students begin their college education, they vary tremendously in the amount of experience they have had in writing academic papers. At many high schools, students write papers regularly and are familiar with the process. Less-prepared students must quickly learn what is expected of them.

Writing an academic paper involves a series of challenging steps. Inexperienced writers often need to seek help starting with the very first step. At most colleges, supportive faculty and staff members are available to assist a student in learning how to succeed with the steps for developing an academic paper.

A CASE STUDY: FACING THE CHALLENGE OF . . . A WRITER'S ROADBLOCKS

Calvin attended a high school in a small town in Illinois, but his ambitions were large as he hoped to become a corporate attorney in New York. Without having felt challenged academically, Calvin was honored at graduation as his high school valedictorian. His academic excellence earned him a scholarship to a college in his state. In his first semester, Calvin followed his advisor's recommendations in choosing classes for a pre-law curriculum. He elected to take English, political science, world history, French, and biology.

When he read the syllabus for his political science class, he discovered that a significant part of his final grade would be based on a ten-page research paper. Even though he knew that writing was important for attorneys, he had virtually no previous experience in writing a serious academic paper. Calvin became concerned when he ate dinner with a few other guys in the class and found out that they each had written a number of lengthy academic papers in high school. Calvin felt lost. He had been fascinated by the 2012 presidential election but was unsure how to decide on a more specific topic. He also was uncertain how to research the paper and organize it.

OVERCOMING THE CHALLENGE OF . . . A WRITER'S ROADBLOCKS

Be prepared to discuss your answers to the following items: (1) Predict how the professor who assigned the paper can assist Calvin in narrowing his topic; provide a sample narrow topic that would be appropriate, given Calvin's general interest. (2) Which office or center is available on your campus to help a student with Calvin's concerns? What specifically does this resource do to provide help for a student preparing an academic paper? (3) Since Calvin's career choice requires skillful writing, explain what Calvin can do during his college years to help himself become a successful writer.

Can You Recall It?

Directions: To review your understanding of the chapter, choose the correct term from the list below and fill it in on the blank. You will not use every term.

supporting and explanatory paragraphs	library
academic paper	outline
proofread	LexisNexis
plagiarize	introductory section
MetaCrawler	footnotes, endnotes
jargon	statement

1. _____ is an example of a fee-based proprietary electronic database that your college or university library may provide for students.

2. _____ and _____ provide the sources of information from which you have taken quotations or evidence. _____ are placed at the bottom of each page, whereas _____ are accumulated as a list and placed at the end of the paper.

3. The term _____ covers many types of writing that may be required in college classes, such as a research paper, an essay, a reaction paper, a literary analysis, or other types of written assignments.

4. The vague terms *interesting* or *many reasons* will be criticized in a thesis _____ because these terms are not clear enough for a controlling sentence.

5. Besides the Internet, a great source of information for writing an academic paper is the _____.

6. An informal or formal _____ allows you to discover the connections and relationships between ideas and to determine which information isn't related to the thesis statement.

7. The thesis statement should appear in the _____ of the paper.

8. The "Spell Checker Poem" cautions you to _____ on your own and not to rely on the computer.

Web Activity: Web Quest

Directions: Step 3 of the seven steps for writing an academic paper involves completing a literature review. One of the primary sources for gathering information is the Internet. In Exercise 2, you wrote a thesis statement. Copy your thesis statement below. Then, search the web for *two specific sources* that provide evidence and support for your thesis statement. Before deciding to include any particular website, be sure to evaluate it according to the criteria in "Evaluating Web Resources" found earlier in this chapter. Provide the exact web page addresses you discover and list them. After each web address, write a brief (two or three sentence) explanation of what information the web source offers that supports your thesis statement.

Your thesis statement from Exercise 2: _____

_____

First specific web source address: _____

_____

Brief explanation of how the web source information supports the
thesis statement: _____

_____

_____

_____

_____

_____

Second specific web source address: _____

_____

Brief explanation of how the web source information supports the
thesis statement: _____

_____

_____

_____

_____

_____

_____

_____

Achieving Your Goals by Researching and Writing an Academic Paper: An Introduction

Suppose in class tomorrow your professor assigns you a ten-page academic paper. Discuss how confident you are that you could write a successful paper. Which topics covered in this chapter can you handle competently and which cause you concern? For the topics that concern you, explore steps you can take to strengthen your skills.

_____

_____

_____

_____

_____

_____

_____

_____

_____

_____

_____

_____

_____

_____

_____

_____

_____

_____

_____

_____

_____

_____

Money Matters: Gaining Financial Literacy

8

In this chapter, you will move toward achieving your goals by

- discovering how to maximize financial resources to afford college.

- learning how to manage your money effectively.

- acquiring control over the use of checking accounts, debit cards, and credit cards.

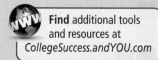

Find additional tools and resources at *CollegeSuccess.andYOU.com*

Self-Assessment: Spending Style Indicator

Step 1: After reading each item, answer either T if the item is True about you or F if the item is False about you. Be sure to answer every item as honestly as you can.

_____ **1.** I bought, rented, or borrowed at least one used textbook for my current classes.

_____ **2.** If I drop a few pennies while making a purchase, I would leave them on the ground for someone else to pick up.

_____ **3.** I am as generous as my friends.

_____ **4.** I usually wait for sales to buy clothes.

_____ **5.** I stick to a budget that I devised for my expenses.

_____ **6.** I usually arrange to get cash without having to pay an ATM (automated teller machine) fee.

_____ **7.** My friends usually tip more generously than I do.

_____ **8.** I buy the latest model cell phone as soon as possible.

_____ **9.** I usually don't take advantage of the giveaways and free entertainment at my college.

_____ **10.** I rarely sell my possessions to earn extra money.

_____ **11.** I try to find the most economical form of transportation when I travel.

_____ **12.** I readily volunteer to chip in extra money when I eat out with friends if we are a few dollars short.

_____ **13.** People in my family think that I spend too much for them on presents.

_____ **14.** When I shop for food, I look for the items on sale first.

_____ **15.** I would not feel comfortable shopping in used furniture stores to furnish my apartment.

_____ **16.** Other students annoy me when they spend a lot.

_____ **17.** I would not be satisfied wearing clothes from a discount store.

_____ **18.** I use coupons to save money at stores and restaurants.

_____ **19.** I expect to get at least one library or parking fine at college.

_____ **20.** I know almost precisely how much money I have with me most of the time.

Step 2: Follow the point guidelines below to calculate your *Spending Style Indicator Score.*

Calculate Your Score

Give Yourself 1 Point If You Answered	Give Yourself 0 Points If You Answered	My Points
1. True	1. False	1. _____
2. False	2. True	2. _____
3. False	3. True	3. _____
4. True	4. False	4. _____
5. True	5. False	5. _____
6. True	6. False	6. _____
7. True	7. False	7. _____
8. False	8. True	8. _____
9. False	9. True	9. _____
10. False	10. True	10. _____
11. True	11. False	11. _____
12. False	12. True	12. _____
13. False	13. True	13. _____
14. True	14. False	14. _____
15. False	15. True	15. _____
16. True	16. False	16. _____
17. False	17. True	17. _____
18. True	18. False	18. _____
19. False	19. True	19. _____
20. True	20. False	20. _____

My Total Points: _____

Step 3: Your total, which can range from 0 to 20, signifies the degree to which you are free or cautious in your attitude about spending money. There are no "good" scores or "bad" scores, simply an indication of your spending style. Here are the score ranges and their implications.

Spending Style Indicator Scores

0–5 You are very free and liberal with money. If you have enough money, you may be able to afford this style, but it could become challenging if you have limited financial resources. You may be envied by some students, but others may not understand your free spending.

6–10 While you are somewhat easy with money, you usually think twice before impulsive spending decisions. Friends will likely see you as comfortable with paying your share.

11–15 You tend toward thriftiness and saving. Although you are appropriately concerned with preserving your resources, you may sometimes come across to some people as cautious with money.

16–20 You value thrift. This value may be very helpful in managing your finances as a college student. Hopefully, you will find ways to enjoy college life along with your ability to save. You may get a reputation as being careful with money.

If you are like many new students, you look at college, in part, as an investment to help you become financially successful in the future. While achieving that goal may seem far off, learning to manage your own financial affairs while you are a student will help you reach future financial success.

For successful money management, knowledge is control. The good news is that once you are an upper-level student, you most likely will be more knowledgeable about money matters. Studies show that experienced college students are much better informed about personal finances than high school seniors.[1] However, you might not yet have had much experience managing your money. As a result, you may lack the knowledge necessary to make the wise financial decisions that will now be required. You can expect to transform into a more responsible money manager during your college years. Although the material presented in this chapter is intended to assist you in that transformation, taking an applied introductory class in economics or finance will also be helpful.

Along with knowledge, your attitudes about money will influence your financial life in college. Your early experiences related to money can form characteristic ways of behaving that currently affect you. For example, you may have learned to be extremely **frugal**, or cautious, with money. In contrast, you may feel free to spend money. These attitudes may stem from modeling your behavior after members of your family. Alternatively, your attitudes toward money may have been influenced by a memorable event in which you gained a prized possession or felt deprived of something important to you that another child was given. You might also be accustomed to getting most things you want and expect that pattern to continue. Since childhood experiences can profoundly influence your attitudes about money, awareness of them can make it easier for you to adjust to your current circumstances.

AFFORDING COLLEGE

The cost of college varies by thousands of dollars from one school to another. Costs are generally lowest in state colleges for residents of that state and highest in private colleges. Some students can easily afford the most expensive schools, while others struggle to pay for even the least expensive colleges. Wherever you stand in your ability to pay for your college costs, it will be very helpful for you to understand your expenses and how to manage them.

A Dollar Saved: Staying on track to graduate on time saves you money by not having to pay for extra semesters.

College Costs

By now, you have paid for tuition and fees for the current segment of the academic year. If you are a full-time student, you paid a fixed amount for tuition. If you are a part-time student, you most likely paid per credit. Your motivation to succeed in school is likely to increase significantly when you realize how much you are paying for the opportunity to learn.

Since you are also paying fees along with tuition, it is important for you to know what these fees cover. The services covered by mandatory fees vary greatly from school to school. They may include free use of such benefits as health and counseling services, career planning and placement, tickets to athletic events, a Wellness Center, and campus transportation. You can learn exactly what your fees cover by going to the student accounts page of your school's website.

Living expenses are another necessary cost of attending college. You may pay for a meal plan along with your room if you live on campus. By now, you know how much additional food, if any, beyond the meal plan you will regularly need. If you live off campus but not at home, you will have to pay for rent and food as well. Those of you living at home may need to contribute to your family's expenses. Finally, there are miscellaneous, but not inconsequential, costs such as textbooks, furnishings, visits home, snacks and eating out, cell phones, laundry, and entertainment.

Unfortunately, expenses are very likely to rise during your years in college. For instance, college tuition has historically increased each year along with other fees. An important strategy for saving extra money for tuition and fees is to plan to graduate on time. This goal can be accomplished by completing your full course load during each academic period, steadily fulfilling academic requirements, and not making a drastic switch of your major.

Paying for College

With such serious expenses ahead of you, what are the leading alternatives for financing your college education? You can consider savings, family support, part-time jobs, and financial aid as ways to pay for college.

Savings

Congratulations if you have enough savings to help pay for college costs. Regardless of the source of your savings, you are off to a good start financially. As you progress, you may need to rely on some of the other alternatives for meeting college costs, which are explained below.

Family Support

Many families contribute to college expenses. Their contributions vary greatly according to financial capability and willingness to help, as well as complex factors such as divorce, job status, family size, and other monetary obligations. When possible, have a mature, face-to-face conversation with your family so that you know how much, if any, financial support you can expect. Since family financial circumstances can change, you may periodically need to adjust the amount of money that you must provide on your own.

Part-Time Jobs

Approximately half of college students work.[2] Student employees are often eagerly sought by campus administrators because their contributions are highly valued. In addition to providing earnings, part-time jobs can help you develop skills, identify a mentor, meet people, and improve your time management skills (see Chapter 3). For full-time students, however, working more than twenty hours per week increases the likelihood of earning low grades and dropping out of college. The ideal number of working hours ranges from ten to fifteen hours per week for full-time students.

On the Job: You can earn money through a part-time job to pay your expenses.

On-campus employment has many advantages compared to off-campus jobs. For example, students working on campus often have supervisors who are sensitive to the special demands of the academic calendar. Many campus supervisors are willing to allow reduced schedules so that student employees can study for exams, visit home, or take a summer internship. Campus jobs also don't require extra transportation or additional travel time. A Student Employment Office can usually provide lists of job openings both on and off campus. Leads on summer jobs and paid internships may also be available through this office. Some colleges offer cooperative education programs that provide students with the opportunity to spend time working in fields related to their majors while gaining practical experience and earning money along with college credits. Another means to defray college costs is to become an RA (resident assistant—see Chapter 2). RAs often receive free housing, free or reduced meal plans, and a financial stipend.

Federal Work-Study is the leading college work program. Eligibility for this program is established each year through FAFSA (see "The Language of Loans" later in this chapter) and other criteria, so even if you don't qualify one year, you may the next. Students are awarded a specific amount of money for the year and must apply for jobs in campus offices. Since the federal government subsidizes a portion of the earnings, campus departments are typically eager to hire work-study students. Most colleges offer additional employment opportunities for students who do not qualify for the Federal Work-Study program. Visit your Student Employment Office to determine the opportunities that exist for you on your campus.

When you have any official employment, you will find deductions in your paycheck for income taxes (federal and possibly state) and Social Security (shown as FICA) taxes. The good news is that you are likely to receive a refund for income tax deductions after you file your tax returns.

Financial Aid

Since this system is complex, students seeking financial aid should make an appointment with a campus financial aid specialist to clarify procedures and learn about any application deadlines. As you progress in school, getting to know a financial aid specialist who is familiar with your needs is recommended. If you did not start college with financial aid and you have achieved outstanding grades or your need level has increased, you may qualify for financial aid for the next academic year. Information about three types of financial aid follows.

Scholarships or Grants

Scholarships or **grants** are a very desirable type of financial aid because they are essentially awards that don't require repayment. According to a 2012 UCLA national survey, 72.6% of college freshmen report receiving a scholarship or grant.[3] Scholarships are often based on merit, while grants are more likely to be based on need. **Pell Grants**, which are need-based federal grants, are sometimes overlooked by students who may qualify for such assistance. Scholarships, particularly from governmental agencies such as ROTC (Reserve Officers Training Corps), may compel repayment if students do not fulfill certain obligations. Furthermore, in order to retain certain scholarships, students may need to maintain a minimum grade point average (GPA). At some schools, academic departments award grants or scholarships to students majoring in their fields who have demonstrated academic promise through grades or research.

GI Bill

The Post-9/11 Veterans Educational Assistance Act of 2008 (GI Bill) provides significant tuition and housing benefits to college students who have served in the military on or after September 11, 2001. Dependents of service members may also be eligible to receive a transfer of education benefits. The website www.gibill.va.gov provides information about eligibility and benefits as well as an application to receive support through this program.

Loans

Loans are the most common form of financial aid. About two-thirds of undergraduates use loans to help them with college costs.[4] In most cases, if you have a loan, you are making an excellent investment in your education and future earning potential. Since you must pay back loans after you complete your education, it is vital to understand the nature of your obligations when you borrow to finance your college education. To help you make the right choices when borrowing, an explanation of loan terminology follows. While all these terms may not be relevant to you now, they may become more relevant later, so keeping these definitions available is a good idea.

The Language of Loans

Annual Percentage Rate (APR) — APR indicates the cost or interest on a loan; it can be stated as 10%, for example.

Consolidation — Consolidation refers to an opportunity to lump all of the loans you have accumulated together, preferably with a lower fixed interest rate.

Cosigner — A person who signs your loan agreement along with you to provide the lending agency additional security that the debt will be repaid. Cosigners are often required for private loans.

Credit Rating — Private agencies establish a number rating to indicate how likely you are to be able to repay your debt. This number can affect your opportunity to obtain loans and the APR (see above) you will receive.

Direct Loans — This loan is arranged between you and your school, usually with relatively low interest rates.

Fees — Some loans require you to pay a percentage of the sum borrowed as a base charge for taking the loan. This fee must be paid back as part of the amount borrowed and also accrues interest.

Fixed Interest Rate — This term refers to an interest rate on a loan that remains the same until the debt is repaid.

Free Application for Federal Student Aid (FAFSA) — This detailed form must be completed to apply for federal loans and other forms of financial aid. If you are twenty-four or younger, your family must participate in the application process.

Grace Period — The amount of time you are given before you must start repaying a loan is the grace period. Upon graduation, you are usually given six months before having to begin paying back a federal loan.

Interest Rate — This term refers to a percentage charged for the use of borrowed funds.

Loan Forgiveness — If you work for certain agencies such as the Coast Guard or Peace Corps after graduation, you may not need to pay back part of a college loan.

Perkins Loans — These low interest loans are provided by the federal government if you have "exceptional financial need." Your school also contributes to the loan, and you must repay your college for the money borrowed.

Private Loans —Students and their families may borrow from banks, credit unions, and finance companies. A college may have a specific arrangement with a lending agency to facilitate these loans. Often, interest rates are higher for private loans than for federal loans.

PLUS Loans (Parent Loan for Undergraduate Students) — Parents may borrow money that will be sent directly to your college by the U.S. Department of Education. Repayment usually must begin within sixty days of the disbursement.

Stafford Loans — This popular governmental aid program consists of **subsidized loans** (see the following page) and **unsubsidized loans** (see the following page). Stafford Loans usually have a low interest rate, permit increasing borrowing amounts annually, and do not require payments until six months after graduation.

State Loans — Approximately half of the states offer loan programs for college students. These fees and interest rates may be lower than those for private loans (see above).

Subsidized Loans — Based on need, these loans feature a deferment of interest until repayment begins. The government pays the interest while you are enrolled in college.

Unsubsidized Loans — Not awarded on the basis of financial need, these loans accrue interest from the day the funds are disbursed.

Variable Interest Rate — The interest rate on variable loans may increase or decrease at set periods based on economic factors. Thus, after you graduate, you could see a significant jump in monthly payback amounts if interest rates rise. Private loans (see above) are likely to have variable interest rates.

Managing your MONEY

Because money becomes so important, you usually need to learn early in your college career to exert some control over your funds. Effective money management can reduce your stress and enable you to benefit from your new educational and social opportunities. Money management will also enhance your development as a competent, independent adult.

While approaches to money management may vary, the bottom line is the ability to balance available funds and anticipated expenses. This challenging task requires awareness and planning.

EXERCISE 1 My Spending Log

Step 1: Beginning today and for the next three days, write down all the money you spend. Include the date, time, amount of money spent, purpose for expense, and nature of payment. The nature of payment may be cash, debit or credit card, check, or some other method. When you cannot immediately record this information, be sure to write it down at the next available opportunity. Use the form provided on the next page and also see the textbook website for more copies. Here is a sample of how your *Spending Log* will look.

Example: My Spending Log

Date and Time	Expense	Purpose	Means of Payment
Tues.,11/5, 10:05 A.M.	$2.14	Coffee with Jen	Cash
Tues.,11/5, 3:20 P.M.	$2.74	Index Cards	Cash
Tues.,11/5, 7:30 P.M.	$18.55	Supermarket	Debit Card
Tues.,11/5, 10:40 P.M.	$4.00	Vending Snack	Cash

My Spending Log

From _____ (today's date) to _____ (three days from today)

Date and Time	Expense	Purpose	Means of Payment

Discuss the challenges of sticking to a budget at *CollegeSuccess.andYOU.com*

Developing and Maintaining a Budget

Using a budget to balance your expenses and income can help you stay financially healthy. According to a Harris survey, 40% of college students report skipping meals because they were low on money. Additionally, 10% of the students said that they had pawned or sold possessions in order to raise money.[5] If these students had developed and maintained a budget, they might have been able to avoid some of these consequences.

A budget is a planning tool. It takes into account your anticipated available funds and your anticipated costs so that you can effectively plan. With the information gained from developing and maintaining a budget, you may decide to limit or increase your spending or to work more or fewer hours so that you can match your income to your financial needs. A budget can be created for a day, a week, a month, a year, or for a specific plan, such as a vacation.

Income

To develop a budget, you must begin by estimating your income. You may have two types of income to help pay your expenses. The first type is **fixed income**, which means it is predictable income. Examples include a set monthly allowance from your family or weekly paychecks from a job. You can consistently count on these sums to assist you in meeting your costs. However, since some fixed income, such as financial aid, may be provided in a lump sum when classes begin, it can become tricky to spread the money throughout several months of a class semester or term. The second type of income is **variable income**, which is less predictable than fixed sources. For example, a relative may send you a check for your birthday or you may earn some spending money by working at a campus event, such as homecoming. You cannot always rely on having this kind of income available.

Expenses

In a successful budget, expenses must be balanced against income. Because not all costs are predictable, it takes a lot of planning to accommodate unexpected expenses in most students' budgets. **Fixed expenses** are those costs that are regular and anticipated. For instance, tuition and housing bills are among the fixed expenses for most college students. **Variable expenses** are costs that are not predictable. When you need to purchase medicine for an unexpected illness, replace your printer cartridge, or go to movies with friends, you are paying for variable expenses. Estimates suggest that the average college student spends $200 to $300 a month for variable expenses.

Going Shopping: Managing your budget allows you to determine if you can afford to go shopping.

Designing a Budget

Directions: Prepare a budget for the month after this one. Use receipts and records from past spending and income to complete the budgetary items. Make your best estimates for variable items or those for which you do not have information. Some commonly included items are listed, but you should add additional costs that apply to you. Do not include cents; instead, round to the nearest dollar.

Step 1: Fill in the blanks below.

Budget Worksheet for the Month of_____, 20__

Estimated Income

Job(s): $_____

Family Support: $_____

Financial Aid: $_____

Other—please specify:

_____: $_____

_____: $_____

_____: $_____

_____: $_____

_____: $_____

              My Total Estimated Income: $_____

Estimated Costs

Cell Phone: $_____

Tuition Bill: $_____

Textbooks: $_____

Credit Card Payments: $_____

Clothes: $_____

Food: $_____

Entertainment: $_____

Transportation: $_____

School Supplies: $_____

Toiletries: $_____

Health Care: $_____

Haircut/Style: $_____

Laundry: $_____

Savings: $_____

Other—please specify:

_____: $_____

_____: $_____

_____: $_____

_____: $_____

_____: $_____

              My Total Estimated Costs: $_____

Step 2: Do the subtraction.

My Total Estimated Income: $ _____

Minus

My Total Expected Costs: $ _____

Resulting Balance: $ _____

Step 3: If you find a **positive balance**, you can anticipate an excess of funds and you can save some for the future or spend more now. On the other hand, a **negative balance** suggests that you will need to reduce your variable spending next month. You can prioritize your fixed costs while deciding which flexible items in your expense budget you can decrease in cost or eliminate.

Step 4: Without having to disclose your personal budgetary circumstances, be prepared to discuss in class your best ideas for balancing a budget.

Cutting Costs

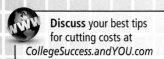

Discuss your best tips for cutting costs at *CollegeSuccess.andYOU.com*

Even if you anticipate a surplus of funds, you may benefit from finding new ways to maximize your money. Here is a list of tips aimed at helping you make the most of the money that you have.

Going Green with Money: Cash Conservation

- Look for local and national college student discount cards. Also, some local businesses may provide a discount just for showing your school ID or offer coupons through your smartphone or computer.

- Purchase or rent used texts at your bookstore or online; however, make sure they are the editions your professor assigns. If you are comfortable with ebooks, or electronic books, you may find the cost less than traditional textbooks.

- Minimize impulse buying. Pause before a purchase of something tempting that will strain your budget. For grocery and toiletry shopping, making a list before you go to the store and then sticking to it may save you from unnecessary purchases.

- Maintaining a car is costly; however, if you need one, many car insurers give "good student discounts" if you are a full-time student and can submit a transcript with As and Bs.

- Look for no-fee checking accounts that require a low minimum balance and offer free ATM withdrawals. Some banks have special student checking accounts that require no minimum balance. Banks sometimes reduce or waive checking account fees if you additionally open a savings account.

- Find a cell phone and texting plan that gives you the best deal for your particular needs. Keep in mind family plans, cell phones without contracts, rollover minutes, and discounts for night and weekend use. If necessary, monitor your usage as your billing period progresses.

- If you earned money and qualify, file for reimbursement of federal income taxes and any state income taxes you paid.

- Find bargains; for example, some students buy used furniture from stores run by charities.

- You may discover bargains for travel by using a student discount card. Also, some airlines offer standby fares for college students or reduced fares for those under the age of twenty-two. In the Northeast and Midwest, some bus companies offer inexpensive, comfortable travel between cities.

- Gambling can cost some students more money than they can afford to lose. Seek help from a campus counseling service if you cannot control your gambling impulses.

- Take advantage of free entertainment on campus. Most colleges offer social events, speakers, movies, and intercollegiate athletics that are free for students. Using your school's gym and health service can also save you money.

- While the campus library is another great free resource, avoid fines for returning books late.

- Avoid costly parking fines if you have a car.

- Consider the costs of smoking. Not only is smoking bad for your health, but cigarettes are also expensive.

- Minimize luxury coffee drinks.

- If possible, avoid extending your undergraduate studies beyond four years.

- Put spare change in a container; it adds up.

- Try to save about 10% of what you earn through part-time and summer employment. If you can accumulate some money, open a savings account at a bank or credit union.

- Some retailers offer a discount to customers who pay cash instead of using a credit card.

- If you are planning for a big expenditure such as a new computer or a trip, regularly set aside enough money in your budget so you eventually have the amount you need.

Becoming knowledgeable about how to pay bills efficiently and at minimum cost to you can be helpful. The methods of payment include checking accounts, debit cards, and credit cards.

Checking Accounts

Managing your own checking account represents a great first step on the road to financial independence; however, not all checking accounts are equal. Factors that can differentiate one account from another include required balances, fees per check, cost of replacement checks, interest paid to you on the balance, and ATM charges. You will want to investigate these factors before opening your checking account.

Checking accounts may be opened at a bank, either in person or online, or at a credit union. **Credit unions** have many of the same services as banks but usually limit their customers to people associated with a certain organization or group. Many colleges are affiliated with a credit union and have branches on campus. Credit unions often charge lower fees and pay higher interest than banks.

For most checking accounts, you will need to deposit at least a minimum amount of money to open the account. You will then receive checks for use in covering your major expenses. Some banks with headquarters or branches near colleges offer special college checking accounts with lower required balances and reduced fees for use. Some of these banks don't even require a minimum deposit. Before selecting a financial institution for a checking account, it is important to read the fine print and ask questions to make sure you understand what the account includes and what it will cost.

A great advantage of paying a bill by check is that a record is generated. That record proves your payment and helps you keep track of your expenses. Most financial institutions provide customers with excellent online registers of their checking account along with the opportunity to pay bills over the Internet. These features can help you maintain your budget and avoid writing checks for more than the current balance in your account. If you **bounce a check**, which means that you exceed your balance, your bank can charge you extra fees.

Debit Cards

Most banks and credit unions provide **debit cards** with their checking accounts. Some of these cards can be used as both debit and credit cards. When used as debit cards, they are similar to checks except their use *immediately* withdraws funds electronically from your checking account. While debit cards can be used to access available funds from an ATM, they can also be used in place of checks to make retail purchases. Even though a debit card may feature a credit card company insignia, use of a debit card is not based on credit but on the funds available in your checking account.

Feed the Piggy: Saving regularly will help you pay for unexpected expenses or special purchases.

A **debit card overdraft** will occur if a payment made with your debit card exceeds the amount of money left in your checking account. When you go over your balance, you will be assessed a fee for each overdraft. The average overdraft fee charged by a bank is thirty-four dollars.[6] Banks refer to this expense as a "courtesy overdraft loan," which certainly sounds better than calling it a fine against your account. That means a twelve dollar pizza would end up costing you forty-six dollars if you exceed your checking account balance. A 2009 study by the Center of Responsible Lending finds that banks had reported earning about $1 billion annually in overdraft fees on debit cards from eighteen- to twenty-four-year-old customers.[7] Fortunately, the Federal Reserve System recognized this cost to consumers and created a new rule in 2010 eliminating the possibility of overdraft fees unless you request the overdraft option through your bank. Without the overdraft option, a payment is declined at the point of purchase if you have insufficient funds in your checking account to cover its cost. The same process applies to ATM withdrawals.

Check It Out: The routing number at the left bottom of your check designates your financial institution, while your specific account number is listed at the center bottom of your check. You will need these numbers for direct deposits to your account and for some phone or online payments.

Here are some other tips about managing debit cards:

- If you are not interested in having a debit card, your bank may be willing to provide you with an ATM card that can only be used for withdrawals from your checking account and not for making purchases.

- In case you opt for the possibility of overdrafts on your account, you can arrange to link a savings account to your checking account at the same bank to automatically shift funds necessary to cover any overdrafts.

- You can ask the bank to notify you by text or email when your checking account balance falls to a designated level so that you can avoid an overdraft.

- To minimize your liability, notify the bank as soon as possible if your debit card is lost or stolen.

Credit Cards

The Credit Card Accountability, Responsibility, and Disclosure Act of 2009 (CARD) includes provisions to protect college students from the dangers of credit card misuse. As a result of this legislation, students under twenty-one cannot acquire credit cards unless they prove that they can independently afford to make the payments or they arrange for a parent or other person over twenty-one to cosign the application. Nevertheless, you probably will want to have a credit card during your college years. Developing a positive credit history through credit card use demonstrates responsibility that will enable you to borrow money at good rates in the future. Favorable rates will help you with important future purchases, such as a car or a residence.

The use of credit cards is very tempting since it seems as if you can use them to buy almost anything you desire without laying out any cash. To a college student, being able to buy things with a credit card and not cash may seem like the magic of Harry Potter's wizardry. However, credit cards can be almost as perilous as the dangers that Harry faced.

The key to handling credit card opportunities involves exerting control. Having a thorough understanding of the way that credit cards work can help protect you from financial harm. The idea is to acquire the information that you need to take control of the process rather than allow the credit card companies to control you. You will need to shop around until you get the best deal. Look for banks that offer credit cards with low credit limits that are specifically designed for college students.

Choosing the right credit card can help you get off to a positive start, in charge of your own destiny. As you will learn from the information that follows, there are many factors to consider when making a credit card selection. To help you understand credit cards, read the following two illustrations of students who handled the use of credit cards with opposite approaches.

Contrasting Credit Card Approaches

Student #1: Matt

Toward the end of his senior year of high school, Matt's parents gave him one of their credit cards with his name on it to use for summer travel and for when he went off to college. Matt cosigned for the card with his parents but didn't bother to learn anything about credit card use.

When college began, Matt's parents directed him to buy books, supplies, and other educational materials with the credit card but to pay for his personal expenses through a part-time job. However, Matt found it so easy to pay for restaurant meals, concerts, clubs, and tickets to professional sports events that he forgot about getting a job. He also began to use his card repeatedly for cash withdrawals to pay for quickly mounting poker debts arising from playing online and in a weekly game with college friends.

During his first few months at college, Matt felt out of control with his spending. As soon as his parents received the credit card statement, they visited him and angrily cut up the credit card, informing him that he would have to pay for his reckless expenditures. Matt felt lost about how he could recover from his debt.

Student #2: Samira

When Samira started her freshman year, she decided that she would wait a month before looking for a part-time job. She planned to limit her trips to restaurants and movies off campus. Instead, she took advantage of the free activities on campus. Samira also decided that when she received her first paycheck, she would accept the offer of her older brother, a successful attorney, to cosign a credit card application for her.

With several available credit card possibilities, Samira found a website that helped her decipher the fine print in the credit card offers. She selected a credit card with no fee, a low interest rate of 9.95%, and a maximum available balance of $500. She understood from her brother that she would be wise to develop a good credit rating by making some small charges and then fully paying them off on time. She planned to keep her low-limit credit card until she graduated and had a decent paying full-time job. She would then apply independently for a card with a higher credit limit.

What do you think about the contrasting approaches to credit card use by Matt and Samira? Are you more similar to Matt or to Samira in how you might handle your credit card use?

Risky Business: You will benefit financially by having fun in ways that cannot bust your budget.

EXERCISE 3 Taking Charge of Credit Cards—What You Don't Know *Can* Hurt You

Step 1: The following multiple-choice items will help you recognize what you need to learn about credit card use. Write the letter for the best answer on the blank line. You aren't expected to be able to answer all of these questions correctly. When you don't know an answer, make your best guess.

_____ **1.** The approximate average credit card debt of college students is _____ at the time of graduation.

  A. $850

  B. $1,550

  C. $2,600

  D. $4,100

_____ **2.** Which statement is most true about a credit card sponsored by your college?

  A. It probably represents the best deal in interest and fees for you.

  B. It will build your credit rating better than any other card.

  C. Because you are a student at that school, you will be protected by your college if you get behind in your payments.

  D. It makes money for your college.

_____ **3.** Credit card companies are eager to provide college students with cards because they

  A. expect students, more than other customers, to have to pay interest and fees.

  B. expect students' families to back them up if they need extra money.

  C. believe that college students are too smart to have problems with their cards.

  D. have found that students are more likely to waste more money on fun activities.

_____ **4.** Which statement is true for students who regularly pay their monthly balance on a credit card cosigned by their parents?

  A. Their parents are violating the Credit Card Accountability, Responsibility, and Disclosure Act of 2009.

  B. Their regular payment will help develop a good credit rating.

  C. Their credit ratings will be hurt if their parents ever make a payment for them.

  D. Their credit ratings will be helped only if they can prove they also have a job.

_____ **5.** Which of these is the ideal number of credit cards for a student to have?

  A. 1

  B. 2

  C. 3

  D. 5

_____ 6. From the time a credit card bill is sent, consumers have at least _____ days to make a full payment before they must pay interest.

   A. 7

   B. 14

   C. 21

   D. 30

_____ 7. Approximately _____% of college students pay off their credit card balances every month.

   A. 17

   B. 27

   C. 37

   D. 47

_____ 8. Which upper limit for a credit card's maximum purchasing power would be most helpful to a college freshman without significant savings or income?

   A. $500

   B. $2,000

   C. $5,000

   D. no limit

_____ 9. Which company is _not_ one of the three major agencies that provide credit ratings?

   A. TransUnion

   B. Equifax

   C. Experian

   D. Pan United

_____ 10. You can order a report of your credit rating once a year from each of the three major agencies that provide credit ratings for a per report cost of _____.

   A. $5

   B. $15

   C. $25

   D. $0

_____ 11. A score from 300 to _____ is usually used to indicate a person's credit rating.

   A. 500

   B. 650

   C. 750

   D. 850

12. A consumer with a low credit rating could be predicted to pay _____ in interest for a new car as compared to a person with a high credit rating.

    A. the same

    B. less

    C. slightly more

    D. significantly more

13. If you have a history of late and irregular payments on credit card debt, and you marry someone with an excellent rating, your credit rating will

    A. move up to the level of your new spouse.

    B. stay the same.

    C. be averaged between your rating and your new spouse's rating.

    D. start fresh, as it also will for your new spouse.

14. If you lose your credit card and notify the issuing company immediately, you will be liable for a _____ maximum of fraudulent charges.

    A. $50

    B. $100

    C. $300

    D. $500

15. Which is *not* a benefit of effective, responsible credit card use by a college student?

    A. It establishes a better credit history for future use.

    B. A credit card is safer to carry around than cash.

    C. It validates your ability to function independently.

    D. It allows you to travel whenever and wherever you want without having to pay up front.

Step 2: Now, check your answers. When you have answered incorrectly, read carefully through the explanation to gain a full understanding of the credit card concepts that you need to strengthen.

Answers and Explanations

1. <u>D.</u> The average student graduates with around $4,100 in credit card debt, which will require significant payment of penalties over time. According to Sallie Mae, a national lender, almost 20% of college graduates have credit card debts of $7,000 or more when they graduate.[8]

2. <u>D.</u> Choosing the right card can be tricky. Your college may promote a specific card with the college logo on it, but choosing that card will probably be profitable for your college but disadvantageous for you. Generally, the best approach is to ignore special offers and use the Internet to research cards that are designed specifically for college students. Through your favorite search engine, search for something like "best credit cards for college students" and begin evaluating the recommended products. Be sure to read sites you know are reliable. In your search, keep in mind that the interest rates and policies are established by the banks and not by the card companies.

3. <u>A.</u> Credit card companies are eager to sign up students because students are unusually likely to have to pay late fees and interest.

4. <u>B.</u> Students authorized by their parents to use cosigned cards will help enhance their own credit rating if they pay their full balances regularly, on time. Conversely, not paying on time can harm their parents' credit ratings as well as their own.

5. <u>A.</u> Since it is difficult for someone inexperienced to manage credit cards, focus on selecting a single card, but one that will meet your needs. If you handle credit properly, you should not need more than one credit card *at a time* while you are in college.

6. <u>C.</u> CARD established a minimum of 21 days for a consumer to make a payment from the time a credit card bill is sent.

7. <u>A.</u> Only about *17%* of college students report successfully paying their credit card debt on time each month.[9]

8. <u>A.</u> Selecting a single credit card with no annual fee, the lowest interest rates you can find, and an upper limit of $500 is recommended.

9. <u>D.</u> How are credit ratings maintained? Three credit bureaus—Equifax, Experian, and TransUnion—track each credit user's payment history and make data available upon request to other companies. For example, if you want to borrow money to buy a car, the car dealer will request your credit rating from one of these credit bureaus.

10. <u>D.</u> You can get a free report about your credit status from each of the three credit bureaus once a year. Watch out for online services that charge for these reports. More information about the free reports is available at www.AnnualCreditReport.com, the website that coordinates this information.

11. <u>D.</u> The credit bureaus often assign a **Fair Isaac Co**rporation (**FICO**) score ranging from 300 to 850. The score is based on your payment history, amount of debt, length of credit history, frequency of credit applications and usage, and current credit obligations.

12. <u>D.</u> A person with a score over 700 is usually considered a good credit risk. In other words, companies are often willing to extend such a person credit. A person with a FICO score of 730 could end up paying $6,500 less in interest costs for a new car than a person with a FICO score of 560.

13. <u>B.</u> Marriage to a person with a good credit rating will not remove a poor credit rating. Paying credit card debt regularly over time can help.

14. <u>A.</u> If your card is lost or stolen, notify the credit card company immediately to cancel that card. You will be sent a replacement card, and you will only be liable for $50 of unauthorized charges.

15. <u>D.</u> If used properly, credit cards can be safer to carry than cash and provide an important resource in an emergency. If you pay your balance on time, you will also develop a better credit rating for the future. A good credit rating is extremely beneficial. It can enable you to get car or home loans and to be eligible to rent an apartment. You also can qualify for lower interest rates when you need loans or credit in the future. In contrast, a poor credit rating can interfere with achieving your goals. For instance, some students have been rejected by medical schools because they are unable to qualify for needed loans.

Step 3: Discuss in class what you learned that is most surprising and important to you about credit card use.

A Few Final Notes about Credit Cards

- When you receive a credit card offer, you must be provided with the following information to consider:

  Annual Percentage Rate (APR)—The APR represents the annual percentage rate you pay on balances when you do not pay an entire monthly bill on time. To find out the interest rate for a monthly balance, simply divide the APR by twelve.

  Default APR—This percentage will be charged to you if you do not pay the minimum due in any month.

  Late Fee—An additional fee will be charged depending on the balance you owe if your payment is late.

  Cash Advance Cost—Although credit cards can be used to obtain cash, the interest rate will be higher than your ordinary interest rate.

  Annual Fee—Annual fees are essentially unnecessary membership fees. Look for a card with *no* annual fee.

  Upper Limits—In case a statement of the upper limit you can charge each month does not appear in the information sent, it should be clearly provided to you before you make your decision. For most students paying their own credit card debts, a maximum of about $500 per month seems appropriate.

- In case you cannot make a full payment, pay more than the minimum due in order to reduce your interest costs.

- The length of time to pay off credit card debt while making minimum payments can be surprising. For example, a person paying $200 each month on a debt of $5,000 with an 18% interest rate will require twelve years and six months to pay off the debt.

- Arrange for your credit card company to send you email or text alerts reminding you before your monthly payment is due and alerting you if you approach your credit limit.

- Collect the receipts for your credit card expenses in a shoe box or large envelope. Each month, when your credit card statement arrives, match each bill on the statement to its corresponding receipt and then shred the receipt. If you find line items on the bill that are not attributable to you, notify the credit card company immediately. Keep records of the date of your communications and the name of the person you consulted.

- Report address changes promptly so that you will not miss bills and pay late fees. You may be able to get a copy of your bill and statement online.

- Be cautious about giving out the numbers for your credit card, student ID, Social Security account, passport, debit card, and driver's license to prevent identity theft. Shred financial documents with identifying information rather than simply tossing them in a wastebasket.

- If you run into trouble with credit card debt, help in managing your payments may be available through a local consumer credit counseling agency. To get referrals, check with your school's Financial Aid Office. Usually, legitimate credit counseling services provide a free initial session to learn about your circumstances.

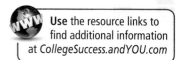
Use the resource links to find additional information at *CollegeSuccess.andYOU.com*

Thinking Critically About . . . Money Matters: Gaining Financial Literacy

Critical thinking involves an active evaluation of information using careful, thoughtful, and reasoned judgments.

1. Why is learning to live within your financial means often a difficult lesson? Discuss instant gratification versus delayed gratification.

2. Categorize the different ways that college students spend money carelessly. What attitude shifts are needed to reduce careless spending?

3. The *Princeton Review* asked 9,955 college applicants, "What will be the biggest benefit of your attending college and earning a college diploma?"[10] Explain why "better job and income" dramatically exceeded the next two choices, "exposure to new ideas" and "education."

4. Discuss the differences between net worth and self-worth.

5. Benjamin Franklin said, "A penny saved is a penny earned." Analyze how this saying relates to college students.

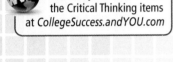
Discuss your ideas about the Critical Thinking items at *CollegeSuccess.andYOU.com*

Online Learning

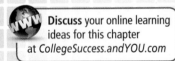
Discuss your online learning ideas for this chapter at *CollegeSuccess.andYOU.com*

The same issues of maximizing financial resources, controlling credit and debit card expenses, and developing and maintaining a budget apply to online students as much as they apply to students in traditional college classes. Since many online students work full-time and have families, money management may be even more essential.

Online students have several means to help them with their financial challenges. For example, they may save money on transportation and child or elder care expenses since they don't need to travel to campus. A necessary expense for online students is the purchase of a dependable, up-to-date computer with high speed internet access. This expense can be softened for students with a 529 college savings plan as they or their parents can withdraw funds tax-free to purchase necessary computer equipment or internet access.

A research study indicates that during a recent economic downturn, the demand for online classes increased significantly.[11] As a result, while more students registered for online classes, many continued to be dramatically affected by economic concerns. In fact, a survey by Educational Dynamics reports that financial challenges are cited as the number one reason that online learners do not complete their degree program.[12] The results show that 41% of the students surveyed give financial challenges as the main reason for quitting their online programs. According to the same study, almost half of the online students who dropped out did not complete even one class, a much different attrition trend than is found for most traditional college classes. Online students may suffer significant financial losses by failing to complete online programs and courses. For example, since many online students borrow to pay for their education, a frequent challenge arises when they must pay back loans soon after leaving college.

CHAPTER CHALLENGE

A WINDFALL

Money management presents all kinds of challenges to new college students. While the most typical challenge certainly involves making limited funds last longer, some freshmen are placed in the seemingly enviable position of suddenly having more money available to them than ever before. This circumstance usually arises when a student receives financial aid for living expenses in addition to core college expenses. Having a lot of spending money available unexpectedly can create temptation to spend it unwisely.

A CASE STUDY: FACING THE CHALLENGE OF . . .
A WINDFALL

With outstanding high school grades and college admissions test scores, Leticia earned a full scholarship to her state's leading public university. Leticia's award completely covered her tuition and fees for her freshman year. After learning of her financial aid in the spring of her senior year of high school, Leticia and her parents decided to have a family conference about how to meet her additional financial needs for the first year of college. Her parents agreed to contribute most of the funding for her room and board, suggesting that Leticia's summer job could pay for the rest. However, they stated that they would be unable to help her with additional spending money. Not knowing at that point if she would have time for a job on campus, Leticia and her family filled out the application for a $5,000 government loan to cover her textbooks, everyday expenses, and a few visits home. The loan was approved with the provision that Leticia would receive a check for $2,500 at the beginning of each semester.

When Leticia received her first check for $2,500, she followed her dad's advice to deposit it immediately in her checking account. Having used $500 of this sum to pay for books, she still had $2,000 in her account. She realized that she could access this money at any time with her debit card.

On the first Saturday after classes began, three girls on Leticia's dorm floor invited her to go to the mall with them. One girl bragged that her dad had given her a credit card and told her she could buy all the clothes and shoes that she wanted. By the end of the shopping day, all the girls had several bags in their hands and big smiles on their faces. They capped the day off with a three-course meal at a seafood restaurant. Upon her return to her room, Leticia began to lose her smile, realizing that she had spent almost $300 in one day.

OVERCOMING THE CHALLENGE OF . . .
A WINDFALL

Be prepared to discuss your answers to the following items: (1) Evaluate the extent to which Leticia's friends probably influenced her spending; (2) Discuss how developing and maintaining a budget can help Leticia avoid overspending; (3) Recommend how Leticia can have fun with her friends at the mall without experiencing a financial hangover.

Key Chapter Strategies

- Take a practical introductory class in economics or finance during your college years.

- Check your college website to find out what free services you receive from your school.

- Get to know a financial aid specialist if you need aid from the school.

- Carefully monitor deadlines for financial aid through your daily planner.

- Develop and maintain a budget.

- Manage your checking account online.

- Avoid costly overdraft charges on your debit card by keeping track of your checking account balance and not opting for overdraft privileges.

- When you qualify, look for a credit card with no annual fee, a low interest rate, and a low maximum for charges.

- If you experience a financial disaster, immediately seek help from your family, an appropriate campus resource, or a community agency.

- Read these books for more information about money matters: *The Money Book for the Young, Fabulous, and Broke* by Suze Orman[13] and *1000 Best Smart Money Secrets for Students* by Debby Fowles.[14]

Can You Recall It?

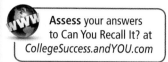

Directions: To review your understanding of the chapter, choose the correct term from the list below and fill it in on the blank. You will not use every term.

APR	overdraft fee	credit union
FAFSA	CARD	variable expense
fixed income	FICO	frugality
debit card	grant	good student discount

1. A cost that does not occur every month is known as a/an _____ when managing a monthly budget.

2. Each person using credit is assigned a/an _____ score by a rating agency to reflect dependability and promptness in paying back debt.

3. A/an _____ usually is provided with a checking account for use in paying for goods and services as well as for obtaining cash.

4. Car insurance companies often provide a/an _____ to students with grades of A and B.

5. The annual interest that must be paid on both loans and credit card debt is called the _____.

6. A/an _____ is a financial aid award that the student does not have to pay back.

7. _____ is the 2009 legislation that includes protection of college students from the dangers of credit card misuse.

8. A/an _____ is a financial agency that may offer better deals than banks.

Directions: Reading popular financial magazines and newspapers is a very useful method of learning more about money matters. Many of the most popular financial periodicals present much of their content free on the Internet. These publications include the *Wall Street Journal, Money, Forbes, Bloomberg Businessweek, Worth, Fortune, Kiplinger's,* and *Young Money* (an online magazine designed for college students and young adults). Look at the content in one or more of these financial publications online and select an article that interests you. Read this article and then answer the following questions about it.

1. What is the title of the article you selected and the name of the newspaper or magazine in which it is published? _____

   _____

   _____

2. Identify the exact address for the website of this article. _____

   _____

   _____

3. Write a summary of this article (see Chapter 5 for information about summaries), including its key points. _____

   _____

   _____

   _____

   _____

   _____

   _____

4. Briefly explain how the content of this article is relevant to you. _____

   _____

   _____

   _____

   _____

   _____

   _____

Achieving Your Goals through Money Matters: Gaining Financial Literacy

This chapter provides you with information and tools to help you learn how to gain control over your finances. As you progress through college and beyond, you can apply what you learned to improve your economic circumstances. In the first paragraph, describe your dreams for your financial situation in ten years. In the next paragraph, explain the steps you will have to take to turn these dreams into achievable goals. Then, in one sentence, state your best advice to yourself for achieving your financial goals.

First paragraph:

_____

_____

_____

_____

_____

_____

_____

Second paragraph:

_____

_____

_____

_____

_____

_____

_____

One sentence:

_____

_____

_____

9

Keeping Healthy and Safe

In this chapter, you will move toward achieving your goals by

- examining how to promote your health and well-being.

- mastering the best practices to stay safe on and off campus.

Find additional tools and resources at *CollegeSuccess.andYOU.com*

Self-Assessment:
Health Court

Imagine that you are in a courtroom on the witness stand. Instead of being in a regular courtroom that is concerned with legal cases, you are in "Health Court" where the judge will rule on how you are taking care of yourself. The judge asks you to testify about each health and safety item below as it applies to you. Just as in a real court of law, you must give truthful testimony. Imagine the judge asking you each question; then circle "Yes" or "I Need Improvement," providing your honest testimony.

Judge's Questions	My Testimony
1. Did you get eight hours of sleep last night?	Yes I Need Improvement
2. Do you exercise at least thirty minutes four times or more a week?	Yes I Need Improvement
3. Do you regularly eat three nutritious meals a day?	Yes I Need Improvement
4. Do you have no more than two alcoholic beverages on a day when you are drinking?	Yes I Need Improvement
5. Do you abstain from sex or always take precautions against sexually transmitted diseases when engaging in sexual activity?	Yes I Need Improvement
6. Do you have a clear understanding of birth control techniques?	Yes I Need Improvement
7. Do you weigh no more or less than ten pounds of the recommended weight for your sex and height?	Yes I Need Improvement
8. Do you avoid taking prescription pills or drugs that are *not* recommended or prescribed by your own doctor?	Yes I Need Improvement
9. Do you avoid feeling overly stressed?	Yes I Need Improvement
10. Do you have no more than two caffeine drinks in a day?	Yes I Need Improvement
11. Have you quit smoking or never smoked?	Yes I Need Improvement
12. Have you had a full physical examination by a physician in the past year?	Yes I Need Improvement

Judge's Questions	My Testimony	
13. Are you responsible in managing your health care needs?	Yes	I Need Improvement
14. Do you remember to keep your door locked where you live?	Yes	I Need Improvement
15. Do you try to avoid walking alone after dark in unsafe areas?	Yes	I Need Improvement
16. Have you had all the recommended inoculations?	Yes	I Need Improvement
17. Has a dentist examined you within the last six months?	Yes	I Need Improvement

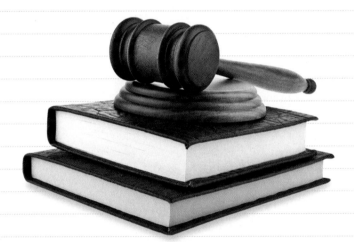

The Judge's Decision: *"Congratulations on those items for which you testified 'Yes.' Continuing to take good care of yourself in these ways will pay off during college and in the future. However, I am asking you to go on six months' probation for the items to which you testified 'I Need Improvement.' During the six months, try to implement changes that will improve your health and safety. This chapter will help you with some of the information you need to begin to improve your health and safety. If you need additional information, consult with your professor or a health professional on campus or in the community. Good luck on your journey to stay healthy and safe."*

Taking good care of your health and safety during your college years offers many rewards. First and foremost, keeping healthy and safe is its own reward. But did you know that taking care of yourself can help you in other ways as well? Taking care of your well-being will smooth your progress along the academic path to success, causing few interruptions for illness or recovery. It also empowers you to become a confident adult who makes healthy choices. The sections that follow provide you with information and tips to improve your sleep, nutrition, fitness, substance awareness, sexual safety, general health care, stress management, and safety on and off campus.

Promoting HEALTH and WELL-BEING

Different students will certainly achieve physical well-being in different ways. For example, one student may perform on a dance team that requires fitness, agility, and daily practice. Another student may simply eat well, take regular vigorous walks, and get sufficient sleep. Both of these students have found their own paths to physical health and well-being.

The Power of Sleep

An important factor in your health is sufficient sleep since sleep fuels your body and mind. When you sleep, both your body and mind rest to restore energy for the next day's activities.

College students report sleeping an average of six to seven hours per night. Generally, students tend to try to catch up on the weekend after sleeping fewer hours during the week. Seven hours per night is less than the recommended healthy level of eight to nine hours per night. Failure to sleep enough can make people tired and cranky the next day. For students, however, a significant effect of insufficient sleep is the loss of concentration for classes, studying, and taking tests. Researchers from Harvard Medical School and the University of Pennsylvania report that getting enough sleep helps memory.[1] Their findings suggest that all-night cram sessions are counterproductive for you.

Sleeping Beauties: Have you ever observed a dog or a cat sleeping? The peacefulness is inspirational. You can achieve this calmness, too.

Getting enough sleep in your first year of college may require some adjustments. Students often share space with a roommate who may snore, play loud music, or keep very different hours. Early morning classes can conflict with staying up as late as most students prefer. According to a survey of students at Stanford University, the average time for going to bed is 2:31 A.M.[2] Some students experience difficulty in switching to this college norm from their previous lives under family supervision when "lights out" was typically much earlier. For students who do fall into this pattern, serious lack of sleep usually results.

The good news is that the solution to most of these sleep challenges is under your control. You can use earplugs for unwanted noises and a sleep mask for unwanted light. You can also hold a mature discussion with your roommates or housemates about making compromises related to each of your sleep preferences. Generally, keeping a consistent sleep schedule during the week will help. You may also develop a relaxing nighttime ritual, such as reading for pleasure or writing in a journal, before simply turning out the lights when you are ready to fall asleep.

Catching Some Zzzzzs: A Key to Smooth Sleep

According to a 2009 survey, over 60% of a sample of 1,125 college students are not as lucky as the peacefully sleeping dog and cat above.[3] These students are rated as poor quality sleepers according to the Pittsburgh Sleep Quality Index. Many of the sampled students also report frequently using sleep medications, a very risky step. If you find yourself tossing and turning, fluffing the pillow, arranging and rearranging the sheet and blanket, and repeatedly checking the clock while trying unsuccessfully to fall asleep or get back to sleep, a simple procedure called the Cognitive Control Sleep Method might work for you.

The **Cognitive Control Sleep Method** uses **cognition**, or thinking, to allow you to manage your restlessness and negative thoughts so that you can fall asleep. The key to this method is staying in the bed while allowing yourself to consciously relax. Sleep specialists have found significant benefits to your mind and body from merely resting all night in bed and not necessarily sleeping at all.[4] With this knowledge, it will be easier for you to relax since you won't stress about getting enough sleep if you're not falling asleep right away. As it turns out, according to the experts, it is relaxing your mind and body in bed—not just sleeping—that is important. The cognitive method involves creating positive mental images and maintaining a positive attitude as you are trying to fall asleep. You relax in bed, allowing yourself to think only of calm, soothing images with self-talk that focuses on optimism, gratitude, and contentment. If catastrophic thoughts such as "This is horrible! I'm not getting enough sleep! I'll fail my test tomorrow!" begin to invade your mind, you can shut them down by returning to the peaceful images and positive words that you find encouraging and inspiring. But the key is to think positively as you relax in the bed, telling yourself that you are gaining rest just from lying down with your eyes closed. As you continue to use the Cognitive Control Sleep Method, you will probably discover the next morning that eventually you fell asleep.

But what if you *don't* fall asleep? Dr. Peter Hauri of Dartmouth College used the Cognitive Method in his sleep lab to help a young woman who couldn't sleep. He states in Goldberg and Kaufman's *Natural Sleep*, "When she came to me she was desperate. I taught her [relaxation] and told her that it didn't make any difference if she slept or just lay there and rested. I emphasized that it's beneficial enough to just lie there quietly. Her . . . insomnia vanished."[5] People who stay in bed all night without falling asleep can be surprisingly well rested the next day. In contrast, people having trouble sleeping who decide to read or watch TV are *not* as well rested the next day since reading or watching TV uses brain cell activities that do not necessarily produce a rested mind. You can legitimately say to yourself that lying in bed and following the Cognitive Control Sleep Method will allow you to be rested enough to meet the challenges of the next day even if you don't sleep at all during the night. There is no need to worry if you just close your eyes, relax, and follow the recommendations above.

Tale of a Sleepy Ruler

"I recall when I was still in my teens reading about a great potentate [ruler], reputedly the richest man in the world, who promised he would give away half his riches to the first person who would offer him a cure for his insomnia. I went to bed that night determined to think of a formula that would help the great man and enrich me. Unfortunately, I fell right off to sleep. (Had I been an insomniac, I might have been the world's second richest man.)

"In succeeding years, I read no headlines announcing the cure. Probably the lucky fellow stumbled upon some simple cure that didn't cost him a dime. . . . Most likely of all, he learned 'not to care' whether he slept or not."

Peter Steincrohn, MD, *How to Get a Good Night's Sleep*[6]

Sleep Interference

Certain substances act as stimulants and can interfere with sleep. The most notable is caffeine, so avoiding beverages with caffeine in the evening may help you fall asleep. Another stimulant you may want to refrain from using at bedtime is nicotine, which can be found in cigarettes and smokeless tobacco. Drinking alcohol in the evening can also interfere with normal sleep stages. On the other hand, a chemical found in milk may help promote your sleep.

If you experience chronic sleep problems, consider seeking a medical evaluation. A common medical cause of sleep problems involves breathing-related disorders, which a physician can identify and for which treatment is available.

Food for Thought

Food, the counterpart to sleep as a source of energy, also presents challenges to a college student. Before college, mealtime and food selections may have been arranged for you. In college, you will be more in control of when and what you eat.

While your diet at college will have important health implications, making the right choices can be difficult. Do you consider your health when selecting food or choose just what looks appealing? And when you are eating or drinking in social situations, do you simply conform to what your friends are having, or do you act with your own best interest in mind? Possessing essential knowledge about nutrition can help you make healthier choices.

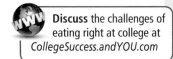

Discuss the challenges of eating right at college at *CollegeSuccess.andYOU.com*

Nutrition Facts

- Eating three regular meals a day, including breakfast, is beneficial. You can seek out a balanced variety of foods in order to obtain the vitamins and minerals you need. More information about the different major food groups is available at *http://www.ChooseMyPlate.gov.*

- Snacks can be useful for providing energy between meals. Fruit and vegetables are examples of healthy snacks to have during the day. Drinking water is also healthful, and water doesn't add calories.

- If you indulge in junk food, you may want to do so only occasionally and then really enjoy it as a special treat.

- At mealtime, a guideline is to stop eating when you are full. Learning to properly manage the size of the portions you eat is helpful.

- Complex carbohydrates are good sources of mental alertness and sustained energy as well as fiber, which helps regulate your body. Foods high in complex carbohydrates include fruits, vegetables, and starches. In contrast, simple carbohydrates (such as sugary snacks) are less healthful.

- Adding high-calorie dressing to a salad or adding butter, sour cream, and bacon to a potato converts an otherwise healthy food into one that is not.

- Calcium is important in bone and muscle development for both men and women. Adequate levels of calcium can prevent **osteoporosis**, a loss of bone density that can lead to fractures and a stooping posture later in life. Consuming dairy foods (such as low fat milk, yogurt, and cheese) three times a day can provide sufficient calcium intake.

- Fat is acceptable as a small part (20% or less) of a daily diet, but consuming too much fat is unhealthy. It can contribute to high cholesterol, eventually causing heart problems. A high-fat meal can also make you feel sleepy during class and studying. Foods with a great deal of fat content include pizza, ice cream, pie, and nuts. You can eat these foods, but only in moderation.

Menu of Options: Selecting nutritious foods gives you energy and promotes your health.

- Too much salt can contribute to high blood pressure. If high blood pressure runs in your family, you might want to study the sodium content of the foods you eat and limit the amount of salt you use in cooking and seasoning.

- Many students drink too many soft drinks. Soft drinks have virtually no dietary benefit and do not take the place of nutritional drinks, such as water, milk, and fruit juices. Note that energy drinks are often laden with caffeine and empty calories.

- Many students are concerned about the legendary "freshman fifteen" weight gain. The **body mass index** has become a popular guideline to determine if you are underweight, normal, or overweight. You can calculate your body mass index at the Centers for Disease Control and Prevention's website, http://www.cdc.gov/healthyweight/assessing/bmi/adult_bmi/english_bmi_calculator/bmi_calculator.html.

- Eating regularly and avoiding long periods without nourishment can help you stay calm. Having a light, healthy snack before an exam or performance can reduce your feelings of nervousness.

EXERCISE 1 Menu Choices: Creating Your Food Diary

Step 1: Keeping a daily food diary is helpful for maintaining a healthy diet. Use this form to keep a food diary of all the food and beverages that you will consume tomorrow. Make a sequential list in the first column of the form for every item that you will eat and drink. In the second column, write the time of day that you consume the item. The third and fourth columns are more subjective. In the third column, write "above average," "average," or "below average" for the portion size of each item that you consume. In making this judgment, compare the amount to what you believe the average college student of your sex and body size would consume. For the fourth column, apply the term "healthy," "neutral," or "unhealthy" to describe the nutritional quality of the food or drink that you consume.

Food Diary for _____ (date)

Food or Beverage	Time	Portion Size (above average, average, or below average)	Nutritional Value (healthy, neutral, or unhealthy)

Food or Beverage	Time	Portion Size (above average, average, or below average)	Nutritional Value (healthy, neutral, or unhealthy)

Step 2: Answer the following questions.

1. What are your reactions to the *Food Diary* results?

   _____

   _____

   _____

2. List three ways you can improve your diet in the future.

   _____

   _____

   _____

Step 3: Discuss in class the food and beverage temptations that are present on a daily basis in a college student's life. What actions can be taken to resist these temptations?

Working Out for Health

Experts agree that regular exercise is the one activity most likely to promote your physical health. They point to studies consistently demonstrating that physical fitness can be helpful in preventing a wide range of problems varying from depression to cancer. Luckily, it is relatively easy to engage in an exercise program with or without fancy gym equipment. To start your own exercise plan, you can ask yourself what your goals are. Are you trying to reduce stress? Is muscular development or weight loss your primary goal? Are you aiming for an all-around healthy lifestyle? You can then develop a realistic, enjoyable program of exercise to meet your needs.

Fitness on Campus

Many campuses feature well-equipped fitness centers with cardio equipment, free weights, machine weights, and playing courts. You probably can arrange for a personalized fitness program through a consultation with one of the staff professionals at your fitness center.

"Wellness Center" is the most popular name for campus fitness centers. The term *wellness* refers to a health philosophy that is holistic because it integrates aspects of both the mind and the body into your choices for health. In addition to physical factors, it takes into account social, spiritual, emotional, and intellectual dimensions, as shown in this Wellness Model.

Here is a table with examples of activities that can help strengthen each of the five dimensions. Your campus may sponsor many beneficial programs centered on these five dimensions of the Wellness Model.

Dimension	Examples of Activities
Physical Dimension	Managing sleep, nutrition, exercise, substance use/abuse, sexuality, health care, stress, and personal safety
Social Dimension	Achieving affection, friendship, and communication
Spiritual Dimension	Engaging in meditation, connectedness, and reflection
Emotional Dimension	Fostering resilience, self-esteem, and optimism
Intellectual Dimension	Developing memory, reading with curiosity, and thinking critically

Usually a fitness program will consist of two exercise forms, aerobic exercise and anaerobic exercise. **Aerobic** exercises—such as walking, running, skiing, inline skating, swimming, bicycling, or aerobic dancing—involve breathing faster and getting your heart to beat faster than normal. These exercises are helpful for **cardiovascular health**, or heart health, as well as stress management. **Anaerobic exercises**, which are not intended to increase respiration or heartbeat, include weight training to enhance your strength and stretching to support your flexibility. Anaerobic exercise can reduce the likelihood of back problems, which are known to bother many college students. Combining aerobic and anaerobic exercises about three or four times a week can result in many physical and emotional health benefits.

The Intersection of Exercise and Diet

Calories are units of measure for energy needed by the body to function. Foods are a source of calories and therefore a fuel for the body. Each food has a caloric value. For example, a medium banana has about 105 calories, and a cup of vanilla soft ice cream has about 377 calories. Experts often cite 2,000 to 2,800 calories as the average recommended daily intake for an active adult.[7]

Every human activity expends a certain number of calories. For example, in a half hour, driving a car consumes 60 calories while playing tennis consumes about 210. Since the relationship of caloric intake and expended calories is a factor in a person's weight and energy level, it can be helpful to have some understanding of caloric values.

EXERCISE 2 **Calorie Counter: For the Health of It**

Assess your answers to Exercise 2 at *CollegeSuccess.andYOU.com*

Step 1: In this exercise, you will estimate the number of calories in a specific well-known food and the number of calories consumed by a common activity. Write your estimate on the line to the right of the food or activity. Your estimates are guesses, and you are not expected to know the exact answer.

Food — **Calorie Estimate**

Orange juice (one cup): _____

Toast and butter (one slice): _____

Scrambled eggs (two): _____

Apple (medium): _____

Regular soft drink (twelve ounces): _____

Hamburger (six ounces): _____

Potato chips (fifteen): _____

Tomato (medium): _____

Pepperoni pizza (one slice): _____

Apple pie (one slice): _____

Activity (approximate burning of calories per half hour)	Calorie Estimate
Volleyball:	_____
Walking two miles:	_____
Sleeping:	_____
Dancing fast:	_____
Racquetball:	_____
Sitting and studying:	_____
Running hard:	_____
Shooting baskets:	_____
Cleaning your room:	_____
Standing:	_____

Step 2: Answer the following questions:

1. What is your opinion of your own calorie consumption through eating and drinking?_____

   _____

   _____

   _____

   _____

2. What is your opinion of your own calorie expenditure through your regular activities? _____

   _____

   _____

   _____

Step 3: After your professor has given the correct answers to Step 1 in class for the numbers of calories, you may want to revise your answers in Step 2 above. Be prepared to discuss in class how students can improve the balance between calorie intake and energy expended.

A Question of Substance

At some colleges, students may be exposed to a variety of mind-altering substances. This situation is sometimes not new, just an extension of high school but with more freedom from family supervision. As a college student, you want to be sure that you are making intelligent decisions about what you consume. Information about the effects of different substances can be useful in helping you make these decisions.

Nicotine

Nicotine is the active chemical ingredient in cigarettes and other tobacco products. It is a stimulant drug that increases blood pressure and heart rate. Even though smoking cigarettes is banned inside most campus buildings, it continues to be a regular habit among some students. Why do these students smoke despite their awareness of such highly publicized long-term negative health consequences as lung cancer and heart disease? The answer lies in the addictive power of nicotine. Very unpleasant symptoms such as irritability and nervousness will occur when nicotine levels drop in a habitual smoker. These withdrawal symptoms are relieved when the smoker inhales nicotine from another cigarette.

Quitting cigarettes is difficult, so smoking becomes a long-term habit for some college students. If you are an addicted smoker who wants to stop, you can find an intervention program on your campus or in your community. Other alternatives are going "cold turkey" or using nicotine substitutes, such as gum, sprays, lozenges, or patches; but you may want to consult a physician before trying one of these alternatives. As a first step to quitting, explore the opportunities for assistance by searching the web pages of your college or consulting a campus health provider.

Alcohol

The consumption of alcohol goes back at least as far as 1700 B.C. in ancient Babylonia. Although alcohol is a drug, it can be consumed safely by most people when used in moderation. Having one glass of wine or one beer is a perfect example of the appropriate use of alcohol for those who are of legal drinking age.

Experts have established a safe upper limit for alcohol use during one drinking occasion. This standard, known as **Anstie's law**, states that most people can safely drink a maximum of one and a half ounces of absolute (pure) alcohol without suffering negative consequences.[8] That is equivalent to two and a half standard twelve-ounce cans of beer. This amount is the *maximum* for anyone to drink on one occasion, although your personal maximum may be less, depending on your body size. And, no, you can't save one day's allowance and add it to the next day. Of course, there are some people who cannot safely consume any alcohol because of health conditions or proneness to addiction.

As a college student, you will need to make your own decision about alcohol use within the bounds of the law and your school's rules and regulations. Recent studies show that college students tend to overestimate how much other students actually drink.[9] For that reason, as well as because of peer pressure, you may feel inclined to drink more than you want. At many schools, **binge drinking** (four or more drinks at a time), which is not safe, has become a common part of the culture.

Tobacco-Free: If you want to stop smoking, help should be available on campus or in your community.

A Student View of Binge Drinking

"Why drink so much that you won't really experience all the fun that you're having? Also, you don't want to spoil your best memories. By the next day, you won't even remember where you were or even who you were with."

Lauren
University of Tennessee

Heavy consumption of alcohol can have negative consequences for both the short and long term. For college students, short-term effects include hangovers, blackouts, victimization by sexual assault, and driving accidents. Excessive alcohol can also be fatal if alcohol poisoning occurs. If friends show signs of **alcohol poisoning**—vomiting, unresponsiveness, confusion, breathing irregularity, or skin discoloration—they need medical attention immediately. Brain and liver damage are among the most dangerous of the many long-term health effects of chronic excessive drinking. Alcohol addiction also can result from consistent heavy use.

It is important to be aware of the legal age for drinking in the state where you attend college. The use of fake IDs has become a federal crime potentially punishable by a fine or jail term.

EXERCISE 3 Self-Assessment of Alcohol Use

Step 1: For the items below, circle the number next to the response that applies most accurately to you.

Alcohol Use Disorders Identification Test (AUDIT)

Developed and given permission to copy by the World Health Organization.

1. How often do you have a drink containing alcohol?

0	=	Never
1	=	Monthly or less
2	=	Two to four times a month
3	=	Two to three times a week
4	=	Four or more times a week

2. How many drinks containing alcohol do you have on a typical day when you are drinking?

1	=	One or two
2	=	Three or four
3	=	Five or six
4	=	Seven to nine
5	=	Ten or more

3. How often do you have six or more drinks on one occasion?

0	=	Never
1	=	Less than monthly
2	=	Monthly
3	=	Weekly
4	=	Daily or almost daily

4. How often during the last year have you found that you were unable to stop drinking once you had started?

0	=	Never
1	=	Less than monthly
2	=	Monthly
3	=	Weekly
4	=	Daily or almost daily

5. How often during the last year have you failed to do what was normally expected from you because of drinking?

0	=	Never
1	=	Less than monthly
2	=	Monthly
3	=	Weekly
4	=	Daily or almost daily

6. How often during the last year have you needed a first drink in the morning to get going after a heavy drinking session?

0	=	Never
1	=	Less than monthly
2	=	Monthly
3	=	Weekly
4	=	Daily or almost daily

7. How often during the last year have you had a feeling of guilt or remorse after drinking?

0	=	Never
1	=	Less than monthly
2	=	Monthly
3	=	Weekly
4	=	Daily or almost daily

8. How often during the last year have you been unable to remember the night before because you had been drinking?

0	=	Never
1	=	Less than monthly
2	=	Monthly
3	=	Weekly
4	=	Daily or almost daily

9. Have you or someone else been injured as the result of your drinking?

0	=	Never
2	=	Yes, but not in the last year
4	=	Yes, during the last year

10. Has a relative, friend, or health professional been concerned about your drinking or suggested you cut down?

0	=	No
2	=	Yes, but not in the last year
4	=	Yes, during last year

Step 2: Now determine your score. All you have to do is add up the numbers you circled for each response. Scores *above* 8 suggest an alcohol problem and merit a visit to a health professional to learn how to reduce your alcohol consumption.

Step 3: Discuss in class the effects of peer pressure to drink. What recommendations can you and your classmates offer to help cope with the pressure to drink?

Other Drugs

Alcohol's effects are increased significantly and possibly dangerously if combined with other drugs. Over the years, some college students have experimented with mind-altering substances besides alcohol.

The current variety of substances most popular with students includes street drugs as well as prescription medications. Unauthorized possession of any of these substances is illegal. Also, regular use of most of these substances can result in drug dependence and addiction. People who use unsanitary needles to administer substances may risk HIV/AIDS or hepatitis infections. Finally, it is impossible to know what chemicals are really being consumed in drugs that are illegally manufactured.

Many people who abuse alcohol and other substances tend to be in denial about the consequences. Therefore, to seek and follow through with help, students who abuse drugs usually must experience very negative consequences, receive great pressure from concerned family or friends, or have unusual insight and courage. For students who have substance abuse problems, help is available. Some campuses have Drug and Alcohol Education and Referral Offices, while many communities have Alcoholics Anonymous and Narcotics Anonymous chapters. Additional information to help you or someone you know with a substance abuse problem is listed on the website for this textbook.

The following chart lists popular recreational drugs along with examples of their common street names, typical methods of administration, effects on academic performance, and negative physical or psychological effects.

Major Abused Drugs

Street Drugs	Street Names	Methods of Administration	Academic Effects	Risks
Club drugs: ecstasy, ketamine, Rohypnol, GHB	X, special K, roofies	Pills; GHB and Rohypnol slipped in drinks	Loss of concentration and memory; anxiety	Dizziness; loss of coordination; coma; death
Cocaine*	Coke, rock, crack	Snorted, injected, smoked, inhaled	Distraction from studies; lack of appetite and sleep	Severe depression; paranoia; convulsions; nasal problems
Hallucinogens: LSD, psilocybin, PCP	Acid, magic mushrooms, shrooms, angel dust	Eaten, snorted, injected	Distortion of thoughts and sensations; loss of abilities	"Badtrips"; flashbacks; reality loss; permanent psychological damage
Methamphetamines*	Speed, meth, crystal meth, crank, ice	Injected, smoked, snorted, pills	Agitation; anxiety; panic; problems with sleep, concentration, remembering	Reality loss; fast heart rate; strokes; death
Marijuana	Pot, weed	Usually smoked; also mixed in tea or food	Loss of memory, motivation, concentration, and problem-solving skills	Panic; respiratory illness; lung cancer; driving accidents
Heroin*	Smack, horse, H	Injected, smoked, snorted	Slow thinking; distraction from goals; indifference	Hepatitis and HIV/AIDS; nausea; coma; death

Prescription Drugs	Street Names	Methods of Administration	Academic Effects	Risks
Steroids: Dianabol, androstenedione, Deca Durabolin	D-bol, andro, deca, roids	Injected	Restlessness; weakness; fatigue	Cancer; fractures; infertility; rage reactions; testicular shrinkage; hair loss
Amphetamines: Dexedrine, Adderall, Ritalin	Speed, uppers, Dex	Pills, snorted	Problems with sleep and appetite; nervousness; depression	Irritability; irregular heartbeat; high blood pressure; seizures
Opiate painkillers:* Oxycontin, Percocet, Percodan, Vicodin	Oxy, OC, Percs, Vikes	Pills, snorted, chewed, injected	Fatigue; weakness; sleepiness; panic	Headaches; respiratory problems; coma; death

*Especially addictive.

Q&As: About Sex

As you hear stories about wild college parties, you may believe that all of your fellow students frequently engage in promiscuous sex. This is not true. Nevertheless, since college students typically experience a combination of new personal freedom, drinking, and maturing bodies, student sexual involvement is not uncommon. In this environment, you have the right to decide how you want to handle your own sexuality. Accepting responsibility for your decisions can help you feel in control during your college years.

Here are some answers to frequently asked questions about sex to help you with your decisions:

Question: How does getting drunk affect sex?

Answer: When students were surveyed, they admitted that they would have preferred to skip 70% of the sex they had while they were drunk. One in five students said they abandoned safe sex practices while they were drunk.[10]

Question: What is the probability of pregnancy if no birth control is used during sexual intercourse?

Answer: For healthy women of college age, about one in five will become pregnant without contraception during the first month of frequent intercourse. Of course, a woman can become pregnant after only one sexual encounter, so protection is always necessary.

Question: What is the "morning-after pill?"

Answer: **Plan B**, known as the morning-after pill, is a form of emergency contraception for use following unprotected sex. This pill is sold over-the-counter at many pharmacies. A prescription is not needed for women seventeen or over. Plan B works most effectively immediately following intercourse, but it will not work for women who are already pregnant. If you would consider using Plan B, you might want to discuss this drug with a health professional, since it has possible side effects.

Question: Is masturbation a normal sexual practice?

Answer: Masturbation is a common form of sexual self-satisfaction that is not harmful. According to a survey of first-year students at California State University at Chico, 46% of women and 94% of men masturbate. Additionally, 88% of the same sample of women and 95% of the sample of men state they have a "strong" or "somewhat strong" sex drive.[11] Some students may have moral objections to the practice, but there is no health concern.

Primary Care: Establishing care with a specific medical professional on campus or in your community pays off both when you are ill and when you need a checkup.

Question: Do I need a regular medical checkup related to my reproductive health?

Answer: It is a very good idea to make this a part of an annual physical exam. Physicians recommend that college men be evaluated for testicular tumors. Women are advised by the American Cancer Society to regularly have a breast evaluation starting at age twenty. Also, according to the Centers for Disease Control and Prevention, a first **Pap smear**, which is a screening that detects some forms of genital infection and cancer, is recommended for women at the age of twenty-one.[12] To perform a Pap smear, the clinician takes a relatively painless scraping from the cervix. The checkup also can present an opportunity to ask questions regarding any sexual concerns.

Question: What is a sexually transmitted infection (STI) or sexually transmitted disease (STD)?

Answer: A **sexually transmitted infection/disease (STI/STD)** is an infection that is spread through vaginal, anal, or oral sexual contact. There are several commonly diagnosed types of STIs/STDs, with the most widespread on college campuses being chlamydia, human papillomavirus (HPV or genital warts), and genital herpes. The types of STIs/STDs vary in symptoms and treatment possibilities. The most dangerous STI/STD is human immunodeficiency virus (HIV) infection. It has been estimated that 25% of college students in the United States have at least one STI/STD.[13] To learn more detailed information about specific STIs/STDs, go online and also visit the office of a health professional. If you think you may have an STI/STD, get a medical screening as soon as possible.

Question: How can I prevent an STI/STD?

Answer: Abstinence is the surest measure. After abstinence, having a condom available when you want it and then using it is one of the best STI/STD preventative measures you can take. This is one reason why both males and females are urged to carry condoms with them if they anticipate engaging in sexual intercourse. Condoms are supplied free on many college campuses. According to a study by the Kaiser Family Foundation, 42% of college males admitted wanting to use a condom when they did not have one available.[14]

Question: How can I find out if I have an STI/STD?

Answer: Since some STIs/STDs do not result in obvious symptoms, this is a good question. You can get tested at a campus Health Service, public clinic, or by a private health professional. Briefly explain your concern to the nurse or doctor, who will know what kind of screening to perform.

Question: How do I know if a sexual partner has an STI/STD?

Answer: It is hard to know whether your partner has an STI/STD without testing. This is a reason to wait for sex until you are in a committed relationship. You and your partner could go together for testing and then share your results with each other. Even if you are uncomfortable going for testing together, waiting for a committed relationship may make it easier to ask your partner about whether he or she is STI/STD-free. Sexual activity with a stranger is obviously risky.

Question: Is there a vaccine to prevent an STI/STD?

Answer: Human papillomavirus (HPV) is one of the most frequent types of STIs/STDs diagnosed on college campuses. It can lead to genital warts and mouth and throat cancers among both men and women and is the leading cause of cervical cancer in women. An HPV vaccine is available to help females under age twenty-seven and males under age twenty-two reduce the risk of human papillomavirus infection and cervical cancer. A vaccine is also available to prevent **hepatitis B**, a liver disease that can be transmitted through sexual contact.

Question: Why is there an abstinence movement among some students?

Answer: Students favoring abstinence usually believe in saving their sexual involvement until they are married. Abstinence is also the only sure way to protect against pregnancy and STIs/STDs. Also, some students believe in waiting to engage in sexual activity until marriage on religious or ethical grounds.

Health Management

You will undoubtedly perform best in college and enjoy your experience most if you stay healthy. Some recommendations to help you take care of yourself are discussed below.

Health Kit and Health Care

Some basic health care items are useful for you to have available in your residence, including a thermometer, a first aid kit, skin ointment, sunscreen, and over-the-counter medications for pain, stomach discomfort, and colds. You will also want to have available any prescribed medicines and medical equipment that are necessary for your well-being. You may also be advised by your physician to take regular vitamins or nutritional supplements.

Health Kit: Having a health kit available is important when you need to use it.

Caution about Tylenol

Acetaminophen is the chemical name for Tylenol, a popular over-the-counter painkiller. Accidental overdose with this drug is the leading cause of liver failure in the United States. The safest daily upper limit is four thousand milligrams or eight five-hundred-milligram extra strength capsules in a twenty-four-hour period. The upper limit for Tylenol use for students who drink alcohol—another drug that can affect liver functioning—is significantly lower. Some of the accidental overdoses result from Tylenol users being unaware that acetaminophen is found in many other medications that they may use along with Tylenol. These include prescription painkillers, cold remedies, arthritis medicines, and other over-the-counter painkillers such as Excedrin and generic acetaminophen.

The warning label on containers of acetaminophen says the following: "This product contains acetaminophen. Severe liver damage may occur if you take:
- more than 8 caplets in 24 hours, which is the maximum daily amount.
- with other drugs containing acetaminophen.
- 3 or more alcoholic drinks every day while using this product."

Liver failure caused by an overdose of acetaminophen can necessitate a liver transplant and may even cause death. Because of this risk, you might check with your health provider or a pharmacist about alternative over-the-counter painkillers *without* the same potential to induce liver failure. If you do choose to use acetaminophen, it is very important to keep track of your dosage and your alcohol intake. In the event that you or a friend experience unusual symptoms after taking acetaminophen, you may want to play it safe and go to a nearby emergency room.

Managing your health care includes paying attention to common illnesses found in a student population. A survey sponsored by campus health services shows that colds/flu/sore throat and sinus infection/ear infection/bronchitis/strep throat are the two categories of medical problems that students identify as frequently interfering with their academic performance.[15] The close contact that students have with each other helps spread these illnesses, and the old rule of washing hands regularly may help you avoid some of these common health problems. If you do develop symptoms of these illnesses, a health professional can provide diagnosis and treatment to minimize their impact.

Your health care needs also include keeping up-to-date with vaccinations. You have probably had mandatory vaccinations throughout your life. However, two vaccines (aside from the HPV and hepatitis B vaccines) to consider that are usually *not* required by colleges but that can prevent potential infections are the vaccines for bacterial meningitis and for the flu. **Bacterial meningitis** is an infection that affects the brain and spinal cord and is spread by close contact with an infected person. Students also sometimes overlook the flu vaccine, which can prevent a disruptive and uncomfortable illness. Flu vaccines are often available on campuses, usually from October to December. You can check with your health care professional about the value of these vaccinations for you.

Health Insurance

More and more colleges require students either to purchase the school's health insurance or to prove that they are otherwise covered. With health costs so high, some kind of group insurance plan is highly desirable.

Dealing with the complexity of health insurance is another difficult rite of passage into adulthood. Therefore, it is important for you to understand your insurance coverage. For example, many policies include **deductibles**, which are required annual payments for treatment before insurance begins paying for your costs. Policies also vary greatly for insurance coverage of prescription medicines. Evaluate the insurance package for these elements as well as the coverage for specialized care, emergency treatment, routine physical exams, and vaccinations. It is a good idea to carry your insurance card with you at all times, just in case you need it for those unexpected mishaps.

EXERCISE 4 **Establishing Your Health Care Portfolio**

Step 1: Managing your own health care requires you to have information and courses of action ready to meet your needs as they occur. You will establish your *Health Care Portfolio* of information by answering the questions that follow. For some of the questions, you will need to make decisions, and sometimes you might need to check local directories or the Internet to get the answers for these questions. After you complete your portfolio, you may want to include this information in your cell phone.

Health Care Portfolio

Who is your current primary health care provider?

Name _____

Address _____

Phone _____

Which emergency room is the closest to where you currently reside?

Name _____

Address _____

Phone _____

What is the name of your health insurance company?

Name _____

Phone _____

Insurance ID# _____

Which local pharmacy do you use or plan to use?

Name _____

Address _____

Phone _____

Identify a local dentist in case you need an appointment.

Name _____

Address _____

Phone _____

Identify a local optometrist in case you need eye treatment.

Name _____

Address _____

Phone _____

Step 2: In class, discuss the benefits of keeping an up-to-date *Health Care Portfolio*.

Stress and Health

With the dramatic life changes and heavy demands that new college students face, significant levels of stress are almost inevitable. According to a survey by the Associated Press and mtvU, a college television network, grades and financial problems are the two greatest sources of stress for students.[16] Gaining control over stress is very important since stress can influence your susceptibility to a variety of health problems ranging from colds to heart disease.

Several physical mechanisms account for the impact of stress on health. Of most importance, stress can compromise the immune system, increasing the likelihood that people exposed to viruses and bacteria will develop a contagious illness. Stress also increases blood sugar, causes muscles to tense, and speeds up the heart.

Does Stress Contribute to Acne?

Many college students suffer from acne; they wonder why they don't have clear faces. Among the factors contributing to acne are high hormone levels, oily cosmetics, hair products, genetics, and menstruation. Not only can stress increase hormone levels, but it also can stimulate oil glands, resulting in clogged pores leading to flare-ups of acne. The good news for acne sufferers is that implementing the stress management tips may reduce acne.

Here is a list of constructive strategies to help you manage stress and protect your health.

The Dozen "Do's" to Manage Stress

1. Sleep about eight hours a night.
2. Engage in regular moderate aerobic exercise. Walking can also reduce stress.
3. Maintain social relationships for friendship and communication.
4. Meditate and reflect.
5. Seek out humor, including opportunities for "belly laughter."
6. Effectively manage your time (see Chapter 3).
7. Use progressive muscular relaxation when you feel tense. You can learn more about the procedures for this technique and observe demonstrations online. (See the textbook website for more information.)
8. Arrange to have fun at least once a week to break up the routine of study and hard work.
9. Take regular (but not *too* long) study breaks to do what you find relaxing, such as listening to music, watching TV, chatting on the computer or cell phone, or playing video games.
10. Practice good nutritional habits, minimizing caffeine and sugary foods.
11. Maintain a positive attitude by visualizing success, staying optimistic, refraining from "sweating the small stuff," and seeking solutions to problems quickly rather than stewing about them or becoming angry.
12. Keep naturally centered without using mind-altering substances.

Discuss your favorite ways to manage stress at *CollegeSuccess.andYOU.com*

If you want to assess your current level of stress, you can complete the "How Vulnerable Are You to Stress?" scale on the website for this textbook.

SAFE-KEEPING

Another component of your physical well-being is your personal safety. Just because you are on a college campus doesn't mean you are completely safe. Your campus may seem like a bubble, free from the real world, and in many ways it is. However, you still want to remain alert. Campus safety administrators realize the potential for harm and try to prevent it. For instance, many colleges have implemented systems for texting students in emergencies and setting up video surveillance around campus. Signing up for the text alerts shows that you are taking responsibility for your safety. You can also take care of yourself through a better understanding of safety risks and what to do to minimize them.

Protecting Your Property and Yourself

The **Jeanne Clery Act** is named for a Lehigh University student who was murdered on campus in 1968.[17] This law requires any college participating in a federal financial aid program to publish annual statistics concerning crimes committed on its campus. Each college also must provide information about campus security policies and procedures. You can read the most recent report on your college's website to learn about the type and extent of criminal events occurring on your campus.

Protecting Your Property

The most common type of crime on college campuses is theft. Statistics from North Carolina State University show that its students were 1.7 times as likely to be victimized by theft as the general community.[18] Objects most commonly stolen from college students include textbooks, backpacks, iPods, cell phones, laptops, tablets, wallets, bicycles, cars, and video games. It may be a good idea to purchase insurance so that you can be reimbursed if a costly theft occurs. Here are some steps Campus Police Departments recommend to help safeguard your property:

- Buy and consistently use a high quality lock for a bicycle. Cables wrapped in wire mesh and U-locks reportedly are effective. Lock your laptop to your desk with a steel cord if possible when it is in your room.
- Engrave identification numbers into valuable personal property. Many campus police offices provide engraving services at no cost.
- Maintain an inventory of your electronic equipment. Be sure to write down their serial numbers. Also, take and store photos of your property.
- If you have a car, keep it locked at all times with no important personal possessions visible. If you leave items in your car, place them in the trunk or cover them.
- Put your name on textbooks in a visible spot such as across the outer edges of the pages. This will discourage a thief from taking your books.
- Keep close track of your purse, wallet, and credit and debit cards at all times.
- Avoid unnecessarily showing off or bragging about your possessions.
- Never leave your property unattended. For instance, use a locker if you are in a gym and keep your backpack or bag with you in the library or a lab.
- Keep the door to your residence locked.

Keeping Track: Carefully monitor your personal items at all times to avoid losing them.

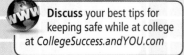

Discuss your best tips for keeping safe while at college at *CollegeSuccess.andYOU.com*

Protecting Yourself

Being alert and cautious both on campus and in the community will help you stay protected. You should identify dark and isolated locations on campus so that you can avoid them. You might also want to become aware of community neighborhoods with reputations as being especially unsafe. At night, it is usually best to stay on well-lit paths and streets while accompanied by at least one other person. Listening to music on earbuds may prevent you from realizing that someone is following you. If you sense you are being followed, you can walk (or run) toward more crowded areas and buildings. You can also locate blue-light phones, used on many campuses for direct contact with the police.

Many campus Public Safety Departments provide night escort services upon request. They recommend that if you drive to campus, park in a well-lit location and have your key ready to open the door as you near your car. Campus safety officials also suggest that you stay alert and aware of your environment. Texting may distract you if you are alone; however, while walking by yourself, speaking or pretending to speak on a cell phone may ward off an intruder.

You do not deserve to feel threatened by other people. Strangers acting suspiciously may make you uncomfortable, and you have the right to act upon that feeling. For example, if you live on campus and a suspicious stranger gains access to your dorm, you can notify the authorities. Alternatively, someone who belongs on campus, such as another student, may begin harassing you. While you may decide to avoid this kind of bothersome person, you can make an official complaint if the person does not stop.

Cell Phone Guard: Staying alert to your surroundings while appearing to talk on a cell phone may ward off an intruder when you are out alone.

A Frightening Lesson

Shannon, a student at a state university, had one evening class. To stay safe, she walked to and from class with her roommate. They also regularly sat next to each other in the classroom. One evening, after class, a male student who sat near them caught up with both of them outside the classroom and began discussing the class. He proposed that the three of them get together to study for an upcoming exam. Shannon politely declined. As the women walked back to their dorm, they both agreed that the guy was really creepy and frightened them. They decided to sit far away from him in the next class. However, Shannon began receiving harassing phone calls from him. She became so scared that she reported the situation to the dean of students. The dean met with the man and ordered him to keep away from Shannon and her friend. He did. Ten years later, Shannon was astounded to read that this man had been arrested for committing a series of rapes.

Preventing Sexual Assault

Carla is a student volunteer with her school's sexual violence prevention team. She participates in programs to help victims of sexual assault and to teach students how to prevent sexual assault. Here is her advice:

"I feel so sad when I hear about a girl who woke up in some guy's bed but doesn't know how she got there. It's usually a freshman girl who doesn't know better. She's usually so ashamed she can't stop crying. When you go out on or off campus, you need to always stick with at least one friend; never go alone in a room with a strange guy. You need to limit yourself to one or two beers so you can think straight. And never take a drink except from a bottle or can you open yourself. Someone could have tried to slip you a date rape drug. If you are alone with a guy, say 'No' if you want to stop. If he goes on, it's rape. I also recommend that you take a self-defense class, just in case."

Male students accused of sexual assault can have their lives damaged, too. When the female's intentions are ambiguous, and he continues, he may be charged with a disciplinary violation or even a crime. Sometimes, it may not seem fair. In one well-known case at Brown University, a male student and a female student who had both been drinking heavily had sex. Subsequently, she regretted her behavior and made a formal complaint, leading to his suspension from school for taking advantage of an impaired person, a violation of the school's code of conduct.[19]

Stalking

Stalking involves the obsessive pursuit of another person. It is estimated that 13% of college women have been stalked, and that 80% of those women knew the stalker.[20] College men also may be victims of stalking. The stalker is often a former or potential romantic partner who has been rejected. Many states have laws against stalking. It is important to document communications from a stalker so that you can provide a log for the police, if necessary. You can report any damage to you or your property if you think it was caused by a stalker.

Social networking channels, such as Facebook, email, Twitter, and texting, have facilitated stalking. Personal information and photos sent via these sites can attract stalkers. Additionally, students who divulge information about their addresses, phone numbers, or plans for the day are giving unnecessary information to a stalker or a thief. It is best to assume that anything you place on your pages will be permanently available to strangers. You may want to check the privacy controls of any site you use to find out if you can make your pages more secure.

Use the resource links to find additional information at *CollegeSuccess.andYOU.com*

Thinking Critically About . . .
Keeping Healthy and Safe

Critical thinking involves an active evaluation of information using careful, thoughtful, and reasoned judgments.

1. Compare and contrast addiction to substances (alcohol, nicotine, drugs) with nonsubstance addictions (compulsions to shop, play video games, gamble, and use the Internet). In your response, express and defend your opinions on the following two questions: Is one type of addiction "better" or "worse" than the other? Is one type of addiction more personally harmful than the other?

Discuss your ideas about the Critical Thinking items at *CollegeSuccess.andYOU.com*

2. Emma discovers that she contracted an STI/STD during the summer before college. Soon after classes begin, she develops a close relationship with a sophomore guy. He wants to have sex, but she isn't sure about revealing her infection to him. Advise Emma on whether she should reveal her STI/STD and provide a reasoned argument for your opinion.

3. Discuss the reasons sex crimes on campus are underreported by students.

4. Argue for or against the following proposition: "College students are responsible for intervening when their close friends engage in very risky behavior."

5. Discuss "ownership" and responsibility for health and safety on campus. Citing specific examples, distinguish between personal versus institutional responsibilities.

Online Learning

Discuss your online learning ideas for this chapter at *CollegeSuccess.andYOU.com*

Although online learners must strive to apply the same health and safety practices as anyone else, some issues are specific to online students. You probably already know about having a comfortable chair that provides adequate back support when you sit in front of the computer. Since you are likely to spend long periods of time sitting, your sitting posture is important. It can be helpful to (1) place your feet flat on the floor, (2) have a ninety-degree angle for your knees, (3) rest your back against the chair, (4) have a ninety-degree angle for your elbows, and (5) rest your wrists in a neutral position. If you do sit for extended periods, you may need to stop working regularly (about every thirty minutes) for some simple stretching exercises. Stretching your fingers, arms, neck, and shoulders to prevent fatigue can help keep your circulation going and facilitate better focus on your work. You might also want to take a brisk walk or get some other form of aerobic exercise.

With such heavy reliance on digital communication, online students may be particularly susceptible to identity theft. **Identity theft** occurs when someone steals key pieces of another person's identity for malicious purposes. Online students can minimize the likelihood of identity theft by avoiding careless online use of their addresses, phone numbers, Social Security numbers, credit card numbers, bank account numbers, student ID numbers, driver's license numbers, and other similar personal identification data. You can learn more about identity theft at the U.S. Department of Education's *Identity Theft* web page:

http://www2.ed.gov/about/offices/list/oig/misused/idtheft.html.

There is a wealth of free information online to help you stay fit and safe. For example, the University of North Carolina at Charlotte created "411 Fit" which can be accessed at https://www.411fit.com/411fit/public/solutions-individual-overview.cfm?, and includes helpful information about nutrition and exercise. See the textbook website for other useful health and safety internet resources.

CHAPTER CHALLENGE

A BURNING QUESTION

The life of a college student has been likened to living in a cocoon, always protected from threat. While a college campus may serve as an intellectual sanctuary, recent tragedies including mass killings and fatal fires, have dispelled the notion that campuses are risk-free environments. Every college must publish crime statistics, and those statistics verify that dangerous incidents do occur on campus. At most schools, from orientation onward, students are regularly reminded to prevent risk by remaining cautious and vigilant. Students are also informed how to proceed if they are aware of a likely danger or if a threat to their campus is actually occurring.

A CASE STUDY: FACING THE CHALLENGE OF . . . WHAT TO DO ABOUT A BURNING QUESTION

Jessica and Ashley were thrilled with almost every aspect of the first few months of their freshman year. As roommates in an eighth-floor, first-year dorm room, they were very compatible and spent most of their free time hanging out together.

The roommates had been appropriately informed about campus safety issues. Jessica and Ashley had attended an orientation session about protecting property, walking around campus safely at night, and avoiding sexual assault. Their residence hall assistant also held a meeting reviewing the dorm's rules for crime and fire prevention. Both sets of parents had warned their daughters to stay safe and expressed concern about their welfare.

As they were walking together back to their room from the elevator one evening after dinner, they thought they smelled smoke. Almost immediately, a girl they didn't know came stumbling out of her room, where they got a glimpse of several candles burning. Ashley remarked to the girl, "You know, you're not supposed to be lighting candles here; it's dangerous because it could cause a fire." The girl mumbled that she was paying attention and not to worry. When they passed the room during the next evening, again they smelled smoke.

OVERCOMING THE CHALLENGE OF . . . A BURNING QUESTION

Be prepared to discuss your answers to the following items: (1) If Ashley and Jessica are concerned about the threat of a fire from the candles, what alternatives do they have for dealing with the situation? (2) Recommend what, if anything, Ashley and Jessica should do. (3) Explain what factors should be considered in their decision.

Key Chapter Strategies

■ Establish a sleep schedule that allows you to maximize your classroom and study abilities.

■ If you have sleep troubles, try the Cognitive Control Sleep Method.

■ Choose nutritious foods and beverages for your snacks and meals.

■ Develop and follow a realistic, regular exercise program.

■ Remember the dangers of drug use and smoking and that help is available if you want to stop.

■ Moderate your alcohol consumption—keep in mind Anstie's law of no more than two alcoholic beverages when you drink.

■ If you are sexually active, be sure you use protection.

■ Have a first aid kit available in your room.

■ Keep your Health Care Portfolio information up-to-date and accessible so you are ready to meet your health care needs.

■ Stay alert to your surroundings and take steps to keep safe.

■ Read this book for more information: *The "Go Ask Alice" Book of Answers: A Guide to Good Physical, Sexual, and Emotional Health* by Columbia University's Health Education Program.[21]

Can You Recall It?

Assess your answers to Can You Recall It? at *CollegeSuccess.andYOU.com*

Directions: To review your understanding of the chapter, choose the correct term from the list below and fill it in on the blank. You will not use every term.

The Jeanne Clery Act	emotional	Oxycontin
nicotine	aerobic	STI/STD
cognitive	osteoporosis	hepatitis B
acetaminophen	calorie	Anstie's law

1. A helpful sleep control technique uses _____ control to help manage restlessness and negative thoughts so you can go to sleep.

2. _____ gives an upper recommended maximum for alcohol use.

3. The chemical name for Tylenol is_____ .

4. Walking, running, skiing, inline skating, swimming, and bicycling are forms of _____ exercise, a type of fitness activity that involves breathing faster and getting your heart to beat faster.

5. A/An _____ is a unit of measure for energy needed by the body to function.

6. Chlamydia is an example of a/an _____ .

7. Both bacterial meningitis and _____ are dangerous infections that can be prevented by having vaccinations.

8. _____ requires most colleges to maintain campus crime statistics.

Web Activity: Go Ask Alice!

Directions: *Go Ask Alice!* is a website originally developed by Columbia University for its students. According to the site, "*Go Ask Alice!* receives over 1,100 inquiries weekly from college and high school students, parents, teachers, professionals, older adults, and others, on every conceivable health topic." Visit the website, which is at http://www.goaskalice.columbia.edu. In the Search Alice! box, choose one of the following four topics: "colds," "sunburn," "allergies," or "back pain." Read some of the questions and answers for the topic you selected. In the space below, identify your topic. Then, write a paragraph explaining at least three useful ideas you learned from the information you read.

My topic: _____

_____

What I learned: _____

_____

_____

_____

_____

_____

_____

_____

_____

_____

_____

_____

_____

_____

_____

_____

_____

Reflection Time

Achieving Your Goals by Keeping Healthy and Safe

Write three paragraphs, one paragraph for each of the following items: (1) Summarize what you do to take care of your health. (2) Summarize what you do to take care of your safety. (3) Discuss three improvements in self-care you would like to make and explain how you can accomplish them.

_____

_____

_____

_____

_____

_____

_____

_____

_____

_____

_____

_____

_____

_____

_____

_____

_____

_____

_____

_____

_____

Adjusting Emotionally

10

In this chapter, you will move toward achieving your goals by

- identifying your personal strengths.

- employing positive strategies to overcome obstacles.

- acquiring information about available support services.

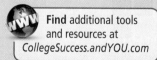

Find additional tools and resources at *CollegeSuccess.andYOU.com*

251

Self-Assessment:
Dimensions of Personal Strength

Step 1: In this "Self-Assessment" activity, you will discover what you believe are your unique personal strengths. Below you will find six sets of adjectives that can describe a person. Check the "Yes" or "No" box to the left of each adjective to indicate if that word can be used to describe you. Please respond to every adjective as honestly as you can.

Dimension 1 Adjectives

Yes	No	
☐	☐	Adaptable
☐	☐	Calm
☐	☐	Effective
☐	☐	Logical
☐	☐	Patient
☐	☐	Practical

Dimension 2 Adjectives

Yes	No	
☐	☐	Kind
☐	☐	Likable
☐	☐	Respectful
☐	☐	Pleasant
☐	☐	Popular
☐	☐	Thoughtful

Dimension 3 Adjectives

Yes	No	
☐	☐	Charitable
☐	☐	Honest
☐	☐	Modest
☐	☐	Sincere
☐	☐	Spiritual
☐	☐	Trustworthy

Dimension 4 Adjectives

Yes	No	
☐	☐	Active
☐	☐	Full of life
☐	☐	Enthusiastic
☐	☐	Intense
☐	☐	Lively
☐	☐	Industrious

Dimension 5 Adjectives

Yes	No	
☐	☐	Capable
☐	☐	Efficient
☐	☐	Creative
☐	☐	Intelligent
☐	☐	Talented
☐	☐	Versatile

Dimension 6 Adjectives

Yes	No	
☐	☐	Charming
☐	☐	Confident
☐	☐	Courageous
☐	☐	Appealing
☐	☐	Inspirational
☐	☐	Fascinating

Step 2: Next, in the box below, record the number of "Yes" responses for each of the six sets of adjectives. Circle the dimensions for which you have a score between four and six. Any *Dimension Score* that is between four and six represents a personal strength for you. The interpretation for each dimension you circled suggests that you view yourself as having the qualities measured by that set of adjectives.

Dimensions of Personal Strength

Dimension 1 Score: _____
Judgment

You see yourself as very successful in solving problems. You take time to evaluate a situation thoroughly before acting, and you stay calm and use reasoning to figure out how to proceed.

Dimension 2 Score: _____
Friendliness

You believe that others view you very favorably. You come across as sensitive and helpful so that others can count on you. You usually maintain a positive attitude.

Dimension 3 Score: _____
Morality

You try to live by high standards. You take pride in being ethical when dealing with others and rely on a deep philosophical meaning to guide your behavior. You have special concerns for less-fortunate members of society.

Dimension 4 Score: _____
Energy

You feel full of zest and display a high level of interest in your activities. You seem to have a battery that is always fully charged.

Dimension 5 Score: _____
Competence

You believe in your own skills. You have the ability to perform well in a variety of activities, and you have likely experienced past successes. You expect more achievements.

Dimension 6 Score: _____
Charisma

You have positive qualities that you believe attract other people to you. You realize that you are admired by others and have the potential to influence them.

Your college experience will help you develop both intellectually and emotionally. Your knowledge will be enhanced through participation in thought-provoking classes and through deep conversations with your friends. This intellectual knowledge, both broad and specialized, can help you become a contributing member of society. Additionally, your emotional development will be enriched by the interactions you have with a diversity of people and by the continued strengthening of your self-confidence.

Along your journey through college, you are likely to encounter some bumps. Academic demands always challenge your motivation and ability. And, of course, there are plenty of other sources of stress—including loneliness, money management, and career decisions. What behaviors can help you emerge successfully through this challenging period? Following are the most powerful behaviors for helping you level those bumps.

Discuss the items on the Action List for Emotional Adjustment at *CollegeSuccess.andYOU.com*

Action List for Emotional Adjustment

- Solve problems quickly and effectively.
- Develop relationships with at least one or two people your age in whom you can confide.
- Work toward harmony with members of your family.
- Maneuver toward financial independence.
- Feel like the worthwhile person that you are.
- Take care of your body and mind.
- Maintain a high level of motivation toward achieving your goals.
- Figure out your path for dealing with sexuality and romance.
- Come to terms with your strengths and limitations.
- Keep yourself from becoming too discouraged when things don't go your way.

The emerging field of positive psychology promotes a constructive framework for personal development. It highlights qualities similar to those you discovered in "Dimensions of Personal Strength" from the "Self-Assessment" activity. This framework offers many ideas for personal success and satisfaction.

POSITIVE PSYCHOLOGY

As the name suggests, positive psychology emphasizes a constructive approach to life. The **theory of positive psychology** states that focusing on personal strengths while maintaining an optimistic outlook will promote happiness.[1]

Positive people, therefore, will look at the glass to the right as "half full" instead of "half empty." They achieve their goals through a variety of constructive experiences that can include helping others.

If you accept the positive psychology viewpoint, you don't ignore the possibility that things will sometimes go wrong. While you learn from your mistakes, you rely on your capacity for **resilience**, or bouncing back quickly, from a frustration or a mistake. Instead of nonstop worry, self-criticism, or self-pity—which usually won't improve a situation—you engage in productive action that will help. You use your positive strengths to solve problems as they arise.

You don't have to be a superhero to have special strengths, according to Martin Seligman, the psychologist who founded the positive psychology movement. Seligman points to **signature strengths**, which are unique attributes for each individual.[2] The defined dimensions for the "Self-Assessment" activity are examples of signature strengths, which you can use to find fulfillment in life. For example, a computer science major with signature strengths of "friendliness" and "morality" might volunteer to teach computer skills to the elderly.

Half Full or Half Empty: Thinking of the glass as half full promotes a more positive outlook.

An Example of Positive Psychology in Action

William Wang, the head of Vizio, a major U.S. manufacturer of flat-panel TVs, exemplifies the positive psychology outlook. In 2000, Wang survived the crash of a commercial jet in which 83 passengers died. When asked how that crash affected him, he stated, "I am a very optimistic person. Optimism got me through my hard times. I think of everything as half full. The event was pretty crazy. I wish I could have stayed longer to help more people. It happened at the time where I hit the bottom of my career also. But actually, the crash gave me more courage—more than anything else. My dreams didn't die. In fact, they were renewed. I always had a lot of guts. After that, I had a little more."[3]

Positive psychology classes are taught at a number of colleges. As part of those classes, students learn about specific changes in their behavior that are likely to promote happiness and self-esteem. Below you will find several behavior changes that can help you become a more positive person. Two sample action plans to implement each strategy are also included.

Ten Core Strategies for Becoming a More Positive Person

Strategy 1: *Increase your happiness by doing little things for yourself.*

Action Plan A—Download a tune you want to add to your collection.
Action Plan B—Buy yourself a little gift that will make you smile.

Strategy 2: *Express your gratitude to someone.*

Action Plan A—Visit the person and express your appreciation directly.
Action Plan B—Write a letter or an email expressing your appreciation.

Strategy 3: *Savor an experience.*

Action Plan A—Slowly eat one of your favorite foods and focus on your enjoyment of every bite.
Action Plan B—Go outside and concentrate on the beauty of nature. Take time to appreciate the beauty of the world around you.

Strategy 4: *Demonstrate your resilience.*

Action Plan A—React to a frustration with a constructive solution.
Action Plan B—Overcome a mistake that you made by deciding how to prevent the mistake or how to respond correctly if the same situation arises again.

Strategy 5: *Plan a fun activity.*

Action Plan A—Imagine doing something fun that you haven't done in a while and make it happen.
Action Plan B—Arrange to have dinner with a friend at your favorite local restaurant.

Strategy 6: *Perform a kindness.*

Action Plan A—Do something particularly helpful for another person.
Action Plan B—Give a compliment to someone who could really benefit from the support.

Strategy 7: *Get away from it all.*

Action Plan A—Visit a place in or near your community or campus that interests you but that you have never visited before.
Action Plan B—Engage in an activity that is not regularly part of your life but which really excites you and takes your mind off your daily challenges.

Strategy 8: *Consider the good that you did.*

Action Plan A—Before going to bed, write a journal or blog entry describing each of your best accomplishments during the day.
Action Plan B—Make a list of your most significant good deeds during the last week.

Strategy 9: *Initiate a social interaction.*

Action Plan A—When you are standing in line or sitting in a class before it begins, start a conversation with a person nearby.
Action Plan B—Visit a neighbor or phone a relative or friend you have not contacted recently.

Strategy 10: *Apologize or forgive.*

Action Plan A—Say that you are sorry to someone you might have hurt.
Action Plan B—Tell a person who said or did something negative toward you that you forgive him or her.

EXERCISE 1 Positive Pursuit

Step 1: Select two of the previous "Ten Core Strategies for Becoming a More Positive Person." Then execute an action plan to accomplish each of the two selected strategic goals. In the space below, identify each strategy you selected and write out the specific method you used for accomplishing your goal.

1. First selected strategy: _____

_____

Action plan: _____

_____

_____

_____

_____

_____

2. Second selected strategy: _____

_____

Action plan: _____

_____

_____

_____

_____

_____

Step 2: Be prepared to discuss in class why it is desirable to become a more positive person.

Emotional Intelligence

Emotional intelligence (**EI**) is an ability that complements your general intelligence.[4] It involves being able to understand yourself, control your emotions, use your emotions for effective problem solving, react with sensitivity to other people, maintain your motivation, and overcome conflict and frustration.[5] Students with high levels of emotional intelligence are often seen as mature and as having the potential for leadership.

Using your emotional intelligence will help you achieve two of the major goals of positive psychology; happiness and satisfaction. Since you have succeeded in gaining admission to college, you probably already have a good foundation of emotional intelligence. Developing your emotional intelligence even further during college can enable you to achieve higher levels of personal and career satisfaction. In the table on the next page, there are some of the characteristics found in college students who display high levels of emotional intelligence.

Characteristics of College Students
with High Levels of Emotional Intelligence

Emotional Intelligence Characteristics	Definition
Empathy	Ability and willingness to recognize and show understanding for the feelings other people are communicating and experiencing
Delay of gratification	Readiness to resist temptations that will interfere with important personal values and goals
Self-awareness	Accurate recognition of your own emotions
Effective relationship management	Skill in negotiation and compromise to overcome disagreements
Self-motivation	Implementation of plans for attaining goals
Respect for others	Acceptance of students and others, including those with different backgrounds and values
Self-control	Capacity for accomplishing tasks without feeling overwhelmed while being flexible enough to adapt to change
Confidence	Belief in the ability to succeed
Emotional regulation	Ability to moderate emotions and express feelings effectively
Acceptance of structure	Working effectively within the framework of college, including the authority of the faculty and administration
Judgment	Ability to make sound, rational decisions not affected by emotion

EXERCISE 2 **Your College EI**

Step 1: Read the following eight scenarios. Each scenario presents a problem that is followed by a potential solution for the problem. Rate each potential solution on the scale ranging from "No Way" to "Definitely" to indicate the likelihood that you would adopt the potential solution as your own.

Scenario 1: You have been emailing a person you have never met. This "friend" claims to live about five hundred miles from your campus. Recently, the "friend" has been expressing a romantic interest in you. Out of the blue, a communication from the "friend" indicates a plan to visit you during the coming weekend and a request for a meeting at the local bus station.

Potential Solution: You respond that you will be there to make your relationship develop further.

No Way   Maybe   Probably   Definitely

Scenario 2: It's early in the semester in a writing class. When your teacher returns your first assignment, you get a much lower grade than you expected along with some highly critical comments. You wonder if the other students were "zinged" as badly as you, but you have another class immediately following the writing class.

Potential Solution: You decide to skip the next class in order to talk to some of the other students in the writing class.

No Way   Maybe   Probably   Definitely

Scenario 3: Your professor assigns a group project that you must complete with three other students designated by the professor. You want to get a high grade on this project; however, you notice in your first meeting with the group that the other members are less serious and motivated than you are.

Potential Solution: You decide to take a leadership role and suggest different tasks and deadlines to each member of the group. You also plan to send reminders to each of them before the next meeting.

No Way   Maybe   Probably   Definitely

Scenario 4: You applied for financial aid on time, but you have not heard any news from the Financial Aid Office. Since you know that other students have heard about their awards, you go in person to the office. You meet with a financial aid advisor, but this advisor cannot locate your paperwork.

Potential Solution: You become enraged, tell the advisor that she is incompetent, and threaten to complain to the college president.

No Way   Maybe   Probably   Definitely

Scenario 5: You are having lunch with several students, including an international student. During a conversation about world politics, this student takes a position that you regard as extreme and unacceptable.

Potential Solution: In a non confrontational way, you ask the student to explain the basis for this extreme position.

No Way   Maybe   Probably   Definitely

Scenario 6: The employer at your part-time job informs you of a major event next week. Even though the employer is usually flexible about your schedule, she says that it will be very important for you to show up for your hours during that period. However, you realize that you have a very busy academic and social schedule and had intended to ask for two particularly busy days off that week.

Potential Solution: As your two busy days approach, you decide to notify your employer that you are sick and will miss those two days of work.

No Way   Maybe   Probably   Definitely

Scenario 7: You learn from several friends that another friend is heavily using drugs to the point of danger, with no insight or willingness to get help. When all of you get together that evening, you verify their concern as your friend is slurring words, acting strange and disoriented, and refusing to eat. Your friend passes out during the evening, and your other friends find a combination of illegal and dangerous drugs in his possession.

Potential Solution: Since your friend's survival is at stake, you convince your other friends to drive him to an emergency room so that he can begin to get help.

No Way   Maybe   Probably   Definitely

Scenario 8: As class ends, you immediately go to the professor's desk to ask a question. The professor exits the room quickly after your conversation. Upon returning to your seat, you notice that the student sitting in front of you walked off without her textbook. She left it sitting under her chair. You do not know this student, and her name is not in the textbook.

Potential Solution: You assume that she will be very upset about losing her textbook. Therefore, you plan to contact other students, and if necessary the professor, to identify the girl so that you can inform her that you have her book.

No Way   Maybe   Probably   Definitely

Step 2: Circle your score for each scenario.

	No Way	Maybe	Probably	Definitely
Scenario 1:	4	3	2	1
Scenario 2:	4	3	2	1
Scenario 3:	1	2	3	4
Scenario 4:	4	3	2	1
Scenario 5:	1	2	3	4
Scenario 6:	4	3	2	1
Scenario 7:	1	2	3	4
Scenario 8:	1	2	3	4

Step 3: Add up your circled numbers to obtain your *Raw Score*. The Raw Score is _____.

Step 4: Interpret the meaning of your *College EI Score* as follows:

24–32 = Above-average college EI

16–23 = Average college EI

8–15 = Can improve college EI

Step 5: Be prepared to discuss in class what students can do to enhance their EI.

College ADJUSTMENT CHALLENGES

A good criterion for considering the significance of an emotional concern is its degree of interference with your everyday life. For example, an issue that gets in the way of your concentration in class, your ability to study, your completion of other regular tasks, or your enjoyment of life deserves attention. Sometimes, just admitting that the issue exists can be a great first start toward overcoming it. Then, discovering and applying new ways of coping may solve the problem.

Following is information about five of the most common adjustment challenges for students along with proven approaches to handling them. The five challenges are sadness, grief, low self-esteem, anxiety, and perfectionism.

Sadness

Feeling blue for brief periods of time is a normal part of life. However, when a student remains sad over several days to the point of being unable to complete daily tasks, there is a problem. Usually, depressive feelings are associated with guilt, crying, irritability, low self-esteem, lack of energy, and pessimism. The onset of a pattern of eating or sleeping too little or too much indicates that the body is also suffering.

An important element in figuring out how to manage persistent sadness involves discovering its basis. Often, depressed people think negatively. They become pessimistic after one negative event, expecting future failures to be unavoidable. They ignore their successes and choose a way of thinking that turns everyday frustrations into catastrophes. Here is a journal entry from a female first-year student who began feeling depressed after auditioning for a play but not getting selected for a role:

> "I am doomed at this school! I suck at everything. I had thought I gave my best performance ever last night. That shows that I know nothing about myself and nothing about theater. Those starring roles in high school were a joke. The drama teacher probably just picked me because I wanted it more, not because I had any talent. Now I have to think about a different major and a new career. Maybe I should just quit school and work as a cashier. I probably couldn't even do that well. I was looking forward to hanging out with the theater kids, but forget that. The girl who got my part told me I did a good job, but she was just being sarcastic. I probably won't ever be able to make friends here. I am a total loser."

As you can see, this journal entry is full of negative thoughts. The author looks at a single negative event in her freshman year as a catastrophe ruining her entire college career. In fact, at many colleges, acting roles are highly competitive and are out of reach for most first-year students. She also minimizes her significant successes in high school. She generalizes from her theater experience to her entire social life being ruined. Her blog is also full of self-criticism as she writes about "sucking at everything" and being "a total loser."

Certainly, this student added to her sad feelings by exaggerating a single instance in her mind. This student's blog entry indicates that she is pessimistic, has low self-esteem, and is considering giving up. However, she could have maintained a more optimistic, positive approach about her lack of success in earning a role. For example, she could have realized that it is very difficult for a new student to be given a role on her first try. She also could have avoided blaming herself, putting herself down, drastically altering her plans, or giving up hope. If she simply described her circumstances with more positive sentences, she could have probably prevented, or at least reduced, her sad feelings. Here is the blog rewritten with more positive sentences that would avoid creating such sad, depressed feelings:

> "I had my first audition last night for one of the leading roles. I thought I gave my best performance, but I guess I didn't do as well as I thought since I didn't get a callback. The drama professor chose a senior. I know I'm really pretty good for a freshman because I've already had a lot of experience in starring roles in high school. It's just that now in college there is a lot more competition from really qualified upper-level students. I think if I take the experience I already have, give myself some more time to learn, and use the talent I have, another opportunity will come along that will be right for me. I'm also going to try to get to know some of the theater kids—the girl who actually got the part I tried out for told me she thought I did a pretty good job with some of my interpretation of the monologue—a compliment from a senior! Yep . . . I'm looking forward to tomorrow's drama class."

Sometimes, a depressed student may fall into a pattern of being passive and feeling helpless. With little energy or enthusiasm, that student may stay at home, eating food and doing class assignments brought by friends. Despite their good intentions, these friends may actually be prolonging the mood problems by making it easier to stay depressed. Occasionally, a strong push to get the unhappy student active again will help overcome the passiveness and helplessness.

Grief

If a student's sad feelings are reactions to a personal loss from a death, a breakup, or another source of grief, the impact can be relatively brief if handled correctly.

Mourning the Death of a Loved One

The death of a loved one can bring about severe emotional pain. Unfortunately, relatives or friends may pass away while you are enrolled in college. When such a tragedy occurs, it is important, if possible, to take part in any services or ceremonies to honor your relative or friend's life. You will then have the opportunity to pay your respects and share your grief with others.

If such an unfortunate situation arises, you or a family member can notify the appropriate academic officer at your school so that you will be excused from the classes you need to miss. In most situations, you will be able to return to college in about a week. Even though life may not feel the same, you can go on to achieve your goals after you mourn your loss.

The worst way of handling the loss of a loved one is to deny your feelings. Actively mourning by facing the loss and letting the tears out will enable you to gain perspective and go forward again more quickly. A helpful mourning method can involve imagining having a final farewell conversation with the deceased person. Try to keep in mind that your cherished friend or relative would probably want you to succeed, so continuing with college can further demonstrate your fondness for that person.

Breaking Up Is Hard to Do

Breakups are a very common part of the college landscape because most students are not ready to settle down in permanent relationships. Although common, the end of an important romantic relationship can be devastating to the unsuspecting partner when it occurs. The emotional pain only needs to last a short time, however, if the breakup is managed effectively.

The key to an effective breakup combines timing with taking control of the relationship. If you are suddenly informed that you are no longer wanted as a boyfriend or girlfriend, you are likely to react with shock and then an assortment of negative emotions. In the midst of these emotions, you may begin thinking about how you can save the relationship instead of facing the likelihood that the relationship is over. This reaction is natural because it is so painful to give up a relationship that has become an important part of you. Sometimes, the person who started the breakup continues to communicate and gives hope to the person who was rejected. If you do not get back together, however, you may begin realizing that the relationship is really over. This is where timing and taking control come into play.

When you realize that the relationship has no future, make the decision that you want it to end as soon as possible. Take control! Instead of being the puppet on the string with your ex-boyfriend or ex-girlfriend as puppet master, simply cut the string. In your mind, practice saying a final goodbye to your former romantic partner. If tears come, that's okay. Then, when you feel ready, directly notify him or her that the relationship is permanently over. You can include best wishes for a good life or not—that's up to you. The key is your making the decision to break up totally.

Your feelings of loss will gradually decrease as the days pass. You will begin looking more toward the future than the past. Some students find it helpful to destroy or discard mementos of the relationship, such as photos or CDs. Over time, you will be able to figure out how to react if you see your ex-boyfriend or ex-girlfriend on campus. Keep in mind that you probably learned a lot about yourself and relationships from your experience. As a result, you will be prepared for a more successful relationship in the future.

Puppet Master: If you feel controlled by your romantic partner in a failing relationship, it may be time to cut the strings.

Discuss your best tips for handling a breakup at *CollegeSuccess.andYOU.com*

A Question of Self-Esteem

Being overly self-critical can certainly be associated with sadness. In fact, everyone has limitations and imperfections to acknowledge. What is the healthiest approach to self-esteem? By college age, it is important for your self-worth to be based on what you think of yourself rather than on other peoples' opinions about you. Some students have to work hard to overcome negative views based on past family criticisms or high school reputations.

Another trap is to compare yourself physically to others, since body image is central to self-esteem. While it's important to improve your body with sound exercise and nutrition, there are certain physical characteristics, such as your height, that you can't change. Generally, a good idea is to accept your body even if you don't look like a movie star.

As long as you are acting responsibly, simply saying "I'm okay" to yourself is psychologically very sound. It will be helpful to cut out negative labels like *boring* or *fat* that you may have the habit of using when you think of yourself. Focus instead on your positive qualities, accomplishments, and good deeds. Consistently believing you're okay will help you continue liking yourself even on those inevitable occasions when things aren't exactly how you want them.

I'm Okay: Accepting yourself and your body strengthens your personal adjustment.

Anxiety

Another important emotional issue that can interfere with your college life is anxiety. Anxiety is a normal experience that may make you temporarily uncomfortable. Some people even seek out experiences that can make them anxious, such as thrill rides or horror movies. Experiencing too much anxiety can interfere with your comfort, your confidence, and your studies. Signs of excessive anxiety can include sweaty palms, stomach distress, difficulty in concentration, trembling, restlessness, and fearfulness. For college students, feelings of being pressured and overwhelmed are leading sources for high levels of anxiety.

You have already read about dealing specifically with classroom speaking anxiety (see Chapter 5) and test anxiety (see Chapter 6), but many students have more general nervousness that may arise at almost any time. If you feel overly anxious, what can you do to calm down? Here are twelve proven self-help techniques to control excessive levels of anxiety.

Twelve Techniques for Reducing Anxiety

1. When you feel anxious, visualize the most relaxing scene that you can imagine. Maybe you will think of walking around a beautiful scenic path or sunbathing at a quiet beach.

2. Eliminate or reduce caffeine intake.

3. Don't allow yourself to stay hungry since hunger contributes to anxiety.

4. If you experience feelings of panic, breathe deeply and slowly. Short, fast breaths will make you more nervous. Also, try to convince yourself that you will not faint, die, or be abandoned. Be realistic about your condition. Nothing catastrophic is likely to happen to you.

5. Work on restoring your confidence. A confident person is less likely to suffer from problems with anxiety. You were okay before you became nervous; you are the same person as you were previously, so you can also be okay now.

6. Be patient. Even if you do feel very nervous, the feeling will pass. Don't emphasize "what if the worst happens" in your thinking.

7. A person is unable to physically experience anxiety immediately after intense aerobic exercise (see Chapter 9). If you participate in a daily aerobic exercise, you will decrease your anxiety.

8. Take a break to engage in absorbing and enjoyable distractions. Do a crossword puzzle, play a video game, or watch a TV show.

9. When you face an experience that makes you nervous, practice or rehearse it ahead of time if possible.

10. Use basic relaxation procedures (see *CollegeSuccess.andYOU.com*).

11. Think about how lucky you are to be in college and how many personal strengths you have.

12. Help others, which will take your mind off yourself.

EXERCISE 3 Calmness Index: The Fearful Fifty

Step 1: Below is a list of fifty items that are known to make some people anxious. For each item, place a check mark in the "Anxious" column if you react to the item nervously or in the "Calm" column if you react calmly. For any item you have not experienced, check your most likely reaction.

The Fearful Fifty	Anxious	Calm
Being around worms		
Having blood drawn		
Speaking to a stranger		
Taking an exam		
Thunder and lightning		
Being stuck in traffic		
Elevators		
Sharks		
Going to the dentist		
Flying in an airplane		
Walking into a party alone		
High places		
Listening to a boring lecture		
Trying a new physical activity		
Spiders		
Witnessing an accident		
Being in a crowd		
Getting a shot from a doctor		
Noise from a vacuum cleaner		
Being alone		
Fireworks		
Difficulty falling asleep		
Helicopters		
Dogs		
Being around coughs and sneezes		
Sirens		
Asking a question in class		
Noisy children		
Hospitals		

The Fearful Fifty	Anxious	Calm
Crossing a bridge		
Amusement parks		
Snakes		
Waiting in a long line		
Driving		
A medical checkup		
Meeting an attractive person		
Movie theaters		
Getting back a test grade		
Seeing blood		
Loud music		
Computer or cell phone not working		
The number 13		
Cockroaches		
Public bathrooms		
Using eyedrops		
Feeling anger		
Nudity		
Speaking before a group		
Mice		
Being in an underground parking garage		

Step 2: Count the number of items you checked as "Calm." The total number is _____. Now, multiply your *Calm Score* by two to obtain your *Calmness Index Score* of _____. This score indicates the percentage of anxiety-producing experiences that you handle calmly. The interpretation of ranges for the Calmness Index Score is shown here:

Calmness Index Interpretation
85–100 = Usually calm
70–84 = Mostly calm
50–69 = Sometimes calm
0–49 = Often anxious

If you scored "Often anxious" or want to reduce your anxiety in certain situations, you can read *The Anxiety and Phobia Workbook* by Edmund J. Bourne[6] or make an appointment at your college's Counseling Center.

Step 3: In class, be prepared to share your favorite techniques for staying calm in situations that typically make people nervous. For example, maybe you listen to music when you are in the dentist's chair.

Perfectionism

Nobody is perfect. Sometimes that's easy to forget. Unfortunately, some college students may not realize they are striving for unreachable standards. While working hard to succeed at college is a sign of healthy adjustment, attaching self-worth to being the best at everything you do is likely to make you anxious and depressed.[7] For instance, you might have sleepless nights worrying that the paper you prepared is not just right. If you are a perfectionist, you might blame yourself for the A- you received on an exam when another student you know got an A+.

Perfectionistic attitudes usually apply to more than just academics. A true perfectionist will want to be number one in every activity. Such activities might include having the most comprehensive music collection, being the slimmest or most physically fit, or being the best at playing video games and sports. Anything less than having the best or being the best is unacceptable to a person with this attitude.

Many perfectionists avoid activities in which they feel they cannot excel. This avoidance behavior will keep them out of many social situations. For example, if a friend invites a perfectionist to play poker or tennis and the perfectionist does not already feel superior in these activities, the perfectionist will likely decline the invitation. Unfortunately, he or she will probably miss out on some fun and new experiences.

Surprisingly, a research study shows that perfectionists are less successful in their jobs than non-perfectionists. Thirty-four insurance agents were rated as "perfectionist" or "non-perfectionist." The findings show that the sixteen who were non-perfectionists earned an average of fifteen thousand dollars more annually than the eighteen who were perfectionists.[8] The best explanation for these results is that the perfectionists' work was hindered by the need to perform so perfectly in their jobs that they created self-doubt.

Imperfect Success: Aim for excellence in college (or video games) but realize you may not always achieve perfection.

There is hope for perfectionists who want to change. Experts in treating perfectionism recommend that people who display this characteristic need to realize that their attitude is more of a liability than an asset. If perfectionists can accept this idea, they can push themselves to engage in activities in which they will not necessarily excel. Learning to relax and accept less than ideal performance may break the link between self-acceptance and perfectionism.

Discuss your attitude about seeking professional help for emotional challenges at *CollegeSuccess.andYOU.com*

Help for EMOTIONAL challenges

For some students, emotional challenges will interfere with their ability to take advantage of educational opportunities. While many students' initial instinct is to turn to friends for help, an increasing number are seeking professional counseling. To meet this need, many colleges provide counseling services. Usually these support agencies have the words *psychology*, *mental health*, or *counseling* in their titles. The most frequently used name is *Counseling Center*. Typical emotional concerns brought by students to counseling services include depression, anxiety and stress, mood instability, eating disorders, substance abuse, sleep problems, academic concerns, relationship issues, victimization, and family conflict.

College students who have a counseling service on campus are lucky since comparable services outside of college are usually either very expensive or difficult to access. It is important to know that seeking counseling is not a sign of weakness or a sign that you are "abnormal." Most college counseling is free, although there are some exceptions. The services are typically aimed at helping students overcome specific issues interfering with their current lives. Such issues lend themselves to short-term counseling. A typical example would be a breakup of a romantic relationship. While devastating, a romantic breakup can usually be overcome with the help of a skilled counselor in a few sessions. On the other hand, some campus counseling services may not provide direct treatment for long-term problems. Since students are usually unable to judge if their issues are treatable at a college counseling service, it is best to make an appointment to find out. At a minimum, the counselor will give expert information along with a recommendation or referral.

One very important point to remember is that communications between a student and a counselor are ordinarily confidential. **Confidentiality** means that college administrators and faculty as well as family members cannot find out what you discuss with the counselor without your written permission. If you seek counseling, you can clarify any limitations to confidentiality with your counselor. Such limitations vary according to state law.

Counselors usually come from the fields of psychology, social work, and mental health counseling. Schools with a training program in one of these mental health professions may include graduate students or interns as counselors. A counselor-in-training will be required to discuss your case with a licensed supervisor. Since counselors-in-training can easily relate to student issues, they often are very effective.

Some counseling services also offer psychiatric consultation. Psychiatrists typically diagnose and treat students needing medication. In such cases, it is highly advantageous for students to combine psychiatric treatment for symptom relief with counseling so that they can learn new strategies for coping with their problems.

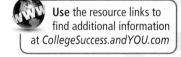

Use the resource links to find additional information at *CollegeSuccess.andYOU.com*

Group therapy is a very helpful form of treatment provided by many college counseling services. In this form of treatment, groups of students meet together with a therapist from the counseling staff. For social issues such as shyness, feelings of inferiority, lack of assertiveness, and relationship conflict, group therapy may be the treatment of choice.

Counseling services often sponsor workshops to teach students about emotional concerns and how to manage them. The centers also typically provide an array of useful self-help brochures available in print or online. You can visit your campus counseling service or check your college's website to access these brochures.

Group Therapy: Many students benefit from this form of counseling.

Thinking Critically About . . .
Adjusting Emotionally

Critical thinking involves an active evaluation of information using careful, thoughtful, and reasoned judgments.

1. Evaluate the extent to which a college administration should involve itself in the emotional health of students. Should the college use its resources to prevent and treat the emotional problems of students? When a specific student is suffering an emotional breakdown, should college officials intervene, and if so, what should they do? Justify your responses to these questions.

2. Some critics of the positive psychology movement argue that happiness should not be a specific personal goal but simply a side effect that sometimes occurs. What do you think? Provide a reasoned justification for your opinion on whether happiness should be a specific personal goal.

3. Analyze the influence of emotional adjustment on students' academic success and physical wellness.

4. Contrast the positive and negative effects of personal computer and smartphone use on the emotional well-being of college students.

5. Examine the reasons why many students prefer to speak to friends about emotional issues rather than to a professional counselor. Indicate how you would decide the point at which a troubled friend should be referred for professional counseling.

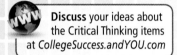
Discuss your ideas about the Critical Thinking items at *CollegeSuccess.andYOU.com*

Online Learning

Here is a list of positive characteristics that are associated with success in online learning:

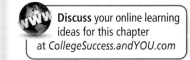

Discuss your online learning ideas for this chapter at *CollegeSuccess.andYOU.com*

- Intellectual curiosity
- Independence
- Drive to succeed
- Discipline and responsibility meeting deadlines
- Skill at written communication
- Goal orientation
- Social satisfaction
- Ability to tolerate frustration from technological issues
- Sensitivity to classmates and professors
- Willingness to collaborate
- Ability to organize

For online students experiencing challenges in adjusting, several resources exist that can help. Many of the websites for college counseling services contain self-help material and self-assessments on a variety of important topics related to emotional adjustment. Additionally, the websites usually include useful links for additional information. Also, some campuses have hotlines that provide information, referrals, and peer counseling for all students.

Most college counseling services provide community referrals to online learners making telephone requests. However, most counseling services do not provide direct counseling through email or telephone to any students, including online learners. A few exceptions exist; for example, some schools do offer telephone, Skype, or email counseling for topics such as stress management, motivation, goal setting, and career choice. Online students with more serious problems are usually referred to specific community agencies.

COPING WITH LOSS

One of the most difficult emotional challenges in life is dealing with the death of a loved one or other significant personal loss. The resulting grief can not only be psychologically devastating but also very disruptive to college students since students must have high levels of concentration and drive for academic success. It sometimes feels as if losing someone or something very close to you is like losing a part of yourself.

For college students, emotionally disruptive losses might include a romantic breakup, parental divorce, sale of the house in which they grew up, loss of a cherished pet, or a natural disaster destroying their family's home and community. The most overwhelming type of loss, though, is the death of a beloved family member or friend.

A CASE STUDY: FACING THE CHALLENGE OF . . .
COPING WITH LOSS

Jill and her "grandmom" had been extremely close throughout Jill's life. Since Jill's parents both worked, Jill stayed with her grandparents every weekday before she began school and every afternoon after school until high school. Grandmom taught her how to sew and grow prizewinning roses. During middle school and high school, Jill confided in her grandmother about some of her personal concerns that she was afraid to discuss with her parents. After her grandfather died when Jill was 15, Grandmom moved in with Jill's family.

About two months after Jill left for college, she got an urgent phone call that Grandmom had suffered a fatal heart attack. Jill felt overwhelmed with pain as she went home for the funeral. While her parents and younger brother were also very upset, Jill really felt that she had a uniquely close bond with her grandmother. Grandmom had been there for her throughout most of her life, but she would not be there any longer. Upon returning to college about a week after the funeral, Jill could not stop feeling overwhelming sadness and had difficulty pulling herself together to go to class.

OVERCOMING THE CHALLENGE OF . . .
COPING WITH LOSS

Be prepared to discuss your answers to the following items: (1) Recommend steps Jill can take to overcome her grief. Include what she should do to manage her academic responsibilities. (2) What can Jill's friends do to let her know she is not alone in dealing with the death of her grandmother? (3) What are the advantages or disadvantages of Jill discussing her feelings of sadness and loss with other people rather than keeping her feelings to herself?

Key Chapter Strategies

- Think of a glass as half full instead of half empty to help keep your outlook positive.
- Maintain confidence about your personal strengths and an optimistic view even when things temporarily do not go your way.
- Display empathy for other people.
- Face the grief that accompanies a loss and mourn effectively.
- Recognize that always striving for perfection sometimes results in frustration.
- Seek counseling if you experience adjustment challenges that interfere with your studies and your happiness.
- Read *Feeling Good: The New Mood Therapy* by David Burns[9] to learn techniques for overcoming negative thinking that can lead to adjustment concerns.

 Can You Recall It?

Directions: To review your understanding of the chapter, choose the correct term from the list below and fill it in on the blank. You will not use every term.

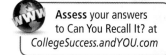
Assess your answers to Can You Recall It? at *CollegeSuccess.andYOU.com*

academic advisor	perfectionism	emotional intelligence
low self-esteem	resilience	confidentiality
anxiety	breakups	positive psychology
grief	Counseling Center	gratitude

1. One way to decrease _____ is to eliminate or reduce caffeine.

2. When you spend a sleepless night worrying about the A- you received on your exam because you know another student received an A+, you are showing tendencies for _____.

3. Focusing on your personal strengths and maintaining an optimistic outlook are features of _____ , which emphasizes a contructive approach to life.

4. One of the worst ways to handle _____ is to deny your feelings and not participate in commemorative services or ceremonies.

5. People high in _____ usually show empathy and the ability to delay gratification.

6. When you or someone you know experiences emotional problems, the best on-campus resource for help is the _____ .

7. The key to effective management of _____ combines timing and taking control.

8. Having a negative body image creates _____ since these two characteristics are related to each other.

Web Activity: Pandora's Music Box

Directions: Music influences our emotions. Listening to music can energize us so that we want to get up and dance or soothe us so that we feel peaceful and calm. Follow this series of steps and then answer the questions below.

Step 1: Go to http://www.pandora.com (Pandora is a personalized internet radio service) and complete the free registration if you are not already registered.

Step 2: Select **Create a Station**.

Step 3: Identify an artist you especially like. Pandora will play music from this artist followed by similar songs and artists. Listen to several songs.

Step 4: Choose one of the songs played that makes you feel joyful or happy. Listen to it, paying special attention to what it is about this particular song that makes you feel so positive. Now answer the questions below.

1. What is the title of your song? _____

_____

_____

2. Who is the artist? _____

_____

_____

3. What aspects of this song cause you to feel so positive? If there is a line or a chorus that especially affects you, write the lyrics here and explain their influence. _____

_____

_____

_____

4. What type of music (jazz, pop, etc.) do you like to listen to the most and why? Do you listen to one type of music when you are feeling certain emotions? If so, which type of music do you listen to for which kind of emotion?

_____

_____

_____

_____

_____

_____

Reflection Time

Achieving Your Goals by Adjusting Emotionally

Write three paragraphs, one paragraph for each of the following items: (1) Discuss what has surprised you the most about the challenges of emotional adjustment to college. (2) Identify which personal strengths have helped you the most with emotional adjustment to college and specifically how they have helped. (3) Explain how other people have provided you with support for your emotional adjustment to college.

_____

_____

_____

_____

_____

_____

_____

_____

_____

_____

_____

_____

_____

_____

_____

_____

_____

_____

_____

_____

_____

11

Developing and Maintaining Healthy Relationships Through Positive Communication

In this chapter, you will move toward achieving your goals by

- learning to communicate in a healthy way with your family.

- finding out how to enhance social success and harmony.

- understanding the challenges of romantic relationships.

Find additional tools and resources at *CollegeSuccess.andYOU.com*

Self-Assessment:
My Sociogram—
A Visual Map of My Social Communication

Step 1: A **sociogram** (developed by psychiatrist Jacob Levy Moreno in the 1930s) is a classic visual method to represent social and communication links among people. Below you will create a sociogram that illustrates your social communication network. You will draw circles, lines, and arrows to create a pattern that shows the nature of your communication relationships based on your answers to the following five questions. First, read and answer these five questions. Please *use a different person* for each answer.

1. Name the family member with whom you communicate most frequently. _____

2. Which student from one of your classes would you most like to work with on a project?

   _____

3. Name a person you like to eat with in the cafeteria.

   _____

4. Name a student with whom you frequently discuss your shared interests. _____

5. Name a student you communicate with frequently through a social networking site (such as Facebook), email, Twitter, or text message. _____

Step 2: Before you create your sociogram, review the following method for drawing the circles, lines, and arrows.

Drawing the Circles

■ Your sociogram will consist of five circles you draw around a center circle that represents you. Each of the five circles you draw will represent your significant social and communication relationships—including family, friends, and other people in your life.

■ You will write the name of a person in each circle based on your answers to the questions in Step 1 above. That means you will name *a different person* in each of the five circles.

■ Let the distance between your own circle and the circle you draw reflect the frequency of communication between you and the person named. The closer to you that you draw the circle, the more frequent the communication.

■ Adjust the size of the circle you draw to represent the power or influence of the person named—the bigger the circle, the more influence or power for that person.

Drawing the Lines and Arrows

■ You will draw lines with arrow tips to represent communication between you and the other person.

■ Use solid lines for arrows that represent strong social and communication bonds and broken lines for weaker social connections.

Your finished sociogram will look something like this example:

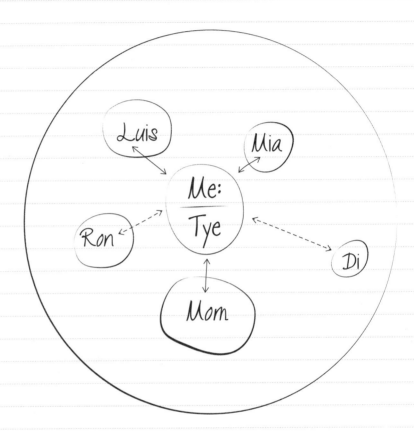

Answer to Question 1:   Mom

Answer to Question 2:   Di, my classmate for a project

Answer to Question 3:   Mia, someone I like to eat with

Answer to Question 4:   Luis, my friend who likes sports

Answer to Question 5:   Ron, my friend at a different school

Step 3: Now create your own sociogram by using your answers to Questions 1–5, and following the directions on the previous page for drawing circles, lines, and arrows.

My Sociogram

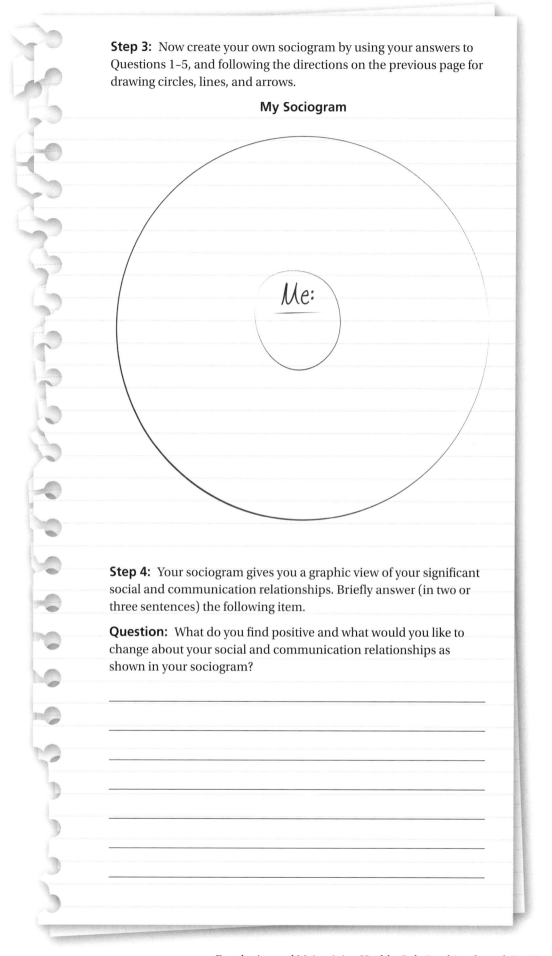

Step 4: Your sociogram gives you a graphic view of your significant social and communication relationships. Briefly answer (in two or three sentences) the following item.

Question: What do you find positive and what would you like to change about your social and communication relationships as shown in your sociogram?

_____

_____

_____

_____

_____

_____

"How can I stay close to my old friends who didn't come to this school?" "How much should I still depend on my family?" "Will I find friends here?" "How can I get along with a roommate?" These are questions that you may be considering as you begin your college years. You have already undoubtedly had experiences that have helped you grow socially. Also, you have probably had to stay patient and deal with some social frustrations during your early college days.

Close friendships established at college often form treasured, lifelong bonds. Students frequently meet their closest lifetime friends through campus organizations, classes, and dorms. While college romances may not become permanent, they often have a great deal of enduring personal impact. This chapter is designed to help you meet the social challenges of college by emphasizing the importance of effective communication in promoting your relationships.

Maintaining FAMILY CONNECTIONS

During college, you will undergo profound changes in the nature of your relationships with your family and high school friends. These changes will reflect the maturity you achieve through your college experiences.

As you transition toward more independence, what role will the adults who reared you play in your life? Even if they didn't attend college themselves, they will certainly have the wisdom of their years to share with you. Ideally, they can advise you, providing you with information based on their experiences while encouraging you to solve your own problems and make your own decisions. They may also give you emotional and financial support, if necessary. At the same time, your family will probably appreciate learning about your challenges and triumphs while maintaining their close relationship with you.

If you have moved away from home, it may be difficult for you to accept all the changes that will occur while you are gone. Younger siblings will grow up, grandparents will age, and economic or health factors might affect everyone. Meanwhile, you will be changing too, maturing and expanding both intellectually and socially.

Family Talk: Effective communication with your family helps in your transition to college.

Communicating with Your Family

You may want to keep up with family events, and your family will want to know what is happening with you. Today's wide variety of communication choices facilitates regular sessions for catching up. An issue arising for some of you, however, involves the frequency and extent of communications with your family. For example, some worried parents expect to phone first-year students twice a day, while you may prefer to place the call yourself and do so less frequently.

You can begin by trying to set the rules yourself. Taking control of communications with your family will convey your developing independence and allow you to manage your time and your emotional reactions to family contacts as you see fit. You can inform your family that you will phone regularly during each week. Of course, emailing, text messaging, and other ways of communicating can supplement your phone calls.

When you phone, you will be happiest if you exert some management over the conversation, particularly if you have a family member who peppers you with questions. While that person may be genuinely concerned about your welfare, you may burn out from constantly being quizzed about the details of your life. Instead, work toward keeping the interchange more equal by respectfully asking your family members similar questions about their social lives, jobs, and family events. Aside from taking the focus away from you, you will demonstrate your interest in your family through these types of questions. Maintaining good communication with your family will help you successfully transition into college life.

Discuss the challenges of communicating with your family at *CollegeSuccess.andYOU.com*

DOONESBURY © 1998 G. B. Trudeau. Reprinted with permission of UNIVERSAL UCLICK. All rights reserved.

EXERCISE 1   Family Empathy

Step 1: Empathy (see Chapter 10) is the ability to accurately recognize and understand the feelings of other people. In this exercise, you will demonstrate how well you understand a family member who has been involved in your preparation for college. The name of the family member you select is _____.

That person's relationship to you is _____.

Step 2: Answer the following questions about the person you just identified.

1. List at least two ways this person helped you prepare for college.

   _____

   _____

2. How do you think this person felt when you began college?

   _____

   _____

   _____

3. What has been most gratifying for this person about your becoming a

   college student? _____

   _____

   _____

   _____

Step 3: In class, discuss reasons family members might worry about students on a college campus.

Families and Commuter Students

Commuter students live off campus. If you are a commuter student who lives with your family, you may have the advantage of their direct support. The emotional support and company provided by family members can be invaluable.

Some commuter students find that family members—particularly relatives or spouses who did not attend college—fail to understand the challenges of being a college student. Commuter students may also have to contend with the lack of a quiet place to study and with time-consuming family responsibilities. Furthermore, conflict may arise if a college student stays up or returns home as late at night as students who live on campus. Keeping the lines of communication open among members of the family is the key for successful commuter student life at home.

If you are a commuter student living at home, it is a good idea to explain the pressures of being a college student to your family. Regularly using a quiet place to study, such as the campus library, can also be helpful. One commuter student who lived too far from campus to use the library studied in his car, parking in a quiet spot during weekend days when his house was too noisy.

Homesickness

After starting college, some students who have moved away from home miss their families and old friends. Such feelings can emerge regardless of your age or distance from home. Homesickness may be intensified by major changes back home, by your feelings of loneliness, or by a sense that there are no students similar to you at your college.

In addition to keeping regular communication going with those back home, here are some suggestions to combat homesickness:

- If geographically and economically possible, plan one visit home during your first four months at college.
- Encourage at least one family visit. For instance, your family might visit during Family Weekend if your school sponsors this event. Additional visits by siblings or friends can also be comforting.
- Work hard to find new social attachments at college. Join organizations to develop friendships and become part of a group.
- Find a mentor (see Chapter 2), a more seasoned person to offer you guidance.
- Be patient as you try to develop social ties and as you await visits with your family and old friends.
- Share your feelings with another student, an RA, or if necessary, a counselor.

Visits Home

You may have eagerly anticipated your first visit home after starting college. It can be great to see your family and friends again and very reassuring to find out that most things are still the way you left them. Don't be surprised, though, if you feel a little different. You are no longer the same person you were when you began college. Your family may have a tough time accepting your emerging independence. For example, they may still expect you to come home early if you go out with friends at night. Or they may look disapprovingly at any big changes you have made to your appearance. These issues are normal for first visits home and simply require a period of adjustment through open and respectful communication. Remember that your family also must adjust to your visits home. By showing empathy for your family, you will demonstrate that you are an adult, and your future visits home can go smoothly for everyone.

SOCIALIZING

Being able to experience fulfilling social relationships can make your college life more satisfying. The two best opportunities to develop meaningful social communication networks are through the development of friendships and participation in campus activities.

Friends

off the mark.com — by Mark Parisi

It might be nice if you could duplicate your old friends and bring them to college with you, but unfortunately, you can't. Maybe you have struck it rich and already found one or more new friends. For most students, though, that quest requires patience. Sometimes, it's just good luck that you have a roommate or neighbor who becomes your friend, or you connect with the student who sits next to you in one of your classes. More likely, you need to stay alert to find friends among people in classes, jobs, and activities.

A great approach to finding a friend is just talking to a fellow student you don't know. Cheerfully initiating a conversation about any topic potentially relevant to both of you might start a pleasant conversation. Even if the result is not a friendship, you will often feel better about yourself after taking such a social risk.

Finding a friend can be a lot different from keeping a friend. You want friends who are dependable and loyal. You will also usually connect best to people who are open about themselves but who are also willing to listen, understand, and provide sound advice if requested. It's also reassuring to have a friend who will reach out to help you if necessary. Of course, your friend will expect the same positive traits from you.

Taking Care of a Friend

Melanie was one of the most popular, lively girls on the fourth floor of the freshman dorm. She was part of a group of guys and girls who hung out, went to football games together, and sat at the same dining hall table for every meal. Tess felt lucky to have been accepted in this group just because she was Melanie's roommate. As finals approached, Tess became concerned because Melanie's behavior had changed dramatically. She became fidgety and was drinking pots of coffee and highly caffeinated energy drinks, plus taking some kind of caffeine pills. When Tess asked Melanie about the pills, Melanie explained that they helped her stay alert while she studied. In fact, Melanie seemed to be studying all night, every night, and not getting any sleep. One evening at dinner a few days before her first final, Melanie looked pale and had dark circles under her eyes. She had no appetite and couldn't stop jabbering. Tess considered contacting the RA or Melanie's parents but didn't want to get Melanie in trouble. A few nights later, however, Tess heard a commotion in the hall and found the rescue squad examining Melanie, who was lying on the ground screaming that some foreign government was out to get her. Tess overheard the paramedics say that Melanie had broken her wrist from falling and that they needed to get her to the hospital. By the next day, Melanie's parents had moved her to a hospital back home. As soon as she was feeling better, Melanie phoned Tess and told her she had been diagnosed with acute caffeine poisoning, which had made her act in such a crazy way. The lack of sleep had caused her to be accident prone. She tearfully told Tess that her parents would not let her return to take her exams or come back to school. Tess felt very guilty, wondering if any of this would have happened if she had tried to help Melanie.

Discuss the qualities you look for in a friend at *CollegeSuccess.andYOU.com*

A benefit of college friendships is that one of your friends might be a gateway to a larger group of compatible people. Feeling part of a group is very comforting and can provide a reliable and enjoyable social outlet, both for your college years and beyond.

Removing Barriers to Social Connections

One of the great advantages of college is the variety of interesting people you can meet. In most classes, you can decide to sit next to anyone you want and strike up a conversation. If you do that enough times, you are likely to be successful in establishing a social connection. Even students who felt like outsiders in high school can find like-minded peers in college. For example, geeky students who love computers and science fiction are often much more successful in finding fellow geeks in college than in high school.

It's been estimated that about half the population has considered themselves shy at one time or another. Therefore, there's nothing abnormal about being a little reluctant to be the person to initiate a social contact. The key to overcoming this hesitance simply involves finding the confidence to try. Even **introverts**, who prefer less social contact, can overcome their usual tendency to keep to themselves. Here are seven steps to help you make a social connection.

Steps to Initiate a Social Contact

1. Visualize successfully starting a first conversation. You might even plan some topics or questions.
2. Choose a person, such as a classmate, to approach before or after class.
3. Look for someone to become your friend who seems like a happy person since a 2008 study of 4,739 people found that happiness extends to friends.[1]
4. Start a conversation by asking an open-ended, class-related question. See if a conversation develops and how the other person reacts.
5. Listen carefully and show interest in the other person's responses.
6. Pat yourself on the back for having the courage to initiate contact.
7. Remember that not every attempt will succeed; no one is successful 100% of the time.

EXERCISE 2 **Making Contact**

Step 1: Begin a friendly conversation with a student on campus you don't know. Then answer the following questions.

1. Where on campus did you meet this student?

_____

_____

2. Why did you select this person?

_____

_____

3. What did you say or ask to begin your conversation?

_____

_____

4. How did your conversation turn out?

_____

_____

Step 2: Be prepared to share your reaction to this experience in class. How easy or difficult was it for you to step outside your comfort zone to complete this exercise?

There are a few attitudes and behaviors that can hinder social connectedness. Spending too much time hiding out with your computer is one. Prejudging other students is another. Saying contemptuously to yourself, "Oh, he's a football player," "He's a science guy," or "She's a princess" involves stereotyping that eliminates considering people as individuals. If you want to open up as many social connections as possible, you can be most successful if you hold back your prejudgments and get to know other students as individuals who have habits, quirks, and preferences, just as you do. Your willingness to initiate open-minded communication is likely to broaden your social relationships.

Dealing with Roommates

The majority of students have not regularly shared a bedroom before coming to college. While adjusting to living with a roommate is a major challenge for many students, the experience can result in as much personal growth as any other part of your college experience. Because of the requirements needed to make this arrangement work, successfully sharing a room with another person furnishes the best training ground possible for living with someone in a future permanent relationship. In both situations, you will need to communicate and compromise in order to succeed.

In Harmony: You and your roommate benefit from open communication and compromise.

To get along effectively with a roommate, friendship is not enough. In fact, high school friends who decide to room together at college often experience disastrous results. Some of the most successful roommates who stick together for four years are not necessarily close friends but demonstrate respect for each other in many ways.

Thoughtfulness can promote your relationship with a roommate. For example, if your family comes to visit you and takes you out to dinner, you might try to arrange for your roommate to be included. When your roommate wants to use the room for a special get-together and you want to study, you might volunteer to go to a study lounge or the library. Even if you and your roommate do become close friends, it's still a good idea for you each to have other friends so that you don't become too dependent on one another.

In learning to adjust to roommates, the first step is to accept their **idiosyncrasies** or unique, quirky preferences. You can usually count on the strange and unfamiliar when you are living with another person for the first time. For example, one student's roommate was a vegan who practiced yoga in the room every night and constantly cleaned because she believed germs were everywhere. On the other hand, your roommate also has to accept your idiosyncrasies (yes—you have them, too). Of course, if something your roommate does truly bothers you, you might try to discuss it in an open, constructive way through respectful communication with one another. It is best not to let even small problems simmer.

Below is a checklist of some of the most typical conflicts that can arise between roommates. Following the checklist is a discussion of some positive ways to overcome these conflicts and maintain harmony.

Typical Roomate Conflicts

- Sharing a small space
- Use of a roommate's personal possessions
- Division of chores
- Preferences of messiness versus neatness
- Noise
- Privacy
- Splitting costs
- Sleep patterns
- Study habits
- Overnight guests
- Incompatible schedules
- Use of the bathroom, if shared
- Room decorations
- Alliances when there is more than one roommate

Other problems can occur as well. For instance, there may be difficulties if a roommate brings a video game system into the room. The National Bureau of Economic Research reports that students whose roommates brought video games to college earn a lower grade point average than comparable students without video game equipment in their rooms.[2] Some roommates may object to the video game system as distracting while others may become addicted to it.

Resolving Conflicts

Conflict resolution is a constructive procedure involving direct interchange to resolve disagreements so that all parties will be satisfied. Applying the technique of conflict resolution can usually work out differences in all sorts of situations involving disputes. The beauty of conflict resolution is that all involved participants "win" through compromise, and tension is alleviated.

The first step in successful conflict resolution involves agreeing to sit down and talk over your differences with the other person in a quiet, mutually respectful manner. The meeting should be face-to-face and exclude other people, including friends. One of you will begin by expressing your feelings and their basis, using an "I" statement. For example, you might say, "I have trouble falling asleep when it is noisy." Then, follow the recommendations for successful conflict resolution in the list of *do's* and *don'ts* on the next page. Accomplishing these steps requires maturity and self-control, but the payoff can certainly be worth the effort for the people involved in the conflict.

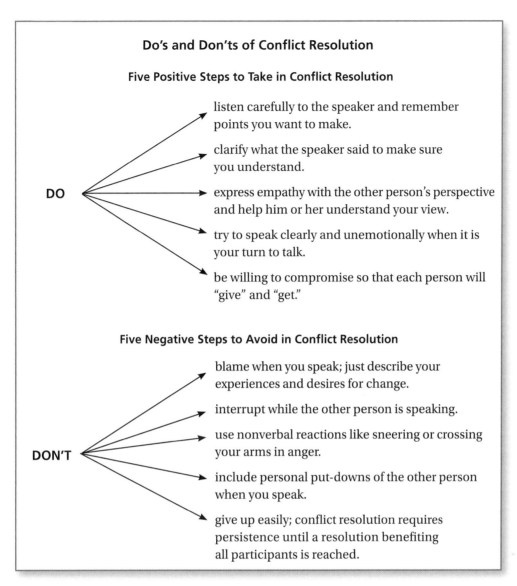

Do's and Don'ts of Conflict Resolution

Five Positive Steps to Take in Conflict Resolution

DO

- listen carefully to the speaker and remember points you want to make.
- clarify what the speaker said to make sure you understand.
- express empathy with the other person's perspective and help him or her understand your view.
- try to speak clearly and unemotionally when it is your turn to talk.
- be willing to compromise so that each person will "give" and "get."

Five Negative Steps to Avoid in Conflict Resolution

DON'T

- blame when you speak; just describe your experiences and desires for change.
- interrupt while the other person is speaking.
- use nonverbal reactions like sneering or crossing your arms in anger.
- include personal put-downs of the other person when you speak.
- give up easily; conflict resolution requires persistence until a resolution benefiting all participants is reached.

After each person has an adequate opportunity to speak, continue to trade roles until each person has been heard and understood. Then, calmly negotiate mutually acceptable compromises and solutions. These agreements can be written down as they are reached.

In conflict resolution, you will not get everything you want. Nevertheless, it is a very fulfilling method because you end up with much of what you want as well as more harmony with the other person. Additionally, learning to engage in successful conflict resolution while in college can have a very positive effect on your future. It requires a combination of empathy plus assertiveness that will be useful in both personal and professional relationships.

When students can't work together successfully to resolve their conflicts, they may be able to use mediation to help them reach agreement. **Mediation** is a formal meeting run by a neutral person who listens to information about the disagreement, makes a clear statement of issues and conflicts, leads a discussion of alternative solutions, and negotiates a compromise acceptable to both students. Similar to the goal of conflict resolution, mediation is aimed at finding a solution that is perceived as win-win by each of the students involved. Some colleges have an **ombudsperson**, an administrator who is assigned to troubleshoot and resolve conflicts between a student and other students, faculty members, or administrators. Aside from an ombudsperson, residence hall and Counseling Center staff members may be able to provide mediation.

Student Programs and Organizations

Most colleges feature a wide array of extracurricular activities and organizations for students. Activities may feature sports, hobbies, intellectual interests, media, special talents and skills, and politics. There are often honor societies, religious associations, international student organizations, and groups sponsored by academic departments. Some students initially become involved in several activities until they can decide to make an enduring commitment to one or two.

Many of you are already very busy with your studies and jobs. Even if you are very busy, participating in at least one campus activity can be rewarding. Such participation can enable you to have fun, meet new people, enhance your credentials for jobs or graduate education, and help others.

> ### The Happiest Students
> "Students who are involved in extracurricular activities are the happiest students on campus and also tend to be the most successful in the classroom." [3]
>
> Dr. Richard Light
> Harvard University

Discuss your reaction to Dr. Light's quote defining the happiest and most successful students at *CollegeSuccess.andYOU.com*

EXERCISE 3 **So What Does an Anime Club Do, Anyway?**

Step 1: Go to your school's website and look for a list of current student organizations. If you cannot find such a list on the Internet, go to the Student Activities Office on campus or consult the campus phone directory to find a list.

Step 2: Even if you are already actively involved in campus activities, select two unfamiliar organizations that could be interesting to you. List them here.

Organization 1 _____

_____

Organization 2 _____

_____

Step 3: Use websites or other resources to learn where and when the organizations meet as well as information about their activities and purposes. Write that information below.

Location and time of meetings for Organization 1 _____

_____

Description and purpose of Organization 1 _____

_____

_____

_____

Location and time of meetings for Organization 2 _____

_____

Description and purpose of Organization 2 _____

_____

_____

_____

Step 4: Based on what you have learned, are you interested in joining either or both of these organizations? Check one: Yes_____ No_____.

Explain your answer. _____

_____

_____

_____

Step 5: Be prepared to discuss in class your perspective on the benefits of involvement in campus activities. _____

Leadership Activities

Leadership skills are useful in all walks of life, and college is a great place to develop or enhance those skills. Campus organizations offer students direct opportunities for leadership experiences. Some students even take the initiative of starting new campus organizations, both to obtain leadership opportunities and to meet like-minded people. Additionally, many colleges provide special training programs to help students understand the characteristics of effective leadership. Learning to be a successful leader can develop the following important set of skills applicable to many careers. In the table on the following page, check the skills that you already have and those that you might want to improve or acquire.

Leadership Skills	Already Have	Want to Improve or Acquire
Decision making		
Planning		
Cooperation		
Sensitivity		
Confidence		
Managing a meeting		
Ability to delegate		
Environmental awareness		
Budget planning		
Being motivated and inspiring		
Influencing others		
Leadership by example		
Setting goals		
Communicating		

If you decide you want to work at enhancing your leadership skills, you can examine the available courses or workshops at your school designed to develop and support campus leaders. Building leadership skills can also strengthen your credentials when you apply for further educational and career opportunities.

Civic Engagement and Service Learning

Civic engagement involves working for the public good by volunteering for community service and participating in community support organizations. Volunteering for public service during college positively impacts you, and it gives you a chance to help others. Campus Compact, a national organization that promotes student service, estimates that 30% of students perform volunteer activities and that these students contribute the equivalent of $7 billion annually to the economy through their civic engagement.[4] Among the most popular student civic engagement activities are one-day service projects and alternative spring breaks, which allow students to spend their spring breaks in organized volunteer activities. Along with the obvious satisfaction you can get from volunteering to help others, you learn skills for the future ranging from leadership to carpentry. You also may have the opportunity to work with people you would not otherwise meet.

Spring Break: Participating in an alternative spring break organized by your college offers you the opportunity to communicate with many people you might not ordinarily meet.

Civic engagement also can be combined with your academic program by taking part in either a nonpaying internship or a service learning class (see Chapter 2). For example, the campus Career Center may arrange for a marketing major to have an internship for the semester at a charitable organization. The student's role might be to help increase the public's awareness of the agency's big annual fundraising event. Unlike internships, **service learning classes** incorporate civic engagement into formal classroom experience. As an illustration, one computer science service learning class was divided into teams to design software to help a local Goodwill agency manage donations, volunteers, budgets, employees, and inventories. Civic engagement through some service learning classes might also involve participation in the political process or many other similar activities.

Social Sororities and Fraternities

Sororities and fraternities are a part of the social scene at a number of schools. Known as **Greek organizations** because their names feature Greek letters, these groups are usually chapters of national organizations with significant traditions. The chapters must govern themselves according to both college and national organization standards. (Some academic honor societies also have Greek names, but their focus is recognition and promotion of academic achievements.)

Greek groups usually engage in significant service activities. They also can provide an important sense of sisterhood and brotherhood as well as mentoring by older members. Furthermore, Greek affiliation can facilitate networking that can prove useful later in the career world. On some campuses, sororities and fraternities sponsor housing. Students who decide to live in these houses may be assigned chores to help maintain the property.

One of the drawbacks, historically, for Greek organizations has been hazing. **Hazing** occurs when a student going through the required pledging process to become a member is harmed, demeaned, harassed, humiliated, or placed at risk as part of the process. Because of pressures from national organizations and college officials, the amount of hazing has been reduced by fraternities and sororities. A number of leading national Greek organizations set up a hotline (800-Not-Haze or 800-668-4293) to report hazing.

More experienced students often advise new students to wait until sophomore year to join a Greek group. By then, you will be able to decide whether you want to pledge. It is important to note that some students interested in joining a Greek organization experience hurtful rejections. If this occurs, you can see it as only a temporary setback, since there will be comparable organizations on campus that will warmly accept you as a new member.

Social Networking through Technology

The resources you have available for digital communication are extensive, including social networking, texting, posting on Twitter, Internet telephoning, and blogging. With computer access, you can easily and inexpensively keep in touch with your friends on campus or anywhere around the country or the world. You also can develop new connections—whether you are a soap opera fan or a World Cup soccer fanatic—through shared interests on sites such as Facebook.

According to a recent study of smartphone users at Stanford University, the phone became "a means to have a social life" and a way to "manage a second identity that emerges on the Internet."[5] Your online persona can affect your social success, so how you present yourself on the Internet is important. Your happy photos, witty comments, cool design features, and interesting journal comments can portray you in a very favorable light. Just your sense of pride in your online communication, even without positive feedback from others, can help build your social confidence.

Social networking sites are great for spreading news quickly. They can instantly publicize events or share your views. Announcements of becoming "single" or "in a relationship" can alert interested people that you are or are not now available. You also may be able to communicate readily with classmates about academic concerns, such as assignments or difficult material.

Proceed with Caution

With the many benefits of digital communication, it's also a good idea to be cautious in order to keep your experiences positive. For example, college officials and campus police agencies have been known to monitor websites for disciplinary violations. Additionally, professors have visited student pages to discover that a student who missed an exam allegedly because of an ill relative was actually vacationing at the beach.

Update: Social networks make it possible for personal information to be shared instantly.

Some students experience problems by spending too much time online. They report lower grade point averages than they want, along with insufficient sleep. They also may isolate themselves from social contact. Excessive participation in activities such as online video role playing games can interfere with the development and maintenance of in-person relationships. If you find yourself averaging more than three hours a day online, try to arrange a personal activity with a friend or start participating in campus groups and activities.

Always consider that anything you place online can be seen by anyone. Even if you use privacy controls, it is easy for friends or acquaintances to forward embarrassing emails or photos without your knowledge. Also, if you post personal data on the Internet, you can become vulnerable to identity theft, cyberstalking, cyberbullying, and computer viruses. For example, students posting their daily schedule online could unknowingly invite thieves, who know when they will be away, to their residences.

Since prospective employers review the internet postings of student applicants, the rule of thumb is to omit anything on your pages that you would not want members of your family to see. Experts also warn that anything ever placed online can be there forever despite your attempt to remove it. When you are applying for jobs, you can use www.LinkedIn.com, a career site that enables you to present a favorable profile, including videos, travel experiences, blogs, part-time jobs and internships, and school activities.

ROMANTIC
RELATIONSHIPS

The freedom of college life affords students the opportunity to explore sex and affection. Many students worry about how to deal with these "hot" issues. Often, the challenging social experiences of the college years will result in a clarified vision of what to look for in a romantic relationship and, ultimately, a long-term partner.

Romance

Writers and musicians idealize love, and college students who study the poems of Elizabeth Barrett Browning or listen to the lyrics of modern love songs search for this ideal. Although finding idealized love in college is uncommon, students can experience a loving romantic relationship with affection, familiarity, companionship, and humor. To achieve and sustain such a successful relationship, the partners will usually need to accept one another unconditionally, with no expectation that the other will change. They will need to communicate openly and directly with each other, even about inevitable disagreements. In working out disagreements, couples who reach decisions through compromise are the most successful.

Couples are also most likely to succeed when each partner maintains separate friendships on campus. That is sometimes difficult when the partners are both members of the same group or when they spend all their free time alone together. However, the benefits of each having separate friends are significant. Each person will have his or her own life to share in the relationship. And in case they break up, each person will not feel isolated and alone. They also will not feel uncomfortable when forced to see each other again in a mutual group.

College Romance: The college years give you time to figure out the kind of person you want for a long-term partner.

Making time to be together is a major challenge for many couples. Individuals may have heavy course loads, jobs, major extracurricular activities, and other commitments. As a result, some couples have limited time to spend together, a circumstance that can burden the relationship. Also, couples may be separated during the summer if they do not stay in school together. Many college couples are able to overcome these obstacles, especially through regular communication while they are apart.

According to U.S. Census data, the approximate average age for a first marriage is 27 for women and 28 for men.[6] The relationships of many college couples may therefore not endure long enough to result in marriage. Nevertheless, a college romance can have a lifetime of importance. It can help you develop confidence, learn how to interact effectively in a close relationship, and form a clearer image of a compatible lifetime partner.

Sex

For college students, decisions about sex and sexuality usually require a period of time and adjustment. "How does sex relate to my moral and religious beliefs?" "Do other students find me physically attractive?" "Will getting sexually involved interfere with my academic success?" "Am I gay, bisexual, or straight?" "If I'm gay, do I come out?" These are just a few of the concerns that college students have about sex. Information about sexuality may be helpful in dealing with these issues.

Students' assumptions about sexual norms at their college may have a dramatic impact on their own attitudes and behavior. Several studies prove that much less sex is actually occurring on many campuses than most students believe. A study conducted on four typical college campuses shows that students overestimate the amount of sexual activity of their fellow students and the number of partners with whom other students have sex.[7] Sex is typically discussed more frequently than it is actually experienced, leaving sexually uninvolved students mistakenly thinking that they are missing out on what everyone else is doing.

Nevertheless, at many campuses, casual sex is more common than sex through committed relationships. Drinking alcohol sometimes precedes casual sex and clouds judgment. Pregnancy and STDs/STIs (see Chapter 9) can be serious consequences of alcohol use combined with casual sex. Sober students may want to help prevent intoxicated friends from putting themselves at risk in such settings as bars, fraternity parties, or spring break celebrations.

Students' sexual values usually can be characterized on a continuum from very liberal to very conservative. The liberal view is exemplified by the sexual philosophy of Albert Ellis, a psychologist who wrote *Sex without Guilt*.[8] Ellis believes that any sex is acceptable as long as it doesn't physically or psychologically injure anyone, including oneself. At the conservative end of the continuum are students who practice chastity. **Chastity groups** for students who choose not to be sexually active exist at many colleges, sometimes sponsored by campus ministries. These groups promote abstinence until marriage and provide support for students who do not wish to engage in premarital sex.

EXERCISE 4 R-E-S-P-E-C-T

Step 1: Read the story below, paying particular attention to the behavior of each of the five characters.

> **Lisette** and **Steve** fell for each other when they met on the first day of freshman English. They were a happy couple for the next few months. However, with Thanksgiving approaching, a dramatic event changed everything. Both **Lisette** and **Steve** were considered attractive students and had been very popular in high school. **Lisette** liked to show off, and friends described her as sexy and seductive. She hadn't realized, however, that she had attracted the attention of **Emil**, a guy who lived in her hall. One night in **Lisette's** room after they both had been out drinking with friends, **Lisette** and **Emil** were kissing passionately when her roommate, **Vera**, walked in on them. Since **Vera** liked **Emil**, she instantly became jealous, and she used her cell phone to secretly take a photo of **Lisette** and **Emil** kissing. She then posted a photo on her web page of **Lisette** and **Emil** kissing. **Steve** was soon bombarded with text messages telling him to look at the photo. He was shocked because he and **Lisette** had promised to stay faithful to one another. **Steve** phoned his older brother, **Bob**, for advice on what to do. **Bob** told him to hook up with another girl to make **Lisette** jealous and get even with her so that they could then forgive each other and make up. He followed his brother's advice, but **Lisette** was furious and broke up with **Steve**.

Step 2: You will find below a list of the characters in the story and columns labeled "Totally Respect," "Somewhat Respect," "Somewhat Disrespect," and "Totally Disrespect." Place a check mark in one of the columns to indicate your reaction to each character's behavior in the story. This exercise clarifies some of your social attitudes.

Character	Totally Respect	Somewhat Respect	Somewhat Disrespect	Totally Disrespect
Lisette				
Steve				
Emil				
Vera				
Bob				

Step 3: For each of the characters, explain the reasons for your ranking and what he or she could have done differently to earn your total respect.

Lisette _____

_____

_____

_____

Steve _____

_____

_____

_____

Emil _____

_____

_____

_____

Vera _____

_____

_____

_____

Bob _____

_____

_____

_____

Use the resource links to find additional information at *CollegeSuccess.andYOU.com*

Step 4: Be prepared to discuss in class your views of Lisette, Steve, Emil, Vera, and Bob.

Long-Distance Love

When beginning college, many students must reluctantly move far away from their girlfriend or boyfriend. Preserving a romantic relationship over distance and time is very challenging. Making such a relationship work requires mutual devotion, regular communication, and perhaps some sacrifice of new social opportunities. In fact, most long-distance relationships do not survive through the college years, leaving a student who has not developed new friendships on campus feeling isolated and left out.

If you want a long-distance relationship to endure, you will need to rely on a successful communication system with your boyfriend or girlfriend. Unfortunately, reliance on typical methods of communication such as telephoning, emailing, posting on Twitter, and text messaging are far from ideal because they are not face-to-face and in-person.

Nonverbal Communication:
When you can't see the speaker, you are limited in understanding his or her communication.

To appreciate this limitation, you need to understand **nonverbal communication**, the cues that are used along with words to give messages their meaning. Nonverbal cues include gestures, vocal intonations, and facial expressions. To accurately understand what your romantic partner is really communicating, you must go beyond the words that are used. Words are limited when it comes to emotional expression. For example, if a boyfriend were to ask his girlfriend over the phone how she's doing, she might respond, "Oh, I'm just great!" Was she being sarcastic or was she really enjoying herself? Research demonstrates that his perception is far less likely to be accurate when based only on nonverbal cues provided by the telephone, without being with her face-to-face.[9]

One nonverbal cue—facial expression—is superior to all others in promoting accurate communication.[10] Of course, direct in-person communication is ideal for important relationship communications because it includes facial expression and all other nonverbal cues. For long-distance relationships, however, alternatives showing facial expressions do exist. For instance, you can communicate using webcams over internet telephone systems. Systems such as Skype are free to use. Regardless of the method that you use to communicate, it will always be wise to check with your partner to make sure you understand the feelings and intentions being communicated.

Thinking Critically About...
Developing and Maintaining Healthy Relationships Through Positive Communication

Critical thinking involves an active evaluation of information using careful, thoughtful, and reasoned judgments.

1. Examine the social challenges that might be faced by each of the following freshmen who live on campus: (1) a 23-year-old veteran who just completed a tour of duty in a war zone, (2) a 19-year-old international student from China, and (3) an 18-year-old on a need-based scholarship who is the first family member to attend college.

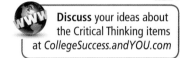
Discuss your ideas about the Critical Thinking items at *CollegeSuccess.andYOU.com*

2. Some parents of college students have been called "helicopter parents" because they remain heavily involved in the students' daily lives. Discuss the advantages and disadvantages for students of having "helicopter parents."

3. George Bernard Shaw, an Irish playwright, is often quoted as having said, "The single biggest problem in communication is the illusion that it has occurred." How does this quote apply to social communication among college students?

4. To monitor students' communication and stimulate class discussions, some professors of online classes admit to posing secretly as fake students in classes. Argue whether this teaching tactic is ethical. Discuss the effects of discovering that your professor had been an active phantom student in an online class that you just completed.

5. Assess the value of leadership experiences for students during college. Identify the positive and negative aspects of becoming a leader.

Online Learning

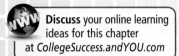

Discuss your online learning ideas for this chapter at *CollegeSuccess.andYOU.com*

Online classes can provide more sense of community than traditionalists might believe. If you are an online student, multiple resources may be available for communications, including web cameras that can enable you to see your fellow students. Friendships develop between classmates who get to know each other through online classes.

Group assignments are used to encourage online students to communicate with one another via their computers. Proponents of online education state that this form of communication effectively prepares future participants in the global economy for transactions around their community and around the world.[11] However, one of the limitations of many online classes is the lack of face-to-face contact available through in-person communication. This circumstance can create inaccurate communications based on the lack of important nonverbal cues such as gestures and facial expressions.

Online learning may be more socially comfortable for some students. For example, it is a great alternative for shy students who are nervous about speaking in classes. Also, online students do not need to worry about other students' reactions to how they dress, look, or sound. There are students who believe their participation in traditional classes might be inhibited because of personal characteristics such as their sex, ethnicity, or unique physical characteristics. These students are not usually distinguishable from other students in online classes.

CHAPTER CHALLENGE

INTERROGATION TIME

Smaller in size than ever, today's families have become increasingly focused on their children. Parents and caretakers shepherd children from one activity to another while carefully monitoring their progress in school. When children hit adolescence, they normally begin to resist some of this adult management and to prize their freedom. Nevertheless, most parents continue to care deeply about their children and try to stay informed about their lives, even when their children go away to college.

A CASE STUDY: FACING THE CHALLENGE OF . . .
INTERROGATION TIME

Ryan is the only child of two very caring parents. He appreciated their support during his childhood as well as throughout the stressful college application process. They also helped him move into the residence hall. As close as he was to his parents, in truth he was very happy to get away from them and have a chance to become his own person. Before his parents left campus after orientation, Ryan agreed to phone home every Monday, Wednesday, Friday, and Sunday evening during his first semester.

During Ryan's first few phone calls, his parents were very excited to hear from him, and he was equally excited to tell them about his new friends and his classes. As the weeks progressed, however, he noticed a regular pattern emerging in their conversations. His parents would ask question after question about him, and he would respond with narratives about his new life. Repeated questions about the neatness of his room, his study habits, and the amount of money he was spending began to put him on the defensive, making him uncomfortable and a bit annoyed. When his roommate asked him why he seemed upset one evening after he had just spoken to his parents, Ryan realized that he had to change the nature of the conversations.

OVERCOMING THE CHALLENGE OF . . .
INTERROGATION TIME

Be prepared to discuss your answers to the following items: (1) Create a strategy that Ryan can implement to make the phone calls with his parents more pleasant for both himself and his parents. (2) What are the possible motivations for all the questions from Ryan's parents? (3) For a student like Ryan, explain the advantages and disadvantages of being an only child.

Key Chapter Strategies

- Establish a regular communication plan with your family.
- For important conversations, use methods of communication that allow you to observe the other person's important nonverbal cues.
- Get involved in student activities and civic engagement—such involvement has many personal, social, and career advantages.
- Consider attending a leadership training program.
- Use conflict resolution techniques to get along with others.
- Protect the image that you project online.
- Read this book for more information on developing and maintaining relationships: *The Shyness and Social Anxiety Workbook* by Martin Antony and Richard P. Swinson.[12]

 **Can You Recall It?**

Assess your answers to Can You Recall It? at *CollegeSuccess.andYOU.com*

Directions: To review your understanding of the chapter, choose the correct term from the list below and fill it in on the blank. You will not use every term.

commuter student	conflict resolution	hazing
ombudsperson	outside mediator	homesickness
idiosyncrasy	sociogram	civic engagement
nonverbal communication	long-distance love	introvert

1. A technique used to settle a disagreement to all parties' satisfaction is

   _____ .

2. A/an _____ is a habit or mannerism peculiar to an individual.

3. Bill is a student who likes to keep to himself. He is probably a/an

   _____ .

4. Figuring out what is said based on facial expression and vocal intonation involves a reliance on _____ .

5. If Greek organizations and other campus groups mistreat students trying to become full members, the mistreatment is called _____ .

6. A student who lives off campus is a/an _____ .

7. Feelings of _____ occur in new students when they long for their family and friends where they previously lived.

8. A/an _____ is a graphic representation of social connections.

Web Activity: Who Am I? A Self-Search

Directions: Complete *one* of the following activities. Choose *either* Activity 1 or Activity 2.

Activity 1: Use a major search engine to look for references to your name on the Internet. If your initial search does not yield results, refine your search by adding the name of your current school, previous school, or special activities in which you have participated or try a different search engine.

I. List up to three specific web addresses where you are mentioned.

1. _____

2. _____

3. _____

II. Write two or three sentences explaining your reaction to what you found about yourself in your search. _____

_____

_____

Activity 2: Review any personal pages that you have placed on the Internet, including those that you no longer update.

I. List two community websites, blogs, journals, or similar personal pages that you have developed.

First website _____

Second website _____

II. Write your personal evaluation for each of these websites. Include what you like and what you don't like.

First website _____

_____

_____

_____

Second website _____

_____

_____

_____

Achieving Your Goals by Developing and Maintaining Relationships through Positive Communication

As you read this chapter, you probably considered your current social status and how you would like it to unfold during your years in college. Write three paragraphs, one paragraph for each of the following questions: (1) How would you evaluate your social adjustment to college so far? (2) What do you find most challenging about creating and maintaining social relationships on campus? (3) How do you want to extend your social development during the rest of your college years?

_____

_____

_____

_____

_____

_____

_____

_____

_____

_____

_____

_____

_____

_____

_____

_____

_____

_____

Appreciating Diversity

12

In this chapter, you will move toward achieving your goals by

- exploring the nature of campus diversity.

- recognizing the challenges to campus multiculturalism.

- discovering the benefits of diversity opportunities.

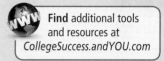

Find additional tools and resources at *CollegeSuccess.andYOU.com*

Self-Assessment:
Similarities and Differences

Step 1: Write your name at the top of the left column below and fill in the blanks describing your characteristics for each item.

Step 2: Select a friend (unrelated to you). Write your friend's name at the top of the column on the right. Ask your friend to provide you with the information you need to fill in the blanks in the right-hand column.

_____

Your name

1. Age _____
2. Hair color _____
3. Eye color _____
4. Sign of zodiac _____
5. Favorite sport _____
6. Favorite color _____
7. Favorite food _____
8. Preferred music _____
9. Best school subject _____
10. Number of siblings _____

_____

Your friend's name

1. Age _____
2. Hair color _____
3. Eye color _____
4. Sign of zodiac _____
5. Favorite sport _____
6. Favorite color _____
7. Favorite food _____
8. Preferred music _____
9. Best school subject _____
10. Number of siblings _____

Step 3: For each of the ten items, circle either "Same" or "Different" below, based on the responses in Step 2.

1.	Age	Same	Different
2.	Hair color	Same	Different
3.	Eye color	Same	Different
4.	Sign of zodiac	Same	Different
5.	Favorite sport	Same	Different
6.	Favorite color	Same	Different
7.	Favorite food	Same	Different
8.	Preferred music	Same	Different
9.	Best school subject	Same	Different
10.	Number of siblings	Same	Different

Step 4: According to the results in Step 3, your number of "Same" items is _____, and your number of "Different" items is _____. The sum must be 10. The following ratings indicate the degree of similarity between you and your friend, based on these scores.

Score	Degree of Similarity
9 to 10 items marked "Same"	Very Similar
7 to 8 items marked "Same"	Somewhat Similar
5 to 6 items marked "Same"	Slightly Similar, Slightly Different
3 to 4 items marked "Same"	Somewhat Different
0 to 2 items marked "Same"	Very Different

Based on this scale, your *Degree of Similarity* with your friend is

_____ .

Step 5: Read the following discussion about the degrees of similarity between friends.

Surprisingly, most friends score "Somewhat Different" or "Very Different" from each other on this "Self-Assessment" activity. Your differences show that you each have unique and special qualities that you bring to the relationship. During your college years, you will meet new people who share both similarities and differences with you. Learning about their experiences and qualities will broaden you educationally while also helping you appreciate the value of diversity in your life.

Regardless of whether you came from near or far to attend your college, you are sure to be around many new people. Getting to know students from different backgrounds presents one of the great opportunities for your educational and personal development during your college years.

Experts agree that college students prepare for their future lives as much by learning from fellow students as they do from classes. Today, most campuses include students from widely diverse cultures, backgrounds, and locations. This diversity contributes significantly to the ability of students to learn from one another.

College administrators generally believe that students' ability to relate effectively to people from backgrounds unlike their own will increase their chances of personal success as well as their contributions to society. For students, campus diversity provides an important opportunity to stretch and grow by developing an understanding of fresh perspectives. Additionally, a multicultural atmosphere provides the opportunity for students to share a rich variety of beliefs, music, artistic expression, and experiences based on their unique heritage.

In reality, all human beings are much more biologically alike than different. According to the Human Genome Project, 99% of any one person's DNA is the same as that of every other person. Consequently, only 1% of a person's genetic makeup accounts for individual differences.[1]

Life would be pretty dull if you and everyone else were totally alike. Fortunately, the sum of your experiences, including cultural upbringing, combines with genetics to produce your unique personal identity.

Discuss what you have observed about the nature of diversity on your campus at *CollegeSuccess.andYOU.com*

NATURE of The DIVERSITY

The *Merriam-Webster Collegiate Dictionary* defines **diversity** as "the condition of having or being composed of differing elements..."* On college campuses, diversity takes many forms, including those discussed in the following sections.

Sex

Through the 1960s, far fewer women than men attended college in the United States, and many students attended single-sex schools during this era. Today, most campuses are balanced with comparable numbers of both men and women. As a result, today's students have an unrivaled opportunity to learn from their peers of the opposite sex.

*By permission, From Merriam-Webster Collegiate® Dictionary, 11th Edition ©2013 by Merriam-Webster, Inc. (www.Merriam-Webster.com)

Religion

College students span the gamut of world religions. You may think that you know something about the spirituality of a student who identifies with a specific religion. However, religious beliefs and practices often vary extraordinarily even within religions.

Christianity, the most extensively practiced religion in the United States, is an excellent example of diversity within a religion. In 2000, 76.5% of people in the United States identified themselves as Christian.[2] The five largest Christian groups in the United States are Roman Catholic, Baptist, Methodist, Lutheran, and Presbyterian.[3] However, there are estimated to be 1200 different Christian groups practicing in the United States with wide variations in beliefs and practices, even within specific sects.

Of course, it is well known that other major faiths—including Islam, Judaism, and Hinduism—feature a variety of spiritual practices and beliefs within each general religion.

As you can see, religious diversity occurs at multiple layers—not only between religions, but also within religions. Add those students who do not affiliate with an organized religion or who identify themselves as agnostics or atheists, and you will recognize how spirituality represents an important dimension of campus diversity.

JUMP START © 2008 Robb Armstrong. Reprinted with permission of UNIVERSAL UCLICK for UFS. All rights reserved.

Race/Ethnicity

The fact that a large number of college students born in the United States descend from immigrants reflects the incredible diversity in heritage among students. Even within what may appear to be a homogeneous racial/ethnic group, great variety exists, which prevents simple generalizations about the group. For example, while black or African American students are descended mainly from western Africa, it is important to note that the families of some students lived in Caribbean or West Indian countries before coming to the United States. Some of those students (Jamaican Americans or Haitian Americans, for example) view themselves as distinct from black or African American students.

Hispanic Americans represent one of the most rapidly increasing ethnic groups on U.S. campuses. Hispanics also are not a unified group. Their roots stem from 26 different nations, with a variety of customs, food preferences, and language use.[4]

Multi-ethnic students contribute further to campus diversity. **Multi-ethnic** students have more than one ethnicity in their family backgrounds. The 2000 U.S. Census was the first permitting citizens to choose more than one ethnic group, with 6.8 million Americans identifying themselves as multi-ethnic.[5] The trend toward increasing multi-ethnicity in the United States is expected to continue.

EXERCISE 1 Proverbial Wisdom

Step 1: Proverbs, or folk sayings, usually reflect cultural beliefs that have been passed on through generations. These beliefs often can apply to all people. Listed below are five proverbs along with their cultures of origin. For each proverb, explain the universal meaning and then describe how the proverb is relevant to your own experiences. Here is an example:

Example: "A gentle hand may lead even an elephant by a hair." (Iranian)

Universal meaning:

People can be the most persuasive to anyone—even someone who is extremely difficult—by being kind and considerate.

Relevance to me:

I shouldn't yell and fight with my roommate if I want cooperation.

1. "Do not judge your neighbor until you walk two moons in his moccasins." (Cheyenne tribe, American Midwest and West)
   Universal meaning:

   _____

   _____

   _____

   Relevance to me:

   _____

   _____

   _____

2. "A wise man associating with the vicious becomes an idiot; a dog traveling with good men becomes a rational being." (Arabian)
   Universal meaning:

   _____

   _____

   _____

   Relevance to me:

   _____

   _____

   _____

3. "When elephants fight, the grass gets hurt." (Swahili tribe, Eastern and Central Africa)

Universal meaning:

_____

_____

_____

Relevance to me:

_____

_____

_____

4. "Fortune will call at the smiling gate." (Japanese)

Universal meaning:

_____

_____

_____

Relevance to me:

_____

_____

_____

5. "If all pulled in one direction, the world would keel over." (Yiddish-Jewish)

Universal meaning:

_____

_____

_____

Relevance to me:

_____

_____

_____

Step 2: Be prepared to discuss your answers in class. What other proverbs based on your background do you know that offer universal meaning?

Sexual Orientation and Gender Identity

In recent decades, administrations at many colleges have become increasingly supportive of homosexual students, faculty, and staff. They have also instituted nondiscrimination policies and supported LGBT student groups. The initials **LGBT** refer to the groupings discussed in the box below.

LGBT Groups	
Lesbian:	Females attracted to other females
Gay:	Males attracted to other males (Sometimes this term is used more generally to refer to any homosexual.)
Bisexual:	People attracted to both males and females
Transgender:	People whose gender identity does not match their physically assigned sex

LGBT students often experience lengthy struggles with their identity until they "come out" either to themselves or to themselves and others.

Geographic Identity

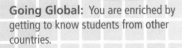

The number of international students studying in the United States adds to the intriguing multicultural fabric of today's college scene. It is estimated that 858,180 foreign students studied in the United States in the 2011–12 academic year. The countries sending the most students were China, India, and South Korea.[6]

While international students can undoubtedly share unique backgrounds with their fellow students, a similar phenomenon occurs with American students from areas under-represented on their campus. For example, a new student from rural Montana studying at New York University would probably bring very distinctive experiences to the school. Wherever you are from, you are likely to have the opportunity to meet people from different geographic areas at your school.

Going Global: You are enriched by getting to know students from other countries.

Additional Examples of Diversity Factors
Age
Disability
Socioeconomic class
Appearance (height, weight, clothing style, for example)
Political preference
Veteran status
Personality type
Academic major
Dietary preference
Special talent (athlete or musician, for example)

Challenges to CAMPUS MULTICULTURALISM

Since students come to college to increase their knowledge and prepare for careers, learning about different kinds of people provides an opportunity to expand social understanding. Nonetheless, several factors can create resistance to the appreciation of diversity.

This notion was acknowledged in the popular song, "Everyone's a Little Bit Racist," in the hit musical comedy *Avenue Q*. The Asian American, African American, Caucasian American, and "Monster American" characters reluctantly admit to the song's message while retaining their close friendships and appreciating each other's unique background. Understanding some of the issues that limit multicultural harmony may help overcome them. Here are some of these issues.

Stereotyping

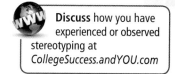

Discuss how you have experienced or observed stereotyping at *CollegeSuccess.andYOU.com*

Human intelligence enables us to develop useful generalizations. A **generalization** is a conclusion based on specific factors. For instance, generalizations from predicted weather changes can allow you to dress comfortably, and generalizations from your knowledge of the nutritional value of different food varieties can help you stay healthy. These generalizations help us manage our lives.

However, one type of generalization applied to other people, stereotyping, can be harmful rather than helpful. **Stereotypes** are negative generalizations about people based on their heritage, sex/gender, or other defining characteristics. Stereotyping interferes with student adaptation to campus multiculturalism. For example, a blond woman and a football player could be stereotyped as dumb just because of one feature of their total beings. Obviously, there are many extremely intelligent blond women and football players.

So-called positive stereotyping can also be problematic. **Positive stereotyping** involves ascribing positive characteristics to people because they fit in a category. For instance, assuming that a tall student is good at basketball can be insulting even if the assumption is true, and it can be doubly insulting if it is false.

When you meet a student from another background, it may be tempting to inquire about "people like you." However, if you put yourself in the other student's place, you will find that this approach may make the other student uncomfortable. Instead, you might simply try to get to know that student as a unique individual, not part of a stereotyped category. You will have a better chance to develop a new friendship with this approach.

The Silo Effect

Another common student pattern impeding diversity is what sociologists label the *Silo Effect*. The **Silo Effect** occurs when students shelter themselves in an exclusionary group of similar people. The proverb "Birds of a feather flock together" conveys the same meaning as the Silo Effect.

This behavior is understandable, because it can be comfortable to hang out with people from backgrounds similar to your own. It can be significantly more difficult to adapt to the communication styles and cultural values of individuals from unfamiliar backgrounds.

Birds of a Feather: The Silo Effect refers to students associating with only students like themselves.

While attempting to foster diversity, most colleges maintain student organizations based on sex, religion, or cultural background. These groups can provide valuable opportunities for students in unfamiliar environments to interact with others from similar backgrounds. However, unless members of these groups take the opportunity to interact regularly with members of other groups, this system can promote the Silo Effect.

The Silo Effect is probably most visible at campus dining facilities. Gathering with other students to eat presents an excellent opportunity for the exchange of ideas and experiences. At your campus, do you see students eating chiefly with students who look and act like each other? The Silo Effect prevents you from gaining appreciation of what others have to offer, encourages **group think**, and discounts the individual worth of others. Can you overcome the Silo Effect?

EXERCISE 2 **Dear Dr. A**

Step 1: In this exercise, you will play the role of Dr. A, an advice columnist like Dear Abby. You will read student letters about complex college adjustment issues related to being part of a multicultural campus. You will then provide advice to the concerned student based on your ideas relating to campus diversity.

Letter 1:

Dear Dr. A,

My problem is my roommate. I am a freshman at a large state university in Wisconsin but I am from Nashville, Tennessee. Overall, I like my roommate, except she continually criticizes the country music I listen to. She says that country music is racist, and that I am insensitive to her by listening to it. Even if I use earphones, she criticizes my taste. I grew up with this music, I love it, and I don't want to give it up. I want to become friends with my roommate, but now I can't. What should I do?

Luanne

Advice for Luanne: _____

_____

_____

Letter 2:

Dear Dr. A,

My new roommate uses a wheelchair, and I don't know how to act with him. He was paralyzed in a serious car crash when he was fifteen. He seems like a pretty cool, regular guy and takes care of himself independently. He has a lot of friends on our floor, and we all eat at the same table most evenings. But the other guys and I don't know how much we should help him out or whether we can talk to him about sports or other things that he might not be able to do. How should I handle this?

Matthew

Advice for Matthew: _____

_____

_____

Letter 3:

Dear Dr. A,

I am a freshman at a community college in California. My problem is the name that my math teacher calls me and the other Latina girls in my class. There are five of us, and he calls us all "Maria" (even though he makes it sound like "Malia"). Not one of us is really named Maria, and no one else in the class is either. The teacher told us his family is from China, so I think he should know better. Not only do I find this to show that he is prejudiced, but he won't remember me when I give a correct answer. What can I do?

Raquel

Advice for Raquel: _____

_____

_____

Letter 4:

Dear Dr. A,

I'm straight, but my friend, Nick, is gay. We both play trombone in the jazz band and hang out together. I've heard some other guys in the band ridiculing Nick behind his back. A few even have teased him directly, like calling him "one of the girls." Nick takes all of this in stride; I guess he had a lot of practice in high school before he came out. He also belongs to a gay pride group on campus, so he gets some support. However, he is my friend, and I want to say something when other guys act stupid toward him. I don't want everybody to hate me, though. Please tell me how to solve this problem.

Brandon

Advice for Brandon: _____

_____

_____

Step 2: During class, share the advice you offered for Luanne, Matthew, Raquel, and Brandon with your classmates. From the recommendations, discuss which suggestions are judged most realistic to help the students solve their problems. Are there other examples of challenges you or other students in class have faced regarding campus multiculturalism? Discuss these challenges and ideas for resolving them.

Culture Shock

When many students arrive on campus after months of planning to begin school, they initially experience feelings of excitement and enthusiasm. Sometimes, for a number of new students, those positive feelings can quickly turn into culture shock.

The stress experienced by people who have to adjust to a completely new social and cultural environment has been labeled **culture shock**. For students, culture shock occurs when they feel so uncomfortable in their new college surroundings that they begin doubting their decision to come to this college. Students with culture shock could not anticipate the dramatic variations they encounter in values, dress, language, and food. As a result, these students often feel lonely and homesick.

While international students are the most likely to experience culture shock, American students can also feel culture shock, even at schools not far from their homes. Colleges often have very different atmospheres than students' hometowns. For example, the main character in Tom Wolfe's novel *I am Charlotte Simmons* felt like a "fish out of water" when she moved from a small rural North Carolina town to a college modeled after Duke University. Charlotte found that most of the students were far different from anyone she had previously known.[7]

Overcoming culture shock usually requires patience, a willingness to try to meet other students, and communications with people from back home. With time, many students who have experienced culture shock come to realize that they are an integral part of a special, unique culture, their own college's culture. By becoming active members of their college community, students can put their special mark on campus culture.

BENEFITS from DIVERSITY

Your college years are a time of discovery. Many students find their political, spiritual, philosophical, and moral attitudes evolving during college. As a result, multicultural interactions can have a tremendously positive impact on your personal development. Research shows that a diverse college experience enhances students' intellectual development, college satisfaction, social skills, character development, career preparation, and citizenship.[8] Each of these six benefits is explored below.

Benefit from Diversity: Intellectual Development

Some students have learned about different cultures through travel or educational programs before they arrive on campus. If you are like most students, you can rely on a diverse college experience to expand your multicultural education. As your cultural boundaries disappear, you may be exposed to interesting new forms of language, art, music, thought, sports, religion, and dance. If you also take classes with multicultural content (for example, world religions, women's studies, sociology, world history, and anthropology), you can boost your ability to think in terms of many cultures.

Studies find that your ability to think critically, creatively, and analytically about complex issues increases through involvement in college diversity.[9] You will also develop more flexibility and open-mindedness in problem solving. Anthony Carnevale of the Educational Testing Service concludes, "Students that are taught in schools with diverse faculty and with diverse student bodies become better critical thinkers, better problem solvers, better communicators, and better team players."[10]

Cross-Cultural Competency: Many college classes provide an opportunity to learn about other cultures.

Benefit from Diversity: College Satisfaction

Through participation in diverse activities and groups, students express more satisfaction with college and increase their probability of graduating. They also exhibit more motivation to learn and greater academic success.

Along with these benefits, students at colleges with diverse populations share a common ground with fellow students from all backgrounds. You wear the same college T-shirts, share the same traditions, and root for the same college team. You live and study together and will proudly have the same alma mater for the rest of your lives.

Benefit from Diversity: Social Skills

Learning to deal with students different from yourself will help you socially. As you become aware of their backgrounds and experiences, you will sharpen your ability to empathize or put yourself in their place. Empathy enhances social understanding and can help you build bridges and make new friends. In fact, research findings show that attendance at a college with a diverse student body increases the probability of having more diversity among friends, fellow employees, and neighbors nine years after starting college.[11]

EXERCISE 3   Getting to Know You

Step 1: Choose a student from this class or another student from campus whose background or heritage is different from yours. Interview this student by asking each of the questions below and writing the answers in the space provided.

Name of the student you interviewed: _____

Question 1 "Where were you born?"

_____

Question 2 "In what community did you spend the most time living before you started college?"

_____

Question 3 "Who lived with you during your first five years of life?"

_____

Question 4 "Who were your most important teachers of cultural tradition?"

_____

Question 5 "Describe your cultural heritage and the major ways that it was expressed when you were a child."

_____

_____

_____

_____

Question 6 "What are your important cultural holidays, and how were they celebrated when you were younger?"

_____

Question 7 "What was the predominant language spoken in your family? What other languages, if any, were used?"

_____

Question 8 "While growing up, who was your hero?"

_____

Question 9 "How was your first name selected?"

_____

_____

Question 10 "What elements of your culture are important to you now?"

_____

_____

_____

_____

Step 2: As you discuss this exercise in class, share the similarities and differences that you find between the student you interviewed and yourself. What is your reaction to what you learned?

Benefit from Diversity: Character Development

Another benefit from diversity experience is positive character development. **Character** refers to personal qualities of honesty, justice, and morality that guide a person to do the right thing. Here are some aspects of personal character development that are often enhanced through multicultural college experiences:

- Compassion for others
- Sensitivity to social justice (fairness for all)
- Self-respect and self-confidence
- Decisions without snap judgments about others
- Respect for others
- Willingness to stand up for worthy causes
- Generosity to the needy
- Ability to be open and honest
- Motivation to contribute to the greater good
- Empathy for others

Benefit from Diversity: Career Preparation

Teaching, medicine, law, engineering, business—students going into these popular professions and others can profit immensely from diversity experiences. The heterogeneity of consumers of services as well as products in the United States will swell in the future, encouraging employers to hire college graduates with multicultural awareness. Graduates' sensitivity to the needs and preferences of the population can lead to creative solutions for businesses and professions.

It can be safely predicted that as the twenty-first century unfolds, there will be fewer Caucasian men in leadership positions than ever before in U.S. history. And those Caucasian men who do ascend to leadership roles will probably have begun their training by interacting on campus with students from backgrounds unlike their own.

Transportation and communication advances have expanded global commerce. Comfort in transactions with people from other cultures, perhaps even the ability to speak in their language, will be extremely advantageous for recent college graduates working in the international marketplace.

From Campus to Career: College diversity experiences help prepare you for personal and career success.

EXERCISE 4 **Where in the World Are You?**

Directions: Assume that you have been hired by a corporation as an international consultant. For your first independent consultation, your supervisor is sending you to a foreign country beginning with the same letter as your last name. Before your trip, your supervisor advises, "Prepare for a successful consultation by learning about the culture of this country."

Step 1: Write the first letter of your last name here. _____

Identify the country that you will visit that begins with the same letter as your

last name. _____

Step 2: Describe the location of this country. In your description, identify two

countries that are its closest neighbors. _____

_____

_____

Step 3: Answer the following questions about this country.

1. What language or languages are spoken?

_____

2. What is the form of government?

_____

_____

_____

3. In the space below, draw this country's flag, with appropriate colors.

4. What religions are practiced in the country? _____

_____

_____

5. Identify the unit of currency.

_____

6. What is the average hourly wage in U.S. dollars for workers?

_____

7. What is the leading industry?

_____

8. Describe special features about clothing or fashion preferences.

_____

_____

_____

9. Name and describe two unique types of food that you would find in this

country. _____

_____

_____

10. What are the major forms of entertainment or recreation in this country?

_____

_____

11. What are especially well-known types of music and art from the country?

_____

_____

Step 4: Be prepared to discuss the following two issues in class:

(1) How has the country you studied responded to the Western idea of progress?

(2) Compare and contrast sex roles in the country you studied with sex roles in the United States.

Benefit from Diversity: Citizenship

A diverse college experience promotes the concept that people from different backgrounds have the potential to understand each other. In a longitudinal study of University of Michigan students from their freshman to senior years, researchers report a number of citizenship benefits from diversity education.[12] Their findings are that students who participated in a curricular diversity program, when compared to comparable students who did not participate, show more democratic sentiments, interest in learning about other groups, commitment to volunteering, and recognition that ethnic differences are not divisive.

Students committed to diversity often become involved in cross-cultural causes. Although a multitude of examples exist, the involvement of students in helping Haiti overcome the effects of its devastating 2010 earthquake represents students reaching out to assist others. Such involvement increases the awareness of local, regional, and international responsibility while establishing an enduring cultural understanding.

A **civil society** includes citizens who understand and respect each other, even when individual differences exist. This means people can choose to debate when they have disagreements, but they strive to listen to one another's viewpoints. The willingness to listen shows respect. With its multicultural context, the college campus is a perfect laboratory for you to experiment through dialogue with other students who have a different background and heritage from your own. Participating in such a way fosters the pluralism that is the basis of today's global society.

One World: Getting to know students from other cultures helps you find your place in today's global society.

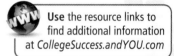

Use the resource links to find additional information at *CollegeSuccess.andYOU.com*

Thinking Critically About . . .
Appreciating Diversity

Critical thinking involves an active evaluation of information using careful, thoughtful, and reasoned judgments.

1. Use an example from your own experience to illustrate an issue related to diversity. Explain what led up to the experience, what occurred, the outcome, and your feelings and reactions.

2. Assess the ways diversity experiences influence the development of critical thinking.

3. Recommend ways for students to gain cross-cultural competency on your campus.

4. Analyze the advantages and disadvantages of the Silo Effect.

5. Many colleges make an effort to recruit a diverse student body. Some students argue that admissions should be based strictly on merit, while others argue that students from under-represented groups should be given admission preference. Take a position on this issue (for or against recruitment of students from under-represented groups) and make a convincing argument.

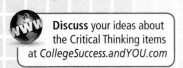
Discuss your ideas about the Critical Thinking items at *CollegeSuccess.andYOU.com*

Online Learning

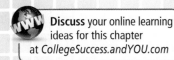
Discuss your online learning ideas for this chapter at *CollegeSuccess.andYOU.com*

In a comprehensive review of research relating diversity to distance learning, Patricia McGee, a faculty member at the University of Texas at San Antonio, challenges a "one size fits all" design for online classes.[13] She concludes that a variety of educational design features and media should be used in online classes to effectively reach students from many different backgrounds and orientations. She also cites the flexibility in the pace of online classes as a factor that can appeal to diverse groups. As a specific example, she notes research support for Hispanic online students benefiting from regular evaluative feedback and collaborative participation in their classes.

Innovative programs have been applied at some colleges to foster diversity experiences in online programs. For instance, the University of Illinois–Springfield, with only 9% minority students, arranged collaborative classes with Chicago State University, with more than 90% minority enrollment.[14] The students taking compatible advanced education classes online at each school were divided into small groups consisting of students from both universities. The groups collaborated on their projects through web audio conferencing and an online course management system.

Online learners have several ways to enhance their appreciation of diversity. For example, they can work for a multicultural organization or become involved in diversity activities in their community. One good opportunity is a volunteer program that may include other college students. Additionally, some online classes, such as world religion, anthropology, and sociology, promote cross-cultural understanding. Distance learners may interact with students from other regions and go on to develop new friendships.

JUDGING A BOOK BY ITS COVER

For most new students, what to expect in a college experience is a scary unknown. Usually, colleges have larger and more diverse student bodies than high schools. It is only natural for students to wonder how they will fit in to this bigger scene and how their social adjustment will affect their goal of achieving academic success.

A CASE STUDY: FACING THE CHALLENGE OF . . . JUDGING A BOOK BY ITS COVER

The valedictorian of an inner-city, predominantly black high school, Cheryl was determined to continue her academic success in college. Cheryl was the youngest of five children, all raised by their single mother. Before she set foot on the campus of her state's foremost university, she had decided that besides focusing on schoolwork, she would participate in a black women's service club, her work-study job, and weekly church services. Her one unknown was her roommate. They had corresponded briefly over the summer, and Cheryl had been surprised to learn that her roommate, Janet, was also black but was an only child who had attended an exclusive prep school in another of the state's large cities.

As soon as Cheryl met Janet, she immediately disliked her. Janet was lighter-skinned, thin, wore very preppy clothes, and seemed full of herself. Cheryl also thought that Janet had more possessions than any college freshman could possibly need. Cheryl decided that she would be courteous, but businesslike, with Janet. This strategy initially seemed to work, as Janet hung out with several girls from her prep school and accepted the cold shoulder from Cheryl by talking to her only when necessary.

When Cheryl attended the first meeting of the black women's service club, she was shocked that Janet was also there. Janet had never indicated that she cared at all about providing service to others.

OVERCOMING THE CHALLENGE OF . . . JUDGING A BOOK BY ITS COVER

Be prepared to discuss your answers to the following items: (1) Evaluate Cheryl's attitude toward Janet. Is Cheryl being fair? What factors are influencing Cheryl's attitude? (2) Summarize what both Cheryl and Janet can do to improve their attitudes toward one another. (3) Create a hypothetical account of how the girls might become close friends.

Key Chapter Strategies

■ Seek out opportunities to learn from diverse students.

■ Share your unique cultural heritage with at least one other student.

■ Make a conscious effort to avoid stereotyping.

■ Become active in a campus organization with diverse membership.

■ Take a course with multicultural content in the curriculum.

■ Expand your diversity experiences by studying abroad or volunteering to work in a needy community.

■ Read this inspiring book: *Mountains beyond Mountains: The Quest of Dr. Paul Farmer, a Man Who Would Cure the World* by Tracy Kidder.[15]

 **Can You Recall It?**

DOWNLOAD

Assess your answers to Can You Recall It? at *CollegeSuccess.andYOU.com*

Directions: To review your understanding of the chapter, choose the correct term from the list below and fill it in on the blank. You will not use every term.

diversity	positive stereotyping	LGBT
multicultural	culture shock	social justice
proverb	transgender	civility
the Human Genome Project	Silo Effect	generalization

1. According to sociologists, the _____ occurs when students stick together in exclusive groups not open to students who are different from them.

2. A/an _____ is a folk saying with deep meaning.

3. _____ can be offensive even though a favorable characteristic is attributed to a student just because that student is part of a certain racial or ethnic group.

4. A college with _____ includes students with a variety of differences in backgrounds and characteristics.

5. Groupings that refer to diverse sexual orientation and gender identification are referred to as _____.

6. _____ is a stress reaction that occurs when new students move to a college community with very different customs, values, and people from those in their home community.

7. A conclusion based on specific factors is a/an _____.

8. _____ involves a respect for others even if they have different opinions.

Web Activity: Musical Mix

Directions: Diversity has been celebrated in many songs. For example, the character Kermit the Frog sang, "It's Not Easy Bein' Green." In that song, Kermit sings, "I am green, and it'll do fine, it's beautiful! And I think it's what I want to be." Using your favorite search engine and the search words "diversity in songs," identify two songs that celebrate diversity, and then respond to the items below about each.

I. Song title and artist:_____

   1. Copy two lines from the song that particularly reflect diversity.

   _____

   _____

   _____

   2. Interpret how these song lyrics express diversity. You may use the meaning of the entire song in your interpretation. _____

   _____

   _____

   3. What is the exact web address for the song lyrics?_____

   _____

II. Song title and artist:_____

   1. Copy two lines from the song that particularly reflect diversity.

   _____

   _____

   _____

   2. Interpret how these song lyrics express diversity. You may use the meaning of the entire song in your interpretation.

   _____

   _____

   _____

   3. What is the exact web address for the song lyrics?_____

   _____

Reflection Time

Achieving Your Goals by Appreciating Diversity

Which unique features of your background do you bring to campus that influence what you think, what is important to you, what you notice about others, and what you want to learn? Explain how these features might contribute to campus diversity.

_____

_____

_____

_____

_____

_____

_____

_____

_____

_____

_____

_____

_____

_____

_____

_____

_____

_____

_____

Selecting a Suitable Major and Identifying a Potential Career

In this chapter, you will move toward achieving your goals by

■ recognizing your values, interests, personality characteristics, and aptitudes that help guide you to select a suitable major and a potential career.

■ matching your personal strengths and qualities to college majors and careers.

■ planning for a potential future career.

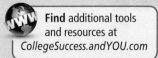

Find additional tools and resources at *CollegeSuccess.andYOU.com*

Self-Assessment: What Is Your Goal in Ten Years?

Step 1: Review the description of each person below. Assume the people described are the same gender as you.

Adrian

An attorney at a prominent law firm, Adrian is single. Adrian dresses in expensive business suits from Bloomingdale's and Neiman Marcus. With a goal in life to become a justice of the United States Supreme Court, Adrian works long hours and has little leisure time. Although interested in marriage, Adrian considers professional success to be the highest priority at this time.

Chris

An artist specializing in landscape painting, Chris spends most of the week alone in a studio. At times, Chris visits attractive outdoor scenes and photographs them to serve as models for paintings. To earn a living, Chris sells some paintings to galleries but also attempts to sell the art at weekend shows in the surrounding communities. Chris is involved with a romantic partner who is available on weekend evenings but does not think that the relationship will become permanent.

Alex

A single personal trainer who works at a gym ten months a year, Alex travels the rest of the time. Alex also plays softball and tennis regularly. With a body that has little fat and is always quite well-toned, Alex is generally considered to be quite attractive looking. Alex lives alone in an apartment and has a pet cat. Having few responsibilities or commitments, Alex dates occasionally but has no interest in sticking with anyone.

Lee

Lee's most cherished goals of getting married and becoming a parent have been achieved. Although Lee has a college degree, Lee has no plans to use the degree in a job. Lee's spouse is a physician with a rapidly growing practice. Lee takes care of two children, ages three and five, with the help of a nanny. Additionally, Lee serves as coach of the five-year-old child's soccer team and spends afternoons at practices and games. The family travels together occasionally on weekend getaways, and the couple takes two weeks a year to vacation away from the kids.

Pat

Pat is a commercial real estate broker who has already arranged the purchase of five buildings worth more than $50 million. Personally collecting 3% of each sale, Pat's net worth recently exceeded $2 million. Pat is arranging to start a hotel chain with a partner in whom Pat has some romantic interest. Pat's primary goal in life is to amass as much money as possible. Pat selects clothing according to what will make the best impression on clients.

Shen

A surgeon at a major hospital, Shen has accomplished this success despite being the parent of three children aged four to nine. Shen's spouse manages a gourmet restaurant and works long hours. Shen has recently become troop leader for the nine-year-old child's scout troop. With such a busy schedule, Shen does not have much time for leisure but does jog daily every morning before helping get the family ready for the day.

Sandy

Teaching first grade at an inner-city school, Sandy is dedicated to getting children off to a good educational start. Sandy's greatest pride is in watching a child learn to read and solve arithmetic problems. To facilitate the learning process, Sandy buys extra educational materials and enjoys taking the children on field trips. Choosing what to wear to work is of little concern to Sandy, who spends spare time volunteering to build houses for Habitat for Humanity. At Habitat for Humanity, Sandy has met a romantic partner who has the potential to become Sandy's soul mate.

Step 2: Based on these descriptions, select which person you would most want to be like in ten years. On the line to the left of each person's name below, rank-order each person: Place "1" for the person you *most* want to be like; place "2" for the person you would *next* want to be like; and so on through "7" for the person you *least* want to be like.

_____ Adrian

_____ Chris

_____ Alex

_____ Lee

_____ Pat

_____ Shen

_____ Sandy

Step 3: Explain *why* you prefer the person you ranked first from the descriptions on the previous page. _____

_____

_____

_____

Below is a chart listing examples of suitable majors and potential careers for people with qualities similar to each person.

Character	Suitable Majors*	Potential Careers
Adrian	Political science, history	Lawyer, executive, politician, public administrator
Chris	Art, music	Web designer, musician, writer, graphic designer
Alex	Exercise physiology, physical education	Gym owner, high school coach, personal trainer, yoga instructor
Lee	Child development, liberal studies	Preschool teacher, writer, tutor
Pat	Finance, economics	Investor, entrepreneur, fund manager, investment banker
Shen	Biology, chemistry	Dentist, physician, research scientist, mathematician
Sandy	Elementary education, sociology	Social worker, principal, teacher, guidance counselor

Note that several different undergraduate majors can lead to many of the careers listed.

Most students attend college not only to broaden and extend their knowledge but also to improve their chances of achieving career success after graduation. However, it is quite normal for new students to be unsure about a specific pathway to achieve this success. In fact, according to research findings, as many as 80% of new students are uncertain about their choice of a major, including those who have officially declared a major.[1]

Since you have the potential to succeed in more than one major and career, taking time to arrive at the best decision makes sense. Even though some of your friends may seem settled into the choice of a major, you can feel comfortable remaining undecided until you are ready to select a major. Actually, statistics indicate that almost half of the students who start out in one major eventually decide to switch to another major sometime during their college careers.[2]

As you progress toward your decision of a major and a career, economic and personal factors may contribute to your choices. For instance, your crystal ball to the future may be cloudy if you select a college major that is not likely to provide opportunities in the career market. "What can I do with a BA in philosophy?" has become a challenging question for some graduating seniors.

How One Student Selected a Major

Ruben, a first-generation freshman, was surprised when his academic advisor suggested that he take an introductory psychology course in his first semester. Although Ruben did not know for sure what the study of psychology was, he followed his advisor's recommendation. As soon as he browsed the textbook, he discovered a number of interesting topics. Ruben's friends had teased him for always wondering about the motives for people's behavior, and now he was going to discover some of the answers. As his first semester progressed, he found himself absorbed by the class and the readings. He also earned a grade of A on the midterm and the final. When he met with his advisor to select second-semester classes, he thanked her for suggesting the psychology class and asked to sign up for another psychology course, Introduction to Personality. Eventually, after continuing success in psychology classes and a volunteer experience in an animal behavior lab, Ruben officially declared psychology as a major and began to read about graduate programs leading to careers in the field.

How to select a
SUITABLE MAJOR and a potential
CAREER

Discuss how much you think a college major should be directly related to a career goal at *CollegeSuccess.andYOU.com*

To help you get started on the path to finding a suitable major and potential career, this chapter explains how your personal characteristics can be matched to college majors and career choices. The values and attitudes that you preferred in the "Self-Assessment" activity can be considered important parts of your personal profile. You might find yourself desiring such fulfillments in your career as power, spirituality, financial reward, technological sophistication, scientific understanding, help to others, protection of the environment, or creativity. Your preferences help identify who you are.

How might you have developed these preferences? Factors in your childhood background can be very important. For example, the career experiences of family members that you observed as a child may have influenced you more than you can imagine. Did you know someone who worked so many hours that he or she had almost no time to spend with family or relax? Did you hear complaints about an unreasonable boss? Have relatives or friends mentioned how much they like being their own boss?

EXERCISE 1   First Impressions

Step 1: Select two older employed relatives or acquaintances, describe their careers, and discuss your perceptions about their degree of satisfaction with their work experiences.

First relative/acquaintance _____

_____

_____

_____

_____

Second relative/acquaintance _____

_____

_____

_____

_____

Step 2: Think about what your relatives or acquaintances liked and disliked about their careers. Write three sentences explaining how their experiences might influence your career choice.

_____

_____

_____

_____

_____

_____

_____

_____

Step 3: Be prepared to discuss in class how your experiences beyond family and acquaintances might have influenced your thinking about majors and careers.

Generally, the key factors for choosing a major and a career involve a combination of your personal values, interests, personality traits, and aptitudes.

Your Values

Your **values** reflect the beliefs and principles that are most important and meaningful for you to fulfill in life. They are among the factors that make you unique. It is easy to understand the importance of satisfying personal values in a career. Returning to the characters in the "Self-Assessment" activity, we can easily identify Chris as satisfying creativity values, Pat as satisfying wealth values, and Sandy as satisfying altruistic values. Surveys find that today's college students place very high values on helping others and being well-off financially.[3]

EXERCISE 2 Values Judgment

Step 1: Below is a list of some typical values. In the column to the right, check the three values that you think are the most meaningful for you to satisfy in your career.

Value	Definition	Meaningful to You
Achievement	Attaining success and status	
Adventure	Seeking fresh and exciting experiences	
Altruism	Helping others	
Creativity	Developing things that are new or unique	
Empathy	Recognizing and understanding the feelings of others	
Fitness	Fostering health and appearance	
Independence	Preferring self-reliance and self-determination	
Justice	Promoting fair treatment for all	
Power	Being in a position to make change	
Preservation	Maintaining history and the environment	
Recognition	Gaining attention and fame	
Science	Analyzing and researching	
Spirituality	Seeking deep, personalized meaning of the human spirit and its relationship to the world	
Wealth	Accumulating money and property	

Step 2: Be prepared to discuss in class how the values you checked can relate to the choice of a college major and career.

Your Interests

Interests refer to what you like to do. Interests include your hobbies, entertainment preferences, dream jobs when you were a child, and types of classes you enjoy most. If you are going to spend a significant chunk of your adult life working, you will be happiest if you find a career that is interesting to you.

John Holland, a psychologist, created a system for categorizing interests. His theory is that all jobs can fit into at least one of six major interest categories that are known as the **Holland Codes**.[4] Below are brief descriptions of the interests indicated by each of the general Holland Code types, along with representative appropriate majors and career choices. The varied majors and careers listed are intended to be examples, and many other majors and careers fit each interest category. You can consult your advisor to learn more about the majors and careers listed.

Holland Codes (designated by the acronym RIASEC)

1. **REALISTIC**
   - Interests: Hands-on, mechanical, practical, outdoors
   - Suitable Majors: Aviation, criminology, forestry, mechanical engineering
   - Potential Careers: Pilot, police officer, forest ranger, engineer

2. **INVESTIGATIVE**
   - Interests: Analytical, computational, research, scientific
   - Suitable Majors: Nutrition, chemistry, biology, meteorology
   - Potential Careers: Dietitian, pharmacist*, veterinarian*, weather forecaster

Work Out: Since you will spend a significant proportion of your life working, finding a job that matches your interests is important.

3. **ARTISTIC**
   - Interests: Artistic, creative, literary, musical
   - Suitable Majors: Broadcasting, dramatic arts, art, English literature
   - Potential Careers: TV news anchor, actor, graphic designer, editor

4. **SOCIAL**
   - Interests: Caring, helpful, listening, people-oriented
   - Suitable Majors: Sociology, religion, elementary education, psychology
   - Potential Careers: Social worker, minister, teacher, rehabilitation counselor

5. **ENTERPRISING**
   - Interests: Managing, marketing, persuading, selling
   - Suitable Majors: Hospitality management, business administration, political science, marketing
   - Potential Careers: Hotel manager, chief executive officer, elected public official, life insurance agent

6. **CONVENTIONAL**
   - Interests: Clerical, data management, organizing, record keeping
   - Suitable Majors: Accounting, agriculture, health management, finance
   - Potential Careers: Accountant, farmer, nursing home administrator, credit manager

*These careers require advanced training beyond a bachelor's degree.

Since jobs may include features from more than one of the interest categories, sometimes careers have overlapping Holland Codes. Here are a few examples of majors and careers with overlapping Holland Codes.

 Discuss whether you think people actually choose a career that incorporates their biggest interests at *CollegeSuccess.andYOU.com*

Examples of Majors with Two Holland Codes

- Advertising (Artistic and Enterprising)
- Dance (Artistic and Realistic)
- Forestry (Realistic and Investigative)
- Information technology (Investigative and Conventional)
- International business (Social and Enterprising)
- Liberal studies (Investigative and Social)

Examples of Careers with Two Holland Codes

- Architect (Realistic and Artistic)
- Banker (Conventional and Enterprising)
- Biology teacher (Investigative and Social)
- Dental hygienist (Realistic and Social)
- Interior designer (Artistic and Enterprising)
- Optometrist (Realistic and Investigative)

EXERCISE 3 **What are Your Interests?**

Step 1: Rank in order your own Holland Code interests from highest to lowest by writing the Holland Code categories (Realistic, Investigative, Artistic, Social, Enterprising, and Conventional) next to the numbers. Beside "1," write the Holland Code category that *most* interests you, beside "2" write the Holland Code category that interests you *next*, and so on until for "6" you write the Holland Code category that represents your *lowest* interest.

1.

2.

3.

4.

5.

6.

Step 2: Next, identify a possible major and career that you are considering and match the Holland Code category or categories that seem to fit. Remember, you may select more than one Holland Code category. For example, pharmacists would have both Investigative and Conventional categories because they must know science, but they also must carefully deal with a lot of paperwork when they fill prescriptions. You might even have more than two Holland Codes.

Major _____

Career _____

Holland Code(s) _____

Step 3: Divide the class into six groups based on each student's number one preferred Holland Code from Step 1 above. In the groups, discuss interests and potential matching majors and careers. After the group discussions, be prepared to share in class what you have discovered about your interests.

Your Personality

The term **personality** represents your consistent unique pattern of relating to the world around you. One dimension of personality is whether you tend to be more introverted or more extroverted. For example, people may see you as more **introverted**, meaning that you gain fulfillment from your own thoughts and feelings. Or they may see you as more **extroverted**, meaning you are outgoing and very involved in relationships with other people. Some careers would clearly favor either a more introverted or extroverted personality style. For example, mathematicians, who spend long hours performing calculations, would likely be more introverted. In contrast, public relations professionals are often extroverted in order to develop and maintain business contacts for their companies.

Another important personality dimension related to major and career choice is assertiveness. **Assertiveness** refers to people's confidence and willingness to stand up for their rights, including the ability to say "no." Unassertive people may feel that their opinions are not heard or respected in social situations. It is important to note that assertive people do not express hostility and do not demean or hurt other people. Instead, they effectively communicate their thoughts and feelings in order to fulfill their appropriate needs. You can expect to develop increasing assertiveness as part of your personal growth during the college years. You can determine your degree of assertiveness by completing the following exercise.

Positively Assertive Developing assertiveness promotes your comfort in leadership roles.

EXERCISE 4 **Are You Assertive?**

Step 1: Circle "True" or "False" for each item as it applies to you.

1. If someone were sitting in my reserved seat when I arrived at a football game, I would tell that person that it is my reserved seat.

    True   False

2. I would accept food that I did not order at a restaurant even if I knew that I would be charged for the extra food.

    True   False

3. I like to give orders to other people.

    True   False

4. I am nervous and uncomfortable when I enter a room where a group is already hanging out together.

    True   False

5. If I were studying in the library and two students sitting near me were speaking loudly, I would ask them to speak more softly.

    True   False

6. If a seller sent me a broken item that I bought on eBay, I would ask for my money back.

    True   False

7. I would be comfortable supervising other people.

        True   False

8. I wouldn't say anything if someone cut in front of me in a long line.

        True   False

9. When people talk loudly near where I am sitting at a movie theater, I either let it go or move to another seat.

        True   False

10. I ask a lot of questions in class.

        True   False

11. I would rather not be in a leadership position.

        True   False

12. If my romantic partner regularly mistreated me, I would not hesitate to end the relationship.

        True   False

13. It is hard for me to give compliments to other people.

        True   False

14. I am uncomfortable talking to authority figures such as teachers and police officers.

        True   False

15. I would complain if someone bothered me by smoking in a nonsmoking zone.

        True   False

16. I would enjoy giving my opinion on live television about a controversial news event.

        True   False

17. I would not protest unfair late charges for a bill I paid.

        True   False

18. I like to stay in the background when my friends are arguing.

        True   False

19. It would be fun to shoot a last-second foul shot that could win my basketball team's game.

        True   False

20. I would be afraid of getting fired if I told my boss that something could be improved where I work.

        True   False

Step 2: Give yourself a score as follows for each of the items that you answered. For example, if you answered "True" to Question 1, give yourself 1 point. If you answered "False" to Question 1, give yourself 0 points. Follow the guide below for points.

Give Yourself 1 Point If You Answered	My Points
1. True	_____
2. False	_____
3. True	_____
4. False	_____
5. True	_____
6. True	_____
7. True	_____
8. False	_____
9. False	_____
10. True	_____
11. False	_____
12. True	_____
13. False	_____
14. False	_____
15. True	_____
16. True	_____
17. False	_____
18. False	_____
19. True	_____
20. False	_____
My Total Points:	_____

Step 3: Check the chart on the next page to evaluate your assertiveness.

Assertiveness Ratings

Score	Assertiveness Levels
15–20	Very assertive personality
10–14	Moderately assertive personality
0–9	Less assertive personality

Very Assertive Personality

You stand up for your rights and say what is on your mind. Assertive people do not have to act rudely or inconsiderately to get their needs met. A very assertive personality facilitates success in fields that require confidence and forcefulness.

Moderately Assertive Personality

You balance your willingness to stand up for yourself with concerns about how your behavior may affect you and other people. You pick your spots for acting forcefully and decisively. Your potential for a leadership position will partly depend on your level of confidence in that position.

Less Assertive Personality

You are less comfortable in expressing your beliefs and upholding them. A low level of assertiveness might limit job performance in decision making, participation in meetings, and relationships with other employees. However, your assertiveness is likely to increase during your college years. Some students decide to attend workshops or counseling to increase assertiveness.

To illustrate further how personality characteristics can relate to a career, consider a sports agent. A sports agent's job is to sign up professional athletes in order to negotiate their contracts. A sports agent should be very extroverted and assertive because of the competition for signing top athletes. To get the athletes the most money, the agent also should be shrewd. However, in order to keep the athletes happy, the agent is expected to be helpful to them in fulfilling many of their other needs. Personality traits of successful sports agents, then, might include extroversion, assertiveness, shrewdness, and helpfulness.

Your Aptitudes

Aptitude is defined as a natural or acquired ability to perform a type of task successfully. When you applied to college, you probably needed to take a test (SAT or ACT) to inform schools about your general level of aptitude. According to a 2010 survey commissioned by the Association of American Colleges and Universities, broad-based abilities such as critical thinking and oral and written communication skills are highly valued by employers.[5]

Your specific aptitudes can help you succeed in certain majors and careers. It is important for you to be honest with yourself about your aptitudes before you decide on a major and a career. According to the National Center for Education Statistics, the four most popular fields of study for college graduates are business, social sciences and history, education, and health sciences.[6] Some of the important aptitudes required for each of these fields are as follows.

Having the Power: Your unique aptitudes provide you with the opportunity to succeed in a variety of activities.

Major Fields	Aptitudes
Business	Leadership, mathematics, communication, organization
Social sciences and history	Writing, memorizing, verbal reasoning, social awareness
Education	Communication, organization, social awareness, motivation
Health sciences	Analysis, mathematics, memorizing, observation

Multiple Intelligences

The theory of multiple intelligences, developed by Howard Gardner of Harvard University, provides a useful framework for evaluating aptitudes.[7] **Multiple intelligences** refer to eight different categories of intelligence, each associated with particular strengths that serve as aptitudes for various majors and careers.[8] According to Gardner, people naturally vary in how well they perform in each of the different categories of intelligence. Examine the chart below to determine the categories for types of intelligence that are most descriptive of your strengths and the examples of majors and careers associated with those strengths.

Multiple Intelligences Chart

Gardner's Multiple Intelligences Aptitude Types	Strengths	Suitable Majors	Potential Careers
Linguistic	Words, languages, reading, writing, memorizing	Spanish, library science, creative writing	Translator, attorney, journalist
Logical-Mathematical	Numbers, scientific thinking, complex calculations, reasoning	Computer science, statistics, physics	Mathematician, physician, scientist
Spatial	Visualization, puzzle solving, art, hand-eye coordination	Art, aerospace engineering, architecture	Graphic designer, pilot, engineer
Kinesthetic	Physical activities, performing, construction	Phyiscal therapy, fitness and recreation, theater	Athlete, firefighter, trainer

Gardner's Multiple Intelligences Aptitude Types	Strengths	Suitable Majors	Potential Careers
Musical	Rhythm, music, pitch, sounds	Music composition, music performance, music education	Conductor, musician, disc jockey
Interpersonal	Cooperation, communication, sensitivity to others	Psychology, sociology, anthropology	Social worker, sales representative, human resources manager
Intrapersonal	Self-reflection, thought-based ideas	History, philosophy, religion	Philosophy professor, minister, writer
Naturalistic	Nurturing, recognizing and classifying things, relating to natural surroundings	Agriculture, forestry, geology	Conservationist, farmer, forest ranger

EXERCISE 5 **Your Top Three**

Step 1: Identify your three strongest aptitudes from the "Multiple Intelligences Chart" on pages 339–340. Write in your strongest aptitude beside the "1" below, your second-strongest aptitude beside the "2" below, and your third-strongest aptitude beside the "3" below.

1. Strongest aptitude _____

2. Second-strongest aptitude _____

3. Third-strongest aptitude _____

Step 2: Be prepared to discuss in class suitable majors and potential careers that correspond to your three strongest aptitudes, including majors and careers not listed in the chart.

MATCHING YOU to a suitable major and a potential CAREER

Values, interests, personality, and aptitudes are important qualities that contribute to major and career choices. Consider how the possible majors and careers in the chart on the following page integrates specific combinations of values, interests, personality characteristics, and aptitudes to suggest a college major that is most likely to prepare students for each field. The possible majors and careers in the chart represent only one alternative for the combination of personal attributes; many majors or careers are possible for these same combinations of characteristics.

Value	Interest	Personality	Aptitude	Possible Major	Possible Career
Spirituality	Social	Helpful	Intrapersonal	Religion	Minister
Science	Conventional	Introverted	Logical-Mathematical	Computer science	Computer programmer
Preservation	Realistic	Adventurous	Naturalistic	Environmental science	Forest ranger
Creativity	Artistic	Helpful	Spatial	Art education	Art teacher
Wealth	Enterprising	Dominant	Interpersonal	Management	Business executive

A single perfect occupational match does not exist for most people. A particular set of personal attributes may actually lead to success in several possible majors and careers. Economic conditions, geographical preferences, and available opportunities are also likely to be important considerations. Many students start out in one major and decide to switch majors with few negative consequences. Similarly, many people end up having more than one career during their lifetimes.

Careers and Stress

In selecting a potential career, you might want to consider how stressful your life will be working in that field. After all, you will probably spend about 40% of your waking hours on the job. Experts believe that the most stressful fields involve responsibility for the safety and welfare of other people.[9] Police officers, air traffic controllers, and preschool teachers are considered to be very stressful occupations. Employment conditions such as an unreasonable boss, job insecurity, a noisy environment, or long hours can also contribute to high levels of stress in almost any field. Executives are one group of professionals particularly challenged by stress because they frequently have to make difficult decisions. Another stressful line of work can be in the health or medical field when another person's life becomes your responsibility. Of course, many people working in stressful professions feel fulfilled because they have matched their values, interests, personality, and aptitudes to their careers.

PLANNING
for a
potential FUTURE
career

Your college probably has a Career Center with advisors trained to help you understand the world of work. A career advisor can provide you with information about the specific job duties of employees in different fields and the requirements for getting into those fields. A career advisor can also help you access pamphlets, brochures, and online information as well as familiarize you with professional networking sites such as www.LinkedIn.com. Additionally, an advisor is able to tell you if a major is appropriate for obtaining opportunities in a particular field. As you get closer to graduation, the Career Center can arrange interviews for you with prospective employers and even help you prepare for interviews.

Résumés and Cover Letters

A very important function of campus Career Centers is to help you develop a résumé and a cover letter for prospective employers. A **résumé** provides an organized description of your educational background, work experiences, and skills that is intended to attract employers to you. Since a résumé is a reflection of you, it will be worth the effort to prepare your résumé carefully and neatly. Employers have cautioned applicants to exclude immature references to themselves, such as email addresses like "sweetbuns@" or "hotbod@." Also, employers who have not solicited your résumé are less likely to open an attachment than to read a résumé that is included in the body of an email communication.[10]

Most Career Centers provide templates for writing a résumé. A good idea is to regularly update a résumé with your latest accomplishments. Then save a copy of your current résumé to paste into an email so that whenever a job opening arises, you will be ready to go into action. At that point, it is a good idea to tailor your résumé to the specific job for which you are applying by adding a job objective that relates particularly to that job opening.

Certain features are generally included in a résumé, such as these:

- Identifying Information—Include your name, address, phone number, and email address.
- Job Objective—State your current goal as specifically as possible.
- Education—This should be chronological with your most recent education entered first.
- Experience—List jobs and volunteer activities starting with the most recent; be sure to describe your most important or relevant job functions. Even a seemingly ordinary job such as babysitting can demonstrate responsibility.
- References—Specific information may appear here, or you can state, "Available upon request."

A **cover letter** generally accompanies each résumé. The cover letter should be carefully written since it is your first contact with a potential employer and creates the first impression. Career Centers usually have models of cover letters for you to follow. If you use your favorite search engine and the key words "cover letters," you will discover a multitude of web resources with suggestions for writing the cover letter, as well as models of cover letters.

Two sample résumés of students seeking part-time jobs on campus are displayed on the following pages. You can build your résumé from such a foundation as you progress through college and use it to apply for part-time jobs and internships. Activities such as volunteering, participation or leadership in campus activities, and part-time employment are great résumé builders for job or graduate school applications.

Finding Your Passion: You can learn a great deal about various professions through the resources of your campus Career Center.

Discuss whether you would prefer to submit a written résumé or a video résumé and why at *CollegeSuccess.andYOU.com*

Sample Résumé

Danelle Mora
P.O. Box 4378
San Marcos, TX 78666
432-786-0009
Acmora221@panamerican.com

Permanent Address
1572 Spring Street
Midland, TX 79701

OBJECTIVE   Seeking a part-time position as a receptionist or file clerk

EDUCATION   Current freshman, Texas State University, San Marcos, TX,
                   Major: Communications
                   High school diploma, Midland High School, Midland, TX,
                   June 2013; GPA: 3.68

WORK   **Preschool Teacher Assistant**, *Early Learning Center*, Odessa,
EXPERIENCE   TX, August 2012–May 2013. Helped teacher with after-school
                   activities; organized and maintained classroom.

                   Pharmacy Technician, *Midland Center Pharmacy*, Midland,
                   TX, June 2011–August 2012. Filled prescriptions in the pharmacy
                   and via drive-through, handled cash register responsibilities,
                   and assisted customers on the telephone.

                   Cashier, *Kmart Super Center*, Midland, TX, June 2010–May 2011.
                   Handled cash register responsibilities, served customers,
                   bagged purchases.

SPECIAL SKILLS   Fluency in Spanish; knowledge of Word and Excel computer
                   applications

HONORS AND   Member, National Honor Society, 2011–2013
AWARDS   Member, Mu Alpha Theta Honor Society, 2012–2013

CAMPUS AND   Varsity Cheerleading Squad, Midland High School, 2012–2013
COMMUNITY   Junior Varsity Cheerleading Squad, Texas State, 2011–2012
ACTIVITIES   Student Council treasurer, Midland High School, 2011–2012

REFERENCES   Available upon request

Sample Résumé

MITCHELL TAYLOR

340 Jones
East Carolina University
Greenville, NC 07858

mitchell.taylor@rmail.net
Phone: 252-328-4179

OBJECTIVE
To acquire a job at the campus bookstore

SKILLS AND STRENGTHS
- Neat
- Organized
- Responsible
- Hardworking
- Cooperative
- Friendly and outgoing

EDUCATION
East Carolina University, Greenville, NC; currently attending; undecided major; expected graduation 2017.

Jordan High School, Durham, NC; graduated 2013

WORK EXPERIENCE
Home Depot, Durham, NC; stock clerk, 2012–2013
Inventoried, stocked shelves, maintained shelves.

REFERENCES
Available upon request

EXERCISE 6 **Your Résumé**

Step 1: Prepare your own résumé. You may follow one of the models above or use a template available on your Career Center's website. Think about any of your special aptitudes, experiences, volunteer activities, or personal characteristics that might appeal to a potential employer. As you prepare your résumé, keep in mind that the usual goal in submitting a résumé is to obtain an interview for a position for which you are applying. Your résumé should distinguish you as being uniquely qualified for the position. For example, if you are applying for a job as a web designer, you will need to include a special skills section listing the computer programs that you use. If you effectively emphasize your strengths, you will have a good chance of getting an interview. Before you send the résumé to anyone, carefully proofread it for typos, spelling errors, grammatical mistakes, and formatting. Also, remember that for the résumé, neatness counts.

Step 2: Bring your résumé to class and be prepared to discuss its strengths and weaknesses. Compare and contrast your résumé with others from your class. Identify any important content that you discovered was omitted from your résumé or deserved more focus. Revise your résumé according to what you have learned from reviewing your classmates' résumés.

Internships

An **internship** is a paid or unpaid formal job experience that provides training for a specific career and usually lasts for one semester or one summer. At some schools, internships also may be completed for academic credit. An internship experience can fortify a résumé in the eyes of prospective employers. Your campus Career Center website is the best resource for beginning an internship search. Since many internships have application deadlines more than six months before the internships begin, career advisors suggest that you start the search early. An updated résumé and letters of recommendation from professors are usually part of the application process. Success during an internship may ultimately lead to a full-time employment opportunity from the sponsoring agency.

Training Time: An internship is an excellent opportunity to gain valuable experience while strengthening your résumé.

A Liberal Declaration

Although she enjoyed many of her classes during the first two years of college, Isabella could not settle on a major. After consulting with her academic advisor, she declared herself a liberal studies major so that she could continue to take a wide variety of interesting classes.

As her college career progressed, she discovered that her favorite areas of concentration were art history and American studies. In fact, between her junior and senior years, she secured an internship at an art museum that featured the works of American artists. While Isabella achieved good grades and loved college, she worried about what she would do after she graduated. During the first semester of her senior year, she decided to interview with prospective employers who did not insist on a specific major as a criterion for employment. Much to her surprise, she received the offer she most wanted—to become a management trainee at a national high-end department store chain. The interviewer explained that Isabella's academic success, personal qualities, and liberal education matched her company's qualifications for this position. She also informed Isabella that her interest in art history and her internship experience could transfer nicely to the world of fashion and jewelry.

Career Assessment

Formal assessment to help you select a major and a career is usually available on campus either at the Career Center or the Counseling Center. Many Career Centers have computer applications to help you match a suitable major and potential career to your personal characteristics. Some of the most well-known computer programs are Discover, Choices, and SIGI (System of Interactive Guidance and Information).

Many Counseling Centers also provide career assessments. At Counseling Centers, a counselor will begin by interviewing you about your background and then will arrange a battery of assessment techniques that meet your needs. The inventories can evaluate your values, interests, aptitudes, and personality characteristics since these are the key factors in occupational satisfaction. Evaluations at a Career Center or a Counseling Center can be extremely helpful either to solidify your choice of major and career or to provide you with new ideas if you need them.

Both Career Centers and Counseling Centers offer a variety of specific assessment techniques to help you understand your strengths and identify appropriate majors and careers. Here are some of the most popular:

- Values Card Sort—Explores your values.
- SkillScan—Helps you to recognize your abilities.
- Clifton's StrengthFinder—Uses a positive psychology approach to identify your strongest talents.
- Strong Interest Inventory—Shows your Holland Codes and corresponding career interest ratings; the college version can be taken online.
- Myers-Briggs Type Indicator— See box below.

The Myers-Briggs Type Indicator (MBTI)

The Myers-Briggs Type Indicator is a widely used personality test that relates several different personality dimensions to career choices.[11] Modeled after the personality type theory of Carl Jung, a Swiss psychiatrist, the Myers-Briggs evaluates preferences along the following four dichotomous factors:

Factor 1: Preference for **Extraversion (E)**—action-oriented external world

or

Introversion (I)—thought-oriented inner world

(Note that Myers-Briggs uses a different spelling for extroversion.)

Factor 2: Preference for **Sensing (S)**—perception of known facts

or

iNtuitive (N)—perception of possibilities

Factor 3: Preference for **Thinking (T)**—judgment through logic

or

Feeling (F)—judgment through emotion

Factor 4: Preference for **Judging (J)**—orderliness

or

Perceptive (P)—spontaneity

Preference scores identify one type (Extraverted or Introverted, for example) on each of these four personality factors. As a result, the four scores represent one of 16 possible combinations of personality types (for example, ENTJ is a combination of Extraversion, iNtuitive, Thinking, Judging). No one preference or combination of preferences is better than any other, since the outcome is an analysis of how people view and respond to their environments.

The Myers-Briggs is widely used in Career Centers, Counseling Centers, and college classes to enhance students' self-awareness. To understand the use of this technique in career counseling, consider a student with an ENTJ combination of Extraversion, iNtuitive, Thinking, and Judging. According to a Myers-Briggs interpretation of this combination of preferences, such a student is especially well-suited to be an executive who is confident, decisive, and a born leader. Majors that might suit an ENTJ student include management and political science. Career possibilities for this combination of personality factors include entrepreneurs, managers, consultants, and attorneys. You can investigate whether the Myers-Briggs is available to be administered to students on your campus.

You now have many resources to consider as you work toward selecting a suitable major and identifying a potential career. A thoughtful approach to the wide array of majors and professions available through your college experience can lead you to a lifetime of career fulfillment.

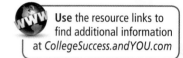
Use the resource links to find additional information at *CollegeSuccess.andYOU.com*

Thinking Critically About . . . Selecting a Suitable Major and Identifying a Potential Career

Critical thinking involves an active evaluation of information using careful, thoughtful, and reasoned judgments.

1. Compare and contrast the concept of a college education for career preparation versus for the promotion of knowledge and citizenship.

2. Children's dreams about becoming athletic stars, firefighters, famous artists, and astronauts are often surrendered by the time they are college students. Discuss the importance and influence of childhood career fantasies on making a career choice.

3. Political scientists, marketing analysts, and social theorists try to understand the values of each generation of college students. Identify the prevailing values of today's college students, including descriptions of behaviors that distinguish this college generation.

4. Analyze why so many college freshmen want to become medical doctors and why so many of those students eventually decide to change their career goals.

5. Provide several sound reasons for accepting this opinion: "No tool or set of tools can give a specific answer to the question 'What shall I be?'"

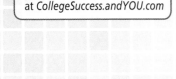
Discuss your ideas about the Critical Thinking items at *CollegeSuccess.andYOU.com*

Online Learning

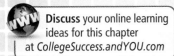
Discuss your online learning ideas for this chapter at *CollegeSuccess.andYOU.com*

The process of selecting a major and career objective is not dramatically different for online students as compared to on-campus students. Online students who are uncertain about occupational goals can take a variety of classes during the first year of college to identify what they are good at and what they like. They can then attempt to find out more about majors and careers that fit their aptitudes and interests.

Some online colleges provide career development services to students through a compilation of carefully selected Internet links. Well-established occupational assessment tests may be included to facilitate career discovery. Some of the most useful links include the following:

- http://www.careerkey.org—The Career Key website provides career guidance including a career assessment test.
- http://thevault.com—The Vault offers in-depth information on job searches, salaries, and specific employers. A Career Center may provide free student access to the fee-based, specialized pages on this site.
- http://monster.com—The popular Monster site features career advice as well as comprehensive information about a wide variety of professions and job opportunities.

Students at online colleges may sometimes select a career goal that is not compatible with the curriculum choices at their school. For example, majoring in fields requiring performance, advanced labs, or special equipment could require a transfer to a traditional campus.

WHERE THE ACORN FALLS

The saying, "The acorn doesn't fall far from the tree," means that children have characteristics that are similar to their parents and often have the capacity to follow in their footsteps. Despite sharing aptitudes with parents who have successful businesses or professions, some students do not wish to go into the same career as a parent. They may have different values or interests or simply desire to create their own set of accomplishments. As a student moves toward adulthood and independence, conflict can result when he or she wants to deviate from parental expectations in the choice of a career.

A CASE STUDY: FACING THE CHALLENGE OF . . . WHERE THE ACORN FALLS

Dwight is a college sophomore at a state university. His only sibling is a 13-year-old sister in middle school. Dwight's father owns a successful office supply business started by his own father and passed down to him. Since Dwight was a baby, his dad has expected Dwight to work in the company after college and eventually take over running it. Dwight's mother has shared this expectation with her husband. They both assumed that Dwight would major in a business field at college to prepare for his career in the family business. As part of his first-year curriculum, Dwight took a variety of classes, including an introductory business class. While he found his business class to be dull and uninspiring, he discovered his true passion was music. He obtained his only A grades during his freshman year in his guitar performance classes, which he loved. He also enjoyed playing guitar in a popular student combo. Although Dwight is not rushing to make a career decision, he has begun to think about how he can explain his disinterest in business and his enthusiasm for music to his parents.

OVERCOMING THE CHALLENGE OF . . . WHERE THE ACORN FALLS

Be prepared to discuss your answers to the following items: (1) Provide a sound argument for Dwight to make to his parents to justify a decision not to join his father's business after college. (2) Recommend what Dwight can do to help his parents understand his desire to pursue music rather than business. (3) Compare and contrast the characteristics required for professional success in business with those required for music performance.

Key Chapter Strategies

- Visit your school's Career Center and its website to find out more about college majors and careers. It is a myth that a Career Center is useful only when you are ready to graduate.

- Consult with your advisors and professors about selecting a major and a career.

- Use what you have learned about your values, interests, personality characteristics, and aptitudes as you consider your future direction.

- Visit your campus Career Center and/or Counseling Center to take advantage of career assessment opportunities.

- Seek a part-time job while school is in session that can help you develop skills and acquire mentoring.

- Realize that success in an internship or summer job can lead to a permanent position.

- Keep an updated résumé and know how to prepare a cover letter.

- Read this excellent book on career choice and success: *What Color Is Your Parachute: A Practical Manual for Job-Hunters and Career-Changers* by Richard Bolles.[12]

  **Can You Recall It?**

Assess your answers to Can You Recall It? at *CollegeSuccess.andYOU.com*

Directions: To review your understanding of the chapter, choose the correct term from the list below and fill it in on the blank. You will not use every term.

Holland Codes	**attractiveness**	**personality**
interests	**SkillScan**	**résumé**
altruism	**assertiveness**	**leadership**
college transcript	**aptitude**	**Myers-Briggs**

1. Your _____ include(s) your hobbies, entertainment preferences, dream jobs, and types of classes you most enjoy.

2. A famous system for classifying jobs into one of six major categories is known as the _____.

3. If you want a career in sales, a personality characteristic generally required is _____ .

4. A/An _____ refers to your natural or acquired abiity to perform a type of task successfully.

5. The unique pattern of relating to the world around you is your _____ .

6. A personal value that indicates you want to help others is called _____ .

7. The _____ Type Indicator is an assessment technique that classifies each person into one of 16 personality combinations.

8. You would prepare a/an _____ to help you get a part-time job or to apply for an internship.

Web Activity: Exploring Your Career Choice

Directions: Select a career that you are considering for your future. Use the United States government's annual *Occupational Outlook Handbook* website (www.bls.gov/oco) and two other career websites of your choice, which you can find by using the key word "careers" in your favorite search engine. Then respond to the following items.

1. Name of the career you selected. _____

2. Write the exact web addresses you used for the additional websites.

    (1) _____

    (2) _____

3. What are the qualifications required for entrance into this career? Be sure to include the educational background and college majors that are preferred.

    _____

    _____

    _____

4. What is the typical starting salary? _____

5. Describe the major responsibilities of a person with this career. _____

    _____

    _____

    _____

6. Name a professional organization for people in this career. _____

    _____

    _____

7. After learning more about this career, list two reasons why this field would be a good match for you.

    (1) _____

    _____

    (2) _____

    _____

Achieving Your Goals by Selecting a Suitable Major and Identifying a Potential Career

In this chapter, you prepared a résumé. As you progress through college, you will have many opportunities to expand your résumé. Write one paragraph for each of the following questions: (1) What pleases you most about your current résumé? (2) What accomplishments and activities would you like to add to your résumé during your remaining college years? (3) How can these accomplishments and activities help you achieve your potential career?

_____

_____

_____

_____

_____

_____

_____

_____

_____

_____

_____

_____

_____

_____

_____

_____

_____

_____

_____

Preparing to Move Forward

In this chapter, you will move toward achieving your goals by

- anticipating the potential challenges of your sophomore year.

- preparing now for success during your junior and senior years.

- beginning to think about life beyond college.

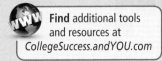

Find additional tools and resources at *CollegeSuccess.andYOU.com*

Self-Assessment:
Ten Degrees of Certainty

Step 1: It is both natural and normal for students beginning college to be unsure about their future plans. In this "Self-Assessment" activity, you will evaluate your current level of certainty for several key topics about your future. Circle a number ranging from 1 ("Very Uncertain") to 10 ("Very Certain") to indicate how sure you are about your plans for the topics listed below.

1. Choice of Major

    1   2   3   4   5   6   7   8   9   10

2. Choice of Career

    1   2   3   4   5   6   7   8   9   10

3. Whether you will begin graduate or professional school immediately after college

    1   2   3   4   5   6   7   8   9   10

4. How you will spend the upcoming summer

    1   2   3   4   5   6   7   8   9   10

5. Achieving the grades that you want

    1   2   3   4   5   6   7   8   9   10

6. Graduating from the college you are currently attending

    1   2   3   4   5   6   7   8   9   10

7. Where you will live after you finish your education

    1   2   3   4   5   6   7   8   9   10

8. How close to your family you will live after college

    1   2   3   4   5   6   7   8   9   10

9. Being able to earn the amount of money you want ten years from now

    1   2   3   4   5   6   7   8   9   10

10. Having a satisfying social life during college

    1   2   3   4   5   6   7   8   9   10

Step 2: Select one item from your self-assessment to which you gave your highest rating. Write your selected item here.

_____

_____

_____

Step 3: Write two or three reasons why you are fairly certain about the item you selected in Step 2.

_____

_____

_____

_____

Step 4: Select one item from your self-assessment for which you would like to have more certain future plans. Write your selected

item here. _____

_____

Step 5: Write an action plan of two or three sentences detailing what you can do to gain more certainty about this item.

_____

_____

_____

_____

_____

_____

_____

For new college students, the first year can be so exciting and demanding that it is difficult to focus on the future. The first thirteen chapters of this textbook are designed to help you successfully navigate the choppy waters of your early college experiences. Hopefully, as you progress through these experiences, you will be able to sustain your successes while also planning to manage new challenges.

The final chapter of this book focuses attention on your future beyond the freshman year. This chapter introduces you to steps you can take to prepare for the challenges that relate to your sophomore, junior, and senior years. As you speak with upper-level students, you will discover that each year seems to have unique features and demands. While different challenges can occur in different years for different students, this chapter provides a general map for planning your journey through the upcoming college years.

Looking down the road to the period after your first year of college can be beneficial, even during your freshman year. For example, you might discover that it can be helpful to begin to think about whether you want to study abroad, which internships seem appropriate for you, and if you want to go directly to graduate school after college. This chapter also explores the major differences between life during and after college. Gaining some perspective on these differences now can ultimately help you achieve your goals.

The sophomore year is so unique that the word *sophomoric* was coined to characterize people who act like sophomores. According to the *Merriam-Webster Collegiate Dictionary*, sophomoric people are "conceited and overconfident of knowledge but poorly informed and immature."* This definition can be interpreted to mean that a sophomore has some knowledge but still has a great deal to learn.

The Sophomore Slump

Today's educators are concerned that second-year students will experience a sophomore slump. The **sophomore slump** involves loss of motivation and enthusiasm because the novelty of being a college student has faded away. At the same time, sophomores often receive less support and attention on campus than freshmen.[1] For instance, special first-year advisors and housing probably will no longer be available. To avoid this slump, sophomores can reenergize themselves and recognize that they may need to function more independently than they did as first-year students.

How to Avoid the Sophomore Slump

Preparing yourself now helps you thrive during your sophomore year. Finding a knowledgeable and supportive academic advisor is a great first step. An academic advisor provides considerable assistance in helping you with the critical task of selecting an advantageous course schedule. Your choice of classes will be important whether or not you already have declared a major. If you have not, you will want to take classes that fulfill general education requirements that can be used with any major. At the same time, you may be able to sample courses from fields you are considering for a major. If you have declared a major, an advisor can help you plan a class schedule combining appropriate courses in your field with electives required for graduation. At some schools, such planning is quite complex and often results in costly mistakes if attempted without expert guidance. (See Chapter 2 for more information on academic advisors.)

*By permission. From Merriam-Webster's Collegiate® Dictionary, 11th Edition ©2013 by Merriam-Webster, Inc. (www.Merriam-Webster.com)

Deciding on a Major

"So what do you want to be when you grow up?" How many times have friends and relatives asked you that question? It's becoming time to think about the answer. Deciding on a major—which is required by the end of the sophomore year at most colleges—often presents a challenge to undecided students. Using all the information you learned in the previous chapter on selecting a major and identifying career goals will help you decide. By your sophomore year, you will have a good idea about your interests, values, personality characteristics, and aptitudes. You may also have some sense if you will want to start a career immediately after graduation or if you would rather attend a graduate or professional school before beginning a career. Your choice of major may be influenced by all those factors. Additionally, you can talk to students in a major you are considering. Once you have narrowed down your alternatives, it will be particularly helpful to meet with an academic advisor or professor from the specific department you are considering in order to get more information about prerequisites or course sequencing.

Adjusting to New Living Arrangements

A dramatic social shift occurs when students who have lived in freshmen residence halls during their first year move either off campus or to campus housing with upper-level students. Students who could previously visit each other by going down the hall may now have to make special arrangements with their old friends in order to hang out. Additionally, some friends may transfer to other colleges before the sophomore year. Although it is important to maintain old friendships, a change in living circumstances creates an ideal opportunity to forge new relationships.

Moving off campus creates several new challenges related to money and time. One new challenge necessitates additional financial demands for budgeting and bill paying. Another challenge occurs for students who cook for themselves. These students find a sizable time commitment is required for meal planning and grocery shopping. Finally, if living off campus involves a commute, students must adjust their schedules to accommodate the time required to get to and from campus.

What's Cooking: Living off campus often involves the preparation of meals.

Establishing New Relationships

To help establish new social connections, the sophomore year is also a perfect time to become involved in campus organizations and volunteer activities (see Chapter 11). Part-time jobs also present very good opportunities to meet other students. For example, becoming a campus tour guide for the Admissions Office is a very popular job for sophomores at many colleges. Mentoring a new student is also a means to contribute to your college community.

Investigating a Transfer

As the sophomore year unfolds, the issue of transferring to another college arises for some students. Community college students must transfer if they plan to graduate from a four-year school. Other students consider transferring for reasons including the following: financial concerns; a desire to attend a more prestigious college; a plan to major in a field unavailable at their current school; a decision to move closer to home or to a romantic partner; and a need to overcome poor grades. Since the grass is not always greener at another college, students intending to transfer will benefit by carefully researching the schools they are considering, including at least one visit while classes are in session. Unless transferring students already have close social contacts at the new school, they can expect a period of occasionally awkward social adjustment. Additionally, transferring students may need time to figure out the academic and financial aid systems and establish relationships with an advisor and professors at a new school.

EXERCISE 1　Year Two for You?

Step 1: Conduct a face-to-face interview with a sophomore at your school. You will be inquiring about this student's experiences as a sophomore and how those experiences compare and contrast with his or her time as a freshman. Also, you will ask this student for recommendations for the rest of your first year to prepare you for next year. The specific questions for you to ask are provided below. Write the sophomore's responses on the lines below each question. After writing down each of the sophomore's responses, write your own reactions to each answer in the spaces provided.

Name of sophomore interviewed _____

1. "What are the major academic differences for you between your freshman and sophomore years?" _____

   _____

   _____

   _____

   Your reaction: _____

   _____

   _____

2. "How has your social life changed between your freshman and sophomore years?" _____

   _____

   _____

   _____

   Your reaction: _____

   _____

   _____

3. "What has surprised you the most about being a sophomore?"

   _____

   _____

   _____

   Your reaction: _____

   _____

   _____

4. "What advice do you have for the rest of my freshman year to help me prepare for my sophomore year?" _____

_____

_____

_____

Your reaction: _____

_____

_____

Step 2: Be prepared to discuss in class the responses to these questions. Determine if there are any trends in the answers or repeated recommendations made by the sophomores who were interviewed.

Your JUNIOR YEAR

By your junior year, you should be settled into your role on campus. Many juniors stop excessive partying, having solidified their values and social networks as they have matured. The challenge is now directed more toward planning for the future.

As in high school, the junior year of college is a busy one, involving preparation for what lies ahead. You will need to establish a timetable for acquiring information about employment or educational opportunities, completing applications, and taking any necessary qualifying tests.

Refining Your Résumé

While you are a junior, you still have plenty of time to enhance your résumé in order to help achieve your goals (see Chapter 13). Since you probably will need recommendations for jobs or advanced educational programs, you would be wise to make sure you have developed adequate bonds with administrators or faculty members. The most effective recommendations show how the recommender has personalized knowledge of a student and do not simply review that student's transcript and accomplishments. Many students are afraid that they do not know the right people to ask for recommendations. They fear that professors will not be interested in them personally. In fact, while it is true that some professors may not be helpful, most teach because they enjoy getting to know students. Two ways for professors to get to know you better so that they can write good recommendations are for you to volunteer to assist a professor with research and to take a small class with a professor, such as a seminar. Impressing an administrator or faculty member through a part-time campus job is another effective means to gain a positive, personalized recommendation.

Work Perk: Volunteering to assist a professor with research may result in a positive letter of recommendation.

Aside from working to get good grades and getting to know your professors, you can also improve your résumé through participation in student activities. By the junior year, you might find yourself in a meaningful leadership role in a student organization. You can also include activities such as public speaking or artistic performance in your résumé. Additionally, significant part-time jobs, volunteer activities, and internships will enhance your credentials.

Studying Abroad

The junior year is the most popular time for students to study abroad (see Chapter 2). Students majoring in architecture, history, a foreign language, international relations, comparative literature, or art history often find that study abroad is unequaled as an opportunity to learn more about their fields. The experience of studying in another country will also broaden all students' cultural perspectives while enhancing their independence.

Although there are many advantages, studying abroad might create challenges for some students. The stress of adjusting to new food, possibly a foreign language, and different customs—while being far from family, friends, and college support services—can be difficult. Since loneliness can be upsetting, communicating regularly with people back home is often very helpful for students, especially early in their study abroad programs. Despite these challenges, most students adjust after a short period of time and enjoy the opportunities offered through study abroad programs.

> **Discuss** what factors you believe students should consider in deciding whether or not to study abroad at *CollegeSuccess.andYOU.com*

Popular Professions Available through Advanced Degrees

Even though you have just started your college studies, it is important to begin thinking about whether you will want to continue your education after you graduate. If you are enrolled in a two-year program, you may decide to work full-time or move to a four-year bachelor's degree program. Many students who earn bachelor's degrees go on to graduate or professional programs after graduation. As a general guideline, graduate and professional programs prefer to accept students who earn at least a 3.0 grade point average as undergraduates. If you develop a plan to continue your education after four years of college, you will need to take tests and go through an application process again. The following descriptions provide information about some popular professions for which students seek advanced degrees. The information includes post-baccalaureate training, which refers to the years after the bachelor's degree. The information represents general guidelines, and exceptions may exist.

Guidelines for Post-Baccalaureate Training

Art/Creative Writing

An advanced degree has helped many creative artists and writers achieve their goals. A number of schools offer two- to three-year master of fine arts (MFA) degrees. In these programs, students extend their artistic skills through the support and constructive criticism of experienced professors. To attend most MFA programs, students must first take the Graduate Record Examinations (GRE), which is similar to the SAT (Scholastic Aptitude Test). The GRE includes sections on verbal reasoning, mathematical reasoning, and analytical writing. Applicants may also be required to present a portfolio of their work.

Business

The MBA (master of business administration) is the standard graduate degree in business. Graduate business students select a major from several fields including, for example, accounting, finance, management, marketing, and real estate. An MBA usually can be earned in two years of full-time study. In order to gain admission into graduate business programs, applicants must take the Graduate Management Admission Test (GMAT). The GMAT includes a verbal section, a quantitative section, and an analytical writing assessment. It is important to note that many of the top graduate business schools require applicants to work for a few years before they will be considered for admission.

Dentistry

Students planning to become dentists usually major in an undergraduate field such as biology or chemistry. Applications to dental schools are ordinarily made during the junior year. Applicants must take the Dental Admission Test (DAT), which includes sections on scientific knowledge, perceptual skills, reading comprehension, and mathematical reasoning. The average length of training after college to become a dentist and earn a DDS (doctor of dental surgery) or DMD (doctor of dental medicine) degree is five years. In the first two years of dental school, students take science and clinical classes. After completing regular course work, students gain practical experience in diagnosing and treating patients. Dental school graduates must pass a licensing test in order to practice.

Elementary/Secondary Teaching

While some students become teachers by majoring in education during undergraduate school, others may not decide on teaching as a career until after graduation. To become a teacher, they would then fulfill teaching requirements through a special postbaccalaureate program. As an alternative, they could earn a master's degree, usually a master of education (MEd) degree or master of arts in teaching (MAT) degree. Most graduate education programs require the GRE (Graduate Record Examinations) for admission, which includes sections on verbal reasoning, mathematical reasoning, and analytical writing. The programs average two years, including practical classroom teaching experience. Most states require passing a certification exam to qualify to become a public school teacher.

Law

To become a lawyer in the United States, college graduates first attend law school, which lasts three years, and obtain a juris doctor (JD) degree. In order to gain admission to law school, applicants must take the Law School Admission Test (LSAT). The LSAT is a four-hour test that includes reading comprehension, logical reasoning, logic games, and a writing section. Once students have completed law school, they need to pass a state's bar examination to be entitled to practice law in that state.

Medicine

By far, the most popular degree in medicine is the MD (doctor of medicine) degree, though some specialized schools award a DO (doctor of osteopathy) degree. A medical school education usually consists of four years of classes and clinical training. The MCAT (Medical College Admission Test), which is required by most medical schools, assesses knowledge of physical science and biological science, and in 2015, adds one section evaluating critical analysis and reasoning and another evaluating knowledge of behavioral and social sciences. Supervised experience after medical school is necessary for licensure. Most medical school graduates satisfy this requirement by specializing in a branch of medicine through a three-year residency after their four years of study in medical school.

Pharmacy

Pharmacy involves assisting people in the correct use of medications. The standard doctorate in pharmacy (PharmD) is earned after two years of college and four years at a College of Pharmacy. The Pharmacy College Admissions Test includes 240 multiple-choice questions assessing general academic ability and scientific knowledge. Aside from their scientific aptitude, candidates for pharmacy are expected to work effectively with details, be willing to double-check their work, and maintain high ethical standards. To practice pharmacy, graduates need to pass a state licensing test.

Psychology

To become a psychologist, a student ordinarily completes a doctoral degree program, usually lasting about five years. Students wanting to become research/college teaching psychologists should seek a PhD (doctor of philosophy) program in a specialized area such as cognitive or physiological psychology. Students interested in applied psychology fields such as clinical or counseling psychology can seek admission to a PhD program or a more practically oriented PsyD (doctor of psychology) program. Either type of program typically requires the GRE (Graduate Record Examinations), which includes sections on verbal reasoning, mathematical reasoning, and analytical writing. Completing a one-year internship and passing a licensing examination are usually mandated by states as conditions for licensure to practice psychology.

Research/College Teaching

Students who are interested in research and college teaching earn a PhD (doctor of philosophy) or an EdD (doctor of education) degree from a university. While PhD degrees are available in almost all academic fields, EdD degrees are awarded exclusively in the field of education. The GRE (Graduate Record Examinations) is usually required for admission to the programs and includes sections on verbal reasoning, mathematical reasoning, and analytical writing. The average length for a PhD or an EdD program is five years. Typically, students take courses in their major field of concentration during the first few years of graduate school and then complete a significant research dissertation or project under the supervision of a professor in their final years. Graduate students may earn a master's degree after completing a thesis during their first few years in graduate school.

Social Work

The traditional graduate degree for social workers is the master of social work (MSW) degree, which takes approximately two years of study along with practical training. Many social work graduate programs do not require an admission test, relying chiefly on a student's college record and recommendations. Graduates of social work programs interested in direct services to other people usually need to pass a test in their state to become a licensed clinical social worker (LCSW). Some social workers interested in performing research and teaching college continue their studies to earn a PhD degree.

14

Your SENIOR Year and BEYOND

Last but Not Least

Seniors often experience a combination of anticipation and apprehension as the end of college approaches. Many buzz around with excitement and nervous energy, sharing plans and opportunities for the next phases of their lives. While some might begin a job or continue their education, other students will defer making ultimate career plans by returning to their families' homes, traveling, or volunteering for service agencies. At the same time, everyone will face the looming loss of the security and companionship that likely were central to the college experience.

Separating from close relationships is one of the hardest parts of graduation. For this reason, it is natural for seniors to feel some sadness as they make preparations for their futures. Of course, arranging visits with college friends and maintaining regular communication can alleviate some of the sting. Couples may face a major decision regarding what to do about their relationships. Planning and openness between the partners will help a great deal. The senior year is usually much happier for couples who concur on a decision for their future, whatever that decision is. Even if the partners do not initially agree, open communication helps couples understand each other's feelings and ultimately reach agreement.

While trying to prepare for your future as a senior, you may experience a decrease in academic motivation, especially as graduation nears. This loss of energy during the senior year is so common that it has been labeled **senioritis**. Some students with senioritis may believe their grades no longer matter for their future. Others direct their energy to activities such as job interviews or graduate school applications instead of to classes. Actually, employers and graduate schools have been known to rescind offers to students who receive dramatically lower grades during the senior year. To prevent such problems, it is a good idea at the beginning of your senior year to choose something new and useful that you might get out of classes during this final year of college. For example, you may want to take interesting electives that were not previously available to you. Alternatively, you might volunteer to serve as a teaching assistant in an introductory class or a lab in your major. Senior year provides opportunities for a new variety of activities outside the classroom as well. For instance, you may want to engage in an extracurricular activity that you didn't have time for during your earlier years, such as playing an intramural sport.

off the mark.com   by Mark Parisi

THE MOLD ON THE SHOWER CURTAIN HAS ADVANCED FROM HYPHAE INTO MYCELIUM...

IT'S STARTING TO RESEMBLE JACKSON POLLOCK'S "CONVERGENCE"

BACHELORS OF ARTS AND SCIENCE

As a senior, you will find that you have a number of transactions to conduct with your college. Many seniors must arrange through the registrar to send transcripts to prospective employers or postgraduate programs. Additionally, seniors who receive financial aid will need to make sure they understand their obligations after graduation. For students who have borrowed through the Federal Stafford Loan Program (see Chapter 8), college Financial Aid Offices must offer exit counseling to provide information about repayment schedules and options.

Another important office for you during your senior year is the Career Center (see Chapters 2 and 13). Many seniors rely heavily on career fairs and interviews arranged by this office to help secure jobs. Career Centers may also transmit your résumé to prospective employers or graduate programs upon request. These offices also can be helpful in linking you to alumni working in the career you are considering.

Dressed for Success: You make a positive impression during an interview by looking professional.

Succeeding with the Application Process

The majority of seniors will apply for jobs, graduate or professional schools, or public service agencies upon graduation. There are usually timetables to follow with deadlines for each part of an application process. Many agencies and programs require completed applications, interviews for promising candidates, and letters of recommendation. Educational programs often also require admission tests, while some professions require licensing or certification exams.

You can increase your likelihood of success in the application process during your senior year by learning how to create a positive image of yourself in interviews. An interviewer's first impression will be based on how you present yourself. You may be surprised at some of the following recommendations on how to enhance your image for interviewers.

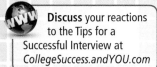

Discuss your reactions to the Tips for a Successful Interview at *CollegeSuccess.andYOU.com*

Tips for a Successful Interview

- If you have papers to bring to the interview, place them in a professional binder.
- Look neat and clean. Use deodorant and breath mints.
- A conservative look is the safest. Avoid piercings, visible tattoos, or wild hairstyles.
- Males applying to formal agencies in business or government are encouraged to wear a dark suit, dress shirt, tie, and dress shoes. For less formal employers, men can wear business casual clothing, such as dress slacks or khakis, a button-up shirt, and loafers. Don't wear baggy clothing for the interview and tuck in all shirts. If facial hair is worn, keep it well groomed.
- Females applying to formal agencies in business and government need to wear professional attire, such as a pantsuit or a skirt suit, each with closed-toe low heel or flat shoes. For less formal employers, women can wear business casual clothing, such as a dress or dress slacks with a sleeved blouse, each with closed-toe low heel or flat shoes. No matter which type of organization, women are encouraged to avoid heavy makeup, display of cleavage, miniskirts, and bare midriffs.
- Clean all clothing and iron any items with wrinkles.

- Prepare for an interview by doing some research to help you understand the organization. When given the opportunity, show that you understand the organization by asking informed questions based on your research. Express enthusiasm about becoming part of this organization.
- To reduce anxiety and build confidence, rehearse by practicing answers to questions that you think might be asked.
- It is critical for you to appear on time or a little early on the day of the interview.
- Be polite and appreciative to the interviewer without going over the top. Firmly shake the interviewer's hand, try to look the interviewer in the eyes, and learn the interviewer's full name. Don't use the interviewer's first name unless you are invited to do so.
- Listen and avoid interrupting.
- Turn off your cell phone and refrain from all digital communication while you are at the interview site.
- Don't exaggerate your accomplishments.
- Follow up the interview with a brief thank you postal letter. Such a letter is likely to solidify your interest in the position in the eyes of the interviewer.

Even as a first-year student, you may soon have interviews for internships, part-time jobs, or other special opportunities. The exercise that follows will alert you to some of the common questions used by interviewers so that you can begin thinking about how you would respond.

EXERCISE 2 **Mock Interview**

Step 1: Write answers on the lines for each of these general questions. Keep your answers honest while trying to impress the interviewer.

Interviewer Asks: "What are your personal qualities that would make us want to select you over another candidate?"

_____

_____

_____

_____

_____

_____

_____

Interviewer Asks: "What are the characteristics of an ideal job for you?"

_____

_____

_____

Interviewer Asks: "If your supervisor asked you to work during a weekend to complete a project, how would you respond?"

_____

_____

_____

Interviewer Asks: "What do you do when something frustrates you and does not go your way?"

_____

_____

_____

Interviewer Asks: "What in your life do you find to be most stressful?"

_____

_____

_____

Interviewer Asks: "Tell me about your comfort level when working with other people on a team assignment."

_____

_____

_____

Interviewer Asks: "Explain to me how effective you are in planning and organizing."

_____

_____

_____

Interviewer Asks: "Provide me with an example of your creativity."

_____

_____

_____

Interviewer Asks: "What motivates you to work to your fullest capacity?"

_____

_____

_____

Interviewer Asks: "What would you do if you discover that a fellow employee is cheating our company?"

_____

_____

_____

Interviewer Asks: "What do you like to do in your spare time when you are not studying or working?"

_____

_____

_____

Step 2: Be prepared to discuss in class what you learned from answering these interview questions.

Taking the Next Step

As you contemplate the future during your senior year, the theoretical framework of Abraham Maslow, a psychologist, can be very helpful.[2] According to Maslow's theory, people must prioritize fulfillment of their most basic life needs before they can accomplish their ultimate goals. To explain this viewpoint, Maslow developed a **hierarchy of needs**, shown in the ladder here.

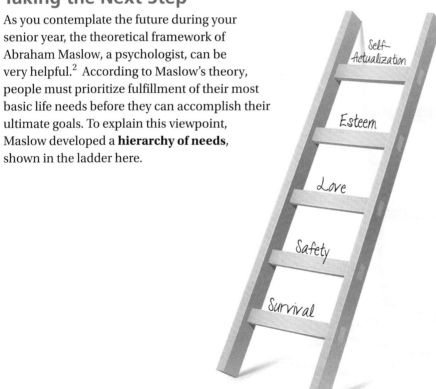

Maslow's hierarchy of needs consists of five levels: the first level involves basic physical survival requirements, such as air and water; the second level is the need for safety and security; the third level is the need for love and belonging; the fourth level is the need for esteem from others and from oneself; and the fifth level is called **self-actualization**. People who reach this highest level of self-actualization have become all that they are capable of becoming. They are able to extend their reach beyond themselves in a creative manner and can apply what they have learned constructively. Maslow estimates that only about 1% of the population reaches self-actualization. Maslow's approach suggests that efforts to ascend to higher levels of fulfillment will be inhibited if people do not satisfy their more basic needs first.

For many recent college graduates, economic factors mean they must temporarily live with their families in order to meet their first and second level needs for survival and safety. A successful return home will often require graduates to accept less freedom than they had during college. Consequently, while living at home, they may be limited in satisfying their fourth level social esteem needs. Nonetheless, they may be able to save money to use once they decide on a path toward independence and possible self-actualization.

If you graduate but don't begin your career immediately, you may go in many possible directions before settling down. Some people volunteer for a service agency, such as Teach For America, AmeriCorps, or the Peace Corps. Others live in an apartment with friends while supporting themselves in a temporary job. Recent graduates who need further education to reach their career goals may begin graduate or professional school soon after graduation. All these choices can help you continue learning and maturing. There is certainly no single path after college that is suitable for everyone.

Regardless of your choice, one of the challenging realities for life after college is still the need for money. Jobs for new graduates often do not pay as much as is hoped for. Graduates continuing their education usually must depend on modest stipends or borrow to pay their living costs. Having an apartment, paying bills, owning a car, and paying taxes can strain a recent graduate's budget. Additionally, paying back loans is often difficult. Recent college graduates attending graduate or professional school full-time or engaging in public service may be able to delay repayment of their college loans until they are employed full-time.

Reaching Out: Service agencies, such as the Peace Corps, offer potential opportunities for recent college graduates.

If you begin on your career path with a full-time job right after college, you may experience a period of adjustment. Your life becomes more structured, you need to conform to your employer's policies, and you must deal with a new set of people. Having the time and energy to maintain a social life can sometimes be difficult. At the same time, a new job can be very stimulating and a great confidence builder. Charlotte Shelton, a management consultant, reports, "The top three things they [today's young professionals] want in a job are positive relationships with colleagues, interesting work, and continuous opportunities for learning."[3] Some ambitious college graduates begin thinking about moving upward in their careers to another employer soon after they begin their first jobs. Professional networking is extremely important in facilitating that form of upward mobility.

Discuss Charlotte Shelton's perception of what young professionals want in a job and what she may have omitted at CollegeSuccess.andYOU.com

Decisions about marriage and parenthood may significantly affect your career plans.[4] Some people experience internal pressure or pressure from their families to marry and start their own families soon after college. The combination of career commitment, marriage, and raising children is extremely challenging. Couples may need to make difficult choices together about their priorities.

EXERCISE 3   The Crystal Ball

Step 1: These items relate to your expectations about life after college. After reading each item, answer either T if you think the item is likely to be "True" about you or F if the item is likely to be "False" about you. Be sure to answer every item with your most honest opinion about yourself as it would apply to the item's content.

_____ **1.** I will earn at least $60,000 a year in my first full-time job.

_____ **2.** After college, my social life will not be as active as it was in college.

_____ **3.** I will have more energy after a day of work than I do after a day of classes.

_____ **4.** My closest college friends and I will communicate regularly after we graduate.

_____ **5.** I won't be able to eat at expensive restaurants after college.

_____ **6.** Following college, I will devote more time to my spirituality.

_____ **7.** It will be difficult being responsible for my own automobile.

_____ **8.** I will have trouble keeping my life organized after college.

_____ **9.** I will be able to spend more time on exercise when I am working full-time.

_____ **10.** I will do a lot of exciting travel during the first few years in my career.

_____ **11.** It will be tough to work full-time, be married, and have a child.

_____ **12.** I will stay just as close to my family in the future as I am now.

_____ **13.** Office politics will probably interfere with my job.

_____ **14.** My supervisor will see that I am so competent that I will become a decision maker in a short amount of time.

_____ **15.** I will only take a job if I can wear casual clothes to work.

_____ **16.** After I succeed in one job, I will succeed in another.

_____ **17.** After college, I won't have the time or opportunity to do as much charitable work to help others.

_____ **18.** The people I meet after college will be less diversified than the people I met in college.

_____ **19.** My self-doubt and insecurities will remain with me after college.

_____ **20.** After college ends, there is a good chance that I will be lonelier.

_____ **21.** It will be easy for me to get the job that I want.

_____ **22.** After I finish college, I will wake up earlier each day.

_____ **23.** I will have less time to keep up with the latest digital communication techniques after I have graduated.

_____ **24.** As an alumnus, I will make increasing donations to my college's annual fund.

_____ **25.** Since there are free classes offered on the Internet, I will regularly complete them.

Step 2: Give yourself a score for each of the items, as indicated below. For example, if you answered "True" to Item 1, give yourself 1 point. If you answered "False" to Item 1, give yourself 0 points.

Give Yourself 1 Point If You Answered		My points
_____	1. True	_____
_____	2. False	_____
_____	3. True	_____
_____	4. True	_____
_____	5. False	_____
_____	6. True	_____
_____	7. False	_____
_____	8. False	_____
_____	9. True	_____
_____	10. True	_____
_____	11. False	_____
_____	12. True	_____
_____	13. False	_____
_____	14. True	_____
_____	15. True	_____
_____	16. True	_____
_____	17. False	_____
_____	18. False	_____
_____	19. False	_____
_____	20. False	_____
_____	21. True	_____
_____	22. False	_____
_____	23. False	_____
_____	24. True	_____
_____	25. True	_____

My Total Points: _____

Look into the Crystal Ball

Am I realistic or idealistic?

Step 3: Your total score, which can range from 0 to 25, indicates the degree to which you are realistic or idealistic about your life after college. Here are the score ranges and their implications.

0–6	**Very realistic**
7–12	**Somewhat realistic**
13–19	**Somewhat idealistic**
20–25	**Very idealistic**

There are no better or worse scores in this exercise, just a reflection in the crystal ball about life after college. Students who are more idealistic may have great optimism about the future. Optimism is a favorable characteristic that fosters happiness and success. Students who are realistic may be more practical. A more practical approach allows you to look at the future in a matter of fact way and possibly exceed your expectations.

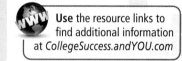

Use the resource links to find additional information at *CollegeSuccess.andYOU.com*

Step 4: Be prepared to discuss in class realistic and idealistic expectations.

Thinking Critically About . . . Preparing to Move Forward

Critical thinking involves an active evaluation of information using careful, thoughtful, and reasoned judgments.

1. Some professors argue that first-year students are too absorbed in their current lives to be concerned about their future college years. Evaluate this argument based on your own experiences and your observations of other students.

2. Analyze the value of study abroad programs.

3. If you are interviewing someone for a job, how would you evaluate the candidate? Identify the factors that would be most important for you.

4. Evaluate why colleges give so much time, effort, attention, and resources to a student's first-year experience. Discuss the educational, social, and civic values of engaging students in a first-year experience.

5. What makes an educated person? Select and discuss five characteristics of an educated person.

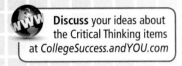
Discuss your ideas about the Critical Thinking items at *CollegeSuccess.andYOU.com*

Online Learning

Discuss your online learning ideas for this chapter at *CollegeSuccess.andYOU.com*

As online students progress beyond their first year of college, they face many unique challenges. For many online students, the requirements to remain self-directed and motivated are the primary challenges. Online students are more likely to succeed if they avoid gaps in their programs. A break from an online program often results in a difficult readjustment when the student returns to classes.

Starting in the first year of an online education program, students can regularly communicate with their professors so that the professors get to know them well enough to be able to write personalized recommendations for job applications or additional education. Finding an advisor for an online student is also very important to help with selecting classes as well as to track the requirements necessary for graduation.

For students who are full-time online learners, the feelings of academic and social isolation may be difficult. Identifying potential friends in first-year classes and possibly taking classes with them again will be helpful. To develop an academic community, online learners can discuss course work with classmates and actively participate in group tasks assigned by professors.

Many graduate and professional degree programs are available for online students. Online undergraduates often discover a very smooth transition to online graduate or professional programs at their own school.

I LOST THE THRILL

Most freshmen receive special attention during their first year of college. At some schools, freshmen residing on campus live exclusively with other freshmen. New students are also assigned special advisors, take classes mostly with other freshmen, and are given extra attention in many other ways by their college.

Once freshmen have succeeded and moved on to their sophomore year, everything changes. The excitement of being in college is gone, and students can be overcome by uncertainty. Sophomores usually don't receive special treatment from their schools as freshmen do. They are usually integrated into normal campus life, living and competing in classes with juniors and seniors. By also not having as clear a direction as many juniors and seniors do, sophomores often feel a bit lost and no longer special.

A CASE STUDY: FACING THE CHALLENGE OF . . .
I LOST THE THRILL

Carla described her first year away at college as "awesome." She had learned to live independently, found great friends, and earned good grades. Even the summer after her freshman year went well. In addition to working at an enjoyable job at a large bank, she hung out with old friends and had a nice vacation with her family. When she returned to college for her sophomore year, her prolonged sense of joy quickly evaporated. She wasn't sure what had happened, but she felt adrift and bewildered on a campus where she had felt so happy just a few months earlier.

Trying to figure out why she felt so lost, Carla thought about the changes from her first year. Although she was still living with her former roommate, she now knew no one else on her floor. This situation was a marked contrast with her freshman year when the students on her floor formed a tight group and were always spending time with each other. She also began to find parties lame, an attitude shift shared by her roommate. Furthermore, Carla was experiencing difficulty in adjusting to her classes. She was not enjoying her three large lecture classes because they were general introductions to content areas that she did not find interesting. Carla liked the content in her two smaller classes better, but they were filled with juniors and seniors who seemed to know more than she did.

Carla told her family, "I feel out of whack. Nothing seems right here anymore. Should I transfer?"

OVERCOMING THE CHALLENGE OF . . .
I LOST THE THRILL

Be prepared to discuss your answers to the following items: (1) Carla realizes that she needs to make changes, but she doesn't know what to do. Recommend changes both in her attitude and behavior that can help restore her enjoyment of college. (2) Suggest ways colleges can minimize the sophomore slump. (3) Identify the campus resources that can help a student like Carla and discuss what each resource can offer to assist her.

Key Chapter Strategies

■ Identify a knowledgeable academic advisor to help you select classes for your sophomore year.

■ Form new social connections through campus organizations and part-time jobs.

■ Continue to update your résumé (see Chapter 13).

■ Establish relationships with professors and administrators who will know you well enough to write letters of recommendation for you.

■ Enhance your civic engagement with volunteer activities.

■ Consider a study abroad program during your junior year.

■ Be sure to prepare for the interview process.

■ Read these books for more information about moving forward: *Book of Majors 2013: All-New Seventh Edition* by the College Board;[5] *College Majors Handbook with Real Career Paths and Payoffs* by Neeta Fogg, Paul Harrington, and Thomas Harrington;[6] and *Sweaty Palms: The Neglected Art of Being Interviewed* by H. Anthony Medley.[7]

Can You Recall It?

Directions: To review your understanding of the chapter, choose the correct term from the list below and fill it in on the blank. You will not use every term.

PhD	hierarchy of needs	sophomoric
GRE	self-actualization	licensure
sophomore slump	esteem	energy
postbaccalaureate training	JD	social work

1. The _____ involves the loss of motivation and enthusiasm for college because the novelty of being a student has faded away.

2. _____ refers to the years after receiving the bachelor's degree when you decide to continue your education.

3. Careers such as social work, pharmacy, and elementary/secondary teaching require_____.

4. Senioritis is the loss of _____ during the senior year.

5. Abraham Maslow developed a/an _____ consisting of five levels, ranging fom level one (basic physical survial) to level five (self-actualization).

6. If you decide to become a lawyer after you graduate, you will have to go to law school to earn a/an _____ degree.

7. To be admitted for some advanced degrees such as the PhD or EdD, you must take the _____ , which includes sections on verbal reasoning, mathematical reasoning, and analytical writing.

8. Maslow estimates that only about 1% of the population reaches the level of _____ to become all that they are capable of becoming.

Web Activity: Lifelong Learning

Directions: A number of major universities provide free classes online. While these classes are not offered for credit, they are the same courses presented on campus by prominent faculty members. The online materials may include lectures, assignments, notes, and readings. The online courses are available to anyone in the world, a truly amazing opportunity for continuing your education after graduation. Listed below are the websites for five universities that have been leaders in offering free online courses and a website that amalgamates free online courses from a number of universities. After reviewing the available classes, select a course that interests you from one of the websites, sign up for the course, watch one lecture, and respond to the items below.

Johns Hopkins University: http://ocw.jhsph.edu/
University of California, Berkeley: http://webcast.berkeley.edu/
University of Washington: http://www.outreach.washington.edu/openuw/
Utah State University: http://ocw.usu.edu/
Yale University: http://oyc.yale.edu/
Coursera.com: https://coursera.org/

1. Identify the university, the class, and the professor you selected.

University: _____

Class: _____

Professor: _____

2. Summarize the content of the lecture that you selected.

_____

_____

_____

3. How difficult was the lecture material for you to understand? Explain.

_____

_____

_____

4. How likely is it that you will take an online course, such as the one you selected, in the future? Explain.

_____

_____

_____

Achieving Your Goals by Preparing to Move Forward

Throughout this textbook, you have learned about methods for achieving your college goals. In this chapter, you have learned about moving forward through the remaining years of college. Reflect on your goals for your remaining college years. List three goals and write two or three sentences for each of them explaining specifically what you can do to achieve that goal.

Goal one for my remaining college years:_____

_____

_____

_____

Specifically how I will accomplish goal one: _____

_____

_____

_____

Goal two for my remaining college years:_____

_____

_____

Specifically how I will accomplish goal two: _____

_____

_____

_____

Goal three for my remaining college years: _____

_____

_____

Specifically how I will accomplish goal three: _____

_____

_____

Glossary

A

Academic Advisor: A staff member who helps students select favorable schedules while fulfilling their graduation requirements and guides them about preparing for education or career opportunities after graduation.

Academic Paper: A formal writing assignment such as a research paper, an essay, a reaction paper, or a literary analysis that asks that students to read, think, analyze, argue, and write about ideas that are relevant for an academic community.

Academic Probation: A student's temporary status caused by grades that do not meet a college's requirement; the student is given a trial period to overcome probationary status.

Acetaminophen: The chemical name for Tylenol, a popular over-the-counter painkiller. Accidental overdose with this drug is the leading cause of liver failure.

Active listening: Dynamically engaging one's full self in understanding the information being presented by a speaker .

ADA: The ADA or Americans with Disabilities Act requires most colleges to arrange accommodations for students who have physical, learning, or psychological disabilities.

Adjunct: A part-time faculty member in an academic department who may have another full-time job related to his or her teaching specialty.

Advance Organizers: The topics viewed during pre-reading that provide a "bird's eye" view of an assignment before it is actually read.

Aerobic Exercises: Physical activities such as walking, running, skiing, inline skating, swimming, bicycling or aerobic dancing that involve breathing faster and getting the heart beating faster than normal.

Alcohol Poisoning: A consequence of excessive alcohol use leading to symptoms including vomiting, unresponsiveness, confusion, breathing irregularity, and skin discoloration. This condition requires immediate medical attention.

Altruism: The value of helping others.

Anaerobic Exercises: Physical activities, not intended to increase respiration or heartbeat, that include weight training to enhance strength and stretching to support flexibility.

Anstie's Law: Proposition that most people can safely drink a maximum of 1½ ounces of absolute (pure) alcohol without suffering negative consequences.

Aptitude: A natural or acquired ability to perform a type of task successfully.

Assertiveness: People's confidence and willingness to stand up for themselves, including the ability to say "No."

Assistant Professor: Less experienced or accomplished faculty members.

Associate Professor: Experienced faculty members who are either on the road to becoming Full Professors or who have not produced enough scholarly work to reach the rank of Full Professor.

Audit: Sitting in on a class but not receiving credit or a grade.

Auditory Learner: A student who prefers to rely on listening skills while learning.

B

Bacterial Meningitis: An infection that can affect the brain and spinal cord, spread by close contact with another person.

Bandwagon Appeal: An error in critical listening based on "joining the crowd" because everyone else presumably believes or accepts an idea.

Bias: An author's preference for one position or viewpoint, often revealed by that author's use of positive or negative words that slant the meaning of sentences.

Bibliography: Alphabetical list of authors and sources used to write an academic paper.

Bibliographic Information: The detailed sources for an academic paper including such information as the author, title, journal or periodical identification, place of publication, publisher, date of publication, page numbers, URLs, creation or modification dates on webpages, and date of access.

Binge Drinking: Four or more alcoholic drinks at a time.

Biological Prime Time: A time period during the day when a student can work consistently better than during other time periods.

Bisexual: A person attracted to both males and females.

Body Mass Index: A popular guideline that uses height and weight to determine if a person is underweight, normal, or overweight.

Bounce a Check: A bank's refusal to authorize payment by a check when the payment would exceed the customer's checking account balance. This event often results in an extra fee for the customer.

Bursar's Office: The student accounts office which maintains financial records, sends out bills to students or their families, and is responsible for collecting the payments.

C

Calorie: Units of energy needed by the body to function.

CARD: Credit Card Accountability, Responsibility, and Disclosure Act of 2009, which includes provisions to protect college students from the dangers of credit card misuse.

Cardiovascular Health: Medical condition of the heart.

Career Center: An office which maintains an array of resources designed primarily to help students find appropriate careers and get placed in jobs after they graduate.

Career College: Schools which emphasize training for specific career goals such as becoming a fashion designer or a chef.

Chastity Group: College organization for students who choose not to be sexually active.

Citation Style: A specific method to list the author, title, publisher, and other necessary components of a bibliographic item.

Civic Engagement: Working for the public good by volunteering for public service and participating in community support organizations.

Civil Society: An enduring social group of people who understand and respect each other, even when individual differences exist.

Clear Thesis Statement: Central thought or main point that uses no vague words.

Club Teams: Non-varsity teams, usually managed by students, that compete with teams from other colleges in equestrian, bowling, skiing, triathlon, and other sports.

Cognitive: Having to do with thought processes.

Cognitive Control Sleep Method: Uses positive thoughts to overcome the negative thoughts that interfere with sleep.

College: Form of higher education emphasizing undergraduate education and culminating with a Bachelor's degree.

College Jargon: Unique terminology used at each school.

Community College: Two-year schools in which students earn an associate's degree. This degree can be a step along the way to a bachelor's degree via a transfer to a four-year college or university program, or it can be a terminal degree.

Commuter: A student who lives off campus.

Complex Carbohydrate: Good source of fiber, which helps regulate important bodily functions. It also increases energy levels. Foods high in complex carbohydrates include fruits, vegetables, and starches.

Concluding Section: A summary of the main points in an academic paper.

Conclusions: Reasoned judgments based on critical thinking applied to reading.

Confidentiality: The rule that college administrators and faculty as well as family members cannot ordinarily find out what students discuss with their counselors without written permission.

Conflict Resolution: A constructive procedure involving direct interchange to resolve disagreements so that all parties will be satisfied.

Connotation: The use of judgments or feelings associated with the use of a word to learn its meaning.

Context Clues: Hints from the surrounding words in a sentence or paragraph that are available to figure out a word's meaning.

Contrast Clue: Understanding the meaning of an unknown word when the opposite of the word is given.

Cornell Note-taking System: One of the most widely used and respected systems of taking notes from lectures.

Cosigner: A financially responsible adult who signs a loan or credit card application along with the main applicant to provide security that debts will be paid.

Course Catalog (or Bulletin): Online list and description of courses, requirements for a major in a program of study, the course numbering procedures, criteria for graduation, and an explanation of the grading system.

Cover Letter: A carefully written first contact with a potential employer that accompanies a résumé and creates the important first impression.

Cramming: Intensive, last-minute preparation for an exam in a short period of time.

Credit Union: An agency with many of the same services as banks. They usually limit their customers to people associated with an organization or group; many charge lower fees and pay higher interest than banks.

Critical Listening: Listening not only to understand but also to evaluate information using careful, thoughtful, and reasoned judgments.

Critical Reading: Clarifies the full meaning and intentions of an author through interpreting, evaluating, and criticizing what is read.

Critical Thinking: Evaluates ideas using careful, thoughtful, and reasoned judgments.

Culture Shock: A stress reaction that occurs when new students move to a college community with very different customs, values, and people than their home community.

D

Dean: An administrator at a college or university who manages a cluster of related academic departments or other support services.

Dean of Students: The administrator of a school's manual of student rights and responsibilities; the Dean of Students office often represents the nucleus for a campus's student services.

Dean's List: An official recognition for high grades that is given after a grading period.

Debit Card: When used, a card that immediately withdraws funds electronically from a checking account.

Deductible: A required annual payment for treatment before health insurance or other insurance begins paying costs.

Defamation: Making a false factual statement, including over the Internet, about someone that is harmful to that person's reputation.

Definition Clue: A context clue in which the exact meaning of an unknown word is provided in a sentence.

Delay of Gratification: A characteristic of emotional intelligence involving a readiness to resist temptations that will interfere with important personal values and goals.

Denotation: Using the literal dictionary definition of a word to understand its meaning.

Diversity: The condition of being different or having differences.

Doctor of Philosophy (PhD): A doctoral research degree held by many professors.

Drop Date: The deadline for withdrawing from a class without penalty.

E

EdD: A Doctor of Education degree.

Editing: Looking critically at written work, thinking about a reader's reactions, and making necessary changes.

Efficiency: Getting the most output or productivity for the least input or work.

Either/Or Fallacy: Assuming there are only two sides or only two possible choices to deal with an issue.

Elective: A course that is not required for either a student's major or minor.

Emotional Intelligence: An ability to understand oneself, control emotions, use emotions for effective problem solving, react with sensitivity to other people, delay gratification, and overcome conflict and frustration.

Empathy: The ability and willingness to recognize and show understanding for the feelings other people are communicating and experiencing.

Endnotes: Footnotes accumulated as a consecutive list and placed at the end of an academic paper.

ESL: English as a Second Language classes, labs, workshops, and tutoring to prepare for classes requiring English.

Eustress: Stress that comes from good events, such as starting college, getting married, obtaining a new job, or winning a big lottery jackpot.

Example Clue: Understanding the meaning of an unknown word when an example of the unknown word is given.

Extroverted: Characteristic of being outgoing and very involved in relationships with other people.

F

Facts: Provable statements established through critical thinking applied to reading.

FAFSA: Free Application for Federal Student Aid which must be completed to apply for federal loans and other forms of financial aid.

Fallacy: An error in reasoning leading to a flawed argument.

Federal Work Study: The leading college work program, sponsored by the government and requiring annual eligibility.

FERPA: The Family Educational Rights and Privacy Act, a federal law which protects the educational records of students eighteen or older.

FICA: Deductions from paychecks to support Social Security.

FICO: Fair Isaac Corporation score, a credit rating score ranging from 300 to 850 based on a person's payment history, amount of debt, length of credit history, frequency of credit applications and usage, and current credit obligations.

Figurative Language: Imaginative language creating impressions for readers to help them understand the meaning of words.

First Amendment: Part of the Bill of Rights of the United States Constitution, affording individuals the right to free speech without regard to political or philosophical preferences.

Fixed Expenses: Costs that are regular and predictable as, for example, from tuition and housing bills.

Fixed Income: Predictable income, as, for example, from a set monthly allowance from your family or weekly paychecks from a job.

Fixed Time Commitment: A regularly scheduled obligation such as a class, meeting, or job.

Footnotes: List of the sources for quotations or evidence used in an academic paper.

Frugal: Cautious about spending money.

Full Professor: Senior faculty members who are usually very accomplished in their scholarly work.

G

Gay: A male attracted to other males; sometimes used to refer to any person attracted to same sex individuals.

Generalization: A conclusion based on specific factors.

GI Bill: A government program which provides significant tuition and housing benefits to college students who are military veterans.

Graduate Record Exam (GRE): A test including sections on verbal reasoning, mathematical reasoning, and analytical writing required for admission for some advanced degrees such as the PhD or EdD.

Grant: A form of financial aid based on need that does not ordinarily have to be paid back.

Greek Organizations: Social sororities and fraternities, which are designated by Greek letters and are usually chapters of national organizations with significant traditions.

H

Hasty Generalization: Drawing a conclusion with insufficient evidence.

Hazing: An occurrence in Greek or other organizations when a student going through the required pledging process to become a member is harmed, demeaned, harassed, humiliated, or placed at risk as part of the process.

Hepatitis B: A liver disease that can be transmitted sexually; there is a vaccine to prevent this disease.

Hierarchy of Needs: Abraham Maslow's theory that levels of basic needs must be fulfilled before ultimate goals can be accomplished.

Hold on Registration: A block on a student's registration imposed by a college for financial, academic, disciplinary, or other factors.

Holland Codes: A system of organizing career interests into six major categories.

Homesickness: A feeling of missing family and old friends for students who have moved away from home.

HPV: Human Papillomavirus is one of the most frequently found STIs on college campuses. It can lead to genital warts among both men and women and is the leading cause of cervical cancer in women; a vaccine is available to reduce the risk of HPV.

Human Genome Project: Research showing that 99% of one person's DNA is exactly the same as that of every other person.

I

Identity Theft: An event that occurs when someone steals key pieces of another person's identity for malicious purposes.

Idiosyncrasy: Unique, quirky preferences.

Inference: Educated guesses derived from critical thinking applied to reading.

Insomnia: Difficulty falling asleep or staying asleep.

Instructor: A full-time or part-time faculty member who specializes in teaching.

Intent to Remember: Mental engagement brought about by planning to recall specific material.

Interdisciplinary Major: A combination of two related fields as a major.

Interests: What a person likes to do; contributes to career satisfaction.

Internship: A paid or unpaid formal job experience that provides training for a specific career and usually lasts for one semester or one summer.

Introverted: Gaining fulfillment from one's own thoughts and feelings rather than from interacting with other people.

J

Jeanne Clery Act: Requires colleges to publish campus crime statistics.

Jargon: Specialized use of language in a subject area or setting.

Juris Doctor (JD): The advanced degree awarded after three years of law school.

K

Key Action Words: Terms used in an essay exam that guide the organization and presentation of the written responses.

Key Qualifying Words: In the wording of alternative answers for a multiple choice test, terms that are all inclusive (include everyone or everything), all exclusive (exclude everyone or everything) or a safe middle position.

Kinesthetic/Tactile Learner: A student who prefers to rely on moving, doing, and touching while learning.

L

Learning Style: A preferred way of processing information that could be auditory (listening), visual (seeing), or kinesthetic/tactile (moving, doing, or touching).

Lecturer: A full-time or part-time faculty member who specializes in teaching.

LGBT: An acronym used to define lesbian, gay, bisexual, and transgender students.

Lesbian: A female who is attracted to other females.

Licensure: A state requirement for the practice of many professions such as social work, pharmacy and elementary/secondary teaching.

Listening Behavior: A self-understanding of attitudes and values toward listening.

Logic/Inference Clue: Information in a sentence that leads to an educated guess about the meaning of an unknown word.

M

Main Idea: The controlling idea for a reader to detect in a paragraph, article, or book.

Major: A declared field of concentration.

Major Details: Supporting facts or statements in a reading passage that prove or explain the main idea.

Mapping: A note-taking method involving drawing diagrams to represent the main ideas and major details as a textbook is read.

Mediation: A formal meeting to resolve conflicts run by a neutral person who listens to information about a disagreement, makes a clear statement of the issues and conflicts, leads a discussion of alternative solutions, and negotiates a compromise.

Memory Dump: As soon as a test is received, every detail a student wants to remember is written down in the margins of the page.

Mentor: Usually a person who has already succeeded with the opportunities and challenges being faced by a student a can advise that student how to achieve success.

Minor: A course of academic concentration with less required courses than a major.

Mnemonic Device: A memory aid trick that you can devise to help you recall information.

Mourning: An active method of dealing with grief by facing one's loss.

Multicultural: An atmosphere that provides the opportunity to share a rich variety of beliefs, music, artistic expression, and experiences based on unique heritage.

Multi-ethnic: Having more than one race in a family background.

Multiple Intelligences: Howard Gardner's framework for aptitudes that includes eight different categories of intelligence, each associated with particular strengths for various majors and careers.

Multitasking: Performing several tasks at once.

Myers-Briggs Type Indicator: A widely used personality test that relates several different personality dimensions to career choices.

N

Negative Balance: Situation when funds do not match expenses in a budget; requires less variable spending in the next budget period.

Nicotine: The active chemical ingredient in cigarettes and tobacco products.

Nonverbal Communication: Cues that are used along with words to give messages their meaning; includes gestures, vocal intonations, and facial expressions.

O

Ombudsperson: A college administrator who is assigned to troubleshoot and resolve conflicts between a student and other students, faculty members, or administrators.

Online College: Institution of higher education in which academic programs are presented exclusively or chiefly online, and communication between students and faculty members usually occurs over the Internet.

Opinions: Beliefs distinguished from facts through critical thinking applied to reading.

Osteoporosis: A loss of bone density that can lead to fractures and a stooping posture later in life. Adequate intake of calcium can help to prevent this condition.

Outlining: A method of taking notes in which the note-taker lists the main ideas and major details, showing their relationship to one another.

Overdraft Fee: A surcharge made by a bank if a payment made with a debit card exceeds the amount of money left in the associated checking account. Customers must give permission in advance for such fees if they want to be able to make payments that exceed their balance.

P

Pap Smear: A medical screening for women to detect some forms of genital infection and cancer; recommended for sexually active women or those 21 or older.

Paraphrase: A technique for reviewing in which each point is stated in students' own words.

Parkinson's Law: A theory suggesting that people have a tendency to take longer than necessary to complete a task when they know that more time is readily available.

Pass/Fail Class: A course that will not result in a traditional letter grade for a student but a grade of Pass or Fail.

Peer Counselor: Advanced undergraduate students trained to advise newer students.

Pell Grant: A need-based financial award from the federal government.

Perfectionism: Striving for unreachable standards.

Personality: A person's consistent, unique pattern of relating to the world.

PhD: A Doctor of Philosophy degree, which is a doctoral research degree held by many professors.

Plagiarism: A form of academic dishonesty that involves copying someone else's written work and passing it off as one's own.

Plan B: The morning after pill, a form of emergency contraception for use following unprotected sex.

Podcast: An audio or video presentation that can be accessed whenever a student chooses.

Positive Balance: Situation when an excess of funds results from budgeting; the extra money can be spent or saved for the future.

Positive Psychology: A theory of psychology which states that focusing on personal strengths while maintaining an optimistic outlook will promote happiness.

Positive Stereotyping: Ascribing positive characteristics to people because they fit in a category.

POSITIVE Time Management: A mnemonic for a step-by-step method designed to facilitate the planning and completion of academic assignments while allowing time for fun. The steps include prioritizing tasks, operating efficiently, scheduling time, itemizing a "To Do" list, tackling procrastination, ignoring distractions, visualizing success, and enjoying achievements.

Post-baccalaureate Training: Educational programs in the years after the bachelor's degree.

Prefix: A word root placed at the beginning of the word.

Pre-reading: A procedure that provides the opportunity to get a "bird's-eye" view of the entire assignment before the reading is actually begun.

Pre-writing: Steps to take before writing an academic paper, such as checking a topic with the professor and becoming familiar with a topic's specialized language.

Prerequisite: A required course for completion of a major.

Prioritizing: Sequentially ordering the completion of tasks according to their importance.

Private College or University: An institution of higher education run independently of a governmental entity.

Procrastination: Delaying the completion of something that should be finished now.

Proverb: A folk saying that may reflect cultural beliefs that have been passed on through generations.

Provost: A high ranking university administrator.

Public Speaking Anxiety: The fear, sometimes almost overwhelming, that some students might experience when they must speak formally to groups of other people.

Public College or University: An institution of higher education run and financially supported under the authority of a state or federal agency.

R

Registrar's Office: An office responsible for course registration, student academic records and the academic calendar.

Resilience: The ability to bounce back quickly from a frustration or mistake.

Résumé: An organized description including educational background, work experiences, and skills that is intended to attract employers to a job applicant.

Review: Going back over a reading assignment from the beginning to the end, looking at each heading, subheading, and first sentence.

Root: A part of a word that contributes to the word's meaning.

ROTC: The Reserve Officer Training Corps programs, offered by many colleges, that involve courses of study and training associated with a specific United States military branch. Successful completion of these programs results in a commission as an officer following college.

S

Scholarship: An award of financial aid based on merit.

Self-Actualization: The highest level in Maslow's hierarchy of needs where people become all that they are capable of becoming.

Senioritis: Loss of energy during the final year of college.

Sentence Outline: Use of complete sentences to show full ideas in an outline.

Service Learning: A class that incorporates civic engagement into formal classroom experience.

Sexual Harassment: A legal concept describing unwanted sexual comments or gestures that contribute to a hostile environment and interfere with academic performance and personal comfort.

Signature Strengths: The unique attributes of each individual.

Silo Effect: Circumstance occurring when students shelter themselves in exclusionary groups of similar people.

SMART Goals: A mnemonic device to help students create specific, measurable, attainable, realistic, and timely long-term and short-term goals.

Social Justice: Fairness for all.

Sociogram: A classic visual method to represent social and communication links among people.

Sophomore Slump: A loss of motivation and enthusiasm during the second year of college because the novelty of being a college student has faded away.

Sophomoric: Immature and overconfident about knowledge but not well-informed.

Specialized Usage: Words and phrases having different meanings in different contexts.

Specific Thesis Statement: Central thought or main point that has been sufficiently narrowed.

SQ3R: Well-known systematic approach to studying a textbook chapter with the steps of survey, question, read, recite, and review.

Stalking: Obsessive pursuit of another person.

Stereotype: A negative generalization about people based on their heritage, sex, or other defining characteristics.

STI: A sexually transmitted infection, also commonly known as an STD or sexually transmitted disease, spread through vaginal, anal, or oral sexual contact.

Stress: A state of tension caused by a change or demand; if prolonged, it can impair health.

Student Affairs: A nonacademic administrative unit responsible for many key areas of student life.

Study Abroad: An official college program placing students in semester or year-long international educational experience.

Suffix: A word root placed at the end of the word.

Summarizing: A method for taking notes from textbooks that involves writing the main ideas and major details in paragraph form as sections of the textbook are read.

Summary: A condensed version of a longer passage.

Syllabus: A guide to a class's schedule of assignments and exams as well as a professor's rules.

T

Teaching Assistant (TA): A graduate student who acquires teaching experience and financial support for assisting a faculty member with a class.

Tenure: A lifetime status awarded to faculty members based on their achievements.

Test Stress: A state of tension before, during, and after college exams.

Thesis Statement: The central thought or main point, sometimes stated in one sentence, for an academic paper.

Tone: The author's feelings toward the subject as revealed by critical thinking applied to reading.

Topic Outline: Uses only short phrases to express ideas in an outline.

Topic Sentence: The controlling sentence in an individual paragraph.

Transcript: A formal cumulative record of a student's grades.

Transgender: A person whose gender identity does not match his or her physically assigned sex.

U

Undeclared: A student's status prior to declaring a major.

Underlining/Highlighting: A note-taking method involving marking the main ideas and major details in the textbook as it is read.

Unified Thesis Statement: In academic writing, a central point or main thought that develops only one dominant idea.

University: Research oriented academic institutions which provide degrees to undergraduate and graduate students.

URL: Uniform Resource Locator or web address, designated by some combination of letters, numbers, and symbols, to be included in bibliographic citations for Internet sites.

V

Values: The beliefs and principles that are most important and meaningful for a person to fulfill in life.

Variable Expenses: Costs to be considered in a budget that are not predictable.

Variable Income: Irregular, unpredictable financial support from earnings or other sources.

Visual Learner: A student who prefers to rely on visual (seeing) skills while learning.

Visualization: A technique that uses mental imaging of success on a task to facilitate the actual accomplishment of the task.

W

Wellness Center: A college fitness center which offers exercise opportunities as well as other varied programs to enhance students' lives.

Wellness Philosophy: A holistic health philosophy that integrates physical, intellectual, emotional, spiritual, and social dimensions.

Word Parts: Prefixes, suffixes, and roots that contribute to the meaning of words.

Endnotes

Introduction

1. Edwin A. Locke, Gary P. Latham, Ken J. Smith, and Robert E. Wood, *A Theory of Goal Setting and Task Performance* (New York: Prentice Hall, 1990).

2. George T. Doran, "There's a S.M.A.R.T. Way to Write Management Goals and Objectives," *Management Review* 70, no. 11 (November 1981): 35–36.

3. Hans Selye, *Stress without Distress* (Philadelphia: Lippincott, 1974).

Chapter 1

1. Erik Blanco, Emily Franklin, Colleen Carmichael, and Alissa Swauger, *u.c.l.a. slang 6*, ed. Pamela Munro (Los Angeles: UCLA Department of Linguistics, 2009).

2. Family Educational Rights and Privacy Act (FERPA), 20 U.S.C. § 1232g; 34 CFR Part 99 (1974). Information on FERPA is available at the U.S. Department of Education website, accessed August 29, 2009,

http://www.ed.gov/policy/gen/guid/fpco/ferpa/index.html.

3. Aysha Bagshi, "Frosh Alcohol Policy Surprise to Many," *Stanford Daily*, October 2007, accessed February 19, 2008,

http://daily.stanford.edu/article/2007/10/16/froshAlcoholPolicySurpriseToMany.

4. I. Elaine Allen and Jeff Seaman, *Online Nation: Five Years of Growth in Online Learning* (Needham, MA: Sloan Consortium, 2007).

5. Jack Canfield, Mark Victor Hansen, Kimberly Kirberger, Dan Clark, and James Malinchak, *Chicken Soup for the College Soul: Inspiring and Humorous Stories about College* (Cos Cob, CT: Chicken Soup for the Soul, 2012).

6. Students Helping Students, *Navigating Your Freshman Year: How to Make the Leap to College Life and Land on Your Feet* (New York: Prentice Hall, 2005).

7. Lao Tse, "Passage LXIV," *The Book of Tao: Tao Te Ching*, trans. James Legge (Rockville, MD: Arc Manor, 2008).

Chapter 2

1. "Students with Disabilities Preparing for Postsecondary Education: Know Your Rights and Responsibilities," *U.S. Department of Education Office of Civil Rights*, September, 2011, accessed March 12, 2013,

http://www2.ed.gov/about/offices/list/ocr/transition.html.

2. R. Michael Paige, Elizabeth M. Stallman, Jae-Eun Jon, and Bruce LaBrack, "Study Abroad for Global Engagement: The Long-Term Impact of International Experiences." Paper presented at the NAFSA: Association of International Educators 2009 Annual Conference, Los Angeles, CA, May 29, 2009, accessed November 21, 2013,

http://www.afs60.de/webcontent/files/MbM_Paige_Et_Al.pdf.

3. Colin L. Powell with Joseph E. Persico, *My American Journey* (New York: Random House, 1995), 31–36.

4. John H. Pryor and Sylvia Hurtado, "Political Engagement, College Choice and Skills for a Diverse Workplace: Results from the 2008 CIRP Freshman Survey," *Association of American Colleges and Universities Annual Meeting*, January, 22, 2008, accessed January 7, 2010, http://www.gseis.ucla.edu/heri/pr-display.php?prQry=28.

5. Surabhi Avasthi, "Wellness: A Holistic Approach to Living," *American Association for Counseling and Development* 33, no. 4, (September 1990): 12–14.

6. "Rice University Sexual Harassment Policy and Procedures," *Rice University Organization Policy No. 830-01*, accessed March 28, 2008, http://professor.rice.edu/professor/Rice_University_Sexual_Harassment.asp.

7. Catherine Hill and Elena Silva, "Drawing the Line: Sexual Harassment on Campus," *AAUW Research Reports*, December 2005, accessed January 10, 2010, http://www.aauw.org/.../02/drawing-the-line-sexual-harassment-on-campus.pdf.

8. Matt Schild, "A Crash Course in Campus Security," *Campus Bound Magazine*, 2000, 92–94.

9. Peter Feaver, Sue Wasiolek, and Anne Crossman, *Getting the Best Out of College: A Professor, a Dean, and a Student Tell You How to Maximize Your Experience* (Berkeley, CA: Ten Speed, 2008).

Chapter 3

1. Purdue University Registrar, "Semester Credit Hours Guidelines," *Purdue University Office of the Registrar*, accessed January 12, 2012, http://www.purdue.edu/registrar/pdf/Credit_Hour_Guidelines.pdf.

2. Cyril Northcote Parkinson, *Parkinson's Law and Other Studies in Administration* (Cutchogue, NY: Buccaneer Books, 1996).

3. Eric Hoover, "Tomorrow, I Love Ya!," *The Chronicle of Higher Education*, December 9, 2005, A30–A32.

4. Maia Szalavitz, "Stand & Deliver," *Psychology Today*, July/August 2003, 50–54.

5. Larry Rosen, "How to Help Today's Wired Students Learn to Focus," *eCampus News*, January 9, 2013, accessed January 9, 2013, http://www.ecampusnews.com/technologies/driven-to-distraction-how-to-help-wired-students-learn-to-focus/.

6. Eyal Ophir, Clifford Nass, and Anthony D. Wagner, "Cognitive Control in Multitaskers," *Proceedings of the National Academy of Sciences*, August 24, 2009, accessed August 24, 2011, http://www.scribd.com/doc/19081547/Cognitive-control-in-media-multitaskers.

7. Doug Valentine, "Distance Learning: Promises, Problems, and Possibilities," *Online Journal of Distance Learning Administration*, 5, no. 3 (Fall 2002), accessed March 6, 2012, http://www.westga.edu/~distance/ojdla/fall53/valentine53.html.

8. Alan Lakein, *How to Get Control of Your Time and Life* (New York, NY: Penguin Group, 1989).

9. John Hoover, *Best Practices: Time Management: Set Priorities to Get the Right Things Done* (New York, NY: Harper Collins, 2007).

Chapter 4

1. Dr. Seuss [Theodor S. Geisel], *I Can Read with My Eyes Shut* (New York: Random House, 1978).

2. David P. Ausubel, "The use of advance organizers in the learning and retention of meaningful verbal material," *Journal of Educational Psychology* 51 (1960): 267–272.

3. Averil Coxhead, "A New Academic Word List," *TESOL Quarterly* 34, no. 2 (2000): 212–238.

4. James I. Brown, *Programmed Vocabulary* (New York: Meredith Publishing, 1971).

5. ACT, "Reading between the Lines: What the ACT Reveals about College Readiness in Reading," March 2, 2006, accessed March 28, 2008, http://www.act.org/research/policymakers/pdf/reading_report.pdf.

6. Francis P. Robinson, *Effective Study*, 4th ed. (New York: Harper and Row, 1970).

7. Aimee A. Callender and Mark A. McDaniel, "The Limited Benefits of Rereading Educational Texts," *Contemporary Educational Psychology* 34 (2009): 30–41.

8. Mark A. McDaniel, Daniel C. Howard, and Gilles O. Einstein, "The Read-Recite-Review Study Strategy," *Psychological Science* 20, no. 4 (2009): 516–522.

9. Ibid., 521.

10. Ibid., 522.

11. William Glasser, "We Learn 10% of What We Read," *Lusenet: Glasser Choice Theory and Reality Therapy*, accessed April 3, 2008, http://www.greenspun.com/bboard/q-and-a-fetch-msg.tcl?msg_id=00AV58. Based on Edgar Dale's "Cone of Experience."

12. Mary Wood Cornog, *Merriam-Webster's Vocabulary Builder* (Springfield, MA: Merriam-Webster, 2010).

13. Kenneth L. Higbee, *Your Memory: How It Works and How to Improve It*, 2nd ed. (New York: Marlowe, 1996).

Chapter 5

1. Neil D. Fleming and Colleen Mills, "Not Another Inventory, Rather a Catalyst for Reflection," *To Improve the Academy* 11 (1992): 137.

2. Laura A. Janusik and Andrew D. Wolvin, "24 Hours in a Day: A Listening Update to the Time Studies," *International Listening Association Convention*, 2006, accessed June 7, 2008, www.listen.org.

3. Andrew D. Wolvin and Carolyn Gwynn Coakley, *Listening*, 2nd ed. (Dubuque, IA: Wm. C. Brown, 1985).

4. Dani McKinney, Jennifer L. Dyck, and Elise S. Luber, "iTunes University and the Classroom: Can Podcasts Replace Professors?," *Computers and Education* 52 (2009): 617–623.

5. Walter Pauk, *How to Study in College*, 7th ed. (New York: Houghton Mifflin, 2001).

6. Carrie B. Fried, "In-Class Laptop Use and Its Effects on Student Learning," *Computers and Education* 50 (2008): 906–914.

7. Malcolm Gladwell, *Blink: The Power of Thinking Without Thinking* (New York: Little Brown, 2007).

8. Madelyn Burley-Allen, *Listening: The Forgotten Skill*, 2nd ed. (Hoboken, NJ: John Wiley, 1995).

Chapter 6

1. Newbury College Academic Support Services, "General Tips for Any Test," *Academic Support Services—Study Skills*, 2007, accessed April 25, 2013, https://www.oaklandcc.edu/ASC/ASCAH/documents/Robinson/General%20Tips%20for%20any%20Test.doc.

2. Yigal Attali and Maya Bar-Hillel, "Guess Where: The Position of Correct Answers in Multiple-Choice Test Items as a Psychometric Variable," *Journal of Educational Measurement* 40, no. 2 (June 2003): 109–128.

3. Richard Pérez-Peña, "Harvard Students in Cheating Scandal Say Collaboration Was Accepted," *New York Times*, August 31, 2012, accessed September 18, 2012, http://www.nytimes.com/2012/09/01/education/students-of-harvard-cheating-scandal-say-group-work-was-accepted.html?_r=1.

4. J. Paul Peter and Jerry C. Olson, *Consumer Behavior and Marketing Strategy*, 7th ed. (New York: McGraw-Hill, 2005).

5. Ed Newman, *No More Test Anxiety: Effective Steps for Taking Tests and Achieving Better Grades* (Los Angeles: Learning Skills Publications, 1996).

Chapter 7

1. Alison Head, and Michael Eisenberg, "How Today's College Students Use Wikipedia for Course-related Research" *First Monday* [Online], 15 no. 3, February 26, 2010, http://www.uic.edu/htbin/cgiwrap/bin/ojs/index.php/fm/article/view/2830/2476 (March 16, 2010).

2. Peter J. Paul and Jerry C. Olson, *Consumer Behavior & Marketing Strategy* (New York: McGraw-Hill, 7th ed., 2005), 337-338.

3. Joseph Gibaldi, *MLA Handbook for Writers or Research Papers* (New York: The Modern Language Association of America, 6th ed., 2003): 53.

4. Jerrold H. Zar, "A Little Poem Regarding Computer Spell Checkers," *Louisiana Tech Geography*, accessed August 22, 2008, http://www.latech.edu/tech/liberal-arts/geography/courses/spellchecker.

5. Gibaldi, *MLA Handbook for Writers or Research Papers*.

6. Geraldine Nagle, *The Arts: World Themes* (New York: McGraw-Hill Irwin, 1997), 63.

7. Ibid.

Chapter 8

1. Stephen Brobeck, *College Student Consumer Knowledge: A Nationwide Test* (Washington DC: Consumer Federation of America, 1993), 23.

2. Elizabeth F. Farrell, "More Students Plan to Work to Help Pay for College," *Chronicle of Higher Education*, February 4, 2005, A1, A32–A34.

3. John H. Pryor, Kevin Egan, Laura P. Blake, Sylvia Hurtado, Jennifer Berdan, and Matthew H. Case, *The American Freshman: National Norms Fall 2012* (Los Angeles: Higher Education Research Institute, UCLA, December 2012), accessed February 19, 2013, http://www.heri.ucla.edu/monographs/TheAmericanFreshman2012.pdf.

4. FinAid, "Student Loans," *The SmartStudent Guide to Financial Aid*, accessed September 5, 2009, http://www.finaid.org/loans/.

5. Harris Interactive, "Upperclassmen Offer Advice to Incoming College Freshmen on Best Way to Avoid Financial Pitfalls," *One-Third of College Upperclassmen Admit Being Financially Unprepared as Freshmen, October 23, 2006*, accessed September 5, 2009, http://www.harrisinteractive.com/news/allnewsbydate.asp?NewsID=1108.

6. Carolyn Bigda, "A Sneaky Bank Fee Gets Higher," *Money Magazine*, September 2007, 54.

7. Center for Responsible Lending, "Quick Facts on Overdraft Loans," *Overdraft Loans*, April 9, 2009, accessed September 5, 2009, http://www.responsiblelending.org/overdraft-loans/research-analysis/quick-facts-on-overdraft-loans.html.

8. Sallie Mae, *How Undergraduate Students Use Credit Cards: Sallie Mae's National Study of Usage Rates and Trends, 2009*, accessed November 21, 2013, http://inpathways.net/SLMCreditCardUsageStudy41309FINAL2.pdf.

9. Ibid.

10. "College Hopes and Worries Results" *The Princeton Review*, 2013, accessed June 16, 2013, http://www.princetonreview.com/college-hopes-worries.aspx.

11. I. Elaine Allen and Jeff Seaman, "Online Education in the United States, 2009," *Learning on Demand*, January, 2010, accessed January 26, 2010, http://www.sloanc.org/publications/survey/pdf/learningondemand.pdf.

12. Education Dynamics, *Education Dynamics Survey: Many Online Learners Never Seek Help Before Dropping Out*, January 6, 2009, accessed March 19, 2010, http://www.educationdynamics.com/downloads/press-releases/survey-stop-out.pdf.

13. Suze Orman, *The Money Book for the Young, Fabulous and Broke* (New York: Penguin, 2007).

14. Debby Fowles, *1000 Best Smart Money Secrets for Students* (Naperville, IL: Sourcebooks, 2005).

Chapter 9

1. Jeffrey M. Ellenbogen, Justin C. Hulbert, Robert Stickgold, David F. Dinges, and Sharon L. Thompson-Schill, "Interfering with Theories of Sleep and Memory: Sleep, Declarative Memory and Associative Interference," *Current Biology* 16 (July 2006): 1290–1294.

2. Greg Toppo, "Schools Use 'Tough Love' to Get in Students' Faces," *USA Today*, January 24, 2006, accessed January 25, 2006, http://www.usatoday.com/news/nation/2006-01-24-campus-deaths-side_x.htm.

3. Hannah G. Lund, Brian D. Reider, Annie B. Whiting, and J. Roxanne Prichard, "Sleep Patterns and Predictors of Disturbed Sleep in a Large Population of College Students," *Journal of Adolescent Health*, August 3, 2009, accessed September 7, 2009, http://www.jahonline.org/article/S1054-139X(09)00238-9.

4. Peter J. Steincrohn, *How to Get a Good Night's Sleep* (Chicago: Henry Regnery Company, 1968).

5. Philip Goldberg and Daniel Kaufman, *Natural Sleep* (Emmaus, PA: Rodale Press, 1978), 76–77.

6. Steincrohn, *How to Get a Good Night's Sleep*.

7. Michael J. Klag, Robert S. Lawrence, Ada R. Davis, and John K. Niparko, *Johns Hopkins Family Health Book* (New York: HarperCollins, 1999), 16.

8. Morris Chafetz, "Carry Nation Had a Drinking Problem: How to Drink Healthily and Why So Many Americans Don't," *Johns Hopkins Magazine*, March 1976, 9–10.

9. Melissa Campbell, "Colleges Act to Reduce Student Drinking," *Hispanic Outlook*, June 2005, 37–39.

10. Ian Birky, "Shared Lives: Separate Realities" (presentation at the Annual Meeting of the Association for University and College Counseling Center Directors, Vail CO, October 9, 2006).

11. Diana Flannery and Lyndall Ellingson, "Sexual Risk Behaviors among First Year College Students, 2000–2002," *California Journal of Health Promotion* 1, no. 3 (2003): 93–104.

12. Centers for Disease Control and Prevention, *Cervical Cancer Screening*, September 5, 2012, accessed September 18, 2012, http://www.cdc.gov/cancer/cervical/basic_info/screening.htm.

13. Rutgers New Brunswick Piscataway Health Service, "Sexually Transmitted Infections," *FYI*, accessed September 8, 2009, http://rhshope.rutgers.edu/health-and-wellness/sexual-health/sexually-transmitted-infections-fact-v-myth.

14. Kaiser Health News, "Many Male College Students Use Condoms Incorrectly, Study Says," *Henry J. Kaiser Foundation*, September 9, 2002, accessed September 8, 2009, http://kff.org/news-summary/study-shows-incorrect-condom-use-common-worldwide/.

15. American College Health Association. *American College Health Association–National College Health Assessment II: Reference Group Executive Summary Fall 2009*, (Linthicum, MD: American College Health Association, 2009), accessed March 31, 2010, http://www.achancha.org/docs/ACHA-NCHA_Reference_Group_ExecutiveSummary_Fall2009.pdf.

16. Edison Media Research, "How Stress, War, the Economy & Other Factors Are Affecting College Students' Mental Health," *New mtvU & Associated Press Poll*, March 19, 2008, accessed November 21, 2013, http://www.mtv.com/thinkmtv/about/pdfs/Stress_War_Economy_mental_health.pdf.

17. Clery Center for Security on Campus, "Complying with the Jeanne Clery Act," *Get Informed*, accessed September 9, 2009, http://clerycenter.org/clery-act-compliance.

18. One Step Systems, "College Students Beware of Theft," *PRLog*, August 13, 2008, accessed September 9, 2009, http://www.prlog.org/10102910-college-students-beware-of-theft.html.

19. Andrew Kurtzman, "Who Is a Sexual Assault Victim? Ambiguity and Political Correctness Change Lives," *The Brown Spectator*, December 2007.

20. Fisher, Bonnie S., Cullen, Francis T. and Michael G. Turner. 2000. Sexual Victimization of College Women. U.S. Department of Justice, National Institute of Justice, Washington, DC.

21. Columbia University's Health Education Program, *The "Go Ask Alice" Book of Answers: A Guide to Good Physical, Sexual, and Emotional Health* (New York: Henry Holt, 1998).

Chapter 10

1. Christopher Peterson, *A Primer in Positive Psychology* (New York: Oxford University Press, 2006).

2. Martin E. P. Seligman, *Authentic Happiness: Using the New Positive Psychology to Realize Your Potential for Lasting Fulfillment* (New York: Free Press, 2002).

3. Costco, "CEO's Drive Helps Company Thrive," *The Costco Connection*, September 2008, 24.

4. John D. Mayer, Peter Salovey, and David R. Caruso, "Emotional Intelligence: New Ability or Eclectic Traits," *American Psychologist* 63, no. 6 (September 2008): 503–517.

5. Daniel Goleman, *Emotional Intelligence: Why It Can Matter More Than IQ* (New York: Bantam Books, 1994).

6. Edmund J. Bourne, *The Anxiety and Phobia Workbook*, 4th ed. (Oakland, CA: New Harbinger Publications, 2005).

7. David Burns, "The Perfectionist's Script for Self-Defeat," *Psychology Today* (November 1980): 34–52.

8. Ibid., 34–35.

9. David D. Burns, *Feeling Good: The New Mood Therapy*, rev. and updated ed. (New York: Avon, 1999).

Chapter 11

1. James H. Fowler and Nicholas A. Christakis, "Dynamic Spread of Happiness in a Large Social Network: Longitudinal Analysis over 20 Years in the Framingham Heart Study," *BMJ*, December 4, 2008, accessed April 18, 2010, http://www.bmj.com/cgi/content/full/337/dec04_2/a2338.

2. Todd R. Stinebrickner and Ralph Stinebrickner, "The Causal Effect of Studying on Academic Performance," *NBER Working Papers* 13341 (August 2007).

3. Alisha Davis, "How to Ace College," *Newsweek*, June 11, 2001, 62.

4. Campus Compact, "Students Contribute $ billions in Services to Communities," *Compact Current*, accessed April 27, 2013, http://www.compact.org/current/issues/2005_Spring.pdf.

5. Pete Carey, "Stanford Student Survey Finds iPhone Users Hooked and Happy," *San Jose Mercury News*, February 28, 2010, accessed March 2, 2010, http://www.mercurynews.com/top-stories/ci_14470072.

6. Diana b. Elliott, Kristy Krivickas, Matthew w. Brault, and Rose M. Kreider, "Historical Marriage Trends from 1890-2010: A Focus on Race Differences, Annual Meeting of the Population Association of America, San Francisco, CA, May 3-5, 2012, accessed April 27, 2013, http://www.census.gov/hhes/socdemo/marriage/data/acs/ElliottetalPAA2012 presentation.pdf.

7. Kristen Scholly, Alan R. Katz, Jan Gascoigne, and Peter S. Holck, "Using Social Norms Theory to Explain Perceptions and Sexual Health Behaviors of Undergraduate College Students: An Exploratory Study. *Journal of American College Health* 53, no. 4 (January/February 2005): 159–166.

8. Albert Ellis, *Sex without Guilt* (New York: Lyle Stuart, 1958).

9. Malcolm Kahn, "Non-Verbal Communication and Marital Satisfaction," *Family Process* 9, no. 4 (1970): 449–456.

10. Ibid.

11. Paula Nechak, "Online Schools Make Community a Priority," *AllOnlineSchools*, accessed September 17, 2008, http://www.allonlineschools.com/online-education-resource-center/online-community/.

12. Martin M. Anthony and Richard P. Swinton, *The Shyness and Social Anxiety Workbook*, 2nd ed. (Oakland, CA: New Harbinger Publications, 2008).

Chapter 12

1. Charles Grimmett, "The Human Genome Project," *Essortment*, 2002, accessed May 19, 2008, http://www.essortment.com/all/humangenomepro_rcaf.htm.

2. P. Scott Richards, Roger R. Keller, and Timothy B. Smith, "Religious and Spiritual Diversity in Counseling and Psychotherapy" in *Practicing Multiculturalism: Affirming Diversity in Counseling and Psychology*, ed. Timothy B. Smith (Boston: Pearson Education, 2004), 276–293.

3. Adherents.com, "Largest Denominations/Denominational Families in U.S.," *Largest Religious Groups in the United States of America*, December 7, 2005, accessed May 21, 2008, http://www.adherents.com/rel_USA.html.

4. Graciela M. Castex, "Providing Services to Hispanic/Latino Populations: Profiles in Diversity," *Social Work* 39, no. 3 (May 1994): 288–296.

5. CensusScope, "Two Race Multiracial Combinations," *United States Multiracial Profile*, accessed April 21, 2010, http://www.censusscope.org/us/print_chart_multi.html.

6. Rahul Choudaha and Li Chang, "Trends in International Student Mobility," *WES Research and Advisory Services*, February 2012, accessed October 12, 2012, http://www.wes.org/ras/TrendsInInternationalStudentMobility.pdf.

7. Tom Wolfe, *I Am Charlotte Simmons*, (New York: Farrar, Straus and Giroux, 2004).

8. Patricia Gurin, "The Effect of Structural Diversity on Classroom and Informal Interactional Diversity," expert report prepared for *Gratz, et al. v. Bollinger, et al.*, No. 97-75321 (E.D. Mich.), *Grutter, et al. v. Bollinger, et al.*, No. 97-75928 (E.D. Mich.) (January 1, 1997), January 31, 2007, accessed May 27, 2008, http://www.vpcomm.umich.edu/admissions/legal/expert/empir.html.

9. Angela Ka-yee Leung, William W. Maddux, Adam D. Galinsky, and Chi-yue Chiu, "Multicultural Experience Enhances Creativity: The When and How," *American Psychologist* 63, no. 3 (April 2008): 169–181.

10. Anthony P. Carnevale, "Diversity in Higher Education: Why Corporate America Cares," *Diversity Digest*, accessed May 25, 2008, http://www.diversityweb.org/Digest/Sp99/corporate.html.

11. Gurin, "The Effect of Structural Diversity on Classroom and Informal Interactional Diversity."

12. Patricia Gurin, Biren A. Nagda, and Gretchen E. Lopez, "The Benefits of Diversity in Education for Democratic Citizenship," *Journal of Social Issues* 60, no. 1 (April 2004): 17–34.

13. Patricia McGee, "Web-Based Learning Design: Planning for Diversity," *Journal of the United States Distance Leaning Association* 16, no. 3 (February 2002), accessed April 22, 2010,
http://www.usdla.org/html/journal/MAR02_Issue/article03.html.

14. Shari McCurdy and Ray Schroeder, "Achieving Diversity through Online Inter-Institutional Collaborations," *Journal of Asynchronous Learning Networks* 10, no. 1 (February 2006), accessed May 30, 2008, http://sloanconsortium.org/jaln/v10n1/achieving-diversity-through-online-inter-institutional-collaborations.

15. Tracy Kidder, *Mountains beyond Mountains: The Quest of Dr. Paul Farmer, a Man Who Would Cure the World* (New York: Random House, 2003).

Chapter 13

1. Michael J. Leonard, "Introduction," *Major Decisions...for Students Who Are Exploring Majors*, March 12, 2010, accessed May 2, 2010, from
http://www.psu.edu/dus/md/mdintro.htm.

2. Ibid.

3. Richard A. Hesel, John H. Pryor, and Edward F.D. Spencer, "Millennial Students: What Do We Know and What Does It Mean for Admissions," *2007 College Board National Forum*, October 24, 2007, accessed May 22, 2010, http://www.artsci.com/documents/CollegeBoardNatForumMillenialPresOct24_07.pdf.

4. John L. Holland, *Making Vocational Choices: A Theory of Personalities and Work Environments*, 2nd ed. (Englewood Cliffs, NJ: Prentice-Hall, 1985).

5. Hart Research Associates, *Raising the Bar: Employers' Views on College Learning in the Wake of the Economic Downturn, A Survey among Employers Conducted on Behalf of: the Association of American Colleges and Universities*, January 20, 2010, accessed May 4, 2010,
http://www.aacu.org/leap/documents/2009_EmployerSurvey.pdf.

6. National Center for Educational Statistics, "Trends in Bachelor's Degrees Conferred by Degree-Granting Institutions in Selected Fields of Study: 1996–97, 2001–2002, and 2006–07," *Digest of Education Statistics*, 2008, accessed August 23, 2009,
http://nces.ed.gov/programs/digest/d08/figures/gi_15.asp.

7. Howard Gardner, *Frames of Mind: The Theory of Multiple Intelligences* (New York: Basic Books, 1982).

8. Howard Gardner, "The 25th Anniversary of the Publication of Howard Gardner's *Frames of Mind: The Theory of Multiple Intelligences*," Howard Gardner, 2009, accessed May 2, 2010, http://www.howardgardner.com/Papers/papers.html.
The authors are aware that Dr. Gardner is considering a ninth intelligence, existentialism.

9. Phillip L. Rice, *Stress and Health*, 2nd ed. (Pacific Grove, CA: Brooks/Cole, 1992), 180–209.

10. Laura Morsch, "10 Ways to Get Your Résumé Tossed," *Young Money*, February/March, 2008, p. 4.

11. Isabel Briggs Myers and Mary H. McCaulley, *Manual: A Guide to the Development and Use of the Myers-Briggs Type Indicator* (Palo Alto, CA: Consulting Psychologists Press, 1985).

12. Richard N. Bolles, *What Color Is Your Parachute? 2013: A Practical Manual for Job-Hunters and Career-Changers* (Berkeley, CA: Ten Speed, 2012).

Chapter 14

1. Sara Lipka, "After the Freshman Bubble Pops," *The Chronicle of Higher Education*, September 8, 2006, 34–36.

2. Abraham H. Maslow, *Toward a Psychology of Being* (New York: John Wiley & Sons, 1999).

3. Anne Fisher, "What Do Gen Xers Want?" *Fortune* 153, no. 1 (January 2006).

4. Jamie Malernee, "Young Americans Waiting Longer to Get Married, Often Until after 30," *Fort Lauderdale Sun-Sentinel*, accessed October 2, 2006, http://www.sunsentinel.com/news/local/southflorida/sfl-cmarriageoct02,0,2996707.story?coll=sfla-home-headlines.

5. College Board, *Book of Majors 2013: All-New Seventh Edition* (New York: College Board, 2012).

6. Neeta P. Fogg, Paul E. Harrington, Thomas F. Harrington, and Laurence Shatkin, *College Majors Handbook with Real Career Paths and Payoffs: The Actual Jobs, Earnings, and Trends for Graduates of 50 College Majors*, 3rd ed. (St. Paul, MN: Jist, 2012).

7. H. Anthony Medley, *Sweaty Palms: The Neglected Art of Being Interviewed* (New York: Warner Business Books, 2005).

Index